CW00701852

The Legitimacy Puzzle in L
*Political Support and Democrac*y ... _Light Nations_

Political scientists for more than two decades have worried about declining levels of citizens' support for their regimes (legitimacy) but have failed to empirically link this decline to the survival or breakdown of democracy. This apparent paradox is the "legitimacy puzzle," which this book addresses by examining political legitimacy's structure, sources, and effects. With exhaustive empirical analysis of high-quality survey data from eight Latin American nations, it confirms that legitimacy exists as multiple, distinct dimensions. It finds that one's position in society, education, knowledge, information, and experiences shape legitimacy norms. Contrary to expectations, however, citizens who are unhappy with their government's performance do not drop out of politics or resort mainly to destabilizing protest. Rather, the disaffected citizens of these Latin American democracies participate at high rates in conventional politics and in such alternative arenas as communal improvement and civil society. And despite regime performance problems, citizen support for democracy remains high. These findings resolve the puzzle – citizen actions and values, even among the disaffected, likely strengthen rather than weaken democratic governments.

John A. Booth is Regents Professor of Political Science at the University of North Texas. In addition to his four coedited volumes and fourteen articles and chapters with this study's coauthor, Mitchell A. Seligson, he is the author of *Understanding Central America: Global Forces, Rebellion, and Change* (fourth edition 2006, coauthored with Christine J. Wade and Thomas W. Walker); *Costa Rica: Quest for Democracy* (1998); and *The End and the Beginning: The Nicaraguan Revolution* (second edition 1985). He has published articles in a wide array of scholarly journals in the United States and Latin America, was an associate editor of *International Studies Quarterly* (2003–2008), and serves on the editorial board of *Latin American Politics and Society*.

Mitchell A. Seligson is the Centennial Professor of Political Science at Vanderbilt University and a Fellow of the Vanderbilt Center for Nashville Studies. He founded and directs the Latin American Public Opinion Project (LAPOP), which conducts the AmericasBarometer surveys that currently cover 23 countries in the Americas. He has been a Fulbright Fellow and been awarded grants from the Ford Foundation, the Rockefeller Foundation, and others and has published more than 140 articles, 14 books, and dozens of monographs. His most recent book is *Development and Underdevelopment: The Politics of Global Inequality* (fourth edition 2008, with John Passé Smith). He serves on the editorial board of the *European Political Science Review*.

For our grandchildren,
Andrew Cruz Lara
and
Maya Rahel, Dalia Ella, and Tamar Marta Levanon
May they grow up in a world of peace and democracy

The Legitimacy Puzzle in Latin America

Political Support and Democracy in Eight Nations

JOHN A. BOOTH

University of North Texas

MITCHELL A. SELIGSON

Vanderbilt University

CAMBRIDGE
UNIVERSITY PRESS

CAMBRIDGE
UNIVERSITY PRESS

University Printing House, Cambridge CB2 8BS, United Kingdom

One Liberty Plaza, 20th Floor, New York, NY 10006, USA

477 Williamstown Road, Port Melbourne, VIC 3207, Australia

314-321, 3rd Floor, Plot 3, Splendor Forum, Jasola District Centre, New Delhi-110025, India

79 Anson Road, #06-04/06, Singapore 079906

Cambridge University Press is part of the University of Cambridge.

It furthers the University's mission by disseminating knowledge in the pursuit of education, learning and research at the highest international levels of excellence.

www.cambridge.org
Information on this title: www.cambridge.org/9780521734202

© John A. Booth and Mitchell A. Seligson 2009

First published 2009

A catalogue record for this publication is available from the British Library

Library of Congress Cataloging in Publication data
Booth, John A.
The legitimacy puzzle in Latin America : political support and democracy in eight nations / John A. Booth, Mitchell A. Seligson.
p. cm.
Includes bibliographical references and index.
ISBN 978-0-521-51589-4 (hardback) – ISBN 978-0-521-73420-2 (pbk.)
1. Legitimacy of governments – Latin America. 2. Legitimacy of governments – Latin America – Case studies. 3. Democracy – Latin America – Case studies. 4. Political participation – Latin America – Case studies. 5. Public opinion – Latin America – Case studies. I. Seligson, Mitchell A. II. Title.
JC497.B66 2009
320.9801´1–dc22   2008042305

ISBN 978-0-521-51589-4 Hardback
ISBN 978-0-521-73420-2 Paperback

Contents

List of Figures

List of Tables

Preface

In democracies, public opinion matters. Political scientists have for several decades pored over the results of public opinion surveys attempting to determine which attitudes and behaviors may be critical for the emergence and maintenance of stable democracy. In the 1970s, however, almost all of Latin America was caught in the grip of dictatorial rule, and carrying out public opinion surveys was dangerous for interviewers and respondents alike. At that time, one of the few places in the region where surveys of public opinion could be carried out openly and safely was Costa Rica, a country that had been democratic since the early 1950s and that had enjoyed a democratic tradition for most of the twentieth century.

It was in Costa Rica that the authors of this volume first began their collaboration, a relationship that has continued and prospered for more than thirty-five years. As graduate students studying at different universities, we had been drawn independently to Costa Rica to write our dissertations. Mitchell Seligson had served there in the Peace Corps and returned to conduct a survey of the political attitudes and behaviors of the peasantry funded by the Social Science Research Council. John Booth went to Costa Rica under the auspices of the Latin American Teaching Fellowship program to conduct a survey for Costa Rica's community development agency (Dirección Nacional de Desarrollo Comunal). During our shared time in Costa Rica, we developed the foundation of a lasting personal and intellectual friendship. We talked shop at length about the challenges of carrying out surveys in a developing country, one that at the time had a poorly developed road system and a telephone system largely limited to urban areas. We shared ideas about the science and art of measuring attitudes and behaviors, sampling, questionnaire wording and design, verification, survey team management, coding, and data management. The learning curve was steep, but this "baptism by fire" has served the two of us ever since, giving us the self-confidence to undertake survey research under challenging conditions. It also set us on a path of sharing our ideas and our datasets, resulting in fourteen coauthored articles and chapters and four coedited volumes. This work is our first book-length collaboration. It is an attempt to solve for us (and hopefully for our readership) what we call "the legitimacy puzzle."

THE LATIN AMERICAN PUBLIC OPINION PROJECT

This book was a long time in the making and involved considerable collaborative enterprise along the way. Beginning in 1976, from a base in the Political Science Department at the University of Arizona, Mitchell Seligson, often in collaboration with Edward N. Muller of the Arizona department and always in collaboration with Miguel Gómez Barrantes of the Universidad de Costa Rica, began a systematic program of carrying out surveys of democratic values in Costa Rica. That program produced a series of surveys, but because dictators governed most of the other countries in Latin America at that time, the environment for extending the democracy survey program to other countries did not exist. By the early 1990s, however, democracy had spread in the Latin American region, and Mitchell Seligson had moved to the University of Pittsburgh. With grants from the Mellon Foundation, Tinker Foundation, North-South Center, Heinz Foundation, University of North Texas, and University of Pittsburgh, and in collaboration with several highly regarded research organizations in Central America and with John Booth, surveys were carried out in the capitals of all six Spanish-speaking Central American countries. Seligson's graduate students at the University of Pittsburgh collaborated on survey design and led the fieldwork. Several of the students involved produced articles and dissertations based on that dataset, and many of them have built successful professional careers based in part on their experiences with this early effort. From this collaborative initiative, the Latin American Public Opinion Project (LAPOP) began to take shape.

A new phase in LAPOP's development began in 1993, when the United States Agency for International Development (USAID) Guatemala commissioned a larger study of that country, allowing LAPOP for the first time to work in languages other than Spanish – in that case five major Mayan languages. The 1993 study was followed by surveys in 1995, 1997, 1999, 2001, 2003, 2006, and 2008. In the late 1990s other countries began to tap into LAPOP's expertise. As a result, studies were carried out in El Salvador, Nicaragua, Paraguay, Bolivia, and Ecuador. The studies in Bolivia and Ecuador also involved working in indigenous languages as well as Spanish. In addition, the project began rendering assistance to some African studies, especially Mozambique, and later Madagascar. Studies began to include corruption victimization and its impact, with projects in Nicaragua, Honduras, and Albania. Important additional funding came from the United Nations Development Program (UNDP), the World Bank, and USAID.

LAPOP's scope broadened further with surveys on war-induced migration (supported by the RAND Corporation) and research on crime victimization and its impact on the economy and the development of democracy. In 2004 the project again expanded with significant new funding from USAID for LAPOP to carry out studies in eight countries simultaneously: Mexico, Guatemala, El Salvador, Honduras, Nicaragua, Costa Rica, Panama, and Colombia. A network of collaborating universities and research centers was established covering each of those countries. In 2004 Mitchell Seligson moved to Vanderbilt as the Centennial Professor of Political Science where his research for this book began and where the LAPOP project is now housed. At Vanderbilt, the project received major new support from the Center for the Americas and the Department of Political Science, as well as a substantial boost in funding from USAID, with additional support coming from the UNDP and the Inter-American Development Bank (IADB). The establishment of periodic surveys in a wider range of countries made it appropriate for the data series to take on a formal name, and from 2004 on, the series became the AmericasBarometer (in Spanish, El Barómetro de las Américas). This book is based on the 2004 AmericasBarometer survey of the LAPOP project.

BACKGROUND TO THE 2004 SURVEY

Public opinion surveys have become very popular in the democratizing world in general and in Latin America in particular in recent years. Unfortunately, far too few of those surveys follow the rigorous scientific procedures that have become accepted as the norm in academic public opinion research in the United States and Europe. Such studies often suffer from poorly designed questionnaires, unrepresentative and nonrandom samples, poor fieldwork supervision, careless data entry, and data analysis that rarely goes beyond univariate presentation of percentages.[1] As a result, such studies can provide grossly misleading results.

The LAPOP project has attempted, we would argue with considerable success, to produce quality survey data that match the highest standards of academic research in the United States and Europe. Because they were envisioned from the outset to allow for reliable cross-national comparisons, the surveys upon which the present study relies were carried out with special rigor and attention to methodological detail, as described in this preface and in the chapters and appendixes that follow. Rather than wrongly assuming that surveys are all "scientific" and would easily provide the "correct" answers, LAPOP researchers recognized from the outset that all survey research, by its very nature, is prone to error (derived from many sources, including sampling, interviewer and respondent inattention, coding mistakes, and data entry failures). The goal was to reduce to the absolute minimum each of those sources of errors. We outline here the steps that we followed to develop the data used in this book.

Our study began with a pilot project carried out in collaboration with Miguel Gómez Barrantes of the University of Costa Rica. As we explain in Chapter 1, even though we had carried out many prior surveys in which one or more dimensions of legitimacy were included, we had not previously taken a comprehensive look at the problem. We therefore embarked on that single-country study in 2002 in hopes of "getting the bugs out" of our instrument and enabling us to see which of our initial hypotheses had empirical support. With that work behind us, we embarked on the multi-country effort that provided the dataset that is the foundation for much of the research presented here.

Teams of scholars from each of the eight countries in which surveys were to be carried out were selected. In order to develop a common sample and questionnaire, the researchers met in Panama City in January 2004, hosted by our Panamanian colleague Marco Gandásegui, Jr., of the University of Panama. To help ensure comparability, a common sample design was crucial for the success of the effort. Each team worked from guidelines for the construction of a multistage, stratified area probability sample with a target N of 1,500 respondents. In Panama, each team met with Dr. Polibio Córdova, president of CEDATOS/Gallup, Ecuador, a region-wide expert in sample design who trained under the University of Michigan's

---

[1] A detailed recounting of the problems encountered in those surveys can be found in Seligson (2005c).

Leslie Kish, the father of modern survey sampling. Refinements in the sample designs were made at that meeting and later reviewed by Dr. Córdova. Detailed descriptions of the sample are found in Chapter 2.

At the conclusion of that meeting, the teams fanned out to their respective countries and engaged in extensive pretests. Problems that were detected in the pretests produced refinements in the instrument (a total of twenty-three distinct drafts were tested before the common instrument was finalized). At that point, translations were made into the major indigenous languages of Guatemala and into English (for the residents of the Bay Islands in Honduras) and the fieldwork was carried out. A sample of questionnaires from each country was drawn and audited and in some cases datasets needed to be corrected or reverified. The country datasets then were merged into a single file, and we began our analysis. This book is a product of that effort.

ACKNOWLEDGMENTS

The 2004 opinion surveys upon which this study is based were made possible by the generous support of USAID. Margaret Sarles, Bruce Kay, and Eric Kite in the Office of Democracy and Governance of USAID, supported by María Barrón in the Bureau for Latin America and the Caribbean, secured the funding and made possible the entire project thanks to their unceasing support. Todd Amani, USAID/Guatemala, assumed the role of coordinating the project at the USAID end. The University of North Texas College of Arts and Sciences and the UNT Development Leave Program freed coauthor John Booth from teaching responsibilities to allow him to dedicate time to the completion of this study.

Critical to the project's success was the cooperation of the many individuals and institutions that worked tirelessly to meet deadlines that at times seemed impossible. These include, for Mexico, Jorge Buendía and Alejandro Moreno, Departamento de Ciencia Política, Instituto Tecnológico Autónomo de México (ITAM); for Guatemala, Dinorah Azpuru and Juan Pablo Pira, Asociación de Investigación y Estudios Sociales (ASIES); for El Salvador and Honduras, Ricardo Córdova, Fundación Dr. Guillermo Manuel Ungo (FUNDAUNGO), José Miguel Cruz, Instituto Universitario de Opinión Pública (IUDOP) de la Universidad Centroamericana (UCA), and Siddhartha Baviskar, University of Pittsburgh; for Nicaragua, Luís Serra and Pedro López Ruíz, Universidad Centroamericana (UCA); for Costa Rica, Luís Rosero-Bixby, Universidad de Costa Rica, and Jorge Vargas, Programa Estado de la Nación; for Panamá, Marco A. Gandásegui hijo, Centro de Estudios Latinoamericanos (CELA), and Orlando J. Pérez, Central Michigan University; for Colombia, Carlos Lemoine, Centro Nacional de Consultoría (CNC), and Juan Carlos Rodríguez-Raga, Universidad de los Andes. Polibio Córdova of Ecuador supervised sample design throughout. A team of graduate assistants worked arduously in numerous aspects of the study: Miguel García (Colombia), Daniel Moreno (Bolivia), Sawa Omori (Japan), and Rosario Queirolo (Uruguay). Miguel Gómez Barrantes, of the Universidad de Costa Rica, provided excellent advice on the questionnaire design. We are profoundly grateful to all of these fine people for their excellent work on this study. Most importantly, we sincerely thank the 12,401 individuals in the eight study countries who took time from their busy lives to answer our questions. Without their cooperation, this study would not have been possible.

Finally, we wish to recognize the roles of our spouses. John Booth thanks his wife and frequent coauthor, Patricia Bayer Richard, for her invaluable support, patience, and excellent counsel throughout this project's gestation. Mitchell Seligson thanks his wife, Susan Berk-Seligson, for making the writing of this book, and all other things, worth doing.

Portions of Chapter 1 and Chapter 5 draw from articles we have published in the *Latin American Research Review* (Seligson 2002a), in *Opinião Pública* (Seligson, Booth, and Gómez Barrantes 2006), and in *Political Research Quarterly* (Booth and Seligson 2005).

1

The Legitimacy Puzzles

Political legitimacy, for decades a bedrock concept in political science and appropriated by journalists and diplomats as part of their discourse on nation-states, is in trouble. Many books and articles have empirically demonstrated a protracted decline in political legitimacy and a rising disaffection among citizens of advanced industrial democracies. Yet the dire consequences of legitimacy's decline, predicted by the seminal works in the field, have not occurred. Wondering why those anticipated crises have *not* materialized has led us to reexamine our understanding of legitimacy theory and to test it with an unusually rich multi-country database.

Modern legitimacy theory originated with Max Weber's three-fold typology from *Politics as a Vocation,* a lecture delivered in 1919 (Weber 1965). He distinguished between "charismatic," "traditional," and "rational-legal" forms of legitimation of the state, arguing that the first two are unstable forms that eventually evolve into the rational-legal form dominated by a state bureaucracy. Weber, however, was not focused on the *democratic* state, and it was not until the 1960s that contemporary legitimacy theory began to emerge. Seymour Martin Lipset's classic work *Political Man* (1961) reviewed the long-term, historical process by which regimes overcome crises and evolve into stable political systems whose right to rule is widely accepted. David Easton then elaborated extensively on the concept of political legitimacy (Easton 1965a; Easton 1975), suggesting various subcategories of legitimacy.

Despite the wealth and stability of established democracies including the United States, surveys show that public trust in government, politicians, and public institutions has declined markedly since the 1960s.[1] As Hetherington (1998) observed for the United States, "With the exception of upturns in the early 1980s and mid-1990s, trust in government has declined dramatically over the past thirty years." Scholars and public figures have repeatedly voiced alarm that democracy itself might thus be threatened by declining legitimacy – that is, by a rise in the proportion of disaffected citizens (Miller 1974; Kornberg and Clarke 1992; Craig 1993; Hibbing and Theiss-Morse 1995; Nye 1997; Nye et al. 1997; Pharr and Putnam 2000a; Hibbing and Theiss-Morse 2001; Hibbing and Theiss-Morse 2002; Dalton 2004).

If legitimacy is as important to political stability as the classical literature argues, then it should have observable effects. Early empirical research stressed the importance of legitimacy for stability in the then-undemocratic Mexico (Coleman 1976; Davis and Coleman 1983). More recently, Rose, Shin, and Munro (1999), using 1997 public opinion data, reported that South Koreans wanted more democracy from their corrupt, popularly elected regime than it was supplying, but that democracy nevertheless remained legitimate and stable despite this deficit. Mishler and Rose (1999) argued that an upward trajectory of public support is important for the survival of new democracies. In their study of surveys from Bulgaria, Czechoslovakia (and later the Czech and Slovak republics), Hungary, Poland, Romania, and Slovenia in the early 1990s, they found that support for the regimes of these postcommunist democracies grew over time. Bratton, Mattes, and Gyimah-Boadi's (2005) study of twelve African countries from 1999 to 2001 reported that, despite a deficit between citizens' demand for democracy and the amount of democracy they perceived, support for democracy was very broad in most countries. Perception of political freedom and evaluation of presidential performance had the greatest impact on citizen commitment to democracy.

Whether discussing new democracies, as do the scholars just cited, or more developed ones, most analysts assume that legitimacy affects system stability. Those who have observed legitimacy's long-term erosion in developed democracies also expect a discernible effect from this change.

---

[1] See the extensive bibliography collected by Norris (1999b) and contributors to her *Critical Citizens: Global Support for Democratic Governance,* and by Nye, Zelikow, and King (1997) and contributors to their book *Why People Don't Trust the Government.* See also Citrin 1974; Miller 1974; Finkel, Muller, and Seligson 1989; Rosenstone and Hansen 1993; Nye 1997; Warren 1999; Pharr, Putnam, and Dalton 2000c, 2002; Gibson, Caldeira, and Spence 2003.

As Russell Dalton, a leader in recent empirical research on legitimacy in advanced industrial democracy, expresses it: "Weakening ties to the political community in a democratic system might foretell eventual revolution, civil war, or the loss of democracy" (Dalton 2004). We know, however, that despite declining mass support, those developed democracies seem nowhere near collapse, and even widespread antisystem protest activity is very uncommon.[2] While it is true that explosive riots wracked Seattle, Washington, in the United States in 1999 and that similar protests occurred in Western Europe, such dramatic outbursts have been sporadic, self-contained, and very limited in their magnitude and frequency. Moreover, such unrest has not come close to destabilizing the regimes of the countries in which they occurred.

These instances of *declining legitimacy with no apparent impact on system stability* nicely frame the central conundrum of research in this field: One might ask, "Where's the beef?" What are and where are the missing effects of legitimacy's observed decline? If institutional legitimacy has indeed declined so much in recent decades, why have we not by now observed at least a few breakdowns of established democracies, or more frequent and widespread protests directed at them? And why do even the newer democracies, with significantly worse performance than developed democracies, appear to enjoy strong popular support?

One answer to these questions might be Easton and Lipset's notion of a "reservoir" of support. They suggest, in effect, that a reserve of legitimacy can accumulate over years of satisfactory regime performance and socialization, and therefore may erode only slowly. As Hetherington (1998) notes, in the 1950s, Robert Lane (1962) found that the average citizen viewed the government as a benign force, providing benefits and protections. But "that was then," as they say. The 1960s are long gone, and citizens in the United States no longer hold this seemingly uncritical view of their political system. The reservoir theory rings hollow as an explanation for the absence of a discernible impact of eroding legitimacy in light of several facts. Institutional legitimacy scores have been

---

[2] Przeworski et al. (2000) find that the only variable that matters in predicting democratic breakdown is economic development: "no democracy has ever been subverted [i.e., broken down], not during the period we studied nor even before nor after, regardless of everything else, in a country with a per capita income higher than that of Argentina in 1975: $6,055. There is no doubt that democracy is stable in affluent countries." The stability of wealthy countries in the post–World War II period, then, would appear to be completely independent of political legitimacy (and all other mass politics attitudes). We have doubts about this sweeping notion.

trending downward in the United States ever since the 1960s.[3] Indeed, one wonders whether there is a bottom to the reservoir. Yet despite this steady decline, citizen behavior does not seem to match. For example, the 2004 U.S. national election experienced a 10 percent voter turnout *increase*, and new citizen campaign finance participation through the Internet surged (Gans 2004). Moreover, in advanced industrial democracies generally, where studies show similar, steady declines in institutional legitimacy, Pippa Norris has nevertheless found impressive increases in citizen involvement in new forms of conventional political participation (Norris 2002). These developments run contrary to what one would have expected in the presence of eroded legitimacy.

Even many newly democratizing countries – ones that could not possibly enjoy any significant accrued reservoir of legitimacy because their regimes themselves were quite new – have survived system-wrenching crises. For example, the post–military rule constitutional democratic system in Argentina emerged more or less intact from extreme economic and political crises in the late 1990s and early 2000s. Moreover, democratically elected governments in Nicaragua and Honduras have retained formal democratic institutions despite extraordinarily poor economic performance over protracted periods. Colombia's government, with a longer experience of electoral democratic rule than Argentina, Honduras, and Nicaragua, has nonetheless struggled with decades of guerrilla insurgency. Aggravated by a horrific record of drug-related violence, the Colombian conflict has at times bordered on civil war. Yet formal electoral democracy has survived, indeed prospered, in that country. Further, the levels of support for democracy reported in African and new European and Asian democracies seem quite high for their actual performance levels, and few if any of those cases have been democracies long enough to build up a reservoir of support for the regimes (Mishler and Rose 1999; Rose, Shin, and Munro 1999, Bratton, Mattes, and Gyimah-Boadi 2005).

The Latin American examples mentioned above seem to suggest that democratic regimes might never fail, irrespective of political or economic performance. But, of course, we know democracies do fail. Not all remain stable. Alberto Fujimori staged an executive coup d'etat that extinguished democracy in Peru, and yet he enjoyed considerable popular support. Bolivia and Ecuador have experienced considerable antiregime protests, riots, and mobilization during the early and mid-2000s, and several of their presidents were forced from office. In Venezuela, a short-lived

---

[3] Excluding a transitory rebound after September 11, 2001.

coup forced out an elected president, Hugo Chávez,[4] who nonetheless managed to resume his post and won an even larger victory in his next electoral contest.

What does legitimacy theory say about these divergent and discrepant cases? Why do long-term and persistent legitimacy declines seem to have no effect on advanced industrial democracies? And why did the Argentine, Nicaraguan, and Colombian democratic regimes survive their crises and turmoil, while those of Ecuador and Bolivia suffered unconstitutional perturbations in the political order clearly related to mass anger at the regime? That such questions must be asked indicates a disjuncture between what legitimacy theory predicts and what is actually taking place: Sharply declining legitimacy in established democracies does not seem to consistently cause anything close to regime breakdown. Some new democracies do fail, conforming to theory that suggests they should break down, while others confound the theory by surviving under apparently high levels of stress. Is there something wrong with the theory that prevents us from making better predictions? Is the theory itself at fault? If so, is political legitimacy then largely or entirely irrelevant to political stability or even protest? Yet, if we throw out the legitimacy "baby with the bath water," then what explains why some nations have been so stable for so long, while others confront regular crises of stability? What is our alternative theory to explain variation in the dependent variable (i.e., stability)?

One alternative approach to the failure of a theory to explain reality is not to critique the theory itself, because it might be fundamentally correct. Rather, one must consider instead whether researchers might have incorrectly conceptualized and measured central concepts. In our case, empirical inquiry into legitimacy may not have asked the right questions or employed the correct variables. Many scholars who support the claims of legitimacy theory but find its inability to make sound predictions disappointing would certainly welcome a finding of this nature.

In this book, we attempt to show that problems of measurement have obscured important aspects of the theory, and we hope that by clarifying the former, we will have advanced the latter. Our review of the scholarly literature below reveals that much remains to be learned about political legitimacy's measurement, which in turn will help reveal much about its origins and its effects on political systems. We believe these legitimacy puzzles

---

[4] Chávez's credibility as a democrat has shrunk rapidly as he has dismantled restraints on the executive. As a result, beyond respect for formal elections, most of the trappings of democracy have been sharply attenuated; yet, by a minimalist definition of democracy based on free and fair elections, Venezuela has remained democratic.

persist in large part because of obstacles to understanding raised by the design of prior research and by the lack of appropriate empirical data on a sufficient range of countries. Thus, while we do not wish to diminish the important theoretical and empirical contributions in the field, many key questions about legitimacy have not yet been asked, while others have not been fully answered. This book, therefore, focuses on solving, to the extent possible, what we consider the three biggest puzzles about legitimacy: What is its structure? What are its sources? What are its effects?

We believe that, with better measurement and with the contours and sources of legitimacy better known, we may yet confirm the theory of democratic legitimacy or a revised version of it. This would then allow us to determine whether the contradictory outcomes in the real word discussed above do indeed fit with the theory. Should we vindicate important aspects of the theory, political scientists and political elites would need to pay careful attention to public opinion data on legitimacy. Alternatively, if even extensive efforts to improve legitimacy's measurement and contextualize its effects do not yield better real world predictions, the time may well have come to reevaluate the utility of the theory or seriously refine it.

We turn now to a review of the scholarly literature on legitimacy and its related notion of "political support," arranged around the puzzles of structure, origins, and consequences. This will facilitate later empirical exploration of the concept in hopes of clarifying legitimacy's structure, examining its sources, and elucidating its impact on political systems.

PRIOR RESEARCH ON LEGITIMACY

Legitimacy (broadly conceived as citizen support for government) is a theoretically rich concept, yet we contend that it remains insufficiently verified empirically. We concur with the recent conclusion of Nathan (2007: 3) that "diffuse regime support is a difficult concept to measure. It is separate from public support for, or the popularity of, specific policies or specific incumbents. It is intrinsically multidimensional and in principle cannot be captured by a single questionnaire item. And the field so far lacks an established, accepted measure or set of measures of this concept." In our view, not only does the construct validity of legitimacy remain poorly verified,[5] but also much remains to be learned about legitimacy's origins or effects on

---

[5] Construct validity refers to whether a variable (or in our case a group of related variables) is internally coherent (internal validity) and measures what it purports to measure in the empirical world (external validity).

political stability. Researchers have assumed, but seldom empirically demonstrated, that citizens' support for their regime somehow affects regime survival chances. It has been argued, for example, that the Weimar Republic fell and Hitler was elected because of the regime's lack of legitimacy. Yet, the complete absence of survey data from Germany in the 1920s and 1930s leaves that assertion untested and, ultimately, untestable. Beyond the German case, observers attribute the widespread collapse of Europe's pre–World War II democracies to legitimacy problems, but no empirical research supports that contention (Bermeo 2003). Determining the consequences of legitimacy decline could be especially important for nascent or younger democracies because even a relatively small loss of system support might undermine their fledgling institutions and undermine democracy itself.

Some scholars, foremost among them Adam Przeworski (1986: 50–53), have observed the failure of legitimacy research to make good predictions about regime survival and have dismissed entirely the value of the legitimacy concept. Przeworski sees legitimacy as a tautological concept: if a regime survives it is legitimate; if it fails it is not. In his critique, which appears in a volume examining the breakdown of authoritarian regimes, Przeworski argues that a country could move from dictatorship to democracy "even if no loss of legitimacy is suffered by the authoritarian system" (Przeworski 1986: 52). He contends that regimes do not collapse when they lose legitimacy but only when their citizens see prospects for a viable alternative system.

As others and we have seen it, this argument suffers from the weakness that individuals would not in fact prefer an alternative regime were the existing system viewed as legitimate. Why would individuals risk the economic and social chaos, not to mention life and limb, if they did not believe that their regime were so reprehensible that the risks were in some way worth it (Humphreys and Weinstein 2008)? The fall of the Nicaragua's Somoza dictatorship is an ideal example: a dynasty that ruled for decades eventually delegitimized itself with a series of disastrous errors of governance that alienated the very sectors that had propped it up for so long.[6] The demise of authoritarian rule in Korea is another well-documented case (Shin 1999: 1–2, 91–92).

Gilley (2009) articulates another weakness in the Przeworski critique. He points out that legitimacy theorists do not argue for immediate

---

[6] The loss of Somoza's legitimacy among both the Nicaraguan population and the international community is traced by Booth (1985) and discussed in Chapter 3 of this book.

breakdown when a dictatorial regime loses its legitimacy. Rather, Gilley contends, there will be lags between legitimacy loss and regime breakdown, sometimes long ones, which is precisely what happened with the demise of the Somoza regime in Nicaragua. Moreover, the limitation of Przeworski's position is that his measurement of legitimacy consists only of the presence or absence of a viable opposition. In contrast, in Gilley's work and in our study, we measure legitimacy independently – as an attitudinal phenomenon. As Gilley (2009: Chapter 5) states, "properly measured, legitimacy ... is the most critical and parsimonious explanation of why countries democratize.... It is the inability of authoritarian rulers to legitimize their rule that critically undermines it."

The Przeworski critique notwithstanding, for many scholars legitimacy is a bedrock concept in political science, one that has two distinct traditions. Weatherford (1992: 150–51) observes that the earliest understanding of legitimacy consisted of "the view from above." This perspective "takes for granted the epistemic assumption that an outside observer, relying on fairly gross aggregate evidence, can measure the legitimacy of a political system and rank it in comparison with other systems" (Weatherford 1992: 150). This approach is exemplified in studies of legislatures, for example (Pitkin 1967), and also in Dahl's early work (Dahl 1956). That perspective has been largely supplanted by an approach that Weatherford calls "the view from the grass roots," which relies on *citizen evaluations* of the legitimacy of their system. This newer approach is, in our view, far more consistent than the former one with the theoretical basis of legitimacy because all definitions of the concept ultimately rely on the *perceptions* of citizens. In the past, however, researchers could not systematically measure such perceptions and thus had to rely upon their own judgments as a *proxy* for legitimacy. With the widespread availability of public opinion data, it has become possible to draw on surveys to measure legitimacy. As we shall see, however, even survey research itself has to date encountered various limitations, which our efforts here attempt to overcome.

Legitimacy's Structure

Almost all empirical research in the field springs from David Easton's (1965a, 1975) pioneering theory, which recast the definition of political legitimacy within the framework of what he called "political support." Easton's framework divided political support into certain components that are more generalized (related to fundamental values) and others that are more specific (the evaluation of well-known leaders). Easton (1975: 435) asked: "Can a valid distinction be made between specific and diffuse support? Should support in either of these modes be construed as unidimensional or multidimensional?" His argument in favor of multidimensionality continues to shape the discussion and research on this question, with some scholars denying the distinction (Rogowski 1974) but most accepting it as the basic starting point for their analyses. In this book, we follow that more widely accepted point of view. We begin our theorizing with Easton's specific/diffuse distinction and build on it to provide what we believe is a subtler and conceptually more defensible empirical definition of the term.

Easton defined legitimacy as citizens' attitudes, specifically "the conviction 'that it is right and proper . . . to obey the authorities and to abide by the requirements of the regime.'" He identified two main dimensions of political support according to their objects – diffuse support (which he further divided into attitudes toward the political community and toward the regime) and specific support (oriented toward the performance of political authorities).[7] Considerable empirical work in the field strongly supports Easton's distinction between specific and diffuse support, and our own empirical findings here support that framework, even though we elaborate upon them somewhat more than Easton initially did. Thus, Rogowski's objection that the distinction was meaningless because citizens themselves did not in fact make it has not found support in the empirical literature (Muller and Jukam 1977; Muller and Williams 1980; Muller, Jukam, and Seligson 1982; Seligson 1983).

More recent theorizing about political legitimacy begins with a discussion by Nye and Zelikow (1997). Norris and others (Dalton 1999; Newton 1999; Norris 1999) build upon this base, refine Easton's conceptualization of legitimacy, and further explicate its dimensionality. Pippa Norris (1999c: 11–12) theorizes that political legitimacy (in the orientations of citizens) has five components based on opinion favoring or critical of certain objects, each defining a dimension: These are the

---

[7] Easton (1965b) elaborated these notions in his earlier work. This has led several scholars to suggest that Easton had a three-dimensional notion in mind (political community, the regime, and the authorities). This is the notion that Dalton (1996, 2004) employs. Our rendering of the thesis as two dimensions in which community and regime are subdimensions of "diffuse support" does not contradict that reading, but merely sees the first two dimensions as distinct from the third. Moreover, many years ago coauthor Seligson's team taught a graduate seminar with Easton at the University of Arizona in which Easton accepted this definition.

political community (the nation), regime principles (core values of the political system), regime performance (the functioning of the regime in practice), regime institutions (the actual institutions of the government), and political actors (incumbent leaders). Following Easton, these range from the general to the specific. Taken together, the discussions by Easton, Norris, and Dalton essentially depict multiple legitimacy dimensions and subdimensions, each based upon a particular political object or class of objects. By implication, individual citizens may be more or less supportive of each dimension, and different countries would thus have varying contours of legitimacy based on their citizenries' mean positions on the dimensions.

While researchers increasingly have grasped the multidimensional nature of legitimacy, empirical measurement has lagged behind. Most empirical research on legitimacy at first relied largely on a handful of "trust in government" items developed by the University of Michigan's Survey Research Center (Citrin and Muste 1999). Those questions asked, for example, "How much of the time do you think you can trust the government in Washington to do what is right?"[8] Efforts to verify empirically legitimacy's multidimensionality lagged well behind Easton's theorizing but eventually progressed through two basic stages. Lowenberg (1971) provoked a debate by arguing that Easton's distinction between specific and diffuse support was not empirically verifiable, and Rogowski (1974) also challenged this dichotomy. In a now classic debate, Miller (1974) argued that the declines observed in the Michigan trust in government series revealed rising political alienation in the United States, while Citrin (1974) countered that the trust measure tapped only superficial discontent with the elected officials of the day. Ensuing articles questioned the reliability and validity of the trust in government items and provided (Seligson 1983) the first empirical verification of diffuse and specific support dimensions (Muller and Jukam 1977; Muller et al. 1982; Seligson 1983; Citrin and Muste 1999).

Despite this promising beginning and notwithstanding the widespread recognition of the importance of disaggregating legitimacy/support, much subsequent empirical research relied on only one dimension. We suspect that this limitation of measurement had more to do with restrictions in questionnaire design than to strong theoretical arguments against the use of a more nuanced, multidimensional perspective. A good example of this

---

[8] See Citrin and Muste (1999: 481–83) for the items.

phenomenon appears in a study based on European survey data. After extensively discussing support's dimensionality, Fuchs, Guidorossi, and Svensson (1995) nevertheless employed a single variable (satisfaction with democracy) in their analysis of European democracies. Similarly, Mishler and Rose (2001) examined only one dimension of legitimacy – trust in government – in their study of 10 postcommunist regimes. In a recent large-scale study using the World Values Survey (WVS), a dataset from over 80 nations, Inglehart and Welzel (2005) examine the ability of legitimacy to predict to two measures of democracy in the period 2000–02.[9] They find little impact in their regression analysis, one that includes as control variables several other predictors of democracy. The analysis, however, follows the same limited approach that others have taken, looking only at measures of confidence in institutions.[10] Therefore, even though the Inglehart and Welzel analysis is commendable for its broad coverage of cases, it does not advance the study of legitimacy because of its unidimensional approach. A recent and equally broadly based attempt to examine legitimacy, based on 54 countries, similarly restricts its initial definition of legitimacy to the single variable of expressing a preference for democracy over dictatorship (Chu et al. 2008: 77). This study then goes on to include several other variables that mix a series of single-item variables including institutional support and satisfaction with democracy. Unfortunately, the analysis presented is correlational, with no dimensional analysis or index construction presented for the legitimacy items used, and no control variables employed in the regression results. In combination, these attributes make interpretation of the results obscure.

In its second phase, legitimacy research moved beyond the diffuse/specific dichotomy to a broader, multidimensional conceptualization. Researchers gradually learned that legitimacy had at least several components. For example, Caldeira and Gibson have focused their research, both within the United States and abroad, on support for particular government institutions (Gibson and Caldeira 1998; Gibson et al. 2003; Gibson 2008). They found, among other things, that courts have higher levels of legitimacy than legislatures (Gibson, Caldeira, and Spence

---

[9] This scale is based on Freedom House scores alone for one measure and, for the second measure, based on a composite index of Freedom House plus the World Bank's control of corruption scores.

[10] In the regression shown by Inglehart and Welzel (2005: 251), two other measures are included as predictors, "approval of democracy" and "democracy-autocracy preference." These, of course, are not measures of legitimacy but measures of democracy, which, as we have argued, may be seen as more or less legitimate.

2005). Other scholars have looked at an even more microsocial level, separating out the legitimacy of the police from that of the larger justice system (Sunshine and Tyler 2003).

A growing trend toward viewing legitimacy as multidimensional had emerged by the early 1990s. An important example was Stephen Weatherford's (1992) all-encompassing notion of legitimacy. He divided legitimacy into two main dimensions, "political components" and "personal components," and employed a structural equation model to analyze numerous items from the 1976 Michigan National Election Study. The political component items emerged from the analysis as "judgments of system performance," which are clearly akin to most notions of legitimacy. The "personal/citizenship traits" components, however, constituted factors apart from legitimacy and should more appropriately be treated as *causes* and *consequences* of legitimacy rather than as legitimacy itself. As will become clear in our analysis, we develop a notion of legitimacy that has antecedents, including some variables that Weatherford included (e.g., interpersonal trust) and consequences (e.g., political participation). However, we do not confound these causes and consequences with the concept of legitimacy itself. Weatherford (1992: 161) concluded his paper by calling for a test of its applicability with other datasets outside the U.S. context, which is precisely what we undertake in this book.

Kornberg and Clarke (1992), continuing the multidimensional approach, used survey data from Canada to examine three "objects of support": community, regime, and authorities. Their analysis tested a unidimensional model consistent with the thesis that support dimensions are not empirically distinguishable. They found that "this [unidimensional] model has a totally unsatisfactory fit" (Kornberg and Clarke 1992: 114) and then presented a confirmatory factor analysis (CFA) identifying separate dimensions for community, regime, and authorities. This pioneering research provided an early confirmation of the empirical validity of Easton's argument for the multidimensional nature of legitimacy. This study was not definitive, however, because it used only a single item (survey question) to measure each dimension and because it tested data from only one country.

The empirical contribution by Kornberg and Clarke to legitimacy's multidimensionality clearly influenced later theorizing by Nye and Zelikow (1997) and Norris (1999c). As a result, researchers increasingly, but not uniformly, began employing multidimensional notions of legitimacy in their survey-based research. However, further efforts to verify empirically the dimensionality itself and explore its contours across different nations nonetheless remained limited. Much research merely assumed, but did not test for, the multidimensional nature of legitimacy. Norris (1999c: 16–21), for example, specified survey items that could tap the dimensional structure she proposed, yet did not empirically analyze them. By contrast, Klingemann (1999) did explore legitimacy's structure. He factor analyzed several items drawn from the WVSs of the mid-1990s from 39 countries and found cross-national evidence for three of the five proposed by Norris – support for political community, regime principles, and regime performance – with national-level variation on each. Of the two missing dimensions (support for regime institutions and political actors), Klingemann (1999: 35) explained and complained: "[A]nalysts face problems of secondary analysis. They are obliged to use those indicators that finally entered the questionnaire, even though alternatives might have been preferred." He also reported that correlations among some supposedly dimension-defining items were low, especially political community (1999 38 n.) Furthermore, Klingemann's factor analysis analyzed the pooled sample of 38 countries but left unclear whether the dimensional structure detected had been confirmed at the individual country level. Thus, his subsequent analysis of support levels by country may not have reflected the same dimensional structure for each country in the sample. In sum, Klingemann advanced importantly beyond Kornberg and Clarke by employing a multinational dataset and by using multiple variables to define the dimensions of legitimacy, but he also confronted serious limitations in the availability of sufficient numbers and diversity of appropriate legitimacy variables in the dataset he employed.

Dalton's (1999) initial work in this field, using a five-dimensional definition that paralleled that of Norris, employed a national-election study series from advanced industrial democracies to examine whether legitimacy varied over time. That study, however, did not confirm empirically the actual dimensionality of the questions used to capture the assumed five-dimensional support structure used in the analysis. Dalton's next major study, however, undertook a more ambitious construct-validation effort. Focusing on eight advanced industrial nations drawn from the World Values 1995–98 survey series, Dalton (2004: 56–62) employed factor analysis on a pooled multinational sample and there uncovered four legitimacy dimensions: support for community, democracy, institutions, and authorities. This array omitted, however, the category of "regime performance" that Norris (1999b) and Dalton (1999: 68–69) had earlier proposed and that Dalton had previously analyzed. Furthermore, he transformed the theorized dimension of "support for regime principles" into the narrower measure of "support for democracy." Dalton (as had Klingemann) used a varimax rotated factor solution (which assumes zero correlation among dimensions) while the theory explicitly assumes the several dimensions of support would be intercorrelated. To address this problem, Dalton (2004: 60 n. 4) mentioned that he performed on the data an obliquely rotated factor analysis that allowed interfactor correlations that confirmed that the dimensions were indeed correlated.[11]

Theory and research to date, while having advanced at each of the mentioned theoretical and empirical stages, still leave us with the first of our puzzles – *what is the structure of legitimacy or political support?* Does this theoretically well-elaborated multidimensional construct actually exist in the minds of citizens of real polities? Further, what is the actual structure of legitimacy in particular political systems? How does the structure of legitimacy depend upon political culture, the many and varied socioeconomic, political, and regime-type contextual variables? In other words, would we expect legitimacy to be the same in well-established as well as nascent democracies? To date, this question has been difficult to answer because most of the data used in construct validation have come from surveys taken in advanced industrial democracies, especially from Europe and the United States.

Legitimacy's Sources

The second legitimacy puzzle concerns the origin of political support. *What causes citizens to support or oppose a regime?* The classic tradition finds the source of legitimacy in either the culture of citizens (a product of socialization by family and peers and of lived experience) or the performance of regimes (Lipset 1961; Easton 1965a). Easton believed specific support would develop from citizens' perceptions of the outputs from authorities to individuals over time. It would vary with "perceived benefits or satisfactions. When these decline or cease, support will do likewise."

---

[11] Dalton ultimately derives the scores for his four legitimacy dimensions using the *un*correlated varimax solution and employs them in subsequent analysis. We will opt in our analysis (Chapter 2) for obliquely rotated factor scores to provide values for the legitimacy norms we uncover. This is a somewhat obscure technical point, but we believe our approach provides measurements somewhat truer to legitimacy theory and appropriately sensitive to the actual empirical nature of legitimacy.

Easton contended that diffuse support is more durable and thus more independent of specific regime outputs than is specific support. Diffuse support would come from three main longer-term sources: education and socialization, personal experience over time, and ideology (Easton 1975: 445–49; Easton, Dennis, and Easton 1980; see also Abramson and Inglehart 1970). The literature on the origins of political legitimacy is too extensive to cite fully, but numerous researchers have identified one or more of these sources of legitimacy.[12]

Ronald Rogowski rejected this approach in favor of what he called "rational legitimacy" (Rogowski 1974). An early advocate of rational choice theory, Rogowski believed that legitimate constitutional arrangements grow out of the rational choices made by individuals. According to Rogowski, once one understands social divisions based on such key factors as class, ethnicity, race, and religion, it is fairly easy to predict what kinds of legitimate constitutions will emerge. Rowgowski's approach to the sources of legitimacy was strongly critiqued, however, by Gabriel Almond (Almond 1977). He argued that Rogowski inappropriately embraced the class basis of rational legitimacy and rejected the culture and performance approaches without testing either. Almond further contended that Rogowski's thesis, if applied to the German Second Reich, would have predicted its breakdown. Yet, in that case, by extending numerous benefits to the middle class, Bismarck managed to prolong the regime's life for nearly 50 years, vindicating a performance approach. Predictions based on social structure, furthermore, allow little room for dynamic analysis (shifting levels of legitimacy). Thus it is not surprising that the Rogowski approach has not been pursued widely in the field.[13]

Recent research on legitimacy's sources examines various categories of influences. Mishler and Rose (2001: 31) classify major approaches

[12] These include Almond and Verba 1963; Dennis et al. 1968; Dennis and McCrone 1970; Muller 1970a; Muller 1970b; Coleman 1990; Putnam 1993; Hetherington 1998; Fuchs 1999; Holmberg 1999; McAllister 1999; Mishler and Rose 1999; Norris 1999a; Rose et al. 1999; Shin 1999; Dalton 2000; Della Porta 2000; Newton and Norris 2000; Norris 2000; Pharr 2000b; Bratton, Mattes, and Gyimah-Boadi 2005; Booth 2006; Nathan 2007.

[13] Another approach to legitimacy that shares some aspects of Rogowski's has emerged from research by Latin American historians. Nolan-Ferrell's review of this literature (2004) detects in several works a perspective drawn from Antonio Gramsci's writings on hegemony (Gramsci and Hoare 1990) and focused on state formation and state building through revolutions (Mexican, Cuban). The main emphasis, as in Rogowski, is class analysis, but the ultimate concern is on the connection of intellectuals to the state rather than the question of interest to us – the evaluation of the state by the citizen.

as cultural or institutional and subdivide each of those between macrosocial and microsocial influences. They argue that the cultural approach (linked to Easton's diffuse support) attributes trust in institutions to "longstanding and deeply seeded beliefs about people . . . communicated through early-life socialization" (p. 31). The institutional approach (linked to Eastonian-specific support) contends that political trust derives mainly from the performance of regimes and institutions and its evaluation by citizens. Mishler and Rose neatly summarize their resulting four types of sources of legitimacy values: national culture (including history), individual socialization (place in the social structure), government performance (public policy and institutional behavior), and individual evaluations (political attitudes, values, and norms) (Mishler and Rose 2001).

Empirical research on the origins of legitimacy usually has viewed and measured legitimacy as a single dimension (indeed, often measured with a single survey question) of support for or trust in government. Most such research has drawn data from large multinational surveys such as the WVS, Eurobarometer, New Democracies Barometer, Afrobarometer, and, most recently, AsiaBarometer. They have examined individuals' traits and positions in society (demographics) with inconclusive or mixed findings (Holmberg 1999; Mishler and Rose 1999; Newton 1999; Rose et al. 1999; Bratton et al. 2005). They have found various political attitudes and behaviors that shape legitimacy, especially democratic and authoritarian norms and evaluations of economic performance (Miller and Listhaug 1999; Dalton 2000; Della Porta 2000; Chu and Huang 2007). In one of the few extended analyses to date using multiple legitimacy dimensions, Dalton (2004) employed a multinational WVS sample of advanced industrial democracies, mainly in Europe, to examine the impact of individual satisfaction with regime economic performance, left-right ideology, postmaterialism, group membership, interpersonal trust, and television exposure. Dalton reported that these variables had somewhat different patterns of influence on the four legitimacy dimensions examined but that such personal traits as education, age and sex had little impact on legitimacy. In another study treating political support as having various dimensions, Bratton, Mattes, and Gyimah-Boadi (2005) employed diverse factors of social structure, culture, and cognition as predictors of commitment to democracy, which is largely analogous to support for regime principles. They also employed numerous other political and economic support items to predict commitment to democracy, raising a question of endogeneity in their analysis (Mattes and Bratton 2007).

Researchers have followed two main strategies when examining the effect on legitimacy of the macrosocial context, shorthand for historical experience, culture, and regime performance. In the first, the context or regime was operationalized mainly as a dummy variable for the nation-state,[14] and impact of regime type (communist or postcommunist) or subnational region (West Germany versus East Germany) was detected by splitting files to compare subsets of data. These strategies produced relationships that, while significant, are difficult to summarize here other than to indicate that macro political-economic-cultural context matters (Dalton 1999; Fuchs 1999; Holmberg 1999; Inglehart 1999; Klingemann 1999; McAllister 1999; Mishler and Rose 1999; Dalton 2004; Gilley 2006).

As a second, and we believe more useful, strategy for detecting macrosocial sources of legitimacy, researchers have measured the political-economic context's effects on political support with the more sophisticated technique of attributing contextual values for each country, for example for its level of democracy, economic performance, or community size (Dalton 1999; McAllister 1999; Miller and Listhaug 1999; Mishler and Rose 1999; Norris 1999b; Dalton 2004; Gilley 2006). This allows for a more finely grained exploration of cultural effects by using graded scoring of contextual characteristics (levels of economic output or quality of human rights performance). It contrasts favorably with the first strategy, which merely lumps all macro effects into single-country dummies. Mishler and Rose, for example, analyzed New Democracies Barometer surveys of post-Soviet polities and found that Freedom House country scores indicating greater system-level political liberties increased individuals' trust in institutions (Mishler and Rose 1999). McAllister (1999: 197) reported for 24 WVS nations that GDP ratios correlated negatively with trust in institutions. Norris (1999d: 232) reported, based on the characteristics of 25 WVS nations, that various government structures (e.g., federalism versus unitary government or parliamentary versus

---

[14] Dummy variables code the presence of a characteristic as 1 and its absence as 0. Thus, in a multinational survey, residents of Guatemala, for example, would be assigned a score of 1 on the variable "Guatemala," while residents of all other countries would receive a score of 0 on that variable. Residents of other countries similarly would receive a 1 for a variable indicating their own country of residence. The baseline country is omitted in regressions. This produces a very blunt instrument for detecting contextual effects because it lumps everything about Guatemala – regime type, economic activity, history, and culture – into one basket, so to speak. One does not, therefore, know what in particular it might be about "Guatemalanness" that produces an observed effect. See our discussion in Chapter 4 of a better strategy.

presidential systems) were modestly but significantly associated with "confidence in institutions." For example, citizens of proportional representation systems had higher levels of institutional confidence than those in majoritarian or mixed systems. Miller and Listhaug (1999: 211–12) tracked the effect of national budget deficits on confidence in government over time in three industrial democracies. They found the contextual trait (budget deficits) to be both directly and indirectly linked to support (the latter mediated through citizens' expectations about government). As we will discuss in more detail in Chapter 4, this methodological approach, while an improvement over previous practice, may have overemphasized the impact of system-level traits upon legitimacy because many of these analyses did not apply multilevel analysis techniques. As appropriate, we will use an analytical technique that can correct for this overvaluation.

In summary, sources of political legitimacy are complex, arising from both institutional and cultural factors and from both micro- and macrosocial origins. The *sources puzzle* we encounter is that various challenges have limited empirical research on sources of legitimacy. First, researchers often have measured political support unidimensionally rather than in its multiple aspects, obscuring part of what is almost certainly a complex pattern of sources of what we now know are different types of legitimacy. Second, the surveys on which analyses of contextual or macrosocial sources of legitimacy have been conducted come mainly from collections of similar nations, such as those in the New Democracies Barometer. This practice has curtailed the range of contextual variation among the samples used in many studies and has thus obscured possible sources. Fortunately, the Afrobarometer and AsiaBarometer data have provided new points of comparison to which we now add our Latin American cases. Third, researchers generally have used dummy variables for countries to summarize multiple cultural, historical, and regime traits. This practice has, in effect, black-boxed regime performance by obscuring valuable information about the sources of legitimacy. Thus it has signaled that contextual factors do matter without telling us why. The full advantage of using graded contextual variables rather than country dummies and of employing the correct analytical technique that does not over-weight contextual factors, we believe, remains to be demonstrated on survey sets that involve broad-ranging variation on key national traits such as static and dynamic measures of economic performance, social welfare performance, or government effectiveness and democracy.

Legitimacy's Effects

The research cited above has recorded a marked decline in the legitimacy of democratic institutions in the United States and many other established democracies in recent decades. Recent pathbreaking work by Hetherington (1998, 2005), focused on the United States, examines the effects of trust, a shorthand term for legitimacy. He found, for example, that declining trust in government brought about a conservative shift in public policies because citizens lost confidence that their government could administer capably such liberal policies as health care (Hetherington 2005). He also found that low trust in the system translated into lower confidence in elected officials (Hetherington 1998). Yet, despite the importance of these findings, they do not directly address the question of system stability we consider here. Many have assumed that eroding legitimacy would necessarily undermine or weaken democratic regimes. We probably should be relieved that the world's established democracies have not fulfilled the legitimacy theorists' darkest predictions by breaking down. Yet, as scholars confronting the *effects puzzle* – the failure of declining legitimacy to produce democratic breakdown – we also must ask why predictions from such an important theory seem to miss their mark. How does legitimacy supposedly work to stabilize regimes, and how does its absence undermine stability? In particular, what are the system-corrosive effects of diminishing legitimacy? Would eroded legitimacy sharply alter the political landscape in some specific ways that might undermine political stability? To pursue these questions, we begin by reviewing the central arguments about legitimacy's effects.

The main answer to this effects puzzle ascribes a critical role to political participation. Classics of political science have recognized that political participation, whether conventional or unconventional, offers benefits and poses risks for political systems. *The Civic Culture* (Almond and Verba 1963) contended that a stable and successful polity would include many more passive, subject-oriented citizens than activist, participation-oriented ones who might engage the system excessively. They thus viewed citizen participation as partly positive, *but only up to a point*. Huntington elaborated on this logic in *Political Order in Changing Societies* by arguing that citizens might participate in politics to such an extent that their demands and protests could overwhelm an emerging political system's institutions and thus lead to its decay and breakdown (Huntington 1968).

Some students of legitimacy have gone beyond broad assumptions to link theoretically aspects of political support directly to citizen participation and regime stability. Two related arguments hold that both conventional and unconventional participation might operate either to strengthen or to weaken regimes (Easton 1975; Coleman 1976; Davis and Coleman 1983; Kornberg and Clarke 1992; Newton 1999; Rose et al. 1999; Norris 1999a; Newton and Norris 2000; Otake 2000; Canache 2002; Norris 2002; Booth and Richard 2006b; Booth, Wade, and Walker 2006). The first contention was that citizens with high legitimacy values (i.e., those strongly supportive of regimes) would more likely engage in conventional political participation within institutional channels. "Much commentary assumes that if people have little confidence in the core institutions of representative democracy. . . they will be reluctant to participate in the democratic process, producing apathy" (Norris 2002: 30). Within-system participation would tend to reinforce and stabilize extant institutions. Politically disaffected citizens would pose little threat to regime institutions because they would not make demands for compliance or change. In essence, these theorists argued that there exists a linear and positive relationship between support and within-channels political activism: *Supportive citizens engage within the system and strengthen it, while disaffected citizens withdraw without weakening it.*

The second contention was that citizens with low legitimacy values would be more likely to engage in unconventional or protest participation. In short, there should exist a linear and positive relationship between low political support and engagement in outside-of-channels participation and protest. For example, "It is widely believed that political cynicism fuels protest activity" (Norris 1999a: 261). Findings on Venezuela in the turbulent mid-1990s and on other Latin American countries indicated that "people tend to oppose political violence and protest when support for democracy is high" (Canache 2002: 136). Indeed, researchers have argued that growing citizen antagonism toward the Nicaraguan and Salvadoran military regimes of the 1970s and early 1980s led to increasing levels of opposition-group activity, protest, and rebellion against the repressive governments ruling those countries (Booth 1991; Foley 1996; Booth 2006). Thus *disaffected citizens may protest or rebel, but supportive or neutral citizens generally do not.* In sum, large amounts of protest or confrontational participation could overtax inflexible institutions and provoke their decay or even overthrow them.

These arguments about legitimacy's behavioral effects, however, tend to dichotomize participation by focusing on participation either within channels (voting or party activism) or outside of channels (protest or, more commonly studied, support for protest).[15] Thus, while minimally recognizing the well-established fact that political participation is multidimensional (Verba, Nie, and Kim 1971; Verba and Nie 1972; Verba, Nie, and Kim 1978), including in Latin America (Booth 1978; Booth and Seligson 1979), the legitimacy-effects literature has not yet fully appreciated the importance of participation's diversity. Merely dichotomizing participation as either engaging within channels or protesting inadequately frames the complexity of citizens' involvement and the multiple arenas in which it may occur.

Bratton, Mattes, and Gyimah-Boadi (2005), in an exception to the patterns noted above, explored the impact of several performance evaluation items on three participation measures in twelve African countries. Although they identified voting and protest as two dimensions of participation, their third dimension, "communing and contacting," included a mixture of partisan activism, electioneering, communal activism, contacting officials, and civil society engagement. Many studies of participation in comparative context suggest that the many items included in communing and contacting likely constitute elements of several distinct modes of participation that more properly should have been disaggregated. Further, in their empirical analysis, Bratton et al. (2005: 297) included various political participation items related to the dependent variable as independent variables in their models. Because nearly all political participation items positively correlate with all others, this decision artificially inflated the explained variation in voting, protesting, and communing-contacting. They report that some performance evaluations have a positive linear relationship to voting and communing, but detect no relationship for protest. While their use of developing-nation cases was encouraging and their effort to disaggregate participation was a step in the right direction, we believe that by not fully "unpacking" participation and not correctly specifying their models, the their analysis was incomplete.

We therefore believe that various possibilities for relationships between legitimacy and political participation remain largely unexplored. First, not all dimensions of legitimacy are likely to affect each mode of participation in the same way. Indeed, for some legitimacy dimensions and participation modes there might be no logical participation effect at all. Second, the simple linear assumptions from the literature cited above, while valid in some instances, appear to understate the possible range of

[15] See, however, a new line of argument by Norris, Walgrave, and Van Aelst (2005) arguing that the theory that disaffection with the political system leads to protest "receives little, if any, support from the available systematic empirical studies of the survey evidence."

legitimacy-participation effects by ignoring nuances of participation in diverse contexts. Citizens with low levels of support might participate in arenas outside of national institutions such as local government, communal activism, or civil society rather than protesting or remaining politically passive.

Third, we are uncomfortable with the assumptions of simple linearity made in most, but not all, previous research.[16] One of the authors of this book, for example, in prior research on Peru, found a curvilinear relationship between legitimacy and approval of coups d'etat (Seligson and Carrión 2002). This finding suggests by analogy that holding extremely polarized legitimacy positions (whether high or low) might move citizens to similarly high levels of participation. In contrast to those who moderately approve or disapprove of institutions (whom researchers since *The Civic Culture* have assumed to participate at moderate rates), citizens who either *intensely approve or intensely disapprove* of government may *both* be moved to high levels of civic engagement. For example, in the 2004, 2006, and 2008 U. S. election campaigns, it is likely that both those most supportive of the incumbent Bush administration and those least supportive of it engaged in high levels of campaign-related activism, causing a marked increase in voter turnout and other types of campaign activism. We believe this relationship would be especially likely to exist in democracies, and especially in those with good human rights climates (as is the case in Costa Rica, a country included in this book). Thus, in a democracy, some legitimacy-participation functions might take on a U shape. Oddly, neither theory nor prior empirical research has sufficiently considered this possibility of disgruntled citizens of democracies increasing their within-channels participation in order to "throw the rascals out." Nor has theory explored which factors cause disaffected citizens to choose among four possible options – increasing their involvement in national-system politics, dropping out of national-system politics and becoming politically passive, shifting their participation from national-system politics to civil society or communal arenas, or engaging in protest or rebellion.

Another concern of ours involves determining the distribution of legitimacy norms among the population. When most people share high legitimacy norms, most citizens would likely engage within institutional channels (voting, contacting officials, party activism). Their behavior thus would tend

---

[16] But see Muller (1979), who argued that violent protest behavior would be found only among those at the extreme low end of system support. Norris, Walgrave, and Van Aelst (2005), however, argue strongly that empirical evidence about support's impact on participation conflicts with this finding.

to reinforce the system's institutions. In contrast, in cases in which there were a large share of discontented or disaffected citizens, national participation levels could decline, depressing voter turnout rates (Seligson 2002a) or shifting participation to alternate arenas (Booth and Seligson 2005). Larger proportions of disaffected citizens could also protest, support antisystem parties, or engage in confrontational participation. With a high ratio of activist malcontents to system supporters, the likelihood of protest or rebellion would increase and thus provoke system instability. In yet another scenario, either relatively flat or bimodal distributions of legitimacy norms in a given country could increase the potential for conflict between large numbers of both activist system supporters and activist malcontents. Mobilization and increased political activism might occur among those at the extremes, increasing the likelihood of violent conflict between pro- and antisystem citizens. One suspects that the situations in Haiti prior to the ouster of President Aristide in 2004 and in Bolivia in mid-2005 would have involved this phenomenon of polarized distribution of legitimacy norms driving pro- and anti-incumbent conflict.

One thing that becomes increasingly clear from this discussion is that multicountry research that aggregates national distributions of legitimacy into a single data point per country sweeps an immense amount of necessary information and nuance under the rug. Without considering the underlying distribution of legitimacy norms in their multiple dimensions, such research could not possibly pick up on the critically important distinctions we have listed here. Yet, a great deal of comparative politics research today does precisely that, aggregating survey data into averages for an entire country.

Finally, we believe that legitimacy norms of mass publics constitute only part of the equation of democratic stability. Situations as stark as those just described attribute dramatic roles to mass publics. But we believe that, more typically, the attitudes and behaviors of elites are critical factors that can interact with masses to sustain or undermine democratic systems. In developing democracies, political institutionalization is typically weak, and elite commitment to democratic norms may be thin. Far more than in developed democracies, young democracies' critical elites (in the security forces, parties, media, business community, state apparatus) and key external actors all can play major roles in undermining system stability by promoting a military or executive coup d'etat or undermining popular support for a democratic regime. Would-be elite plotters against democracy may draw courage and even mass support when large portions of the citizenry become disgruntled about national institutions, actors, and regime performance. Widespread low legitimacy norms could tempt strategically positioned antidemocratic actors to curtail democratic liberties or try to overthrow or undermine a democratic regime (Cameron 1998). Schedler (2006) has described "electoral authoritarianism" – increasingly common in contemporary Latin America – in which elected presidents limit democracy to elections but little else.

We believe that the most likely scenario for the destabilization of democracies will involve widespread multiple discontent (low legitimacy of various kinds) among a nation's population. Awareness of widespread popular disgruntlement could tempt antidemocratic elites to implement electoral authoritarianism or to stage an executive or military coup. In a country with few politically discontented citizens, in contrast, antidemocratic elites would be much harder pressed to justify undermining or demolishing democracy and could anticipate less public support.

We now have completed the discussion of our theoretical expectations concerning legitimacy's shape, sources, and effects. It is time to move from theorizing to the actual data in order to take our first look at how some of these theoretical issues play out in practice. To do so, we turn to the case of Costa Rica.

LEGITIMACY IN COSTA RICA

We have conducted research on Costa Rica and its political system for three decades, much of it on public opinion, political support, and political behavior. We were originally drawn to the country for some of the very characteristics that made it both interesting and suitable for investigating aspects of legitimacy. As one of Latin America's few democracies in the early 1970s, Costa Rica was a place where survey research was possible. Today Costa Rica is widely recognized as Latin America's oldest, most stable democracy. Freedom House (2004), which measures democracy worldwide, has consistently given Costa Rica very strong democracy ratings: in 2003 it scored a combined score of 3, with the very best possible score, obtained by the United States and other advanced industrial democracies, being a 2.[17] Other studies have reached the same conclusions

---

[17] Costa Rica received a score of 1 on "political rights" and 2 on "civil liberties" on a scale that ranged from a best possible score of 1 and worst possible score of 7, for a total of 3. The other countries in our study scored as follows on the combined Freedom House measures: Guatemala 8, El Salvador 5, Honduras 6, Nicaragua 6, Panama 3, and Colombia 8.

(Vanhanen 1975; Bollen 1980; Vanhanen 1997; Booth 1998). Earlier in Costa Rica's history, however, the country was not a democracy. Elections were often fraudulent and constitutional rule was interrupted twice during the first half of the twentieth century (Molina Jiménez and Lehoucq 1999). But for over half a century, since 1950, Costa Rica has held free, fair, and competitive elections, has experienced a regular rotation of rulers and parties, and rarely has experienced violations of human or civil rights (Yashar 1997; Booth 1998; Booth 2006; Booth and Richard 2006b; Booth et al. 2006). In the 1970s, when elected regimes fell throughout Latin America, and in the 1970s and 1980s, when revolution and unrest occurred in nearly all of Central America, Costa Rica remained democratic, with its competitive two-party system intact. By the 1990s the country had evolved into a two-party system dominated by the social democratic National Liberation Party (Partido de Liberación Nacional – PLN), which had formed in the early 1950s, and the Social Christian Unity Party (Partido de Unidad Social Cristiana – PUSC), which arose from a coalition of conservative parties in the 1980s.

Costa Rica provided an ideal exploratory case for us for this larger project because of the existence of a series of surveys conducted there beginning in 1978 that permitted us to track one aspect of political legitimacy across two decades. One of the first relevant findings of that research was to demonstrate the validity of the "reservoir of legitimacy theory," or the theory that those regimes that enter crises with high legitimacy are likely to survive even severe challenges to their stability. Costa Ricans' support for the political system remained high despite an extreme economic crisis in the early 1980s (Seligson and Muller 1987; Finkel et al. 1989). This finding provided evidence suggesting that a reservoir of system support built up over many years prior to the economic crisis of 1982 was sufficient for Costa Rican democracy to weather the storm.

More recently, Seligson (2002d) extended the study through 1999 after a precipitous decline in voter turnout in 1998 from a persistent 80 percent to 70 percent.[18] This trend that continued into the 2006 national elections

---

[18] Not only did turnout decline from its normal level of 80 percent of the electorate, but also votes for minor parties in the 1998 presidential race quadrupled from about 2 percent to over 8 percent, and the number of minor parties more than doubled from seven to 13. Even more striking, at the level of the legislature, this change was even sharper. There, minor parties expanded their votes from 12 percent in 1994 to 24 percent in 1998. The system of proportional distribution of legislative seats heavily favors the major parties such that this 25 percent vote for minor parties translated into only 12 percent of the seats. Even so, this was more than twice the number of seats held by those parties in the prior election.

from which 35 percent of registered voters abstained is the highest level
in half a century.[19] The 1998 election in particular shocked Costa Ricans
and political observers accustomed to consistently higher voting rates
and raised the question of whether the change was transitory or more
fundamental. The possible transitory factors were another sharp economic crisis (1995–97), election campaign–related scandals, and media
coverage stressing popular frustration. Fundamental shifts were hypothesized, such as a profound decline in institutional legitimacy. To test
these competing explanations, Seligson (2002d) used the Political Support-Alienation Scale, which had been widely tested in Germany, the
United States, Israel, and Latin America (Muller 1979; Caspi and Seligson
1983; Seligson 1983; Booth and Seligson 1984; Seligson and Muller 1987;
Booth and Seligson 1994). The Political Support-Alienation Scale has as
its core a set of five items tapping "diffuse support" and asks for evaluations on a 7-point scale of court performance, political institutions, protection of citizens' rights, and pride in and an obligation to support the
national political system. The data for this project were unusually rich for
Latin America, where surveys are often ad hoc and rarely repeat identi-
cally worded questions over long periods. Eight surveys with 4,744
respondents were conducted between 1978 and 1999, a product of
long-term cooperation between Seligson and Costa Rican scholar and
statistician Miguel Gómez Barrantes.[20]

[19] A 2007 referendum (on the free trade agreement with the United States and Central
America) produced an even higher level of abstention of 41 percent. Referenda in Costa
Rica have been very rare, so there is no comparable figure with which to determine
whether the referendum turnout is high or low.
[20] In 1978 Seligson and Gómez Barrantes undertook a pilot study of the greater metropolitan area of San José, Costa Rica, using items derived from the German and U.S. studies
initiated by Edward N. Muller. The collection of data in subsequent years was funded
jointly by the University of Arizona and the University of Costa Rica, with support from
the U.S. National Science Foundation for the national survey data. The 1999 study was
funded by a grant from the Ford Foundation to Facultad Latinoamericano de las Ciencias
Sociales (FLACSO), El Salvador, which did comparable surveys in a few other countries in
Central America. All interviews were face-to-face, and samples were drawn from the
Gómez national sampling frame based on the official census maps and population data.
The sample sizes for each year are 1978, N=201; 1980, N=280; 1983, N=501; 1985,
N=506; 1987, N=927; 1990, N=597; 1995, N=505; 1999, N=1,428. The sample
designs for all of the studies except 1987 and 1999 were focused on the greater metropolitan area of San José. The 1987 survey, with support from the National Science
Foundation, and the 1999 survey, with support from the Ford Foundation, were national
in scope, and thus have the advantage of both allowing direct comparisons with the
metropolitan area and permitting us to see if those results differ substantially from national results. Since they did not, it is reasonable to generalize from the smaller samples to
the nation as a whole.

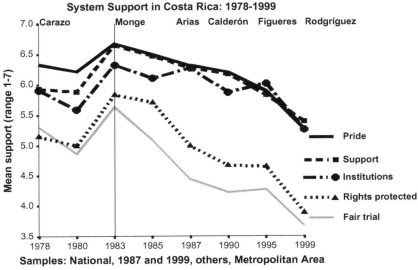

FIGURE 1.1. Costa Rican system support trends

Figure 1.1 reveals the trends in system support for each of the five core items in the Political Support-Alienation Scale (each scored on a 7-point basis) from 1977 through 1999. It shows first that Costa Ricans rsquo; system support on all items was positive and at the high end of the scale through 1983. Despite an economic recovery after the crisis of the early 1980s, declines in each indicator of support were registered and continued through 1999. This revealed that Costa Rican institutional legitimacy patterns were running parallel to those of industrial democracies.

Seligson then combined all the items into a single scale he labeled "system support" and examined its impact on voting in the 1998 presidential election. This revealed that system support was indeed positively and significantly correlated with voter turnout and suggested a "threshold effect," such that only when system support was very low might potential citizens abstain (Muller 1979). Indeed, in Costa Rican surveys up through the 1995 survey, almost no citizens reported very low system support despite falling support averages.

Figure 1.2 reveals clearly the anticipated threshold effect of low system support on voter turnout. For presentation purposes in this graph, the system support scale was divided into 10 increments, from one to 10. When system support was at two or below, voting in 1998 declined dramatically, to near the 50 percent mark for President and below 50 percent

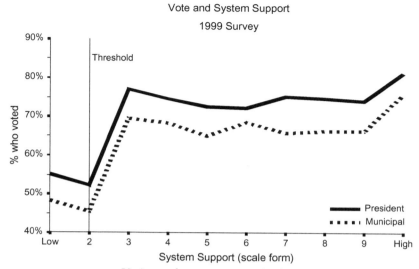

FIGURE 1.2. Voting and system support in Costa Rica, 1999

for municipal elections.[21] Review of prior surveys revealed that almost no respondents reported such low legitimacy values. Thus, in those years there were too few Costa Ricans with extremely low system support for there to have been any notable impact on turnout.[22] Until 1998, levels of discontent, while rising, had not yet crossed this threshold; however, by 1998 the threshold had been crossed, and voter turnout fell. After further analysis to tease out possible intervening or confounding effects, the legitimacy-voting turnout relationship held. We also later analyzed (previously unpublished) survey results collected after the 2002 election in which Costa Rican voter turnout declined slightly to 69 percent. The 2002 findings confirm those from the 1999 survey that very critical (low supporting) Costa Ricans voted at sharply lower rates.

A PILOT RESEARCH PROJECT: THE 2002 SURVEY

These findings and the further decline in Costa Rican turnout in the 2002 and 2006 elections strongly suggest that Costa Rica was experiencing a dynamic participation shift driven by declining system support of the sort that largely

---

[21] Municipal elections since have been separated from national elections.

[22] As we will make clear in Chapter 2, system support as measured in these studies corresponds very closely to a legitimacy dimension we identify as "support for regime institutions," one of several dimensions of legitimacy.

had eluded prior research. This situation offered a golden opportunity to examine the impact of legitimacy decline in a stable democracy, and thus cried out for more intensive research on political legitimacy and its potential effects on Costa Ricans' political behavior. Believing that this Costa Rican shift in legitimacy and attendant political behavior might also have implications for legitimacy research in general, Seligson, Gómez Barrantes, and Booth collaborated in late 2002 on a national sample survey of 1,016 Costa Rican voting age citizens to explore political legitimacy further.[23] This survey allowed us to examine the structure and effects of legitimacy in contemporary Costa Rica at a level of detail not previously undertaken elsewhere, including in Costa Rica.

Based on our review of the literature as described above, in this pilot study we sought to solve several problems, beginning with a detailed examination of the structure of political support (Booth, Seligson, and Gómez Barrantes 2005; Seligson, Booth, Gómez Barrantes 2006). One such problem was that recent empirical studies of legitimacy employed pooled multinational databases and comparative analysis rather than one national database with clear single-government referents for legitimacy. We believed that a detailed analysis of legitimacy's structure in one country would, at the exploratory stage, avoid clouding the picture of political support by having a single set of institutions under consideration. Second, we wanted to improve upon the common analytic technique of exploratory factor analysis by employing the more sophisticated CFA because the latter would provide more detailed information about patterns within complex data.

---

[23] The survey was based on a national probability sample designed by Miguel Gómez Barrantes. The sample is representative of the national population 18 to 69 years of age and was designed as multistage stratified, clustered, and probability proportionate to size (PPS). Specifically, the nation was divided into five geographic strata: the greater metropolitan San José area, other urban areas in the Central Valley, rural areas in the Central Valley, the remaining urban areas, and the remaining rural areas. The metropolitan sample was further stratified into three socioeconomic zones: high, medium, and low. Within each stratum there was a two-stage selection process. The first stage consisted of selecting census segments from the 2000 national census, using PPS techniques, and within each segment a cluster of eight households was designated. The second stage, at the household, followed the sampling procedures suggested by Sudman (1966). The resulting sample totaled 1,016 cases and was weighted to reflect the actual distribution of the population as provided by the 2000 census. The questionnaire included multiple items for each object of evaluation, including local government. We drew upon the conceptualization of legitimacy dimensions in Norris (1999c), other items commonly used to measure political support in other studies, and additional questions of our own. Exploratory analysis allowed us to identify a core set of items related to the dimensions of legitimacy and to eliminate some others from subsequent analysis.

Third, we wanted to use multiple variables to search for each legitimacy dimension, a more reliable way to build indicators than the usual reliance on a single item. Fourth, we wished to include new items related to support for local government, an institutional arena that had been previously overlooked but was likely to prove important because local governments often have much greater contact with citizens than do more remote national institutions. Finally, we explored some alternative ways to measure support for regime principles and regime performance that would avoid using the word "democracy" in the items, as other researchers had done (Klingemann 1999: 36–38; Norris 1999c; Dalton 2004). We avoided the use of "democracy" in the items to avoid possible social desirability response bias. (We will discuss these issues in much greater detail in Chapter 2 as we introduce our larger eight-nation analysis.)

Appendix Table A.1 details the trimmed and revised list of support items that we employed in our pilot study of legitimacy's structure in Costa Rica, grouped by anticipated legitimacy dimension, following the scheme established by Norris (1999c: 10). The list also includes our alternative conceptualizations of regime principles and regime performance, and orientation toward local government. Note that, in order to reduce the measurement effects of differently coded items in subsequent statistical analysis, we recoded all the items in Table A.1 to a range of zero to 100.

Figure 1.3 represents the key results of our CFA of the legitimacy/support norms.[24] Note that for technical-statistical reasons related to the nearly consensual support of Costa Ricans for both of the political community items (Appendix Table A.1), the responses varied so little that we dropped them from the CFA. It is appropriate to conclude from the percentages of positive responses to those questionnaire items, however, that perception of political community was a strongly held belief among

---

[24] Confirmatory factor analysis provides a graphic representation of patterns of correlated variables associated with dimensions (latent factors) found to lie within the data space. It represents these in a graphic form identifying the sets of variables (named in rectangular boxes) that contribute to each latent dimension. Small ovals to the left of the variables represent error terms. Latent dimensions are named within larger ovals and positioned to the right of the variable boxes. Arrows from variables to dimensions represent the significant paths of relationship. The coefficients beside the arrow between each variable and its latent dimension indicate the correlation between the latent structure and the variable itself. Paths not significant at .01 were deleted. Paths with coefficients of less than .01 contributed little to the analysis but added a number of lines and arrows that made reading the diagram of the model too difficult to justify the added complexity. (For readers familiar with path analysis, please note that this CFA figure does not represent a causal model, although its graphic representation bears some similarity to one.)

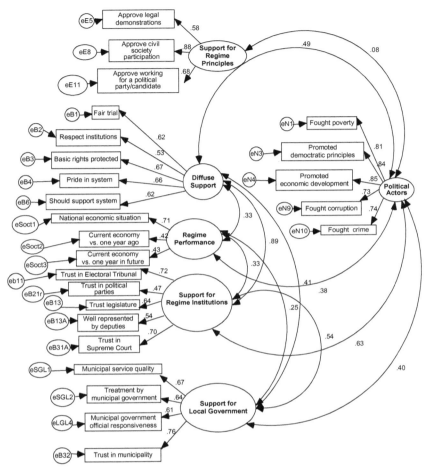

FIGURE 1.3. Confirmatory factor analysis of legitimacy items, Costa Rica, 2002

Costa Ricans. As to the remaining structure of legitimacy, CFA (Figure 1.3) clearly confirmed that political support in Costa Rica had six additional dimensions clustered around specific referents. First, we were reassured when we found that four of these latent structures corresponded straight-forwardly to the dimensions predicted by Norris and others – support for regime principles, support for regime performance, support for regime

---

[25] The overall fit of the model as measured by the C.F.I. was .878, with 25 observed variables and 31 unobserved variables. This diagnostic gives us confidence that the results are reasonably clear and coherent.

institutions, and support for political actors.[25] Here, then, was strong confirmation of the theoretical expectations about legitimacy's dimensionality.

Second, suggesting that legitimacy is somewhat more complex than prior research had found, we uncovered in our CFA (Figure 1.3) two variants in the dimensions of legitimacy not expected by Norris and others. We identified two dimensions of national institutional support rather than a single latent structure. One of them invoked evaluation of the broader functioning of regime institutions, or diffuse support, as discussed above. We also noted that these two institutional dimensions closely associated with each other (the coefficient between them was .89 out of a possible 1.0), suggesting that the distinction between them should not be overdrawn. This provided us with an issue to explore in further comparative research on legitimacy's structure, which we do later in this book.

Another and novel institutional legitimacy dimension in Figure 1.3 derives from citizens' support for local government. This dimension was not anticipated in theorizing by Norris or other researchers, which is surprising given the "all politics is local" orientation of much political science research in the United States. In Costa Rica it appeared as an evaluation distinct from those for other political institutions and coalescing around support for Costa Rica's municipal governments. (Costa Rican municipalities, called *cantons*, are roughly equivalent to a U.S. county.) We concluded that the exclusion of support for local government no longer could be justified, and local support items should be incorporated in our further research.

We also found by using CFA that, as expected, most of the six dimensions of legitimacy found in Costa Rica were positively related to each other and many of the relationships among them were statistically significant. Of 15 dyads possible among the six dimensions, 11 had significant coefficients of association (indicated by the values alongside the double-headed arrows in Figure 1.3). Not surprisingly, the strongest association between any two latent structures was between support for regime institutions and diffuse support because these two dimensions were initially expected to constitute only one dimension. The pattern of remaining association among the dimensions in Costa Rica, we believe, generally comported with what one might expect from citizens of a democracy that was more than 50 years old, had democratic roots that preceded the inauguration of continuous formal democracy, and was well institutionalized and politically stable. Several additional dimensions had moderate correlations with others, while a few were not significantly related.

Based on the theory, we had expected that Costa Ricans would evaluate the more abstract referents of their national political community and its governing principles most positively and would evaluate less positively the more concrete regime institutions and actor performance with which their own experience might be greater. Evidence in Appendix Table A.1, in the form of index scores on each item and mean scores for each latent dimension's set of variables, supports this expectation of different levels of support by dimension. The very abstract perception of a national political community had the highest level of support, followed by support for core regime principles. Mean support thereafter successively declined as the specificity of the reference to institutions and concrete actors and situations increased.

Seeking to explore further the puzzle of legitimacy's impacts on political participation, we developed measures of each Costa Rican legitimacy dimension for further analysis (Booth and Seligson 2005). Exploratory factor analysis of 14 civic engagement items identified several modes of political participation in Costa Rica, and from them we developed single indicators for each of four modes: voting, presidential contacting, partisan activism/instrumental contacting, and communal activism.[26] Multiple measures of participation in six different organizations also provided an index of civil society activism. Finally, the survey included a single item on protest participation, a direct measure of unconventional political activity. We anticipated multiple possible relationships between the multiple legitimacy items and the multiple participation modes, including no relationship for many that might not be germane. We hypothesized, following the standard literature cited above, that more approving citizens might be more involved in within-system participation modes, while more disaffected citizens might be more likely to protest. We also anticipated that disgruntled citizens might actually engage more in some within-system modes but would do so in arenas outside the national government's purview (local government, communal problem solving, and civil society).

---

[26] Following Verba and Nie (Verba et al. 1971; Verba and Nie 1972) and our own prior research in Costa Rica (Booth and Seligson 1978b; Seligson and Booth 1979c) we used exploratory factor analysis to examine the 14 participation items. "Voting" was composed of those reporting having voted in the first-round and runoff presidential election. "Presidential contacting" consists of reporting having contacted the president or contacted the first lady. "Partisanship/instrumental contacting" consists of attendance at political party meetings and contacting each of the following: legislative deputy, ministry or national agency official, cantonal (county) council member, or the *síndico* (another local representative). "Communal activism" consists of affirmative responses to five items concerning contributing to community problem solving activities.

Finally, we expected that some relationships between legitimacy and participation might be U-shaped, with both the most supportive and the most disaffected citizens participating intensely.

Multiple regression analysis, including several demographic variables as controls, produced the following main findings. All five possible hypothesized relationships between legitimacy and political engagement were detected. Voting was higher among those believing in a national political community and more supportive of regime institutions and local government. This finding, then, supported the initial studies in our research program that found voting behavior in Costa Rica sensitive to declining legitimacy. Protest was higher among those with low support for regime principles. Several factors provided evidence of what we called "arena shopping" by Costa Ricans: Citizens highly critical of the regime's performance contacted the president more, citizens with low system (diffuse) support were engaged in more partisan activism/instrumental contacting and communal activism, and citizens critical of the regime's institutions were more active in civil society. Further, two participation modes had a curvilinear relationship to legitimacy norms. Of particular interest was the fact that communal activists came from among those citizens most critical and those most supportive of local government. Finally, as expected, not all legitimacy dimensions were germane to all types of participation, leaving a number of insignificant relationships. In short, this initial foray into a multidimensional exploration of political legitimacy in a developing democracy buoyed our determination to press on for a deeper, comparative look at the legitimacy puzzle.

DISCUSSION AND PLAN OF THIS BOOK

Our pilot study of a 2002 national sample survey of Costa Ricans, using multiple rather than single items for each anticipated object of support, strongly confirmed that the Eastonian model of legitimacy as amended by Norris, Dalton, and others existed roughly as predicted. We also found several significant local nuances in legitimacy structures in the Costa Rican case. The most interesting and novel of these is the political support dimension for local government and the curvilinearity of the relationship between some dimensions of legitimacy and some forms of political behavior. We therefore concluded that there might be rich local legitimacy effects to be identified and explored in future research.

Our analysis of the effects of multiple dimensions of support upon a much more diverse array of modes of political participation confirmed some prior hypotheses but also identified previously unsuspected effects. These findings raised many questions as to how legitimacy might affect political participation, in all its diversity, in a broader range of polities than previously studied. It strongly suggested that there are many more participation choices than allowed by the simplistic dichotomous framework of either staying involved in the system if content or dropping out or protesting if alienated. We believed that this preliminary evidence pointed to some of the answers to our legitimacy puzzle, namely why is it that burgeoning numbers of disgruntled citizens do not necessarily destabilize democratic systems. We believed that what we had uncovered was that disgruntled citizens of democracies actually pursue interests in multiple alternative arenas afforded by different sectors of the political system – local government, civil society organizations, and community. Further, we believed we had found evidence that in democracies critics of government performance step up their within-system participation rather than withdraw.

We believe that the present study has the potential to address additional aspects of the puzzles of legitimacy. We began our research with studies of the structure and impact of political support in Costa Rica. Our early findings there led to a full-scale pilot study that elucidated in much greater detail both structure and effects questions. That prompted us to pursue this issue cross-nationally because many of the questions raised in the literature can be answered only by comparing nations with somewhat distinctive political systems. The data we employ come from eight northern Latin American countries, all formally electoral democracies but ones in which the nature and performance of political regimes ranges widely from peaceful and stable to violent and unstable: Colombia, Costa Rica, El Salvador, Guatemala, Honduras, Mexico, Nicaragua, and Panama. The analysis we undertake here builds upon the pilot research and allows us to address key questions about political legitimacy in diverse settings where many democratic regimes are younger and less well established than in the industrial democracies and where regimes' economic and political performance vary widely. It also builds comparatively on pioneering legitimacy research on other developing democracies in Asia, Eastern Europe, and Africa, while addressing some important lacunae in the field.

Studying legitimacy's three main puzzles within our comparative framework gives us several opportunities for theory testing. First, we can explore legitimacy's measurement, structure, and sources in countries whose democratic institutions differ from each other more than do those in which most survey-based legitimacy studies thus far have been carried out – mostly advanced industrial democracies, but also several postcommunist European countries and some in Asia and Africa. As we explain below, our cases range from a long-standing and peaceful democracy (Costa Rica) to post–civil war democracies (El Salvador, Guatemala, and Nicaragua). We include a fledgling democracy recently emerged from one-party authoritarianism (Mexico), democracies that have taken firmer root since the early 1990s (Honduras and Panama), and finally a democracy still in the throes of a protracted guerrilla war (Colombia).

Second, the diversity of our sample of nations provides very wide variation in government performance and economic development. Finally, since all of the countries have Spanish as their only or predominant language[27] and because all share a common colonial heritage, our study is far less plagued than have been others with concerns about intercultural differences of meaning and questionnaire translation (Lijphart 1989; Elkins and Sides 2007). In short, our sample involves diversity in terms of the political and regime performance settings while providing homogeneity of linguistic, cultural, and historical background. This enables us to focus squarely on our key variables (both dependent and independent), which are the various forms of legitimacy. It allows us considerable opportunity to examine both the micro- and macrosocial sources of political support because the nations and samples vary substantially in many respects. Of course, our risk in carrying out the study was that legitimacy itself might not vary much across this sample, in which case our ability to test the theory would have been compromised. However, as we show below, there are in fact wide variations in legitimacy across these cases.

In Chapter 2 we explore the structure of legitimacy overall in our eight nations, comparing it to other evidence available and seeking to draw further conclusions about how the legitimacy construct travels outside of the advanced industrial democracies and Costa Rica. We also examine whether there are significant national variations in legitimacy. A confirmation for eight Latin American nations of the patterns of legitimacy seen in the older industrial democracies and Costa Rica could increase confidence in the modified and expanded Eastonian conceptualization of democratic legitimacy.

---

[27] The survey in Guatemala did include speakers of Mayan languages, and our survey was translated into five of those languages to accommodate those individuals. It also included a small number of English speakers in Honduras on the Bay Islands, which our survey incorporated with an English language version of the questionnaire. Details of these language issues are contained in Chapter 2.

Chapter 3 introduces the countries in the study and lays out some of their cultural, linguistic, and political similarities. It also explores the variety of their national histories and the performance of their economies and governments. These are the reference structures within which political culture develops and citizens evaluate and interact with their governments. Chapter 4 examines the sources of legitimacy, exploring microsocial (socioeconomic and socialization factors, victimization by crime and corruption, political engagement) and macrosocial factors (economic development, democracy, political violence) that shape legitimacy in these Latin American countries.

Chapters 5–7 address the effects puzzle. Does legitimacy actually matter in the real political world? Does it alter the political landscape of a nation? Does legitimacy affect critical cultural factors such as holding democratic versus authoritarian norms, or vice versa? And, in particular, does legitimacy shape whether and how citizens participate in politics by voting, contacting officials, or engaging in civil society, party activism, campaigning, or protesting? In sum, does legitimacy shape social and political capital in some meaningful way? Chapter 5 focuses on how legitimacy norms affect political participation, a key component of democracy. In Chapter 6 we examine legitimacy's contributions to what might be regarded as negative political capital (antidemocratic norms, support for revolutionary change, and vigilantism). Chapter 7 examines how legitimacy shapes Latin Americans' demand for democracy (preference for elected governments) and their perceptions of the supply of democracy in their particular countries. Chapter 8 provides a summary and conclusions and examines the potential impact of legitimacy norms on the eight countries under study.

2

The Structure of Legitimacy

In Chapter 1 we reported on prior research showing that legitimacy in Costa Rica in 2002 manifested distinct dimensions organized around specific referents such as regime principles, regime performance, regime institutions, and political actors' performance. Having confirmed that the Easton/Norris/Dalton view of legitimacy had construct validity in at least one Latin American nation, we now move on to explore the structure of legitimacy in a broader comparative context.

The field of comparative politics has long been concerned with the problem of cross-national validity of its concepts, including those that emerge from survey research. The classic *Civic Culture* (Almond and Verba 1963) and *Civic Culture Revisited* (Almond and Verba 1980) provided readers an extended and cautionary discussion of cross-national comparability of survey questions. Unfortunately, despite this early concern, nearly all cross-national survey research today begins with the assumption that survey questions do, indeed, "travel" and that concepts defined in one context work in all others. This assumption, recent research has shown, is probably unrealistic, at least to some degree, in surveys in which there is sharp variation in the cultural traditions of the nations included in the surveys. A recent paper, for example, carries out a series of structural equation models using data from two different cross-national surveys and finds evidence of nonequivalence of measures (Elkins and Sides 2007). As already noted, and as we will argue in greater depth in Chapter 3, our study has the advantage of working with a set of nations that have many long-term cultural similarities. Furthermore, our questionnaire was built upon many years of our prior efforts to explore legitimacy in these nations, leading up to the Costa Rica pilot described in

Chapter 1. Even so, we did not want merely to assume that the concepts would work in our sample of eight countries. For that reason, we spend considerable time in this chapter examining the cross-national validity of our legitimacy questions.

We employ a 2004 multinational dataset, incorporating virtually identical legitimacy items that include Costa Rica, our baseline country, and seven other Latin American nations. Because Costa Rica is Latin America's longest-lived democracy, it is possible that the clear structure of legitimacy that we observed there is unique or at least unusual. One must wonder whether this same structure would also exist in a broader array of countries, especially very young democracies or those having recent experience with long-term civil conflict. We therefore need to examine whether a similar structure of legitimacy exists in other Latin American countries that are also electoral democracies but range widely in size, political stability, wealth, and the age of their democratic regimes.

Our review of prior research in Chapter 1 revealed several challenges to the validation of the legitimacy construct. The first we call the "cross-national trap;" it occurs in studies that employ pooled multinational databases and comparative analysis without adequately controlling for context.[1] The problem arises from the fact that much of legitimacy that has been measured *per se* is oriented toward particular real world political systems and the performance of their institutions and actors. In cross-national samples, each citizen who evaluates political actors' performance, for example, is reacting to his or her own nation's community, regime, government, or performance problems.[2] These reference points vary from nation to nation within pooled samples, resulting in a heteroskedasticity problem in cross-national databases (Seligson 2002c). Thus, in our view, legitimacy's dimensionality and contours should be examined comparatively, taking care to determine whether multinational and national constructs are comparable, in order to confirm that the anticipated legitimacy constructs exist and have meaning in particular cases.[3]

We will address that problem by incorporating key variables that measure national context so that we can examine both context and individual

---

[1] Important early exceptions are Preston et al. (1983) and Kornberg and Clarke (1992).

[2] For a similar argument related to political participation, see Norris (2002).

[3] The problem is akin to establishing the dimensionality of political participation as examined by Verba, Nie, and Kim (1971). They discovered the multidimensionality of participation to be universal but the particulars of its structure to be defined by national institutional context.

variation simultaneously. Put simply, if key components of legitimacy are linked to system performance (e.g., GDP levels and growth, or democratic performance) then we would expect that, *ceteris paribus*, citizens who live in countries that perform better would exhibit higher levels of political support. The structure of legitimacy, however, may remain largely the same across national contexts. We also expect variation that cuts across individuals, such that respondent socioeconomic status, for example, could influence individual levels of legitimacy. We argue, therefore, that only by examining individual and contextual variation can we expect to approach a full understanding of political legitimacy among the mass public.

The second problem is that much of the research on legitimacy that has used multiple questionnaire items and sought to uncover a multidimensional view of the phenomenon has assumed the dimensions do not correlate with each other. That assumption emerges from the uncritical application of the statistical tool used to uncover dimensionality, namely, orthogonally rotated factor analysis.[4] Since theory suggests that the dimensions of legitimacy should be correlated with each other, the usual orthogonal varimax rotational solutions to factor analysis and factor scoring contradict the basic theoretical argument. Empirical work (Kornberg and Clarke 1992; Canache 2002), including that from our pilot study in Chapter 1 of Costa Rica, confirms that legitimacy's dimensions are in fact intercorrelated. One partial solution is to use an oblique rotation in factor analysis. However, as we noted in Chapter 1, advances in structural equation modeling, especially as regards confirmatory factor analysis (CFA), allow us to overcome a number of limitations of exploratory factor analysis. We here primarily employ CFA to obtain a clearer picture of latent dimensions within data, their strengths, and their interrelationships.

The third obstacle is the "slender reed" problem, which arises from the high cost of survey research. In opinion surveys it is usually preferable to employ multiple related questions to confirm the construct validity of a key concept such as interpersonal trust or legitimacy. However, using multiple items to represent each legitimacy dimension is expensive because doing so absorbs so much critical questionnaire space. Thus empirical work on legitimacy and other attitudes often relies on a tiny number of items – sometimes only one – as we noted above. This limitation especially affects large, general-purpose national and comparative survey projects. It also affects case studies of support in particular democracies (Fuchs 1999;

---

[4] Dalton (2004) is an exception, applying an oblique solution to his factor analysis work.

Holmberg 1999; Rose et al. 1999). An upshot of this problem is that many comparative studies in which large, cross-national datasets are used simply lack the necessary items to allow the luxury of multi-item indexes. One welcome exception to the problem is the study of African nations by Bratton, Mattes, and Gyimah-Boadi (Bratton et al. 2005), which employs diverse items to build performance indexes. In our view, a more adequate explanation of the actual structure of legitimacy requires at least two opinion-survey items related to each object believed to define a dimension (Dalton 2004). Our research design for the eight-country study satisfies this requirement.

Fourth, in reviewing the literature, we were surprised by the dearth of research on legitimacy/support at the local level. Because much research has shown that citizens interact most with the governments closest to them, we are genuinely surprised that most researchers have ignored the legitimacy of local government (a welcome exception is Rahn and Rudolph 2005). This lacuna is especially troubling in the developing world, where decentralization has become a mantra for many structural reform programs favored by development agencies that seek to "give the government back to the people" (Cornelius 1974; Véliz 1980; Nickson 1995; Crook and Manor 1998; Cornelius, Eisenstadt, and Hindley 1999; Diamond 1999; Eaton 2001; Hiskey and Seligson 2003; Eaton 2004; Montero and Samuels 2004; Falleti 2005). Further, there is emerging evidence that local government provides an alternative venue for participation from national-level politics (Booth and Richard 1996) and that citizen support for local government leads to engagement at the local level (Booth and Seligson 2005). This evidence suggests that a possible explanation for the fact that declining national legitimacy has not led to more regime crises is that disaffected citizens may turn to alternative arenas and participation modes rather than withdraw, protest, or challenge national governments. We include in our design several items related to support for local government.

Fifth, more thought needs to be given to "support for regime principles," which Dalton defines as "the broad parameters within which the political system should function" (2004: 6). Norris cautions, "since democracy remains an essentially contested concept, open to multiple meanings, there is no consensus about which values should be nominated as most important" (Norris 1999c). We strongly agree with Norris, yet her solution, and that of most other researchers, has been to utilize survey questions that refer directly to "democracy." We see two problems when the word "democracy" is included in questions attempting to measure regime principles. First is the problem of social desirability response set (Krosnick 1999), which can make it difficult for respondents to express support publicly for dictatorship against the perceived greater social desirability of democracy. Second, surveys have shown that particular publics interpret this term very differently. For example, one study found that most Costa Ricans defined democracy in terms of freedom, while Chileans saw it in terms of capitalism and free enterprise or free trade (Seligson 2001b). Yet despite such problems, Norris (1999c: 16–17), Dalton (2004: 58–59) and Klingemann (1999) relied on items that ask about approval of "democracy as the best form of government" and a preference for "democracy" over "dictatorship." We believe that this approach to operationalizing regime principles suffers from both response set and potential conceptual confusion on the part of respondents of differing socioeconomic status as well as those living in different national contexts.

The discrepancy in interpreting democracy among respondents and the potential for response set strongly suggests (to us at least) that researchers should avoid the term democracy per se when attempting to measure regime legitimacy norms and ask instead about key *principles of democracy* using more neutral terminology. One key feature of democracy – indeed, its central definition – is citizen participation in politics (Pateman 1970; Cohen 1973). Our strategy here, therefore, is to substitute for the typical regime principles questions (that mention democracy) several alternative items focusing instead on respondents' approval of political participation, which lies at the conceptual heart of democracy. While we do not claim that participation is the only dimension of democracy that defines democratic regime norms, we do think that it is an essential, and we would risk saying universal, element of democracy.

A final difficulty lies with how prior research has operationalized "regime performance." Here too we believe it unhelpful to use items that include the term "democracy." Earlier work has shown that items that measure satisfaction with democracy (Canache, Mondak, and Seligson 2001) in fact confuse satisfaction with regime performance and satisfaction with democracy as a system of government. While not everyone agrees with this concern (Anderson and Guillory 1997), we strongly prefer not to conflate the two concepts even though the items used to measure satisfaction with regime performance are suggested by Norris (1999c: 18).[5]

---

[5] Norris notes, however, that her choice of items was limited by the cross-national databases available to her, since unlike the research we present in this book in which we designed the study to measure legitimacy, Norris and others have had to rely on omnibus surveys in which legitimacy was inevitably only one small component of an overall research project.

Klingemann (1999: 36–37) employs Norris' regime performance items, but adds others that we believe are more appropriate. He uses questions clearly tapping regime performance by asking, "How are things going?" and "How satisfied are you with how the people in national office are handling the country's affairs?" He also, however, includes items measuring confidence in specific institutions (in this case, the parliament and the central government), which conceptually overlap with and blur the important distinction made by Norris between support for regime principles and support for regime institutions. Thus, Klingemann's dimensional analysis effectively eliminates institutions as a distinct dimension of legitimacy.

Dalton (2004: 59), in contrast, employs a scheme in which support for regime institutions does emerge as a separate dimension, but he does not find a dimension measuring regime performance. Mishler and Rose (1999) use yet another tool to measure regime performance, with which they compare the current regimes in Eastern Europe to their communist predecessors. We regard this as very helpful in postcommunist countries but less so in countries not experiencing such dramatic regime changes. We propose instead widely used and face-valid regime performance questions – the standard sociotropic items on the performance of the economy. While these items are limited to the economic sphere, they are so widely used in so many surveys, and the performance of the economy is such a critical factor in citizen evaluation of government that we believe that their use is amply justified.

In sum, we believe that in the following analysis we explore legitimacy's dimensionality and construct validity using appropriate methodology and avoiding the problems that we note above. We will be sensitive to both national-level and cross-national structure outcomes. We will employ multiple items for each of the possible legitimacy dimensions in order to enhance the opportunity to establish the validity of dimensionality and the possible relationships among dimensions.

THE DATA: THE 2004 EIGHT-NATION SURVEY

A study of democratic values and behaviors must gather data on the values of *all* citizens, not just the active ones, the politically "important" ones, or those who live in major towns and cities. Indeed, the major advantage of studying surveys rather than election results is that in elections many people do not vote, and often it is the poor or the rural voter who is underrepresented in elections.[6] Surprisingly, however, many studies carried out in Latin America that claim to represent the views of the nation are based on samples that systematically underrepresent certain sectors of the population (Seligson 2005c).[7] Frequently, the biases that crop up in samples emerge because of cost considerations, which in turn are a function of the dispersion of populations over wide areas or of the multilingual nature of the national population, which makes it difficult and expensive to conduct the interviews in all of the languages that are widely spoken in a given country. Sometimes samples are designed, as one "expert" told one of the authors, to represent the "politically relevant population."

In sharp contrast to this all-too-common ad hoc approach to sampling, here the effort has been to draw samples fully representative of the entire voting-age population of each of the eight countries in the study (map Figure 2.1 and Table 2.1). We believe that we have accomplished this goal within the limitations of the science of sampling and with appropriate consideration for cost effectiveness.[8]

The sample design itself made use of the principle of "stratification" in order to increase the precision of the results. The impact of stratification on our samples may be easier to understand by comparing it to drawing

---

[6] This point was made forcefully by Verba in his presidential address to the American Political Science Association (Verba 1996).

[7] One widely cited source of survey data from Latin America is the LatinoBarometer, which is organized by the director of the commercial survey firm, MORI, Chile. The main advantage of that dataset is that it is available on a yearly basis for as many as 18 countries (Lagos 1997, 2008). The disadvantages, from our point of view, are that the samples often are not national and not comparable since the designs vary from country to country and year to year. Most importantly, however, many of the key dimensions of legitimacy are not included in the questionnaires.

[8] In the field of survey research, larger samples are always better, but cost is always a factor to be considered. Consider the impact of sample size on the precision of the results. In this study we determined that a sample of 1,500 respondents per country would satisfy our objectives and still remain feasible from a cost point of view. With a sample of this size, using what is known as simple random sampling (SRS), 95 times out of 100 results are accurate to within ±2.5 percent of the result that would have been obtained had 100 percent of the voting-aged adults been interviewed. (In fact, we do not use SRS, but rather a complex sample, and report on the design effects impact in Appendix D.1.) Is that good enough? That depends on the trade-off of greater cost for greater precision. If we had doubled the sample to 3,000, the accuracy would have improved to about ±2.2 percent, or an increase of only .3 percent for a doubling of the sample size and fieldwork costs. How does the 2.5 percent figure compare to research in other fields? Quite well. In national elections in the United States, it is common to see samples of only about 1,000, and in most medical research testing new drugs and procedures, samples that are far smaller are common. So, we believe that the sample size selected for this study is appropriate.

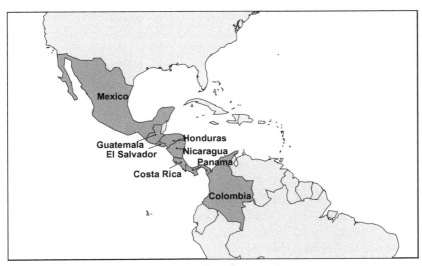

FIGURE 2.1. Sample countries

TABLE 2.1. *Unweighted sample size, by nation*

	Frequency	Percent
1. Mexico	1,556	12.5
2. Guatemala	1,708	13.8
3. El Salvador	1,589	12.8
4. Honduras	1,500	12.1
5. Nicaragua	1,430	11.5
6. Costa Rica	1,500	12.1
7. Panama	1,639	13.2
8. Colombia	1,479	11.9
Total	12,401	100.0

Note: Data collected January–March 2004.

winning raffle tickets. Let us assume that there are eight high schools in a school district and the district has decided to have a raffle to raise money. Those who are running the raffle want to be sure that there is at least one winner in each of the eight schools. If the tickets are all pooled into one bowl, and winners drawn at random, it may well turn out that one or more schools would be left without a winner. Indeed, all winners might come from a single school, although such an outcome would be unlikely. In order to make sure that all schools had at least one winner, rather than placing all of the raffle tickets in one bowl and drawing all winning tickets at random, the raffle organizers place the tickets from each school in separate bowls and then draw one ticket from each. This is precisely the procedure we followed in this study: We divided the sample by country (our first level of stratification), subdivided the countries into regions, and further subdivided them into urban and rural areas. Stratified samples are more precise than simple random samples because they guarantee that no single important component of the population will be left outside of the sample. In this project, our first decision was to stratify the sample by country so as to guarantee that by simple random chance alone the population of any one country would not be excluded. For still greater precision, we further stratified the samples within each country: We divided each country into at least five strata representing the major geographic divisions to assure representation of all regions.[9] The sample design details of each country explain any omissions that remain, but they are very minor when they occur and are justified by cost considerations. For still more precision we subdivided each of the country-level strata into urban and rural areas based on national census definitions. Many other similar surveys in Latin America largely exclude rural areas because of their inaccessibility or survey costs, but we chose not to include them.

The next stage in sample design involved determining the neighborhoods in which the interviews would take place. We referred to these as "primary sampling units," or PSUs. The teams obtained census maps from their respective census bureaus and, using population data segments, randomly selected the maps from within each stratum and then randomly selected the segments in which the interviews would be carried out. Each stage of selection involved using probability proportional to size (PPS) criteria so that the probability of any one unit being selected was in direct proportion to the most recent population estimates. This gave each voting-aged adult in each country an equal and known probability of being selected, a fundamental criterion for a scientifically valid probability sample. Thus, respondents living in sparsely populated rural

---

[9] For the most part, we did not exclude any region unless the cost of access was extreme. In Honduras, for example, even though only a small portion of the population does not speak Spanish, we developed an English version of the questionnaire for use on the Bay Islands to include that population. Similarly, we developed translated versions of the questionnaire in the major Mayan languages for Guatemala. We did, however, exclude some tiny islands off the coast of Panama (the home of the Cuna Indians) and other similar islands in Central America.

villages had the same probability of being selected as respondents in large cities.

The final stages of selection involved choosing the household and selecting the respondent. Choosing the household involved a systematic selection of housing units within a PSU (using the census maps and locally updated information to correct for changes since the census was taken). We determined that between six and eight interviews would be carried out in each urban PSU and between ten to twelve in each rural PSU. We allowed larger clusters in rural areas than in urban areas because rural areas with far lower housing density require increased travel time. Clusters are commonly used as they provide an appropriate trade-off between cost and precision. Since the residents of each PSU are likely to have more in common with each other than with residents living in the country at large – for example, similar incomes and levels of education – the selection of a "cluster" of households in a given area produces a somewhat reduced level of precision, but at great cost savings. By clustering respondents in a neighborhood and interviewing several of them, an interviewer can be much more efficient. The result is the introduction of what is known as "intraclass correlation," a factor that can widen the confidence intervals. Appendix D.1 contains a discussion in which these design effects are estimated and reported for key variables in the study.

Once the household was selected, respondents were chosen based on the "next birthday system" to ensure random selection within the household. However, given the national dispersion of our samples, multiple callbacks at a household to locate an absent respondent who originally had been selected would have been too costly. We thus employed a quota sampling methodology at the level of the household (Sudman 1966) in order to balance the sample demographically in terms of gender and age. These quotas were also based on census data for each country.

Finally, we anticipated the potential problem of the refusal of some sampled respondents to cooperate. Had we targeted only 1,500 interviews per country, we might have obtained a smaller sample size than planned for the level of accuracy desired. As a result, in each country an estimate of noncoverage was included and an oversample was drawn to compensate. The total pooled sample of respondents was 12,401 (Table 2.1).

VARIABLE SELECTION

The immediate challenge in studying the structure of legitimacy is to determine questions that reasonably can measure its various components.

Norris's contribution (1999c) helped us greatly by clearly conceptualizing legitimacy dimensions and linking them to questions used in many large-scale, multination surveys. As in our earlier study of Costa Rica in 2002, we included items developed specifically for the Norris scheme and included in her comparative study drawn from the World Values Survey and the Eurobarometer surveys. Because Norris's list was not inclusive, we added items used to measure political support in other studies that referenced a wide array of institutions and actors (Muller and Williams 1980; Muller et al. 1982; Finkel et al. 1989; Seligson, Grijalva, and Córdova 2002; Booth and Seligson 2005; Booth and Richard 2006b). We included measures of support for political actors and their policies, specifically the incumbent presidents of each country. We also benefited from Afrobarometer studies of public opinion and democracy. They include various measures of evaluation and support: economic performance, government policy performance, delivery of economic welfare, government political performance, and the performance of various political actors including presidents, local councilors, and legislators (Bratton et al. 2005: 83–84).[10]

Again, we believe that measuring support for core regime principles based on approval of "democracy" per se is inappropriate because it may both elicit a social desirability response set and sow definitional confusion among respondents. We focus instead on the essence of democracy – political participation – and employ three questions measuring approval of political participation. In our initial attempts at studying the dimensionality of legitimacy we employed Norris's items, which proved only weakly related to each other and to other legitimacy dimensions. We decided to replace them because of a more fundamental concern about social desirability and definitional confusion. In measuring regime performance we encountered similar potential conceptual confusion between support for regime performance and support for regime institutions. Because incumbent regimes are usually held responsible for national economic performance (whether fairly or not), we employ here two standard sociotropic items related to the performance of the national economy. Finally, in order to capture the local government dimension, we add a set of items evaluating local government as the reference object (Seligson et al. 2002).

---

[10] That work goes beyond government institutions and also includes trust in churches, banks, and businesses, for example Bratton et al. (2005: 107–08).

Table 2.2 lists each of the support items we employed grouped by anticipated legitimacy dimension following the conceptual scheme established by Norris (1999c: 10). We compiled this list after a process of trimming a larger list of available potential items. The list in Table 2.2 also includes our alternative conceptualizations of regime principles and regime performance and items for orientation toward local government. Note that, in order to reduce the unit and measurement effects of similarly structured clusters of items in subsequent statistical analysis, we recoded all the items in Table 2.2 to have a range of 1 to 100.

FINDINGS: THE STRUCTURE OF LEGITIMACY

Table 2.2 lists the variables we used to form our dimensions of legitimacy, grouping them into the structure we expected to find from our dimensional analysis. To anticipate what we found in the analysis below, we list here those dimensions, arranged from the most diffuse (in Easton's terms) to the most specific:

1. Existence of a political community (the most basic and diffuse of the six dimensions)
2. Support for core regime principles (basic support for the key norms of democracy)
3. Support for regime institutions (the classic conceptualization of legitimacy as being focused on the institutions of state)
4. Evaluation of regime performance (the classic sociotropic items on economic performance)
5. Support for local government (an object of legitimacy frequently encountered by the citizen but usually overlooked in legitimacy studies)
6. Support for political actors or authorities (an evaluation of the efficacy of incumbents)

We analyze the structure of the questionnaire items included in Table 2.2 in three steps. We first use exploratory factor analysis (principal components with a varimax rotation), as does most prior published research on the dimensionality of political support. The results provide a reasonable first approximation of dimensionality for the eight-nation pooled sample (see Appendix Table A.2), producing a six-dimension solution. However, they also yield several problems: First, one variable – confidence in the municipality – distributes its loadings between two legitimacy dimensions with this technique designed to assure the orthogonality of

TABLE 2.2. *Variables and expected dimensions of political legitimacy, pooled eight-nation sample*

Object of Support (listed from most general to most specific)	Operationalization of Variables	Mean	Standard Deviation
I. Existence of a Political Community	1. To what degree are you proud to be a _____? (7-point scale: recoded into a great deal = 100...not at all = 1). 2. To what degree do you agree that in spite of our differences, we _____ s have a lot of things and values that unite us as a country? (7-point scale: recoded into very much agree = 100...very much disagree = 1).		
	Political community mean and standard deviation	67.40	12.29
II. Support for Core Regime Principles	I am going to read you a list of some actions or things that people can do to achieve their goals and political objectives. Please tell me to what degree do you approve or disapprove of people taking these actions: (10-point scale, 0 = strongly disapprove; 10 = strongly approve, transformed to a 1–100 range) 1. That people participate in a legally permitted demonstration. 2. That people participate in a group that tries to resolve community problems. 3. That people work in an election campaign for a party or candidate.		
	Regime principles mean and standard deviation	67.77	18.43

III. **Support for Regime Institutions**

All of the following are on a 7-point scale: 0 = none...7 = much, transformed to 1–100 range):

1. How much do you think the courts of _____ guarantee a fair trial?
2. How much do you respect the political institutions of _____?
3. How much do you think citizens' basic rights are well protected by the _____ political system?
4. How proud do you feel to live under the _____ political system?
5. How much do you think one should support the _____ political system?
6. How much do you trust the _____ [national election bureau]?
7. How much do you trust the _____ [national legislature]?
8. How much do you trust the political parties?
9. How much do you trust the supreme court?

Regime Institutions mean and standard deviation

50.76

17.08

IV. **Regime Performance**

1. How would you rate, in general, the economic situation of the country? (5-point scale: recoded into very good = 100...very poor = 1)

(continued)

TABLE 2.2 *(continued)*

Object of Support (listed from most general to most specific)	Operationalization of Variables	Mean	Standard Deviation
	2. Do you think that over the next 12 months that the economic situation of the country will be better, the same, or worse than it is now? (5-point scale: recoded into much better = 100...much worse = 1).		
	Regime Performance mean and standard deviation	44.45	15.29
V. Support for Local Government	1. How much trust do you have in the municipality? (7 point scale: 1 = none...100 = much)		
	2. Would you say that the services that the municipality is providing the people of your canton (county) are very good (100), good (75), neither good nor bad (50), bad (25), very bad (1)?		

3. Do you think that the mayor and municipal council respond to the people's demands much of the time (100), some of the time (67), seldom (33), never (1)?

4. If you had a complaint about a local problem and took it to a member of the municipal council, how much attention would be paid? Much (100), some (67), little (33), never (1)?

Local Government mean and standard deviation 45.62 17.39

VI. Support for Political Actors or Authorities

All on a 7-point scale (nothing = 1 . . . much = 100): Referring to the government of ____ [incumbent president], how much has that government:

1. Fought poverty?
2. Combated government corruption?
3. Promoted democratic principles?

Political Actors mean and standard deviation 48.84 23.19

the factors.[11] Thus the varimax-rotated solution does not cleanly separate support for regime institutions from support for local government. When we turn to a factor analytic solution more in tune with the theoretical expectation that the support items would indeed be correlated with each other rather than independent, an oblique (oblimin) rotation of the factor analysis results (Appendix Table A.3a, b), it still yields a distributed loading for this item between support for local government and regime institutions. The oblimin rotation did produce a factor correlation matrix indicating the anticipated correlations among the six dimensions (Appendix Table A.3a, b).

While tending to confirm our expectations, these factor analysis results have weaknesses, which leads us to utilize the superior technique of CFA to explore the structure of legitimacy. We prefer CFA for several reasons. First, it uses the full information in the dataset via the employment of maximum-likelihood estimation rather than "listwise" deletion of missing data.[12] Perhaps most usefully, CFA tests the strength or coherence of latent structures, identifies the degree of association among them, and allows us to represent these relationships graphically.

Figure 2.2 graphically reveals the structure that CFA detected among the individual items (denoted by small boxes with variable names) in the form of the latent factors, or dimensions, of legitimacy to which they are linked (indicated by the larger ovals with dimension names). The reader should note that we are not providing a causal or "path" diagram here, but a model that illustrates the relationship between each latent dimension of legitimacy and its underlying variables, as well as the linkages among the various factors. The single-pointed arrows pointing from the

---

[11] Orthogonal means that each of the dimensions is completely uncorrelated with all of the other dimensions – essentially, that the identified dimensions have no association among them.

[12] Listwise deletion of missing data results from the fact that on most items in a survey there are missing data (unanswered questions) for some respondents on most of the variables. Statistical routines normally delete all the cases (respondents) for which there are missing data on any variables in order to do their calculations. Where there are many variables in a routine, as in our factor analysis, the effect of compounding the missing data for each variable (dropping out multiple cases for each variable) can lead to a potentially large attrition in the sample size. Here we would have lost 29 percent of our cases, reducing our sample N from 12,000 to 7,379. Maximum-likelihood estimation of missing values is a technique used to estimate missing data using the values of all other variables in the sample for each case as the basis for that missing case's estimation. Its advantage is to produce a full sample of cases for the key variables in question.

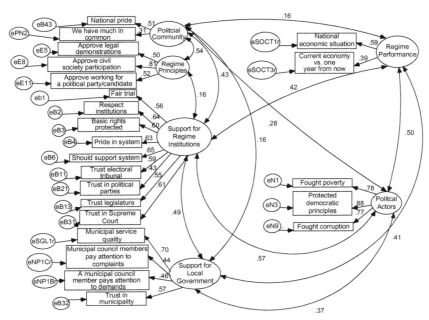

FIGURE 2.2. Confirmatory factor analysis of legitimacy, eight-nation sample, 2004

factors to specific variables indicate which variables make up that factor, and the coefficients next to the arrows provide the strength of relationship (coefficient range 0–1.0). The double-pointed arrows between pairs of factors indicate the association between each pair of factors, with the adjacent coefficients indicating the strength of association. Small ovals adjacent to the variable boxes represent error terms. We have omitted all arrows for relationships (paths) not significant at the .01 level because they increased the diagram's complexity while adding little meaningful information. The overall fit of the model, as measured by the C.F.I., was .891, with 23 observed variables and 29 unobserved variables.

Our further analysis of these results proceeds in three stages. First, we discuss the individual legitimacy dimensions to deepen our understanding of the structure of political support in the eight study countries. Second, we examine relationships *among* the latent factors. Third, we examine the relative levels of support for each of the legitimacy dimensions in order to determine whether, as predicted in the literature, more general and distal referents have greater support than those with specific and proximate referents.

Dimensional structure

The first and most important finding confirms that legitimacy has multiple dimensions based on citizens' orientations toward various political objects. Figure 2.2 reveals six dimensions of legitimacy (the figure's larger ovals) clustered around specific referents for the pooled eight-nation sample. Five of these latent structures correspond straightforwardly to the dimensions predicted by Norris and company – belief in a political community, support for regime principles, support for regime performance, support for regime institutions, and support for political actors.

These dimensions are reasonably coherent internally, though they vary in internal strength. The strongest dimension is the evaluation of political actors, with coefficients of association between the three component variables and latent dimension ranging from .77 to .88. This makes sense because the items used here invoke the performance of the incumbent president, who in each country receives considerable attention and performance evaluation by national media. In Latin America, politics is heavily centralized, with a primary focus on the incumbent president and his/her administration (generally thought of as the various ministers who comprise the cabinet). In less centralized systems around the world, the "support for authorities" may well expand beyond the presidency, as we think it would especially in federal systems. But in the Latin American context – even in a country like Mexico, which is federal (the other seven countries are all unitary) – *the* authorities typically means *the* president and his/her cabinet. Indeed, presidents arguably get more coverage than do other institutions identified in the analysis, or regime principles or national community. Another coherent dimension is support for regime institutions (coefficients of the variables with the latent factor itself range from .43 to .64 with only one below .55). This too makes sense because, like presidents, governmental institutions conduct business that affects the lives of citizens and receive media attention. Other coherent dimensions are regime principles (coefficients of association range from .51 to .81) and support for local government (coefficients range from .44 to .70). Weaker latent dimensions are support for regime performance (its two items' coefficients with the latent dimension are .59 and .39) and perception of a shared political community (coefficients of .51 and .31).

Overall then, we believe this eight-nation model vindicates the Eastonian idea that political legitimacy is multidimensional, especially when taken in conjunction with our previously discussed findings on Costa Rica (Chapter 1) and the work of Dalton (Dalton 2004). What really stands out is that here we have taken the construct validation effort for political support to Latin America – well outside of the industrial democracies included in various World Values Surveys and other cross-national surveys. We have thus confirmed that, in a pooled sample of eight Latin American nations, the structure of legitimacy is indeed multidimensional and that the dimensions are like those Norris and others predicted. Indeed, given the broader array of items that we were able to employ in the effort, we have here what is arguably the most comprehensive multidimensional construct validation effort for legitimacy performed to date.

Aside from their shared Latin American culture and nominal electoral-democratic regime types, the eight study countries are arguably more politically *dis*similar among themselves than the peaceful, well-established nations Dalton and other scholars have previously examined (the United States, Japan, and European nations). For example, at the time of our survey in 2004, Costa Rica was a long-term, stable democracy, while Colombia's civil war was ongoing. Guatemala, El Salvador, and Nicaragua had seen their intense civil wars end only eight, 12, and 14 years previously, respectively. Mexico was emerging from long-standing one-party authoritarian rule. That the CFA analysis produces such clear results for a sample drawn from eight Latin American countries of varying degrees of stability and political peace gives a strong indication that the dimensional structure has construct validity in the Latin American electoral democracy setting. That is, multidimensional democratic legitimacy exists, and the items used to detect it measure what they are supposed to measure.

Figure 2.2 also reveals a variant in the dimensional structure of legitimacy not expected by Norris and others but that we had postulated and identified in our Costa Rican analysis in 2002 – citizens' support for local government. Thus, we have strongly confirmed a local government legitimacy dimension and believe that its absence from virtually all prior studies that examined support for the political system was a serious oversight. This is particularly true given growing evidence that local government legitimacy significantly affects other attitudes and behaviors. For example, Seligson and Córdova Macías (1995) report, using a two-stage least squares analysis, that greater support for local government institutions in El Salvador led to greater support for the national government. Booth and Seligson (2005) report that Costa Rican citizens with higher support for local government voted more and engaged more in civil society. We shall explore questions related to the impact of support for local government and other dimensions of legitimacy in the remaining chapters of this book.

Relationships among dimensions

We now examine the relationships among the latent factors. First, as expected, CFA reveals that most of the six dimensions of democratic legitimacy found in Costa Rica associate positively with each other and that many of the relationships among them are statistically significant. Of 15 dyads possible among the six dimensions, 12 (80 percent) have significant coefficients of association (indicated by the double-headed arrows in Figure 2.2). This indicates a fair amount of association among the political support dimensions in the eight-nation sample.

The strongest single association is between the dimensions of support for institutions and for political actors (.57), a relationship quite similar to the one found in the single-nation study of Costa Rica in 2002. Support for regime institutions has a moderate coefficient of association with support for local government (.49), again similar to the 2002 Costa Rica results. Other strong associations among legitimacy dimensions are between belief in a political community and support for regime principles (.54) and between support for political actors and regime performance (.50). This last finding demonstrates that, for these eight countries, about one quarter of the support for incumbent presidents derives from citizens' evaluations of national economic performance. This provides an important clue as to why it is a difficult job to be president in a troubled economy. In essence, irrespective of the policy tools a president has to work with or where the responsibility for a recession might lie, much of a president's evaluation derives straightaway from citizen evaluations of the economy.

Support for regime institutions correlates with perception of a political community at .42 and with support for regime performance also at .42. Local government support and support for regime performance associate at .41. There are several more weakly linked dyads (political community–actors at .28 and political community–regime performance, political community–local government, and institutions-actors all at .16. The insignificant relationships are all for dyads between regime principles (operationalized as support for democratic political participation rights) and regime performance local government, and political actors. Taken together with the relatively weak regime principles–regime institutions association, this pattern indicates that support for basic democratic norms (regime principles) is the dimension least linked to the other five. In short, support for democratic principles stands apart from the evaluation of the performance of governments in northern Latin America. This finding suggests that democratic principles, as such, have become nearly consensual norms and thus may survive poor government performance.

In terms of number of significant linkages, support for regime institutions has positive ties to all the other dimensions, while support for local government, regime performance, political actors, and political community all have significant ties to four of the other five. In summary, we find, as hypothesized, clear patterns of association among the empirically detected legitimacy dimensions across eight Latin American nations. Most of the six support factors associate with four or five of the other factors. The single exception is regime principles (support for participation rights), which has positive links to only two – a weak one to institutions but a fairly strong one to political community. This multinational pattern – moderate overlap among most legitimacy dimensions but weaker links to the others for support for regime principles – resembles the findings already detailed for Costa Rica (Figure 1.3).[13]

Relative levels of support

Here we explore the relative levels of support among the dimensions predicted by legitimacy theory. We expected our respondents to evaluate the more abstract referents of their national political community and its governing principles most positively. We further expected that they would evaluate less positively the more concrete dimensions of regime institutions and actor performance with which their own experiences and political knowledge might be greater. The differences in question here are those between our respondents' views of their particular *patrias* (fatherlands) – their governments in general and democracy – versus the performance of incumbent presidents, municipalities, and economies.

Figure 2.3 illustrates each legitimacy dimension's mean for the pooled sample and clearly supports the hypothesis of different levels of support by dimension. First, the more abstract and distal legitimacy dimensions, which are perception of a political community and support for regime principles, have the highest mean national scores, about 67 on 100-point scales. These means are more than 15 points higher than the next most positively evaluated referent, regime institutions. Thus, our Latin American respondents on balance view their national political communities

---

[13] The pattern is somewhat confounded by the exclusion of political community from the Costa Rica analysis for statistical reasons, but the absence of relationships among regime principles and all but one other factor is shown in Figure 1.3.

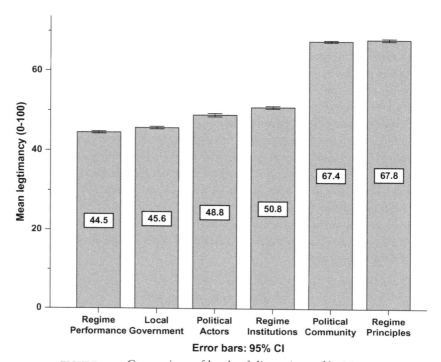

FIGURE 2.3. Comparison of levels of dimensions of legitimacy

with some sense of shared destiny – a whole-sample average of 67.4 out of 100. In contrast, the more proximate references – specific institutions, regime economic performance, local government, and political actors – garner much weaker support. The score for regime institutions – 50.8 points for the whole sample – indicates that support for national institutions barely reaches the midpoint. Support for political actors falls below the scale midpoint at 48.8. Finally, support for local government and regime (economic) performance fall about five points below the scale midpoint at 45.6 and 44.5, respectively. Taken as a whole, the eight-nation data reveal essentially two tiers of support – strong positive support for political community and democratic principles, and lower support for the more concrete and proximate referents.

How much do these sample mean scores vary among the eight nations? We know that the performance of these regimes in economic and political dimensions has been dramatically different, which leads us to anticipate some breadth of distribution around the whole-sample means. Is local variation actually reflected in the specific levels of evaluation by country?

Several macropatterns in political support seem particularly significant. All eight Latin American study countries' means are at or well above the scale midpoint on political community and regime democratic principles. This result indicates that majorities of citizens are committed to the national political community and to democratic norms. Second, most countries' means (except Guatemala's and Nicaragua's) are at or above the scale's midpoint of 50 on support for regime institutions. The legitimacy of particular governmental institutions is clearly lower than that of the two more abstract dimensions in all nations.

For further detail, Appendix Table A.6 presents country means and pooled-sample standard deviations on the legitimacy dimensions. We will examine about national differences in greater depth in Chapter 3 in a broader discussion of the eight Latin American nations in our sample. Here we briefly highlight some common patterns. There are small individual-country distributions around the eight-nation pooled mean for perception of political community, support for regime principles, support for regime performance, and support for regime institutions. Dalton (2004) reports a similarly narrow range of variation in support for institutions among his industrial democracies but broader distributions on democratic values and community. In Latin America we see broader distributions, instead, for local government and political actors. For local government, the outlier on support is Colombia, where citizens indicate markedly higher local government support than in any other country. Political actors in Colombia, Costa Rica, and El Salvador enjoyed much greater support in 2004 than did those in the other countries, especially Nicaragua, Panama, and Honduras.

The most troubling macro pattern revealed in Figure 2.3 and Appendix Table A.6 is for regime economic performance. All evaluations are at or below the scale midpoint of 50. Except for Colombia, respondents also rate their local governments in the low 40s on the 100-point scale. Nicaraguans' and Guatemalans' evaluations of their regimes' institutions fall only in the 40s on the scale. Thus, the national scores reflect serious performance evaluation deficiencies in several nations' economies and local governments. Evaluation of political actors is very low in three of the eight countries, and support for institutions falls below the scale mean of 50 in two. These findings do not suggest by any means that northern Latin America is in imminent danger of democratic breakdown; however, they do allow us to identify economic performance and local government as problem areas for most governments, and actor performance as problematic for several countries.

NATIONAL PATTERNS OF LEGITIMACY

The last major question for this chapter is whether local variations exist in the structure of political legitimacy identified using the pooled eight-nation sample. The central issue is how well or how fully each country's individual legitimacy structure corresponds to that identified in the pooled sample discussed above. Not all national EFA results reveal a structure identical to that for the eight-nation pooled sample (as shown in Figure 2.1 and Appendix Tables A.2 and A.3). Nevertheless, in the eight-country EFA results for each of the six dimensions (not all presented to conserve space), 38 of the total of 48 possible national dimensions are essentially identical to those for the pooled sample. Support for regime principles and local government are present without any divergence in all eight countries. Legitimacy structures of Mexico, Nicaragua, and Colombia very closely approximate the eight-nation structure. These results provide a strong indication of the general validity and utility of the eight-nation pooled legitimacy structure.

Let us now, however, explore some of the local differences. First, in Honduras, Panama, and Guatemala, the support for regime institutions items were split into two dimensions that separate support for national institutions in general (often referred to as diffuse support) from support for specific institutions (specific support). (An illustration of this pattern is available in Appendix Tables A.4a and b, the EFA structure for Guatemala, and is indicated by components one and five in the table.)[14] We are not surprised by this division of support for regime institutions into two correlated factors in several cases for two reasons. First, such a difference is anticipated in Easton's (1965b, 1975) discussions of political support, which predict a division of legitimacy's dimensionality between the more abstract and general (diffuse) and the more specific referents. That is precisely what we observe here – the items cluster around specific institutions (supreme court, parties) versus general institutional performance (protection of rights, pride in the system). Second, in each case these two distinct institutional support factors are the most intercorrelated among all the legitimacy dimensions for the three countries involved. Pearson's *r* coefficients between the diffuse and specific institutional support dimensions range from .343 to .436, indicating significant conceptual/empirical overlap between them.

---

[14] Note that the results of the 2002 Costa Rican EFA and CFA that we reported in Chapter 1, also found the splitting of institutional support into two separate (but strongly intercorrelated) factors.

Another divergence from the eight-nation solution is shared by El Salvador and Costa Rica. There, the support for political actors and evaluation of regime performance dimensions merge into a single dimension. This is not surprising, given that the political actors items ask for evaluation of the incumbent president, and the regime performance items tap into the evaluation of national economic performance. We conclude that in El Salvador and Costa Rica, the presidency and its performance have become more directly associated with economic performance in the minds of citizens than in the other countries. This may work to the advantage of Salvadoran and Costa Rican presidents as long as their relative economic performances remain among the best in the region. However, should their economies sharply decline, these countries' presidents may eventually pay more dearly for the downturn in their citizens' economic circumstances than presidents of the other six nations.

Another divergence between the eight-nation legitimacy dimensional structure and the individual-country results is that a few dimensions are more weakly defined or constituted than most of the others. The political community dimension is weak, for example, in Guatemala and in Colombia. In each case, one of the perceptions of a national political community items also loads heavily on (associates with) other legitimacy dimension. For example, among Guatemalans (Appendix Table A.4a, b), the item "In spite of our differences, we Guatemalans have a lot of things and values that unite us as a country" divides its loadings between political community and the regime principles dimension. Interestingly, in Guatemala the political community dimension also picks up an association with one of the variables from a weak regime performance dimension. An examination of the data reveals a somewhat unexpected finding: Guatemalans who believe their economy is strong average several points *less* on the political community scale than those who think the economy is unhealthy. These results, as we will demonstrate later, reflect certain characteristics that make Guatemala a somewhat distinct case in our eight-nation survey.

In Colombia, the weakness of the political community owes statistically to the fact that one of its components ("In spite of our differences, we have a lot of things and values in common") has almost no association with political community at all and associates more strongly on regime principles (Appendix Table A.5a). Conversely, the Colombian political community dimension picks up an association from two diffuse support items ("pride in system" and "one should support the system"). In Colombia, the confidence in the municipal government item loads more strongly on the support for the national institutions dimension than on the one for support for local government. This difference probably is related to the same factors that cause Colombia's evaluation of local government to be by far the highest of all the eight countries (see Appendix Table A.6) and may arise from system characteristics and policies there that favor local government's strength and effectiveness.

We suspect that these somewhat divergent findings about the structure of legitimacy in Colombia and Guatemala arise from both countries' long histories of violent civil conflict. Civil war ended in Guatemala in 1996 after raging for 36 years. In Colombia, civil war of one type or another has been under way since 1948 and continues at this writing without much hope of resolution in the foreseeable future. Citizens of these two countries have experienced decades of severe disruptions of political order rooted in these conflicts. It would be unreasonable to expect that so much violence would fail to affect citizens' perceptions of government and, indeed, the cognitive map of those perceptions that we have been exploring here. We will address further in following chapters the matter of how sociopolitical history, especially of violence and repression, may affect the structure, levels, and effects of legitimacy in Latin America.

In summary, there are only modest differences in the dimensional structure of legitimacy between the national and the combined eight-nation samples. On balance none of these fairly small differences suggest that we should modify the six-dimension structure we identified above in this chapter. Accordingly, we will employ the six legitimacy dimensions as our key variables for the remaining analysis.

CONCLUSIONS AND MEASUREMENT DECISIONS: OUR KEY VARIABLES

We conclude this chapter by noting that the multidimensional conceptualization of political legitimacy as suggested by Easton and as amended by Norris, Dalton, Klingemann and our own prior research has validity in the Latin American context. By identifying six dimensions of support for government that exist in a culturally and linguistically coherent but economically and politically divergent set of electoral democracies outside of the highly developed industrial nations (see Chapter 3), we have added considerable empirical weight to the literature on legitimacy's structure. We conclude that, in constitutional electoral democracies, multidimensional legitimacy exists largely as it has been theorized. Thus, our findings have considerably reduced at least one of the puzzles about legitimacy.

This empirical advance allows us to take the next logical step, which is to use our measures for the six dimensions we have identified – support for political community, regime principles, regime institutions, regime performance, regime actors, and local government – in further empirical analysis.

3

Countries in the Study

The classic theory on the emergence of state legitimacy comes from Lipset's *Political Man* (1961). Lipset describes a long historical process in which nations overcome a series of crises and so build the confidence of their citizens. "The stability of any given democracy depends not only on economic development but also upon the effectiveness and legitimacy of its political system. Effectiveness means actual performance, the extent to which the system satisfies the basic functions of government as most of the population and . . . powerful groups . . . see them" (Lipset 1961: 64). He further argues that modern democracies' legitimacy derives on a continuing basis from their ability to overcome crises concerning the role of religion in society, the establishment of citizenship rights for the working classes, and the distribution of income (Lipset 1961). Thus, states face an ongoing struggle of performing successfully in order to avoid legitimacy crises. Later Easton (1975) persuasively argued that states can build a "reservoir" of legitimacy to get them through difficult times but that a long-term failure to perform drains that reservoir. In order effectively to study legitimacy and test how it might vary among nations, we need a sample of countries with diverse governmental performance in various areas. In this chapter, we justify our selection of country cases by demonstrating their wide performance differences.

Given the breadth of activities in which modern states involve themselves, on what particular types of performance should we focus? Lipset focused largely on economic development measured comparatively in terms of gross domestic product (GDP) per capita. However, he also included aspects of social development, measured in terms of literacy. By adding this second dimension, Lipset recognized that some states with

66

similar levels of economic development nevertheless differ widely in their delivery of social services that affect the lives of individuals. Infant mortality, for example, varies considerably among states with similar GDP levels, as do literacy and life expectancy. Therefore, in order to study adequately the performance of states, one must consider social development in addition to economic development as defined by economic activity per head.

Another important area of state performance involves political and democratic development, including respect for human rights and civil liberties and providing for citizen influence on politics. These aspects of performance fall under Lipset's rubric of citizenship for the working class, that is, the extent to which nonelites have effective access to full participation in the polity. Participation in politics is the heart of democratic praxis. Citizens must enjoy freedom to acquire information and participate in decision-making processes (Pateman 1970; Dahl 1971; Dahl 1998). The ability of the poor, for example, or of women, indigenous peoples, or racial minorities to the exercise of basic political rights or human rights lies at the heart of democratic development.

Exclusion from full citizenship may occur because poverty denies citizens sufficient resources to allow them to take part in politics. De jure exclusion based on discriminatory laws or unequal legal status may deprive whole groups from citizenship. De facto exclusion from citizenship takes many forms. Powerful actors may manipulate the law, governmental institutions, the media, information, and economic resources to deny others an equal opportunity to exercise effective citizenship. Repression may intimidate citizens, preventing them from participating freely and without fear of reprisals, or may coerce them into compliance with a regime they might otherwise seek to modify or even replace. The exclusion of broad groups of citizens from participation, whether by accident, system design, or repression, constitutes a significant performance failure for a putatively democratic regime. To study political legitimacy fully, therefore, one needs a sample of countries that vary – as our eight nations do – on the key regime traits of human rights performance and the effectiveness of democratic institutions.

As interesting and suggestive as the theory has been, much of the prior research on legitimacy has been carried out in the United States, Canada, Japan, Australia, and Western Europe.[1] These nations vary little in their

---

[1] This literature is cited extensively in Chapter 1.

relatively high economic development levels and human development indicators. Our research design from the outset has sought to broaden the field on which legitimacy research is carried out. In order to explore better legitimacy's structure, sources, and effects, we need cases in which economic, social, and political development vary sharply. Nevertheless, it is also helpful to adhere to a "most similar systems" design, in which many of the historical, cultural, and regional factors are held constant, because this strategy increases our confidence that our surveys do not suffer from variation in respondent interpretation of our survey questions. That is, by studying culturally similar systems, we ensure that our questions tap into the same phenomena in each country (Sartori 1970). Using the same questionnaire in vastly different cultures carries the risk that concepts and measures may not travel well across cultural and geographic boundaries. It is thus advantageous to be able to rule out differences in long-term historical origins or major cultural dissimilarities that might cause variation in key variables. We need to be able to focus directly on the theoretically important variable of the performance of regimes as the driving force in the development of legitimacy.

We therefore focus on a single world region and work with a group of eight geographically contiguous countries – Mexico, Guatemala, El Salvador, Honduras, Nicaragua, Costa Rica, Panama, and Colombia. We chose these countries for several reasons. First, as already noted, this particular region offers an excellent opportunity to study legitimacy because its countries vary in economic, social, and political development while nevertheless sharing many cultural and historical similarities. Second, as scholars, the authors of this volume have together devoted many decades to studying them. Our personal familiarity with the cases, we believe, makes interpretation of the quantitative research more reliable. Third, we have been collaborating on aspects of this legitimacy research for decades, and this study offered the opportunity to address the central questions of this area of research in a broader comparative context than previously possible. Finally, in 2004, funding availability made it possible for us, with a great deal of freedom, collaboratively to design and study the measurement and structure of legitimacy as well as its sources and its effects. As detailed in the acknowledgements section of this volume, the United States Agency for International Development (USAID) made a generous grant to the Latin American Public Opinion Project, now at Vanderbilt University, to carry out nationally representative surveys in these eight countries along with our partner research institutions in each of them.

THE EIGHT NATIONS – COMMON FEATURES

Before discussing the differences among our eight cases, we should note their commonalities. All eight nations are geographically contiguous in northern continental Latin America. They are overwhelmingly Spanish-speaking nations that share a political culture derived from the common experiences of Spain's conquest and colonization of the Western Hemisphere during the sixteenth century. In all eight nations the predominant social and political culture is that of a culturally Spanish, ethnically *mestizo* population. Despite Hispanic cultural dominance, each of the countries has important ethnic/cultural minority populations. Guatemala, Mexico, and Panama today retain significant indigenous populations, although indigenous communities of varying sizes exist in all the countries. Similarly, there are Afro-Latin American populations in all of them, the largest in Panama and Colombia (Andrews 2005).

All eight countries have similar – indeed, even partly shared – political histories.[2] Six of the nations (all but Colombia and its break-away province, Panama) once constituted colonies within the Spanish viceroyalty of New Spain. Mexico's struggle for independence from Spain began in 1810 and culminated in 1821. In that year, the five southernmost colonies separated themselves from the emerging Mexico and established the federated Central American Republic. In 1839, the federation broke apart into the five modern Central American countries (Woodward 1976). Similarly, what are today Colombia and Panama made up part of another, adjacent Spanish viceroyalty, New Granada. After declaring independence in 1813 and consolidating itself in 1819, Colombia became, along with Venezuela and Ecuador, part of the independent Republic of Gran Colombia. Venezuela and Ecuador broke away from Colombia in 1830, and modern Colombia took its final form when, assisted by U.S. military intervention, Panama seceded from Colombia in 1903.[3]

From the sixteenth to the eighteenth centuries, a dominant *criollo* economic class evolved among families who received from the Spanish crown extensive *encomiendas* (trusts) of land and extractive resources including precious metals. These elites (including the Catholic Church), backed by colonial militaries, employed coerced indigenous labor and imported African slaves to accumulate great wealth. As the Spanish colonial system

---

[2] For the colonial history, see MacLeod (1973).
[3] For a detailed review of this history see Cardoso and Pérez Brignoli (1977), Pérez Brignoli (1989), and Hall, Pérez Brignoli, and Cotter (2003).

enterprise deteriorated in the late eighteenth and early nineteenth centuries, this wealth translated itself into military and political power as landed elites used their resources to rebel against Spain. At the time of independence, emerging national elites flirted with elections and popular participation in politics but soon turned to undemocratic politics. Across all eight countries authoritarian political structures arose from nineteenth century struggles – often intensely violent – between conservative and liberal factions among the elites and their *caudillo* (strongman) leaders as they battled for political control of the new nations (Mahoney 2001).[4] After repeated civil wars (Costa Rica being the sole exception to this pattern), liberals eventually secured ruling power everywhere by the late nineteenth or early twentieth centuries. With varying success, progress-oriented liberal dictators promoted modernization of the state and transportation systems and pursued economic development based on exporting *hacienda*-based agricultural commodities (Seligson 1980; Seligson 1984; Paige 1993; Booth, Wade and Walker 2006; Schneider 2007).

In the latter part of the nineteenth century and early in the twentieth century, the United States rapidly expanded its economic and military influence in the Caribbean Basin, affecting all of the countries in this study. Four countries experienced direct U.S. military intervention (Hall et al. 2003: 230–31). Seeking to build a canal across the Central American isthmus in Colombian territory, the United States encountered resistance from Colombia regarding proposed lease terms. In 1903, U.S.-backed Panamanian elements promoted a secession movement and U.S. Marines landed to secure the success of the movement. Panama signed a concessionary canal treaty that turned the new country into a virtual colony holding vital U.S. economic and strategic assets.

Between 1909 and 1932, U.S. armed forces intervened repeatedly in Nicaragua, a potentially alternative canal route, to protect the U.S. canal monopoly and suppress liberal-conservative civil conflict. U.S. occupation of Nicaragua for most of this period brought the establishment of a Nicaraguan National Guard. Control of the guard provided the basis for and key instrument of power for the dynastic Somoza family dictatorship.[5] For

[4] Conservative and liberal proto-parties arose in the late colonial era and eventually developed into specific parties under these and other names in separate countries. When we refer to a specific liberal or conservative party, instead of a broader movement or tendency as we do here, we will capitalize the party names.
[5] For Nicaragua's political history, including U.S. intervention, see Walker (1981), Booth (1985), and Booth, Wade, and Walker (2006).

three decades after 1880, U.S. investors in Mexico received concessionary treatment during the Díaz dictatorship. The Mexican revolution of 1910–17 elicited repeated U.S. military intervention: U.S. forces blockaded and bombarded Mexican port cities to suppress the revolutionaries; the U.S. ambassador was implicated in the overthrow of revolutionary president Madero; and U.S. forces unsuccessfully pursued revolutionary general Pancho Villa around northern Mexico.

While not directly subjected to U.S. military intervention, the remaining countries in our study nonetheless experienced extensive U.S. political and economic influence throughout the twentieth century.[6] U.S. firms invested widely throughout northern Latin America. The United States pushed cooperative multilateral security arrangements as the threat of European and Japanese fascism and militarism loomed before World War II. Containment of communism dominated the era from 1945 to the early 1990s, a period marked by the Inter-American Reciprocal Defense Treaty and the formation of the Organization of American States. The United States covertly intervened in Guatemala to overthrow the democratically elected Arbenz government in 1954 (Schlesinger and Kinzer 2005). In the wake of the Cuban revolution in 1959, the United States expanded its economic and military aid to most of the countries in our study. The Alliance for Progress helped fund economic infrastructure development in the 1960s. Emphasizing anticommunism, the United States provided economic and military assistance to friendly regimes (several of them military dictatorships) in Colombia, Nicaragua, Guatemala, Honduras, and El Salvador to suppress both leftist insurgents and other domestic critics.

By the 1970s, the Panama Canal had lost much of its geostrategic significance for the United States, allowing the Carter administration to return control of the canal to Panama and begin to reduce U.S. military presence there (Schoultz 1987). The Nicaraguan revolution of 1979, however, reignited fears of communist influence in the region and led several U.S. administrations into a new wave of direct intervention in the 1980s. The United States sought to overthrow the Nicaraguan revolution by funding counterrevolutionary forces (the *contras*), imposing economic sanctions, and isolating Nicaragua diplomatically. The United States provided massive civilian and military assistance to El Salvador to resist its

---

[6] Gil 1971; LaFeber 1983; Schoultz 1987; Atkins 1989; Smith 1996; Schoultz 1998; Booth 2006.

own revolutionary movement (Dunkerley 1988; Montgomery 1994). Honduras, too, received extensive U.S. economic and military aid to cooperate against Nicaraguan and Salvadoran revolutionaries. The Reagan and first Bush administrations used economic aid and heavy diplomatic pressure to persuade Costa Rica, a country without a military, to oppose the Nicaraguan revolution.

Additional U.S. influences on the countries of our study in the late twentieth century included pressures to adopt electoral democracy and neoliberal economic development models (Weyland 2005). In the wake of ugly disclosures about violations of human rights by U.S.-supported regimes in Chile and Vietnam, Congress placed human rights conditions upon U.S. assistance to developing countries (Schoultz 1981). During the Reagan administration's burgeoning involvement in Central America, Congress became increasingly reluctant to fund U.S. military intervention or economic aid to Central American regimes with poor human rights records, including Guatemala, El Salvador, and Honduras. The Reagan administration thus began to pressure its Latin American allies away from military rule and toward electoral democracy in order to secure from Congress continued funding for programs to contain leftist influence in Central America (Carothers 1991). This emergent U.S. preference and pressure – backed by other influential international actors – encouraged Honduras, Guatemala, and El Salvador to revise their constitutions and adopt electoral regimes. Even revolutionary Nicaragua, led after 1979 by Marxists, drafted a new constitution in 1987 and conducted open elections in 1984 and 1990. This stratagem, intended by the Sandinista leaders to adapt to the changing international environment and to check U.S. support for the *contra* rebellion, provided the means by which Nicaraguans voted out the revolutionary party in 1990.

The United States invaded Panama in 1989 to oust the uncooperative military regime of former U.S. ally Manuel Noriega and thus allow the real victors of a fraudulently manipulated election to assume office. Mexico, by the late 1990s almost the last of Latin America's authoritarian regimes, followed its own path toward formal electoral democracy. Election reforms implemented in the late 1990s under the watchful eye of the international community permitted Vicente Fox and the National Action Party in 2000 to wrest power from the Institutional Revolutionary Party that had ruled Mexico for 71 years (Camp 2007).

Regarding economic policy, from the 1980s forward proponents of neoliberalism (advocating free trade, capital mobility, economic deregulation, small public-sector shares of national economies, fiscal austerity, reduced public employment, and privatization of public sector firms and services) successfully pressed these policies upon Latin American countries. Widely adopted under pressure from the United States and international lenders, such neoliberal policies have had varying effects from country to country (Lora and World Bank 2007; Payne 2007). Colombia, Costa Rica, El Salvador, and Mexico, for example, grew economically during the 1980s and 1990s. In contrast, the economies of Honduras and Nicaragua performed particularly badly (see the following section). Moreover, neoliberal policies have limited the latter governments' use of critical policy tools with which to address poverty within their gravely poor economies.

One final area of overarching similarity among the countries studied warrants mention – formal governmental systems (Payne 2007; Ropp 2007). All eight nations are constitutional electoral democracies of the liberal variant. At the time of our surveys all eight nations had civilian presidents who had been elected in fair and free elections. Their constitutions provided for separation of powers into three or four branches (legislative, executive, judicial, and in several a fourth branch consisting of an autonomous electoral authority) and gave each branch certain checks and balances on the others. Most of the countries had constitutionally strong executives (Costa Rica is again an exception). Legislatures were unicameral in the six smaller countries but bicameral in the largest two, Mexico and Colombia. Mexico, with its huge population and extensive territory, had a federal structure of government while the other seven nations were unitary. Despite previous military rule at some time in all eight nations, Costa Rica and Panama had effectively no standing armed forces at the time of our study, and the armed forces of the remaining six nations were subservient to elected civilian leaders.

KEY DIFFERENCES AMONG THE EIGHT COUNTRIES

Despite their similarities, the eight countries in the study vary in a number of important ways in their social, economic, and political performance, which theory tells us should affect the legitimacy of their regimes.

Table 3.1 compares the eight countries in terms of population characteristics. In their population size and surface areas, Mexico and Colombia are large in comparison to the other six much smaller nations strung along the Mesoamerican isthmus that lies between them. One striking difference among the nations is the extreme population density of El Salvador (320 persons per square kilometer). Guatemala (113 per square kilometer) has

TABLE 3.1. *Population characteristics*

Country	Population (millions) 2003	Surface Area (1000 square km)	Population Density (per Square km)	% Indigenous
Mexico	102.3	1,975	52	30
Guatemala	12.3	109	113	41
El Salvador	6.5	21	320	1
Honduras	7.0	112	63	7
Nicaragua	5.5	129	43	5
Costa Rica	4.0	51	78	1
Panama	3.0	78	39	6
Colombia	44.4	1,139	39	1

Sources: Interamerican Development Bank (2004), Central Intelligence Agency (2005).

TABLE 3.2. *Economic performance*

Country	GDP Per Capita 2003 (PPN in U.S. dollars)	Percent Real GDP Per Capita Growth 1982–2000	Percent Real GDP Growth Per Capita 1950–2000
Mexico	$8,540	10	192
Guatemala	3,880	2	82
El Salvador	4,570	27	57
Honduras	2,450	−14	14
Nicaragua	2,470	−74	−18
Costa Rica	8,260	29	138
Panama	5,870	4	202
Colombia	5,247	48	144

Sources: Heston, Summers, and Aten (2002), Interamerican Development Bank (2004).

the second most densely settled population while the six remaining countries are far less densely settled. The ethnic makeup of the nations also varies markedly. Guatemala and Mexico have the largest percentage of indigenous populations at 41 and 30 percent, respectively.

The study nations vary dramatically in economic performance, as revealed in Table 3.2. In purchasing power (PPN) equivalents, Mexico at $8,540 and Costa Rica at $8,260 were the wealthiest nations per capita in 2003. In contrast, GDP per capita for the two poorest countries in the study, Honduras and Nicaragua, were less than one-third of the levels of Mexico and Costa Rica. The remaining four nations were arrayed between these exceptionally high and low levels of per capita income. Economic performance over time reveals another facet of the

TABLE 3.3. *Social development performance*

Country	Percent Literate (c. 2004)	Life Expectancy (in years, c. 2004)	Infant Mortality (per 1000 births, c. 2004)
Mexico	92	74	24
Guatemala	71	65	36
El Salvador	80	70	33
Honduras	76	66	32
Nicaragua	68	69	32
Costa Rica	96	78	9
Panama	93	75	19
Colombia	93	72	19

Source: Central Intelligence Agency (2005).

picture. Growth for 1982 to 2000, a period that began with a serious recession afflicting all of Latin America, ranged from reasonably good growth for Colombia, Costa Rica, and El Salvador (48, 29, and 27 percent respectively overall GDP growth per capita), to slow growth in Mexico, and economic stagnation in Guatemala and Panama. Performing far worse still between 1982 and 2000 were Honduras and Nicaragua, which respectively *lost* 14 and 74 percent of their 1982 GDP per capita for this period. Finally, Table 3.2 offers a five-decade performance record of change in GDP per capita. Mexico and Panama enjoyed roughly 200 percent per capita income increases, followed by Costa Rica and Colombia with about 140 percent increases. In contrast, Guatemala and El Salvador grew relatively little over the entire 50-year span. For the worst five-decade economic performances, however, Honduras had a scant 14 percent increase, while Nicaragua had a net *loss* of 18 percent of GDP per capita. We will test in Chapter 5 whether these striking economic performance differences affected citizens' legitimacy levels.

Social development performance measures are presented in Table 3.3, again with notable differences. Governments' differential investments in the social welfare of their citizens are evident. Adult literacy rates around 2005 varied from about 70 percent in Nicaragua and Guatemala upward to the low 90s in Mexico, Panama, and Colombia. Costa Rica, with its historic emphasis on public education, is at the top of the literacy array at 96 percent. Life expectancy likewise clustered in three tiers. Honduras, Nicaragua, El Salvador, and Guatemala ranged between 65 and 70 years life expectancy while Colombians, Panamanians, and Mexicans expected to live between 72 and 75 years. Costa Rica, which had long invested in public medical care for its population, in 2004 had the region's best life expectancy of 78 years. Infant mortality per 1,000 births also clustered in three tiers – Guatemala, El Salvador, Honduras, and Nicaragua in the low to mid-30s, and Panama, Colombia, and Mexico in the mid-20s. Again Costa Rica, with an extensive program of low-cost public access to health care, stood out with only nine infant deaths per 1000. We will test in Chapter 4 whether these social development performance differences affected citizens' legitimacy levels.

Political performance varied dramatically among our nations during the decades prior to our survey, as revealed in Table 3.4. The age of formal electoral democracy (the current regime type in all eight) ranged from the youngest, Mexico, at five years as of 2005, to Costa Rica, at 56 years of continuous electoral democracy. Five of the Central American nations – Guatemala, El Salvador, Honduras, Nicaragua, and Panama, became electoral democracies only in the 1990s. Over the very long haul, the average annual democracy scores for the 1900 to 1989 period as computed by Vanhanen range from a high of 8.81 for Costa Rica to a low of 2.05 for Mexico. In the very short term, democracy levels as measured by our version of the combined Freedom House index for the countries in 2003 ranged from a low of 6 for Colombia, which had an active civil war under way, to a high of 11 out of a possible 12 for the much more stable Costa Rica and Panama.[7] The political terror scale – a measure of violence with a range of 1 (low) to 5 (high) – also varies sharply across the countries. Costa Rica was the least violent in 2003, followed by Panama and Mexico. Colombia's ongoing civil war accounted for its political terror scale score of 5.

Two overall measures attempt to summarize various aspects of the political systems we are studying. The World Bank Institute's Rule of Law measure, shown in Table 3.4, attempts to capture political stability. The index scores range from a low of 23.7 for Honduras to 72.2 for Costa Rica. Colombia, Guatemala, El Salvador, and Nicaragua all score poorly on rule of law, with Panama and Mexico in the scale's midrange. Another overarching World Bank Institute measure of political performance is its

[7] Freedom House (2004) uses two scales of political rights and civil liberties, each ranging from 1 to 7 (with 1 as the best performance and 7 the worst). For the sake of convenience and logic here, we combine these into a single measure that we consider a measure of democracy. We add the two scales together to provide a 12-point democracy scale (ranging from 2 to 14), then invert it so that the most democratic score is the highest and the least democratic the lowest. We then subtract two points to give the recoded FH scale a range from a theoretical high point of 12 to a theoretical low point of zero.

TABLE 3.4. *Political performance*

Country	Total Years of Continuous Democracy as of 2005	Mean Vanhanen Democracy Score 1900–1989[a]	Freedom House Overall Democracy Score (2003)[b]	Political Terror Scale Score (2003)[c]	World Bank Institute Rule of Law Index[d]	World Bank Institute Government Effectiveness Index[e]
	High = more democracy	High = more democracy	High = more democracy	Low = less violence	High = more rule of law	High = greater effectiveness
Mexico	5	2.05	10	2	52.1	50.8
Guatemala	9	2.52	6	3	31.6	32.4
El Salvador	13	2.54	9	3	39.7	56.8
Honduras	9	2.53	8	3	23.7	38.4
Nicaragua	15	3.19	8	3	32.0	47.6
Costa Rica	56	8.81	11	1	72.2	86.5
Panama	16	4.69	11	2	55.7	57.3
Colombia	31	4.20	6	5	40.4	4.9

Sources: Booth, Wade, and Walker (2006), U.S. Department of the Army (1988), World Bank Institute (Kaufmann, Kraay, and Zoido-Lobatón 1999; Kaufmann, Kraay, and Zoido-Lobatón 2006); Vanhanen (1997), Freedom House (2004), Gibney (2005a, 2005b).
[a] Vanhanen's democracy score measures system competitiveness and voter turnout; range 0–100.
[b] The revised Freedom House (FH) score sums both FH's political rights and civil liberties measures, with value scale reversed here (range = 0–12).
[c] Range = 1–5.
[d] Rule of Law Index; range = 0–100.
[e] Government Effectiveness Index; range = 0–100.

Government Effectiveness Index. Colombia had the worst performance on the effectiveness measure at 4.9 while Costa Rica performed the best at 86.5. In sum, our study countries' democracies vary in age, long-term performance, and short-term performance. Political violence, rule of law, and government effectiveness also range widely.

THE EIGHT NATIONS – VARIATIONS ON A THEME

Despite their common historical and cultural-linguistic experiences and the formal similarities of their governmental structures today, much about each of these nations is unique. This section introduces the countries and some of the key economic and political facts that contribute to each one's distinctness.

Mexico[8]

The largest country in the study in population and area, Mexico is also the most industrialized and most prosperous. Yet, its history and national development have been marked by social and political conflict, often epic in scale.

Initiated by a liberal movement of peasant and middle-sector rebels led by the *criollo* priest Miguel Hidalgo y Costilla in Guanajuato in 1810, the Mexican independence movement eventually secured freedom from Spain by uniting factions of wealthy liberal and conservative landholders. After decades of postindependence civil strife among factions of the landed elite as well as territorial losses to the United States, liberals led by Benito Juárez won control of Mexico in 1857. A conservative-backed French invasion and occupation in 1861 brought renewed civil war. Liberals eventually ejected the French and returned to power in 1867, but governance turned dictatorial under Porfirio Díaz (1876–1911). Ruling with an iron hand, Díaz disdained native Mexicans' development capacity and used extensive economic concessions to promote foreign investment. Rich in natural resources, Mexico during the Porfiriato rapidly developed extractive industries, transportation, and manufacturing.

Díaz's repression and the expropriation of indigenous lands combined with growing economic problems to provoke in 1910 a multifaceted

---

[8] Excellent sources on Mexican history, politics, and development include Levy, Bruhn, and Zebadúa (2006), Camp (2007), Grayson (2007), and Meyer, Sherman, and Deeds (2007).

revolutionary insurrection by southern indigenous rebels, northern mestizo peasant rebels, and middle- and upper-class political reformers. After deaths that may have reached into the millions and an internecine struggle among the revolutionaries, a coalition of political reformers prevailed. The resulting 1917 constitution provided for a presidential system, federalism, anticlericalism, economic nationalism, and a strong economic role for the state. Democracy and stability eluded the new regime as revolutionary strongmen struggled over power while official anticlericalism culminated in the Cristero rebellion. In 1929, former President Plutarco Elías Calles formed the Revolutionary Party (eventually the Partido Revolucionario Institucional – PRI), which united revolutionary factions behind a series of powerful presidents. Some of the social claims of the revolutionaries were addressed with land and labor reforms instituted by president Lázaro Cárdenas (1934–40), who also nationalized Mexico's oil industry. The PRI's authoritarian machine controlled unions and elections and penetrated all branches and levels of government. This secured decades of political stability, allowing the military to decline steadily in political importance, and facilitated state-led economic modernization that produced high economic growth rates until the 1970s.

By the 1960s, technocrats had assumed control of the presidency and reduced the role of the PRI's traditional leadership in the Mexican states. The revolution's successes waned as dissent in the late 1960s brought heavy repression. Risky economic decisions spawned by the oil-price run up of the 1970s caused a debt crisis and recession in the 1980s that was followed by another in the 1990s. Pressured by international lenders to adopt neoliberal economic reforms, Mexico privatized banking and important components of the large public sector, streamlined the state apparatus, curtailed welfare programs, reformed the constitution to liberalize peasant agricultural property, and liberalized the rules of foreign investment. The political system, long dominated by the PRI, became critically weakened, suffering a near loss in the 1988 election of Carlos Salinas de Gortari. PRI electoral fraud was so pervasive that it was difficult to know which candidate actually received the most votes. Salinas's administration was marked by corruption, draconian economic austerity programs, a highly unpopular push to join the North American Free Trade Agreement (NAFTA) with the United States and Canada, and the assassination of Salinas's designated successor to the presidency. Popular anger over protracted economic difficulties and NAFTA, the prodemocracy Zapatista insurgency in Chiapas, and external pressures led PRI president Ernesto Zedillo to implement electoral reforms that allowed major opposition party gains in 1997 and a presidential victory by the National Action Party (Partido de Acción Nacional – PAN) in 2000 (Magaloni 2007).

Most observers mark 2000 as the birth of a fully democratic electoral regime in Mexico. Control of Congress eluded PAN president Vicente Fox and stymied policy making in the first post-PRI administration, however. The PRI and the Revolutionary Democratic Party (Partido Revolucionaria Democrática – PRD) each held a large bloc of votes that prevented a PAN congressional majority. The PRI, PAN, and PRD each controlled various state and local governments, and interparty electoral competition remained intense in by-elections and candidate jockeying for the 2006 presidential elections. At the time of our study, Mexico was the youngest democratic regime among our eight nations, and had the weakest prior history of democracy as measured by Vanhanen's 1900–89 index (Table 3.4). On the assumption that both historical and recent experience with functioning democracy likely affect legitimacy norms, we are not surprised that Mexicans ranked sixth in their support for democratic regime principles (Table 3.5).

Despite the economic turbulence in the 1980s and 1990s, Mexico remained the wealthiest country in our study, with relatively high life expectancy and literacy rates. The economic turbulence of the 1980s and 1990s may account for Mexico's rank of only sixth among the countries in evaluation of regime performance, which taps mainly into economic evaluations (Table 3.5). These data, however, somewhat obscured the uneven distribution of wealth between Mexico's industrial north and the intensely poor southern states where the country's large indigenous population is concentrated and where a rebellion by the Zapatista Army of National Liberation (Ejército Zapatista de Liberación Nacional – EZLN) broke out in 1994. These inequalities and ethnic turmoil in the south likely contributed to Mexico's ranking lowest among the countries on a sense of national political community (Table 3.5).

Guatemala

Guatemala, the largest of the Central American states, dominated the federated Central American Republic that separated from Mexico at independence.[9] Guatemala's disproportionate influence over the new nation, along

---

[9] This section draws on several sources: Historical Clarification Commission (1999), Jonas (2000), Seligson (2005a), and Booth et al. (2006).

TABLE 3.5. *Mean legitimacy score (and rank) by country, 2004*

Legitimacy Dimension	Mexico	Colombia	Costa Rica	El Salvador	Guatemala	Honduras	Nicaragua	Panama
Political community mean (rank)	63.4 (8)	67.4 (5)	72.3 (1)	69.9 (2)	64.0 (7)	65.3 (6)	67.7 (4)	69.2 (3)
Regime principles mean (rank)	64.2 (6)	68.1 (4)	73.4 (2)	64.0 (7)	59.3 (8)	65.8 (5)	71.0 (3)	76.5 (1)
Regime performance mean (rank)	42.9 (6)	47.7 (3)	46.5 (4)	48.0 (2)	43.2 (5)	36.2 (8)	41.4 (7)	49.7 (1)
Regime institutions mean (rank)	53.8 (3)	49.8 (4)	58.9 (1)	54.4 (2)	45.7 (7)	49.2 (5)	45.6 (8)	48.8 (6)
Local government mean (rank)	45.7 (3)	55.0 (1)	45.0 (5)	46.9 (2)	45.3 (4)	44.5 (6)	41.0 (8)	41.5 (7)
Political actors mean (rank)	53.7 (3)	61.0 (1)	55.0 (2)	53.1 (4)	50.2 (5)	38.1 (7)	42.3 (6)	37.4 (8)

with liberal-conservative competition, spawned civil wars that eventually brought about the collapse of the federation. Conservative dictators predominated in the fully independent Guatemala until liberals took control in 1871. Later, liberal dictator Justo Rufino Barrios aggressively modernized the country by developing a national army and bureaucracy, promoting road and railway construction, and encouraging coffee cultivation by largeholders using land taken from indigenous communal holdings. Government-implemented debt-peonage and vagrancy laws forced indigenous people to work on the coffee plantations. These policies made coffee Guatemala's major export and greatly concentrated land ownership.

In the late nineteenth century, the United Fruit Company (UFCO) gained control of Guatemala's banana cultivation and exports and used resulting revenues to acquire vast landholdings and take over most public utilities. Liberal Manuel Estrada Cabrera's dictatorship (1898–1920) promoted the continued expansion of the coffee and banana export sectors. After worker unrest driven by the onset of the world recession in 1929, the new liberal dictator Jorge Ubico reasserted state control over the rural labor supply. Ubico ruled until 1944 when student and labor-backed pro-democracy military reformers forced his resignation.

Guatemala's democratic "revolution" of 1944–54 began with the election of President Juan José Arévalo, whose government instituted widespread social and political reforms. Arévalo's successor, Col. Jacobo Arbenz, elected in 1950, won enactment of further reforms, especially of the agrarian sector. A newly legalized communist party supported the Guatemalan government, and peasant unions spread rapidly. Landowner interests and UFCO (with close ties to the Eisenhower administration) reacted with alarm to the appropriation of fruit company lands and arms purchases from Czechoslovakia. The United States in 1953 began destabilizing Guatemala with financial and diplomatic pressures, propaganda, and covert actions. A U.S.-engineered "insurrection" by Guatemalan army rightists, an invasion by CIA-sponsored rebels, and CIA air support forced Arbenz to resign when the army refused to support him.

Repression of labor and peasant movements resulted in the jailing and murder of scores of people. Coup plotter and president Carlos Castillo Armas forged an anticommunist alliance between the military and business interests that would dominate Guatemala for decades. The regime reversed prior reforms and aligned itself with the United States. In 1960, Guatemala's first Marxist rebel groups appeared and began to emulate Fidel Castro's Cuban insurrectionary strategy in what became a 36-year-long insurgency. During this era Guatemala embraced the new Central American Common

Market and also became a major recipient of U.S. economic and military assistance under the Alliance for Progress. Despite the insurrection, Guatemala's economy grew rapidly in the 1960s and 1970s.

In 1963, with U.S.-assisted counterinsurgency operations ballooning but ineffective, the army seized power and retained it for most of the period until 1985. Left and center parties were suppressed, and all remaining parties nominated military officers for the presidency. The military's preferred candidates won fraudulently manipulated elections. Rampant repression by the armed forces and associated civilian death squads afflicted the population, especially indigenous Guatemalans, political opponents, and regime critics. By its end in 1996, the civil war had displaced 1.5 million people. The Historical Clarification Commission attributed 90 percent of the almost 200,000 deaths to government security forces (Historical Clarification Commission 1999).

Guatemala began slowly to liberalize under military tutelage in 1981. An election for a civilian constituent assembly was held. The assembly's 1985 revision of the constitution exculpated the military for its human rights abuses. Centrist parties were allowed to participate in the 1985 election. Christian Democrat Vinicio Cerezo won the presidency but governed under heavy military restraints while the civil war continued. External pressures for a peace settlement, democratization, and human rights improvements moved the military to agree to peace in 1996. Formal electoral democracy in Guatemala dates from this accord, the provisions of which allowed former rebel groups into the political arena as legal parties and brought significant military reform. Rightist and business elements coalesced behind a shifting array of parties after the peace accord. Post–peace accord governments have embraced neoliberal economic policies.

Although at this writing its civil war had ended and formal electoral democracy had been established, Guatemala remained plagued by poverty, violence, high voting abstention, low voter participation, lower democratic norms (Seligson 2005a; Booth and Richard 2006b; Booth and Richard 2006a), and multiple social pathologies: "Little had been done to address the rights of Guatemala's indigenous population.... While human rights abuses declined, activists and workers remained targets of violent repression. Crime and impunity, including both the proliferation of gangs and continued activity by security forces, threatened Guatemala's fragile peace" (Booth 2006).

Guatemala's weak current democracy and governmental performance, its limited prior experience of democracy (Table 3.4), and its protracted history of ethnic strife and discrimination likely contributed substantially to Guatemala's ranking last or next to last among our eight countries on perception of a national political community, support for democratic regime principles, and support for national institutions (Table 3.5). Guatemalans thus distinguished themselves among all respondents by having extremely low average legitimacy positions on three of the six legitimacy dimensions. We anticipate that this may have important implications for other key political attitudes and behaviors of Guatemalans and may give important clues to Guatemala's future political stability.

El Salvador

Tiny in surface area but densely populated and deeply torn by conflict, El Salvador made surprising strides in politics and economics after the settlement of its civil war in 1992. Like its neighbors, El Salvador emerged from the Spanish colonial period in 1823 as part of the Central American federation.[10] Liberal regimes in the nineteenth and early twentieth centuries promoted agricultural exports, especially coffee. Liberal "reforms" forced smallholders and indigenous communities off potentially good coffee land. Coffee production concentrated among a few politically dominant agricultural families while most Salvadorans became increasingly poor (Paige 1997).

In the 1930s, the Great Depression forced down coffee prices and workers' wages. This decline sparked mobilization by peasant unions and urban workers. Prompted by an abortive leftist uprising in 1932, a new military government and landowners brutally massacred tens of thousands of workers. The ensuing dictatorship of General Maximiliano Hernández Martínez protected coffee interests and promoted modernization projects. Subsequent military regimes ruled into the late 1970s using a military-dominated political party in coalition with powerful economic interests.

Under this government El Salvador joined the Central American Common Market, and with aid from the Alliance for Progress promoted economic infrastructure development. Resulting changes included agricultural diversification, manufacturing and commercial investment, and further concentration of land ownership. Moderated repression in the 1960s allowed the reformist Christian Democrats to win the mayoralty of the

---

[10] This section draws upon Anderson (1971), Webre (1979), Baloyra (1982), Montgomery (1982), Werner (1989), Seligson and Córdova (1992), Montgomery (1994), Seligson (1995), Seligson et al. (1995), Seligson and McElhinny (1996), Williams and Walter (1997), Heston et al. (2002, 2006a: Ch. 6), Booth et al. (2006).

capital, San Salvador. Economic growth was rapid during the 1960s and early 1970s, but after the oil price shock of the mid-1970s inflation soared, the economy stagnated, and unemployment rose rapidly.

The military regime responded to growing popular unrest and calls for political reform by stealing the 1972 election and escalating repression. The military formed paramilitary groups to repress perceived opponents. A leftist guerrilla insurgency began in the early 1970s, eliciting soaring regime repression against labor, students, peasants, opposition party leaders, social workers, the press, and Catholic religious figures. Some 13,300 political murders occurred in 1981 alone. Five guerrilla groups formed in the middle- and late 1970s and began fighting the government while mobilizing popular-sector civil society opposition. When the Sandinistas in Nicaragua overthrew the Somoza dictatorship in July 1979, El Salvador appeared headed for the same outcome. Elements of the military, certain economic elites, and the Christian Democrats thereupon engineered a coup on October 15, 1979, and quickly received support from the United States. The junta ostensibly intended to stop regime repression and promote political reform in order to prevent civil war, but anticommunist hardliners quickly took over and instead escalated the violence. The five guerrilla groups then joined into the Farabundo Martí National Liberation Front (Frente Farabundo Martí para la Liberación Nacional – FMLN), which forged a political broad front, promoted protests, and initiated open guerrilla warfare.

The Reagan administration in the United States provided extensive military and economic assistance and personnel to the Salvadoran junta while pressing for formal electoral democracy in hopes of winning centrist forces away from the insurgents. A constituent assembly wrote a new constitution, Christian Democrat José Napoleón Duarte won a deeply flawed election in 1984, and government human rights abuses slowly diminished. This strategy, including U.S. assistance that eventually totaled about $6 billion, gradually proved successful. The rightist Nationalist Republican Alliance (Alianza Republicana Nacionalista – ARENA), representing neoliberal and bourgeois interests, won the next presidential election (and several more into the mid-2000s).

With the war stalemated, the death toll rising toward 70,000, and hundreds of thousands displaced (Comisión de la Verdad 1993), first the FMLN and later the Salvadoran government began considering a negotiated settlement. Pressure for a peace agreement grew from Latin American and other Central American nations. Ultimately, the end of the Cold War in 1989 and the Nicaraguan revolution in 1990 allowed the Salvadoran and U.S. governments to support peace negotiations. Negotiators reached an accord in 1992 that reduced military forces, brought about police reforms, and allowed former insurgent groups to demobilize and enter the political arena as parties.

The birth of full electoral democracy in El Salvador dates from the peace accord. The FMLN demobilized and competed in elections with mixed success. Leftists consistently lost the presidency after the peace agreement, but from the late 1990s forward, leftist candidates won many mayoralties including in the capital city. By 2003, the FMLN held the largest block of legislative seats (37 percent) – won at the expense of the Christian Democrats and ARENA – but again could not capture the presidency in 2004.

In the economic arena, El Salvador's ARENA governments wholeheartedly embraced neoliberalism. Privatization of government enterprises, tariff reductions, and promotion of assembly plant free trade zones brought a spurt in economic growth during the 1990s; however, this boomlet later cooled. When criminal gang activity burgeoned among young Salvadorans repatriated from the United States, the government responded with a draconian antigang policy.

Despite El Salvador's conflicts over economic policy, high levels of criminal violence, and external interference in elections, Salvadorans seemed to be developing a level of comfort with their national political-economic situation by the mid-2000s. Political terror levels since the early 1990s had fallen more than anywhere else in Central America, and real economic growth per capita had averaged 1.5 percent per year from 1982 onward – Central America's second best performance.[11] Voter turnout was the second highest in the eight countries of the study, and support for government institutions was the second highest in Central America (Booth et al. 2006). Our political support indicators (Table 3.5) show that Salvadorans rank second among citizens of our eight countries in their level of perceived national community, evaluation of regime performance, support for regime institutions, and support for local government. These are higher evaluations than we expected given El Salvador's violently authoritarian track record prior to the 1992 peace accord. The dimension in which Salvadorans rank second to last among the eight countries is support for democratic regime principles. This ranking appears commensurate with the country's limited history of democracy and still brief period of democratic governance. We

---

[11] Calculated from the 2002 Penn World Table (Heston et al. 2002).

surmise, however, that a continuation of the improved performance by the current democratic regime reflected in both economic statistics and in other legitimacy norms may over time strengthen Salvadorans' support for democratic regime principles.

Honduras[12]

Fragmented by broken terrain, and with poor soils and few natural resources, Honduras remained for the most part a subsistence economy through the nineteenth century. Its people were among the poorest in the hemisphere, yet compared to its neighbors, Honduras was relatively politically stable. Political and economic elites were regionally based rather than nationally integrated. Coffee cultivation, a powerful force driving socioeconomic change in several other countries in this study, came to Honduras much later and had only a modest impact. Commercial banana production by foreign firms began around 1900 along the northern coast, but because this region was sparsely populated at that time, it displaced few peasants or indigenous peoples. Land shortages developed only in the mid-twentieth century, when foreign market demands led wealthier Hondurans to begin concentrating land ownership (Durham 1979). Absent significant rural protest or a need to manage an agrarian proletariat, the Honduran military remained weak compared to those in Guatemala or El Salvador. Banana workers' unions developed relatively freely, leaving Honduras with the region's largest organized workforce.

After independence, nonideological *caudillos* dominated politics until Liberals became and remained ascendant from the mid-1870s until 1932. The Liberal Party of Honduras (Partido Liberal de Honduras – PLH) promoted modernization and encouraged foreign investment. A conservative National Party (Partido Nacional – PN) appeared in the 1920s and won power when the Liberal Party split in 1932. PN efforts to deny liberals power through elections brought about a military coup in 1956. At first intervening to referee the PN-PLH conflict, the armed forces quickly embraced a more active political role. For four subsequent decades the military either ruled directly or powerfully influenced civilian leaders from behind the scenes. U.S. military assistance, aimed at containing communism, bolstered the Honduran military's strength and enhanced its domestic

---

[12] This section drawn especially from Ropp (1984), Seligson, Jones, and Nesman (1984), Stanfield et al. (1990), Rosenberg (1995), Mahoney (2001), Cuesta (2007).

political power. At first neutral between the PN and PLH, the military began
to ally with the National Party and became more repressive of labor and
peasant movements during the 1960s. Honduras joined the newly formed
Central American Common Market in 1960, but the accord helped the
Honduran economy little and generated a backlash of popular protests.

Air Force Col. Oswaldo López Arellano seized power in 1963. Disad-
vantageous trade with Central America and the brief 1969 war with El
Salvador (the so-called Soccer War)[13] escalated public unrest. López
Arellano stepped down in 1969, but the National Party–Liberal Party
civilian coalition government that followed failed to address growing
popular turmoil. López Arellano seized power again, this time initiating
populist programs that included agrarian reform. Embarrassed by a corruption scandal, in 1975 López Arellano transferred power to two subsequent military rulers whose governments made little economic progress.
Eventually, pressured by the Carter administration, worried about the
breakdown of the Common Market, and troubled by Nicaraguan revolution and Salvadoran civil war, the military in 1980 called elections for
a constituent assembly and began gradually extricating itself from power.

The presidential election of 1981 nominally returned power to a civilian
president, Robert Suazo Córdova, a member of the Liberal Party. Despite
civilian rule, U.S. military aid rapidly re-inflated the military's political
power. Honduras actively cooperated with the Reagan administration's
harassment of Nicaragua's Sandinistas, accepted massive U.S. military
aid, and allowed anti-Sandinista counterrevolutionaries to operate along
its southern border and conduct raids into Nicaragua. In 1984 President
Suazo provoked a constitutional crisis by seeking to alter the constitution in
order to be reelected. Senior officers, disgruntled about Defense Minister
Col. Gustavo Alvarez Martínez's support for Honduras' deepening involvement in the U.S.-Nicaraguan conflict, removed Alvarez and pressured
Suazo to allow the regularly scheduled election. National Party candidates
won the next two presidential elections and the military retained its enormous influence while human rights performance deteriorated.

In 1994 human rights lawyer and liberal Carlos Roberto Reina won the
presidency and began to curtail human rights abuses and military power.
Several officers were tried and convicted for human rights crimes. Reina's
successors have alternated between the national and liberal parties. By the

[13] The misnamed conflict stemmed from Honduran anger about Salvadoran peasants'
squatting on Honduran land, border security, and tensions over trade imbalances.

early 2000s, Honduras largely had consolidated formal democratic rule, having seen the military's political role diminish sharply and having experienced several peaceful turnovers of power by incumbents to opposition party candidates. Ongoing rights abuses related to rampant urban crime have, however, kept (our version of) Honduras' Freedom House democracy score at only 8 out of a possible 12 points. Honduras scored worst among our eight countries on the World Bank rule of law index and second worst on the Bank's government effectiveness scale.

Despite the improved regime political behavior after 1994, Honduras' economic and political performance remained very poor. The country was the second poorest among our study's nations and experienced a 14 percent decline of GDP between 1982 and 2000. Honduras's overall economic growth per capita from 1950 to 2000 was a scant 14 percent. Life expectancy and infant mortality ranked second worst. In short, serious performance issues abounded for Honduras at the time of our survey. It is thus not surprising that Hondurans evaluated the performance of their regime (focusing on economic matters) worse than citizens of any other country in our study, and the performance of their political actors (incumbent president) second to worst among the eight nations. Indeed, at the time of our study Hondurans were, on average, deeply dissatisfied with the national performance and the stewardship of the administration of President Ricardo Maduro.

Nicaragua

Nicaragua, despite a reasonable store of natural resources and access to two oceans via a lake and river system, has seen its natural advantages offset by a history of partisan conflict and geopolitical machination.[14] The Spanish settled in the Pacific lowlands, where landed elites developed proto-parties by the late colonial era. After independence these partisan clan-factions cemented a strong party identification among elites and masses by fighting repeated civil wars during and after the breakdown of the Central American Republic. This violent partisan competition combined with external efforts to control Nicaragua's potential transit route across Central America to mire the nation's politics in violence and impeded economic development.

---

[14] Material on Nicaragua is drawn from Walker (1981), Booth (1985), Seligson and Booth (1993), Booth and Seligson (1994), Seligson and Macías (1996), Seligson and McElhinny (1996), Stein (1998), Booth et al. (2006).

In the mid-nineteenth century, Britain and the United States struggled to dominate access to Nicaragua; the Americans eventually prevailed. California's gold rush intensified U.S. interest in Nicaragua as a quick transit route between the east and west coasts of the United States. Competing transit companies sought advantage with Nicaragua's warring political parties. Liberals backing one firm invited American William Walker and a mercenary army to help them. Walker, however, seized power for himself and announced his intention to annex the country to the United States. Conservatives then allied with Cornelius Vanderbilt, owner of the competing transit company. Vanderbilt armed Conservatives from around Central America, who defeated Walker in the National War of 1857. Their 1857 defeat effectively froze the liberals out of power until the 1890s.

The spread of coffee cultivation in the late nineteenth century required cheap labor and land previously held by free peasants and indigenous people. Elites used laws, fraud, and violence to seize much of the northern highlands for coffee cultivation. Modernizing liberal dictator José Santos Zelaya (1893–1909) crushed rural resistance and promoted modernization, education, and a stronger government and military. When the United States decided to build a trans-isthmian canal in Panama, Zelaya sought competing proposals for a Nicaraguan canal. The United States then provoked a conservative rebellion against him by introducing U.S. troops to install a conservative government. For most of the period from 1912 to 1933, U.S. Marines occupied the country to ensure that no Nicaraguan canal would be built, guarantee a pliable government, and suppress a nationalist rebellion by Augusto Sandino.

U.S. forces formed the nonpartisan National Guard to help pacify the country. When U.S. Marines and the guard failed to defeat Sandino after a multiyear counterinsurgency, President Hoover withdrew U.S. troops in late 1932. Meanwhile, a liberal opportunist, Anastasio Somoza García, employed nepotism and his ties to the U.S. ambassador to finagle himself into command of the National Guard. He then assassinated Sandino in 1934 during a cease-fire and used the guard to seize power in 1936. From then until 1979 Somoza García, one of his two sons (Luis Somoza Debayle and Anastasio Somoza Debayle), or a puppet occupied the presidency. The rapaciously corrupt dynasty relied upon the National Guard and U.S. diplomatic support to maintain power. They courted American economic and military aid by supporting the Allies in World War II and anticommunism thereafter.

The Central American Common Market and U.S. aid through the Alliance for Progress stimulated an investment, industrialization, export agriculture, and economic boom in the 1960s and early 1970s. This growth, however, intensified inequality and mobilized new reform-oriented working- and middle-class unions and parties. The regime responded by suppressing unions, restraining wages, using violent repression, rigging elections, and buying off opposition to retain control. When several armed insurgencies developed in the early 1960s, a ruthless counterinsurgency program backed by U.S. military aid suppressed most of the rebels. The catastrophic 1972 Managua earthquake and the regime's corrupt, inept response angered many Nicaraguans. The 1973 OPEC oil embargo ballooned inflation and unemployment, sparking further civil and armed resistance. These challenges elicited brutal repression that drove regime opponents, including some economic elites, into a coalition with the Sandinista National Liberation Front (Frente Sandinista de Liberación Nacional – FSLN) guerrillas.

Spontaneous popular mobilization and protest following 1978 challenged the Nicaraguan regime's resources and allowed FSLN military gains. In 1979, the Marxist-led FSLN was growing, broadening its civil coalition, and attacking the guard on several fronts. Allies of President Anastasio Somoza Debayle began fleeing Nicaragua in 1979 after the Carter administration began to withdraw support because of human rights abuses. In July of 1979 Somoza fled (later to be assassinated), the guard collapsed, and FSLN took power.

The Nicaraguan revolution began as a broad coalition, but the FSLN soon consolidated its power by marginalizing other anti-Somocistas while maintaining political pluralism. The revolution implemented many programs to improve public education, health, and well-being. It also confiscated the property of the Somocistas and established a mixed economy. Eventually capital flight, elite antagonism, the Sandinistas' own inept policies, and external hostility crippled the Nicaraguan economy. The Reagan administration imposed an economic embargo on Nicaragua and funded a violent counterrevolutionary force of liberal exiles and internal opponents (the *contras*) to attack the new regime. Elections were held in 1984 in which the FSLN's Daniel Ortega Saavedra became president. Despite retaining political pluralism and writing a new constitution in 1987, the Sandinistas could not placate their accumulating enemies or reverse their deepening economic difficulties. In the 1990 election, the FSLN lost to a coalition headed by Violeta Barrios de Chamorro. The revolution ended with the handover of ruling power.

Despite the revolution's end, economic recovery in Nicaragua remained elusive and political tensions high. Exiled liberals, many former allies of the

Somozas, returned to Nicaragua in 1996 to contest and win that year's election with Arnoldo Alemán as president. This effectively left Nicaragua with a two-party system. Liberals led by Alemán (later jailed for public corruption) and the Sandinistas led by former president Daniel Ortega dominated political life. The conservative party collapsed, and smaller parties were badly weakened. Ortega as FSLN head and leader in the legislature and Alemán as president collaborated to alter the electoral system and constitution to favor continued dominance by their two parties. After a subsequent liberal presidential term by Enrique Bolaños, Ortega and the FSLN won the 2006 presidential election despite U.S. threats of dire consequences.

Nicaragua, with formal liberal democracy as the main legacy of the revolution, remains a nation of deeply seated problems. As shown above, as of the early 2000s Nicaragua's economic performance remained nothing short of disastrous. Nicaragua was almost as poor as Honduras, had experienced a 74 percent contraction in its GDP per capita between 1982 and 2000, and in 2000 had an 18 percent *lower* GDP per capita than it had had in 1950. Life expectancy was below the regional mean while infant mortality was well above the average. Governmental performance was poor to mediocre on scoring systems evaluating rule of law, government effectiveness, political terror, and democracy.

Table 3.5 suggests that Nicaraguans, with such poor governmental performance continuously evident to them, should rate various aspects of their political regime poorly. Indeed, they ranked the performance of political actors sixth among the eight nations, the regime's performance seventh, and both regime institutions and local government eighth. Such a comparatively low level of popular evaluation of the administration of incumbent president Enrique Bolaños, of the regime's economic performance, and its political institutions suggests that we should look for other important political attitudes and behaviors among Nicaraguans that could have implications for political stability.

Costa Rica

Costa Rica excels in many ways among the countries in our study.[15] It has the lowest political terror level, consistently scores near the top of the

---

[15] Material on Costa Rica is drawn largely from Hiltunen de Biesanz, Biesanz, and Zubris de Biesanz (1979), Gudmondson (1986), Seligson (1987a), Seligson and Muller (1987), Seligson and Gómez (1989), Fischel (1990), Carey (1996), Yashar (1997), Booth (1998), Wilson (1998), Seligson (2002d), Sánchez (2003), Seligson (2007).

Freedom House democracy measure, and earns the highest marks of any country in our sample on government effectiveness and rule of law (Table 3.4). It ranks second in GDP per capita among our study countries and has experienced steady economic growth in recent decades (Table 3.2). A nation that has long invested in education and social programs, Costa Rica enjoys First World social indicators – life expectancy of 78 years, 96 percent literacy, and 9 per 1000 infant mortality.

It was not always so. Costa Rica began as the poorest and most isolated of the Central American republics, and only after the 1950s did its governments address effectively many problems it had long shared with the rest of the countries in our study. The roots of Costa Rica's exceptional performance may lie in its early poverty. Isolation from the rest of the isthmian colonies and Europe and scant mineral resources discouraged European in-migration. The relatively small indigenous population was unable to support the *criollo*-dominated, coerced-labor *hacienda* system that emerged elsewhere in Latin and Central America. While social stratification and economic inequality existed among Costa Ricans, their levels remained relatively modest when compared to other countries in the region. Much of the population became yeoman farmers.

Because Costa Rica had few indigenous people and because land was widely available to peasants into the mid-nineteenth century, the labor supply was scarce. Rural wages remained high as cultivation of coffee for export spread. Coffee lands eventually concentrated in the hands of big producers, millers, and exporters. Many of the displaced peasants were, for a time, absorbed into the workforce of banana plantations that developed as an adjunct to railroad construction in the late nineteenth century. Harsh working conditions in the railroad and banana industries and unfavorable commodity price cycles generated labor organization and conflict in the early twentieth century.

Costa Rican politics escaped the intense partisan conflict common around the region in the early nineteenth century. Since the liberals prevailed in Costa Rica's early national political development, the partisan civil wars of neighboring countries did not occur, and government was mainly civilian rather than military. Indirect and often rigged elections occurred, managed by factions that had arisen among a small elite of coffee producer-exporters. Nineteenth century presidents were often dictators. Costa Rica experienced military rule after the National War of 1857, which led to the expansion of the army. Liberal dictator Tomás Guardia (1870–1882) pressed modernization with rail and road building and expanded popular education. Increased literacy expanded the electorate, although elections remained indirect and corrupt. By the 1890s, conflict between the liberal government and the Catholic Church and a Catholic party, as well as mobilizing working class interests, contributed to an increased popular voice in politics, albeit not to democracy.

Early twentieth century political reform led to more free and open elections and campaigns, raising expectations for cleaner politics. A military coup in 1917 generated mass protest and elite resistance, resulting in the return of civilian, constitutional rule in 1919. The economically turbulent 1920s and 1930s stimulated increasing working and middle class mobilization in Costa Rican politics. Following a successful banana workers' strike in 1934, communist-led unions gained significant influence. The Great Depression's social dislocations drove increased conflict among organized workers, middle class organizations, and the old *cafetalero* political elite. Congress enacted election reforms in the 1920s and again in the 1930s, but this failed to calm class and interelite conflict.

In 1940, the patrician president Rafael Calderón Guardia broke with the coffee-growing political class and allied his government with the communist labor unions and the Catholic Church. Assisted by communist legislators, Calderón and his successor Teodoro Picado enacted Costa Rica's first labor and social security laws. Counter-mobilization by middle and upper class politicos grew rapidly. In addition to Calderón's policies and alliance with the communists, election fraud and legislative tampering with the presidential election results were the catalysts for a brief but violent civil war in 1948. A coalition of elite politicos angry at Calderón and middle class elements, dominated by a junta of social democrats led by José "Pepe" Figueres Ferrer, rebelled and defeated the Calderón government and its communist allies. Under the National Liberation junta, a 1949 constitutional revision abolished the small army (defeated in the war), enfranchised women and blacks, established an impartial election system, and adopted many social-democratic policies including the retention of Calderón's labor and social security reforms. In 1949, the junta passed power to the putative victor in the 1948 election.

Having relinquished power, the rebel movement converted itself into the National Liberation party (Partido de Liberación Nacional – PLN). From then until the 1990s, the PLN set the tone of Costa Rican political life. Returning to power in 1953 with José Figueres as president, the PLN enacted laws providing widespread health and social security coverage, benefits retained by the conservative coalition governments that periodically alternated with the PLN. Post-1949 elections were scrupulously honest. The PLN won the presidency seven times and the opposition won it six times between 1949 and 1998. Democracy became firmly consolidated in Costa Rica during these decades.

After the mid-1980s, Costa Rica experienced great economic challenges, changes in its party system, and political strains, all the while maintaining its democratic institutions. The OPEC oil embargo and a rigid foreign exchange rate caused a debt crisis that required the implementation of several structural adjustment agreements with international lenders. These externally imposed deals forced Costa Rica to abandon much of its social democratic economic development model, shrink its state apparatus, open its economy to foreign capital and competition, and curtail some social services and education spending. The pain inflicted by structural adjustment fell most heavily on the PLN, which was forced to implement the agreements and thus betray its policy traditions and social base. Meanwhile small, new parties proliferated while the conservative coalition merged to form the Social Christian Unity Party (PUSC), which won the presidential elections of 1990, 1998, and 2002. The once-dominant PLN captured only 31 percent of the vote in 2002 and appeared destined to become a minor player. But a corruption scandal involving two recent PUSC presidents allowed the PLN to recapture the presidency in 2006 while the PUSC itself broke down almost entirely. While many questions remain about the trend in declining legitimacy and the future of Costa Rica's party system, the nation remains the longest-lived and most successful democracy in Latin America.

Costa Rica ranks relatively high on many of the concrete social, economic, and political indicators. In Tables 3.2–3.4 Costa Ricans' legitimacy norms appear to reflect this relatively good standing. Costa Rica ranks the highest among our eight nations on average perceived national political community and on support for regime institutions. It ranks second on the evaluation of regime principles and political actors (Table 3.5). To the extent that relative legitimacy values shape other attitudes and behaviors related to system stability, we expect that Costa Rica's prospects are reasonably sanguine.

Panama[16]

Panama's special geopolitical position uniting the North and South American continents has shaped its economic and political development since the colonial era. Spain used Panama's wasp-waisted isthmus as

---

[16] Material on Panama drawn mainly from Ropp (1982), Ropp (1984), Zimbalist and Weeks (1991), Pérez (1995), Pérez (2000), Ropp (2007).

a vital transit route between South and Central America and between the Pacific and Atlantic oceans. The resulting merchant classes that developed around trade and transit prospered and constituted a political and economic oligarchy that dominated Panama's politics for many decades. From the nineteenth century on, working classes also developed but shared little benefit from the national economic system. In the twentieth century in particular, the working classes periodically challenged oligarchic interests when mobilized by populist leaders. The United States and its armed forces have repeatedly intervened to shape Panama's politics and economics, and indeed proved critical to the modern nation's birth and perhaps to its transition to democracy eight decades later.

After declaring its independence from Spain in 1821, Panama united with the larger state of Gran Colombia. With the exodus of Ecuador and Venezuela, however, Gran Colombia broke apart in 1831, leaving the Panamanian isthmus effectively part of Colombia. Later in the nineteenth century, Panama attempted to separate from Colombia several times but failed. As in Nicaragua, the other great trans-isthmian transit route, the California gold rush of the 1850s and the development of the western United States drove both transit company development and national politics. In contrast to Nicaragua, Panama's success in eventually obtaining a canal became a key to its relatively greater subsequent prosperity. But as in Nicaragua, transit-related geopolitics and external interference shaped politics profoundly for many decades.

Railroad companies first linked Panama's coasts in the 1850s, followed some decades later by efforts to build a waterway to connect the Atlantic to the Pacific that had been dreamed of since colonial times. When French efforts to build a canal failed in 1889, the United States sought control of the effort under the leadership of U.S. president Theodore Roosevelt. Colombia, at that time in the midst of an intense civil war, refused a highly concessionary U.S. canal rights lease proposal. Colombia's rejection led the United States to conspire with pro-independence liberal Panamanian forces antagonistic to the conservative government in Bogotá and to the canal concession's owners in 1903. The quickly kindled Panamanian independence movement prospered when U.S. Marines – conveniently stationed offshore nearby – landed to secure the new nation's separation from Colombia. Immediately after its birth as an "independent" nation, Panama's new leaders signed a treaty granting canal building and operation rights in perpetuity to the United States – the very deal previously rejected by Colombia.

Canal construction under U.S. aegis brought new racial and ethnic groups to Panama as construction workers, contributing Afro-Caribbeans,

Chinese, and others to the rapid growth of the working class. Completion of the canal in 1914 brought new trade and development opportunities, but the loss of jobs resulting from the completion of the enormous project and the foreign monopoly of the canal's operation concentrated and distorted the canal's economic benefits. Subsequent decades of hard times for workers intensified during the Great Depression in the 1930s and brought the political mobilization of hard-pressed working classes.

Arnulfo Arias led the populist Panameñista Party (Partido Panameñista – PP) to electoral victories in 1940, 1949, and 1968 on a platform of anti-American nationalism and racial exclusivism. His program offended the United States and canal operators, the national commercial bourgeoisie and their political parties, and the growing Panamanian armed forces, all of whom who variously conspired and intervened to oust Arias from office each time he was elected (Ropp 2007). U.S. security interests related to the canal and its vital military and economic roles in World War II and the Cold War prompted repeated direct intervention in Panamanian affairs by U.S. troops based in the Canal Zone for the express purpose of suppressing nationalistic unrest. Eventually, however, as intercontinental ballistic missiles and the size of U.S. military vessels reduced the canal's geostrategic import, successive U.S. administrations negotiated to amend the canal treaty as a means to defuse U.S.-Panamanian tensions and popular unrest.

In 1968 General Omar Torrijos ousted Arnulfo Arias from office yet again and pushed both the PP and the fragmented parties of the bourgeoisie off the political stage. Torrijos, a leftist populist, initiated programs, modeled on those of the Peruvian armed forces, that benefited the impoverished majority of Panamanians. Torrijos promoted the Revolutionary Democratic Party (Partido Revolucionario Democrático – PRD) to mobilize the working classes in support of the military regime. The regime's nationalistic push in 1977 finally culminated the long-running negotiations with the United States to amend the canal treaty. The agreement between Torrijos and President Jimmy Carter eventually shifted ownership and effective control of the canal and Canal Zone to Panama and removed several United States military bases from the country by 2000.

Despite these accomplishments, military rule became increasingly corrupt, especially after General Manuel Antonio Noriega took power following the 1981 death of Torrijos in a mysterious air crash. While relying on the popular base of the PRD to mobilize internal support and organize governments, Noriega also grew increasingly repressive. To stay in power he manipulated various forces that included the United States' antileftist involvement in Central America's conflicts, other Latin American nations, drug smugglers who used Panama as a way station, the Panamanian security forces, and the fragmented domestic opposition parties. Nevertheless, the opposition, including the PP and various parties of the old commercial elite, grew increasingly restive.

In 1989, under strong internal and external pressure, Noriega held elections to placate his critics but then fraudulently manipulated the count. Washington's newly elected Bush administration invoked the current U.S. policy of promoting electoral democracy in the region as well as Noriega's drug connections and human rights abuses to justify intervention. Taking advantage of the remaining U.S. bases in the Canal Zone, the United States invaded Panama in December 1989. U.S. forces prevailed quickly, but with considerable loss of Panamanian lives, and captured and extradited the dictator to the United States for trial. The defeated Panamanian military was disbanded while the putative victors of the 1989 election – a coalition of bourgeois reform parties led by Guillermo Endara – assumed power.

Since the U.S. invasion, elections and the process of establishing electoral democracy have remained reasonably free and fair. With the military out of the political equation, the fragmentation of class forces and parties has not allowed any single segment or party to dominate Panama's politics. The presidency has passed from one party to another on multiple occasions and civil liberties performance has been good, earning the country high ratings on the Freedom House democracy measures. Ernesto Pérez Balladares of the PRD won the 1994 presidential election despite the PRD's ties to the Torrijos- and Noriega-era regimes. Mireya Moscoso, widow of Arnulfo Arias of the Panameñista Party, became the first woman elected to the presidency (1999–2004) as head of the Arnulfista Party, a renamed PP that invoked her late husband's populist legacy. Following corruption scandals in the Moscoso administration, the Arnulfistas suffered a humiliating defeat in 2004. Martin Torrijos, candidate of a coalition headed by the PRD and son of the late dictator who had overthrown Arias in 1968, won the presidency in 2004.

From 1989 until 2003, just before our study, Panama remained largely calm politically and socially, in part because its per capita economic growth was the second best among our eight countries.[17] In addition to

[17] Table 3.2 shows Panama's real GDP growth from 1982 to 2000 as only 4 percent, but this is heavily influenced by the reversals caused by the U.S. economic embargo and political turmoil of the late 1980s. Overall, Panama's GDP growth from 1950 to 2000 was the highest among our eight countries.

this strong economic performance, Panama also performed comparatively well on the World Bank's government effectiveness and rule of law indexes, reflecting a reasonably capable government and less corruption than in most other countries in our study. Panama's delivery of social welfare, as indicated by high life expectancy (at 75 years ranked second among our eight nations) and by low infant mortality, also revealed a decent performance both absolutely and in comparison to other countries in the region. These strong performance indicators may help explain Panama's relatively high ranking among our eight nations on regime performance and support for regime principles at the time of our study (Table 3.5). In contrast, though, Panamanians' evaluation of their political actors' performance was the lowest in our study, and the evaluation of local government second lowest.

Colombia[18]

From its high Andean regions, where most of the population resides, to the tropical lowlands of the Orinoco and Amazon basins, Colombia is geographically diverse and relatively resource rich. Latin America's fifth largest nation in territory (second largest in our study) and third largest in population (over 44 million), Colombia exports oil, gemstones, apparel, flowers, and coffee. Illicit trade in narcotics has in recent decades fueled crime, intensified violent domestic political conflict, and challenged the national government's resources by strengthening leftist guerrillas and rightist paramilitaries.

Colombia emerged from the Spanish colony of New Granada in 1821 as the political center of Gran Colombia. Ecuador and Venezuela broke away in 1831, and in 1903, Colombia lost its restive Panamanian province to a U.S.-backed independence movement, leaving the nation with its modern boundaries.[19] By its national period, Colombia's population consisted of a majority of *mestizo* and European-origin Spanish speakers. The remaining indigenous population lived mainly in the tropical lowlands, and an Afro-Colombian population, descended from slaves, resided mainly in coastal zones. Colombia became and remains highly socially stratified by race and by class. Those claiming Spanish extraction

[18] This section draws on Booth (1974), Martz (1975), Peeler (1985), Hartlyn (1988), Peeler (1992), Wiarda and Kline (1996), Rodríguez-Raga and Seligson (2004), Seligson (2006b), Ropp (2007).
[19] Gran Colombia changed its name to Colombia in 1858.

and wealth, whether old or new, reside at the top of the status hierarchy while laborers and those of mixed or other races occupy lower status positions. Recent decades of intense rural political violence have accelerated migration to the cities, resulting in rapid urban population growth.

Political party identification also divides Colombians. From the late colonial era, landed families of both liberal and conservative inclination fiercely contested control of the national and local governments and patronage. They deployed peasant armies raised from their landholdings to gain power and the spoils of office. These conflicts cemented partisan loyalties among the peasantry by region and locality, and built into Colombia's polity a propensity for explosive civil conflict. Even though civilian rule remained the norm, Colombia's liberals and conservatives waged violent war against each other several times. Liberals emerged ascendant from the 1860s until 1886, followed by conservative dominance until 1930. Growing working class discontent and economic hardship in the 1930s favored a liberal return to power during this decade. In 1946, however, a liberal electoral schism gave the conservatives control of government despite their minority status. Tensions escalated and a riot known as the *Bogotazo* erupted the capital city in 1948 following the assassination of a popular liberal presidential aspirant. Heavy-handed behavior by conservative officeholders and efforts by liberal leaders to arm and mobilize peasant supporters quickly metastasized the conflict from the capital city into a broad national civil war, known as *la violencia*, that would last for decades and leave 200,000 dead.

The violence could not be contained by civil forces, prompting a military coup in 1953 by Gustavo Rojas Pinilla. Liberal Party and Conservative Party leaders then began negotiating a settlement and in 1958 reached the National Front accord, which, with the help of another military coup, formally ended the interparty conflict by instituting a power sharing arrangement and restoring civilian rule. Under the accord, liberals and conservatives alternated in the presidency for several presidential terms. Unfortunately, decades of slaughter in the countryside and the interelite accord produced groups of violent bands that would not lay down their arms in 1958. Some became bandits. In the wake of the Cuban revolution, other groups took up Marxist banners and turned on the politico-economic elite. By the 1960s the Colombian government, hampered by a weak national army, was unsuccessfully contending with several leftist guerrilla movements.

From the 1970s on, criminal organizations that produced and exported cocaine became powerful, operating in the absence of a strong governmental presence in the countryside. Over time, leftist rebels began protecting drug production to finance their activities. Both landowners and the weak national military organized and tolerated paramilitaries to protect them from guerrillas. Eventually the paramilitaries, too, became entangled in protecting narcotics production and trafficking. Colombia became rife with political and criminal violence, with government forces, rebels, drug gangs, and rightist paramilitaries attacking not only one another, but also public figures, ordinary citizens, and those in the media who dared report on their activities. Human rights conditions deteriorated badly despite the continued operation of a formal electoral democracy. Colombia requested and received extensive aid from the United States to combat narcotics production and trafficking and sought to negotiate cease-fires with the rebels. Settlements with two major guerrilla groups in the late 1980s somewhat abated violence. The Armed Forces of the Colombian Revolution (Fuerzas Armadas de la Revolución Colombiana – FARC) and the National Liberation Army (Ejército de Liberación Nacional – ELN) did not settle with the government or demobilize. Around 2000, the government ceded to the FARC a cease-fire zone to encourage peace negotiations. The FARC then refused to negotiate further and used the territory to regroup and recruit.

Colombia thus entered the twenty-first century with a troubling mix of high political and criminal violence that continued despite the operation of a formally functioning electoral democracy. Given the country's turmoil, Colombia's World Bank Institute government effectiveness score is understandably the lowest by far of our eight nations due to the nation's persistent insurgency and the inability of the government – even with outside help – to stifle rampant criminality and insurgency. On the other hand, Colombia's recent economic performance in terms of growth of GDP per capita since 1982 (48 percent) has been the best among the eight nations we study. While Colombia has resources, considerable potential for development, and a steady record of economic progress, the afflicted nature of its political performance in recent decades remains deeply problematic. On most items, Colombians' ranking on their regime's performance evaluations lies in the middle of the pack compared to the citizens of the other seven nations. On two legitimacy dimensions, however, Colombia stands out. It has the highest approval of all for local governments and for the administration of presidential incumbent Alvaro Uribe.

THE CENTRAL RESEARCH QUESTION

One of our central critiques of prior legitimacy research is that the most comprehensive and detailed of these studies have been done mainly in highly economically developed industrial democracies. Meanwhile, studies of developing countries and new democracies, while valuable, typically have addressed legitimacy less systematically or somewhat tangentially. The widespread availability of survey data has made First World democracies an obvious target for research. Nonetheless, this advantage also has a drawback: while these developed nations do vary somewhat among themselves, they are – compared to most of the rest of the world's nations – far more prosperous, stable, and democratic. We have argued that the nations where legitimacy has been most studied are ones in which we would not expect the levels to be especially low. Indeed, while research has shown important variation in levels of legitimacy across the advanced industrial democracies, that variation is likely constrained (skewed) to the positive end of the continuum.[20] Moreover, there exist within such countries relatively few significant sectors of the populations who would express very low levels of legitimacy norms.[21] These nations deliver high levels of socioeconomic well-being and opportunities for civilian participation in politics in a relatively safe environment. They have long histories of political stability. Because a fundamental tenet of legitimacy theory argues that support emerges from and is sustained directly by citizens' evaluations of government performance, it would surprise us to find that levels of legitimacy in the advanced industrial democracies are relatively low. This absence of wide variation in political, economic, and social welfare performance in such environments, we believe, limits the ability of these studies to examine comparative legitimacy levels and effectively test legitimacy theory.

Our eight nations have been selected to correct for this effective sampling bias in the most comprehensive previous legitimacy research and to

---

[20] Not everyone would agree with us on that assessment. For example, the classic article by Arthur Miller made the case that trust in government had declined threateningly low levels in the United States as a result of the Vietnam war and other events (Miller 1974). But we are not confident that the "trust in government" scale used really was tapping legitimacy as we define it in this book. For discussion on this point see Muller (1979) and Muller et al. (1982).

[21] Fringe groups have existed and will continue to exist in every society (e.g., the Symbionese Liberation Army of the 1970s in the United States and the Red Brigades in Germany at that same time), and extreme individuals (e.g., Timothy McVeigh) will emerge from time to time. Yet, we have no reason to expect, if legitimacy theory is valid, that such groups and individuals would be widespread in the advanced industrial nations.

deepen knowledge of legitimacy in developing countries. We have chosen nations that are constitutional democracies (at least formally so) and that have reasonably free, fair, and regular elections but are much less successful performers, on average, than the advanced industrial democracies usually studied. We do not include dictatorships in our sample, since doing so would take us into an entirely different theoretical realm (i.e., legitimacy in nondemocracies).[22]

Despite their common features of history, geography, language, and culture, our eight nations range broadly in their performance in economic, social welfare, and political arenas. They have had very different histories of democratic governance. At the time of our surveys, their citizens experienced widely divergent levels of personal security and political stability as indicated by political terror scores ranging across the entire 5-point range of the scale. Their governments varied widely in their effectiveness and levels of corruption. Social welfare indicators circa 2003 revealed between-nation differences of up to 22 years in life expectancy and 28 percent in literacy. Infant mortality varied by a factor of four. In economic performance, the nations also diverged considerably: national GDPs per capita varied by a factor of almost 3.5, and 1982–2000 GDP/capita growth ranged from – 74 percent to + 48 percent. Such marked contextual variations in political, economic, and social welfare performance should allow us to explore the origins, nature, and impact of citizens' legitimacy norms. We believe that the eight-nation dataset we have built thus offers the best opportunity thus far to political scientists to assess legitimacy theory in widely ranging political systems.

We have already demonstrated in Chapter 2 that a multidimensional structure of legitimacy predicted by theory and partially anticipated in previous empirical research exists in our eight-nation pooled sample and in each of the nations considered separately. As we have also seen in Chapter 2 and in this chapter, citizens' average legitimacy norms vary among the six legitimacy dimensions and among the countries. For perception of a national community and support for democratic regime principles, respondents are strongly and consistently on the positive end of the legitimacy scales. On the other four more specific legitimacy dimensions, in contrast, mean scores range from just at the scale midpoint for support

---

[22] There is also the practical problem of conducting survey research on political attitudes and behavior in dictatorial regimes. Authoritarian governments discourage, bar, or interfere with surveys, and citizens do not feel free to answer sensitive questions honestly.

for regime institutions to mean scores in the 40s out of 100 for evaluation of local government, political actors, and regime performance (see Appendix A.6). Each legitimacy norm itself varies substantially both for the pooled dataset and within each national sample.[23]

In sum, there exists both considerable variation in the objective performance of our eight nations and in the various types of legitimacy ascribed to them by their citizens. At least on its face, these patterns of legitimacy seem to square with the concrete social, economic, and political performance we have reported. An ocular inspection of the relative legitimacy levels shows Costa Rica and Panama to have high evaluations by their citizens on the largest number of dimensions. In contrast, Guatemala, Nicaragua, and Honduras reveal very low evaluations by their citizens on multiple legitimacy dimensions. Legitimacy theory strongly suggests that these performance patterns should matter for legitimacy norms and, if they do matter, that they should in turn affect other important political attitudes and behaviors.

These variations in political support should help us investigate more clearly than before a variety of key components of the legitimacy puzzles this book seeks to solve. Specifically, in Chapter 4 we examine the sources of legitimacy, including national context. We ask in that chapter where legitimacy norms come from and believe we provide some clear answers to that question. We then change our analytical strategy, converting citizen support from the dependent variable into an independent variable that should affect other phenomena. That allows us to investigate the impact of legitimacy norms on political behavior and key political attitudes in Chapters 5–7. Finally, in Chapter 8 we will explore how the patterns and combinations of legitimacy norms we observe at the national level might affect particular countries' microlevel politics and prospects for political stability.

---

[23] For the pooled sample, variation within the dimensions is smallest for the perception of political community (with a standard deviation of 12.3 scale points), but larger for other dimensions, especially evaluation of actors (standard deviation = 23.2 scale points). Standard deviations within dimensions for each nation – not shown to conserve space – are consistent with the standard deviations for the pooled sample.

4

The Sources of Political Legitimacy

So far we have shown that political legitimacy in eight Latin American countries is multidimensional, but we do not yet know the sources of these legitimacy norms. Among the many aspects of society, politics, and individual traits, which factors contribute to higher or lower levels of the six dimensions of legitimacy we have identified? This deceptively simple question has interested legitimacy theorists, but empirical work to date, limited by the lack of a comprehensive multidimensional view of legitimacy, has not yet tested a comprehensive explanation. The goal of this chapter is to seek to answer this question and to provide the most comprehensive explanation possible for the eight countries studied here.

Prior research, cited extensively in Chapter 1, has pointed to three main sources of legitimacy norms: the macrosocial performance of the political system, individual attributes of citizens, and citizens' attitudes and experiences at the microsocial level. The better governments and their economic systems perform, the argument goes, the more likely it is that citizens will evaluate them positively (Hayen and Bratton 1992; Pritchett and Kaufmann 1998; Diamond 2008). On this point there has been much research that has tended to distinguish between longer-term and shorter-term performance.[1] Longer-term factors supposedly influence, to use Easton's term, "diffuse support," while shorter-term performance has a greater effect on more "specific support." However, while that research has been skillful and often comparative, much of it has not clearly distinguished

---

[1] See, for instance, the contributors to Norris's *Critical Citizens* (1999b) and Pharr and Putnam's *Disaffected Democracies* (2000a).

among multiple legitimacy dimensions and their various predictors. Our approach, which emphasizes the distinctiveness of the dimensions of legitimacy, is to investigate how each dimension might arise from the performance characteristics of political systems.

We believe that the logic of the literature just cited is correct. Better longer-term performance should contribute especially to the more diffuse types of support. Among our dimensions, perception of a political community falls into the diffuse category. We thus expect a nation's long-term experience with democracy to increase the perception of political community. To a somewhat lesser extent, support for regime democratic principles also constitutes a diffuse support dimension because it focuses on democratic values rather than the performance of specific components of government. However, the brevity of democratic experience in some of our study's countries may obscure the effect of the history of democracy on support for regime principles. Finally, we expect that such clearly defined referents as the regime's economic performance and those of political actors and local government will be linked to fairly specific and short-term perceptions and experiences. For example, we expect those who are better off economically and those who voted for the winner in the most recent presidential election to evaluate political actors and regime performance more positively than those who are poor or who did not support the incumbent president.

The second potential source of legitimacy norms comes from citizens' positions within society and their own traits and resources, which we will label with the shorthand of "socioeconomic and demographic factors." Prior research usually has included these microsocial demographic factors as control variables, yet this approach often has been narrow and included little more than sex, age, education, and income. Moreover, these variables (with the exception of sex) normally have been used in their continuous form, thus preventing the researcher from understanding precisely which specific age cohorts or education levels might be associated with variation in legitimacy norms. We will add additional variables including religious identification and size of community of residence – factors that we believe are especially important in Latin America (and perhaps elsewhere). In addition, following current practice in econometrics, we will use refined measures of several of these potential explanatory variables that subdivide the individual variables into a series of "dummy variables" that allow us to examine, for example, the levels of education or the age cohorts that are specifically associated with variation in levels of legitimacy.

The third potential source of system support is also microsocial – citizens' experiences and attitudes. Here we encounter social-psychological explanations such as a willingness to trust others (Almond and Verba 1963; Easton 1965a; Gamson 1968; Almond and Verba 1980; Hardin 1991; Fukuyama 1995; Newton 1999; Mishler and Rose 2001; Uslaner and Brown 2005; Diamond 2008; Herreros and Criado 2008) and social culture and social capital, especially as the latter is shaped by involvement in civil society or voluntary organizations (Almond and Verba 1963; Almond 1980; Lijphart 1989; Coleman 1990; Inglehart 1990; Inglehart 1997a; Inglehart 1997b; Putnam, Pharr, and Dalton 2000; Mishler and Rose 2001; Paxton 2002; Paxton 2007).

The socialization of individuals has both macrosocial and microsocial aspects. Individuals exist within a political culture partly defined by national history and mediated by institutions such as the education system and political regimes. But individuals also derive their attitudes and appraisals of such institutions from personal experience based on schooling, economic standing, and life's events and problems. For example, formal education, especially postsecondary education, tends to inculcate both empathy and support for political tolerance. We therefore expect higher levels of education to increase citizens' sense of national community and support for regime democratic principles. Similarly, becoming a crime or corruption victim might have little to do with diffuse support for democratic principles but could well undermine evaluations of specific regime institutions, actors, or performance.

We organize our discussion of legitimacy's sources around macrosocial and microsocial factors. The macrosocial sources of legitimacy include the national or context-level institutional and performance factors that form the basis for an individual's development of legitimacy norms. Microsocial factors are unique to individuals, including their socioeconomic and demographic characteristics. We review each of those in turn, and then proceed to model these factors simultaneously in regression equations. We emphasize that we do not believe that all legitimacy dimensions derive from identical sources. Prior research suggests, for example, that important historical events can create age-cohort effects on attitudes (Inglehart 1997a). We anticipate such effects among our respondents but also expect diverse effects across dimensions. For example, we see no reason to assume that a revolution would affect support for democracy in general and the evaluation of one's own local government in the same way. And, while having more formal education may increase support for democratic principles, it could also supply the analytical tools that might lead to negative evaluations of badly performing regime institutions or actors.

MACROSOCIAL SOURCES OF LEGITIMACY

The focus of macrosocial analysis of the sources of legitimacy is the performance of regimes or of social and economic systems on a large scale. The central assumption is that well-performing systems will garner public support and vice versa. At first glance, testing this proposition would seem straightforward; all one needs to do is to add a measure of regime performance to our explanatory models (i.e., our regression equations) for each of our six dimensions of legitimacy and observe whether performance is a significant predictor. One would think that the only decision to make would be to select the specific variable or variables that appropriately capture regime performance. In fact, the problem is far more complex, both in terms of the functional form of variables used to measure performance and in terms of how we incorporate them into our models. Therefore, before we attempt to determine whether performance does indeed impact legitimacy norms, we must spend some time explaining that complexity, the choices we had to make, and the decisions we ultimately made.

Our first important concern is how to measure regime performance. Should it be measured relatively or absolutely; dynamically across time or statically? Each approach has its merits. For example, it is widely assumed that the economic performance of a society is best revealed in terms of the overall output per head, usually expressed as some measure of gross domestic product (GDP) per capita. For example, Mexico in 2003 (the year prior to our survey), with its GDP per capita of US$6,121, was far more successful economically than Honduras (GDP per capita of US$1,001) (United Nations Development Program 2005). Based on these data, one might reasonably expect Mexicans to have evaluated their government's economic performance more favorably than Hondurans in our 2004 survey. It would be reasonable to assume further that macroeconomic performance measured as GDP per capita would explain at least some of the variation in individual-level legitimacy scores on some, if not all, of the six legitimacy dimensions that we have identified.

But do citizens really think about, or evaluate, their national economic system in terms of levels of national wealth? Do they really say to themselves, "I live in a rich country, and therefore I believe my regime is worthy of support?" Or, do they take their national level of wealth as given and neither praise nor blame their regime for the level achieved? If the response is the latter, the GDP per capita could be irrelevant to citizen legitimacy norms, even though so much of the literature emphasizes the importance of performance in shaping those very norms. On the other hand, it may well be that *dynamic* aspects of system performance do indeed matter and shape citizen legitimacy norms, but that scholars have underutilized this approach. Change over time, whether improvement or decline, can provide a critical and perhaps more relevant way of examining performance and explanation of legitimacy norms. For example, it may well have mattered to their respective citizens that the Costa Rican economy improved its overall output per capita about 35 percent between 1975 and 2003 while Nicaraguan economic output actually declined by 76 percent over the same period (United Nations Development Program 2005). Costa Rica's long-term growth rate, despite ups and downs along the way, might have had a positive impact on citizen evaluation of legitimacy. Costa Ricans may have been thinking about next-door neighbor Nicaragua's economic performance, measured dynamically in terms of its rate of growth, and seen it as manifestly poor.

We hypothesize that citizens of both countries would have been aware of Nicaragua's protracted and disastrous economic decline contrasted with neighboring Costa Rica's progress and that their respective legitimacy evaluations reflected that performance difference. One dramatic manifestation of Nicaraguans' awareness of the relatively more favorable economic performance of their southern neighbor is that hundreds of thousands of Nicaraguans have migrated to Costa Rica to take advantage of job opportunities there that do not exist at home. How, then, will these dynamics of economic change over time affect Nicaraguans' and Costa Ricans' evaluations of their government's performance? Should one not reasonably expect, ceteris paribus, that the Costa Rican government would receive higher evaluations from its citizens on a record of positive economic growth, while Nicaraguans would give their government much lower evaluations based on a record of economic decline over time?

In order to capture the absolute as well as shifting nature of regime performance as described above, we employ both static and dynamic measures of performance at the system level in our analyses (see Table 4.1). At the level of economic performance alone, we shall employ both GDP per capita in absolute terms and changes in GDP per capita over time. We did not want to limit the measurement of economic performance to economic growth alone. We thus decided also to consider economic distribution in terms of income inequality. Economic success in terms of positive GDP performance, if not translated into a broad distribution of wealth, could leave most citizens disappointed (even angered) by a system that allows little wealth to trickle down. In addition, we wanted to measure the performance of the regime in delivering key

TABLE 4.1. *System-level performance measures, eight Latin American nations*

	Human Development Index (HDI) 2003	Percent Change in UNDP HDI 1975–2003	Gross Domestic Product Per Capita 2003	Percent GDP Per Capita Change 1990–2003	GDP Per Capita (PPP) 2003	Vanhanen Mean Democracy Score 1900–1989	World Bank Government Effectiveness Index	Gini Index of Income Inequality	Freedom House – Combined and Scale Polarity Reversed
Mexico	0.814	1.18	6121	16.8	9168	2.05	61.9	54.6	10.00
Guatemala	0.663	1.30	2009	13.2	4148	2.52	32	59.9	6.00
El Salvador	0.722	1.22	2277	25.2	4781	2.54	35.6	53.2	9.00
Honduras	0.667	1.29	1001	2.4	2665	2.53	27.3	55.0	8.00
Nicaragua	0.69	1.18	745	10.8	3262	3.19	17.5	43.1	8.00
Costa Rica	0.838	1.12	4352	31.2	9606	8.81	66.5	46.5	11.00
Panama	0.804	1.13	4319	28.8	6854	4.69	53.6	56.4	11.00
Colombia	0.785	1.19	1764	4.8	6702	4.2	45.4	57.6	6.00

Sources: Freedom House (2004), United Nations Development Program (2005), The World Bank Institute (Kaufmann et al. 2006), Vanhanen (1997).

services to its citizens, so we attempted to tap into system-level measures of education and health.

In a study focused on legitimacy, the performance of democracy should also carry weight. For this reason, we considered measures of political rights and liberties, government effectiveness, the rule of law, political stability, and the long-term history of democracy. In addition, we also considered institutional differences among the countries since so much of the "new institutionalism" in contemporary political science focuses on the impact of institutions on outcomes (Anderson and Guillory 1997). For example, one recent study, using Afrobarometer data, showed that institutional variation had an impact on satisfaction with democracy (Cho 2005). Bratton, Mattes, and Gyimah-Boadi (2005) also use Afrobarometer data to examine institutional effects on attitudes, but they measure the institutional context not at the macrosocial level but at the microsocial level in terms of individual experience with civil society and political participation. These measurements may miss important macrosocial features of national institutions.

One difficulty we had with pursuing that line of research was that our cases are in some respects very similar institutionally. All of the countries in our study are presidential and all have similar party, legislative, and judicial systems. There are, of course, certain differences; for example, in the manner in which the countries select electoral tribunals or replace judges. But these appeared to us to be so subtle when compared to the striking differences in democratic experience, economic development, and distribution that we decided not to pursue that line of inquiry. Given a larger sample of countries for which we could have employed a larger number of context variables, examination of these institutional variations could prove to be important predictors of legitimacy. But, doing that risked affecting another valuable aspect of our research design, namely, that the eight countries have many historical and cultural similarities, allowing us to concentrate on key differences.

In sum, we attempted to measure economic performance, economic distribution, and the performance of democracy in both static and dynamic terms by considering a long list of candidate indicators for contextual effects. When we did so, we encountered two problems in considering such a multitude of contextual variables. First, many of these indicators covary with each other within our eight-nation sample, some with correlation coefficients of over .90. This problem, collinearity, is common when working with such macrolevel variables and bedevils many econometric analyses that use country-level data. When two or more independent variables are highly correlated with each other, the proper interpretation of collinear variables' contribution to regression models becomes problematical and even impossible. There are various solutions to this problem, none of them ideal. One frequently used solution is to create an index combining several underlying, collinear variables. We have followed that approach to the extent possible. For example, in order to capture both economic and social development we used the United Nations Human Development Index (HDI), which combines GDP per capita, infant mortality and several measures of educational achievement. Selecting the other variables became an exercise in reviewing the field and choosing our contextual (system-level) variables very carefully so that they were both substantively and theoretically important, yet not collinear.[2] Table 4.1 lists the system-level performance variables, widely variant among the countries, that we employ to analyze legitimacy's sources.

The second problem we faced in incorporating these variables into our analysis was determining the best analytical technique to examine the effect of both system- and individual-level measures. For many years, social scientists merely added variables for system-level traits to individual-level cases for regression analysis. However, this procedure can heavily overstate system-level effects, largely because they involve single data points that are then associated with, in our case, 1,500 individual cases.[3] Education researchers analyzing student performance often have found themselves concluding incorrectly that context, rather than individual variables, was the only thing that mattered in student performance. A technique called hierarchical linear modeling (HLM) was developed to correct for this problem and has become the standard for modeling data including both individual- and system-level variables. However, the fact that we have only eight nations in the study means that we can effectively include only one system-level variable (although many individual-level variables) at a time in our HLM regression as we search for the sources of legitimacy.[4]

---

[2] Our standard is that no pair of variables included in analysis should be correlated at more than r = .60.

[3] Technically, when context-level information is added to individual scores, the independence assumption of OLS regression is violated. Moreover, this approach makes the often-untenable assumption that the regression coefficients are the same for, in our case, countries in the dataset.

[4] The problem of avoiding having more variables than cases is an old one in regression.

Simply put, we wish to avoid having more system-level variables than country cases in our analysis, a problem that affected small-N studies in comparative politics and one that we have avoided by our large national samples in which we have hundreds of respondents per country. Therefore, our applications of HLM when the number of "system-level" cases (i.e., data at the level of the nation) is low, is to be conservative in the use of system-level (i.e., level-2) variables. To carry out this analysis, we employ the software package HLM6 (revision 6.02), which at this writing is the most advanced HLM software available. Our approach is to examine each of the variables in table above, one at a time, to determine which, if any, produced a statistically significant impact on our six legitimacy dimensions.[5]

MICROSOCIAL SOURCES OF LEGITIMACY

Perhaps because the legitimacy of a political system primarily inheres to a state apparatus or particular government, and because much of the analysis of legitimacy has involved the reaggregation of findings from individuals to national-level aggregates, there has been relatively little attention to microsocial sources of legitimacy, especially demographics.[6] Because we believe that demographic variables warrant systematic attention as possible sources of legitimacy, we will incorporate them into our empirical analysis in addition to microsocial variables related to culture and personal experience.

Demographic variables

Governments in Latin America often serve women poorly in terms of their health needs. On that ground, women might be expected to express lower legitimacy norms than men. On the other hand, women have, at times, been observed to be slightly more conservative than men. Women might, therefore, tend to be more supportive of the political community or institutions than men. Thus, we include the respondent's sex in the analysis.

---

[5] We determined that a probability criterion of .10 rather than .05 would be the most reasonable in this exercise given our small number of system-level cases. We believe that the more rigid criterion could force us to overlook potentially significant system-level effects (i.e., a Type II error), and since our approach is always one tailed (i.e., the direction of the relationship is clearly predicted in each model by our hypotheses), the .10 level seems justified.

[6] For exceptions see Newton and Norris (2000) and Norris (2000).

(Details and distribution characteristics for the variables described here may be found in Appendix Table B.3.)

Age may contribute to legitimacy norms. For example, younger citizens may engage less with the political system because they have less at stake in terms of family, property, and the like. They likely also experience higher rates of unemployment and have lower incomes than do older citizens. As a consequence, one might expect younger age cohorts to be more negative toward certain system characteristics, especially economic performance and evaluation of institutions. In contrast, through several decades in the middle of one's life a person usually develops a greater stake in society that may lead to greater support for the system, other things held equal. Notwithstanding, the elderly, often confronted with difficult economic circumstances, may be on average more prone to criticize a government's economic performance. An alternative hypothesis is that, in new democracies, older citizens might retain allegiance to a prior nondemocratic regime. Or, in contrast, they might well have memories of prior dictatorial repression and therefore evaluate democratic systems more positively than the young who lack such experiences. In order to evaluate the possible effects of age, we have divided our sample into various age cohorts, and include all but the youngest in the subsequent analysis (the youngest cohort serving as the excluded base group in the regressions). There are dummy variables corresponding to membership in the age groups 16–20, 21–30, 31–40, 41–50, 51–60, and 61 and older.

Religion, a particularly salient attachment for many Latin Americans, is often hypothesized to shape citizens' attitudes and engagement with the political system (Camp 1994; Norris and Inglehart 2004). Membership in particular denominations may expose one to certain political cues that might shape one's evaluations of the polity. Members of persecuted or unpopular religious minorities, for example, may feel alienated from the system. In contrast, members of a predominant religious denomination may feel validated in their positions and comfortable with the political status quo and thus manifest higher legitimacy. Particular public policies, for example concerning abortion or divorce, may influence members of one or another religious group to support or oppose national institutions. In Latin America, the rise of protestant evangelical groups has become an important trend in recent decades (Stoll 1990) and we want to determine its impact, if any, on legitimacy. We are able to identify various religious or denominational groupings in our surveys – Catholics, non-Catholic Christians (protestants), persons who profess no religion, and members of other religions.

Individuals' levels of formal education may affect their legitimacy beliefs. We expect citizens with more education-provided information and greater skills for evaluating a regime's policy or economic performance to have lower levels of legitimacy norms where performance lags. In contrast, those less formally educated may have absorbed more patriotic socialization through early schooling, but have less capacity for critical analysis of various facets of regime performance than persons with more advanced education. Other factors equal, we expect those with less formal education to be more supportive of regime institutions, regime performance, and actors, and those with more education to be less so. In contrast, education strongly correlates with holding democratic norms in most studies of most countries, so we expect respondents with more formal education to express more support for regime democratic principles. These expectations underline the importance of our multidimensional approach to legitimacy, since without it, we could not capture these variations in the potential impact of education. We divide the education levels of our respondents into five cohorts – no education, primary, secondary, college, and postgraduate education – using the no-education group as the base for the regressions.

A final important demographic trait is one's level of economic resources measured as income or wealth. Having a high income or a high level of personal wealth, we believe, should incline citizens to evaluate their government's economic performance and institutions positively. The poor, in contrast, might reasonably view government institutions, actors, and economic performance negatively. In our measure of income, 10.5 percent of respondents refused to answer or answered "don't know," thus providing an unacceptable level of missing data.[7] As an alternative strategy of estimating income, used the possession of certain household artifacts as a reasonable proxy for the wealth of our respondents, including items ranging from having indoor plumbing to various appliances, automobiles, and computers. This approach has advantages over using respondent-reported income: First, it greatly reduced the missing data problem: the resulting index of wealth had only 0.1 percent missing data, a much more acceptable level.[8] Second,

---

[7] The deletion of over 10 percent of the cases in our regressions would have produced results based on a subsample of our entire national probability samples. The result is that we would have lost some confidence that the findings are consistent with those that we would have had using the entire national samples.

[8] The simple bivariate correlation between income and our wealth index is .63, indicating that the wealth measure is tapping into some of the same traits as income.

household condition is a more stable characteristic than income, which can vary sharply from month to month and year to year.

Personal experiences and attitudes

Legitimacy research has focused more on personal experiences and attitudes than on other variables as possible sources of support for political systems and governments. Norris (2000) has reported a slightly negative impact of television exposure on institutional trust in the United States. Putnam (1995) famously has identified increased watching of television as an important source of declining social capital, which in turn erodes trust in the political system. Information plays a key role in citizens' political assessments (Mondak 2001). Thus we begin with one behavioral and one cognitive variable that are related and have been frequently linked to citizens' attitudes – exposure to the news media and basic political knowledge. The effects that either of these might have upon citizens' support levels would, we believe, depend upon the performance of government. The more one sees, hears, or reads the news, and the more concrete factual knowledge one has about the situation of her country, the more likely this exposure would be to affect support for institutions, actors, and regime performance, whether positively or negatively (see Appendix Table B.3 for details).

When one considers the likelihood of support for a government, a critical factor is whether one has voted for the government in power. Anderson et al. (2005), making a direct link to legitimacy theory, have argued and shown in a large, cross-national project that persons who voted for the government or party in power are substantially more prone to support the institutions of government, its political leaders, and its economic performance than those who voted for the loser in the last election. As a consequence we have constructed a variable that indicates whether our respondents voted for the presidential winner in the last national election prior to the survey. Its inclusion will allow us to determine to what extent support derives from being on the winning side in the last election and, independent of that, what other factors also contribute to legitimacy in its multiple dimensions.

A personality trait of trustfulness (Easton 1965a; Easton 1965b; Gamson 1968; Newton and Norris 2000) also likely affects evaluation of government. Persons disposed by experience or by their personalities to place trust in others would be more likely to believe that government attends to or promotes their interests. Thus, more trusting people would be expected, other factors equal, to have higher legitimacy norms on all legitimacy dimensions. This thesis has been tested by studies of social capital and democratization, although its direct application to legitimacy has been uncommon (Inglehart 1988).

Life satisfaction refers to the expression of contentment or satisfaction with one's own life (Newton and Norris 2000). Legitimacy researchers have assumed that those with higher levels of life satisfaction would tend to evaluate government performance, the national political community, and regime institutions and actors more positively than citizens discontented with their lives. Inglehart (1988) found that life satisfaction, when aggregated to the macrolevel, associated positively with the longevity of democracy.[9]

There are various experiences and attitudes stemming from them that might affect legitimacy levels. One is the stressful experience of having been the victim of a crime. Citizens victimized by crime might conclude that their victimization could have been prevented by more vigilant or effective public security efforts. The crime victim might blame the state for his/her plight and thus hold lower legitimacy norms than nonvictims (Della Porta 2000; Pharr 2000b). A related attitude has to do with the fear that one is not secure or safe from crime in his/her own neighborhood. Citizens who are fearful of criminal violence that might befall them would, by the same logic, likely hold lower evaluations of institutions, of actors, and possibly of the regime than persons who feel more secure (Córdova and Cruz 2007).

A final issue, one largely overlooked by legitimacy research so far, concerns the kind of community in which a citizen lives. In Latin America, cities, towns, and rural areas vary widely in the degree to which they have governmental institutions and vital services linked to quality of life. As the authors learned from decades of traveling extensively in Central America and Mexico studying peasants and communities and observing elections, in smaller towns and villages, basic services such as electricity, clean water, sewer systems, and paved streets can be rudimentary or nonexistent. Health services may be scant, and secondary schools may exist only in larger towns or cities. The larger the town or city, in contrast, the more likely it is that there will be local government offices, national government offices and services, health clinics and hospitals, and a full public service infrastructure. We believe that a citizen's access to or lack of access to such

---

[9] Of course the causality of this association reasonably may be argued to flow in either direction and possibly both. That is, the longer a democracy survives, the happier its citizens may become because of the inherent virtues of democracy. This increasingly satisfied citizenry could in turn reinforce the stability of the democratic system.

services and opportunities may affect his support for the system. We thus anticipate that living in a larger community will increase the expectation of good public services, which, if available, would positively affect evaluation of government performance, actors, and institutional norms. On the other hand, if such expectations go unmet, residents of more urban settings are likely to be more critical of the system. In contrast, we expect residents of smaller communities to have greater support for local government than residents of bigger ones because of the relative ease of access to local government in rural villages and towns. We distinguish in the following analysis between residence in rural areas, small towns and cities, medium and large cities, and the national capital of each country (see Appendix Table B.3 for details).

RESULTS

In order to proceed with the analysis involving multilevel data, our first step is to ascertain whether the contextual level, in this case the country-level variables we outlined earlier in this chapter, significantly and meaningfully contribute to the explanation of our six dimensions of legitimacy. This involves determining the amount of variability accounted for by the context-level variables. Our analysis showed that this contribution was quite limited.[10] This means that for our eight countries, far more of the variation derives from individual characteristics than from contextual factors. Thus, the main focus of our analysis pivots on the individual

---

[10] We determined the maximum possible contribution of the context variables (i.e., system-level, also called "level-2 variables") by computing the so-called "null model," also known as the "fully unspecified model" (FUM). This involves computing the intra-class coefficient (ICC), which is merely the ratio of the system-level variance to the total variance (i.e., the sum of level-1 and system-level variance). Most multilevel analyses strive for an ICC of 20 percent or higher, and a rule of thumb in our experience is that when the ICC is lower than 10 percent the added value of multilevel modeling is too small to be worth the added complexity. We employed an ANOVA test with random effects using STATA's XTMIXED program to compute these results (and rechecked them with HLM 6). In our dataset, we calculated the ICC as follows: political community = 6 percent; regime principles = 9 percent; institutions = 7 percent; regime performance = 8 percent; political actors = 13 percent; local government = 5.9 percent. Thus only the actors dimension shows promise of explaining sufficient variance at level 2 to make an important contribution to our modeling of the predictors of our legitimacy dimensions. The explanation as to why the actors dimension was higher than the others, however, has to do with the idiosyncratic factor of the momentarily high level of popularity of the president Alvaro Uribe of Colombia, which we do not take to have important theoretical significance for our research.

effects. For sake of completeness, however, we do examine the multilevel models and report on those results here.

Political community

We begin our analysis with the most diffuse of our six dimensions of legitimacy, namely, the citizen's perception of the existence of a political community. This perception invokes the idea that there is a broad societal community – a nation of shared interests and concerns that exists irrespective of one's wholly private or familial interests. Table 4.2 presents the results of an HLM analysis of the legitimacy norm of perception of political community.

The first finding concerning the perception of political community is that only one system-level variable had any impact on this norm even though we modeled each of the variables in Table 4.1. As a methodological note, the diagnostic indicator, we shall emphasize to show that there exists a significant relationship between the dependent and the independent variable in our regression tables, is the t-ratio. The rule of thumb for the strength of relationship is that a system-level variable does not contribute in a statistically meaningful way to the dependent variable if the t-ratio falls below an absolute value of 2.0, which corresponds with a probability of relationship greater than .05 (a likelihood of occurring randomly less than one time out of twenty). The greater the absolute value (i.e., positive or negative) of the t-ratio, the stronger the influence of the independent variable on the dependent variable, other variables in the model held constant. A negatively signed relationship means that more of the independent variable predicts less of the dependent variable. We designate significant relationships in the following tables by presenting the t-ratios in boldface type.

Above all the economic, social welfare, and income distribution variables, only a country's prior history of democracy, measured as the mean Vanhanen (1997) democracy index for 1900 through 1989, proved to significantly affect the perception of political community. In concrete terms, Costa Rica, with the highest value for Vanhanen's mean 1900–89 democracy scores (Table 4.1), ranks first among the eight countries on its citizens' perception of political community (Table 3.5). Conversely, Mexico and Guatemala, with low scores on democratic history, are the two nations whose citizens least perceive a national political community. This finding strongly suggests that a national track record of democratic governance creates a sense of shared national community. This is true when,

TABLE 4.2. *Sources of a perception of the existence of a political community – hierarchical linear model*

Fixed Effect	t-ratio	P
System-Level Variable		
Intercept	99.265	0.000
History of democracy	3.246	0.020
Individual-Level Variables		
Women	4.825	0.000
Age 21–30	−0.334	0.738
Age 31–40	1.375	0.169
Age 41–50	1.435	0.151
Age 51–60	0.785	0.433
Age 61 and older	1.488	0.137
Catholic	−0.774	0.439
Christian non-Catholic	1.034	0.302
No religion	−1.374	0.170
Primary education	3.314	0.001
Secondary education	5.313	0.000
College education	0.668	0.504
Postgraduate education	2.416	0.016
Wealth	1.624	0.104
Media contact	2.308	0.021
Political information	3.643	0.000
Voted for presidential winner	7.290	0.000
Interpersonal trust	7.996	0.000
Life satisfaction	7.415	0.000
"Have you been the victim of some criminal act during the last year?" No = 0, yes = 1	−2.310	0.021
"How safe from crime do you feel in your neighborhood?" 1 = not at all . . . 4 = much	−2.993	0.003
"Has a public official solicited a bribe from you in the last year?" No = 0, Yes = 1	−2.791	0.006
Capital city resident	−0.723	0.470
Large city resident	0.869	0.385
Medium city resident	−0.282	0.778
Small city/town resident	−1.747	0.080

Note: Method of estimation: restricted maximum likelihood; $\sigma^2 = 134.17$; λ for intercept = 0.975; $\tau = 3.629$; P-value <.001; maximum number of level-1 units = 12,401 (unweighted); maximum number of level-1 units = 8; $r^{2(\text{level 1 and 2})} = .061$. Degrees of freedom system-level = 6; degrees of freedom individual level = 11,640.

other factors held equal, neither economic development nor economic progress, more equitable income distribution, or human development progress had any significant impact on national community. An anomalous case is El Salvador, where the history of democracy is also extremely limited but the citizens' sense of political community ranks second highest among the eight nations. We suspect that what distinguishes El Salvador from Guatemala and Mexico, but which we cannot control for in our model, is the former's far greater ethnic homogeneity. This factor may mitigate somewhat the depressing effect of a weak prior record with democracy.

Turning to demographic sources in Table 4.2, we find that women share a higher sense of political community than men. All levels of education except college contribute to political community. Secondary education has the strongest positive impact, suggesting a continued political socialization effect for schooling. Individual wealth makes no contribution to a sense of political community, and neither do religious affiliation or the size of the town or city in which one resides. In contrast, contact with the media and having political information contribute positively to a sense of political community. Having voted for the winning candidate for president in the last election also contributes strongly. This adds political community to the list of kinds of legitimacy Anderson et al. (2005) identify as stemming from voting for the winning side in a national election.

As expected, higher levels of both interpersonal trust and life satisfaction contribute strongly and positively to a higher sense of national political community. In contrast, and as expected, being a crime victim, feeling unsafe from crime in one's own neighborhood, and being solicited for a bribe by a public official all significantly lower a citizen's sense of political community. Traumatic experiences, negative perceptions of personal safety, and victimization by acts of official corruption all undermine a sense of common nationhood among Latin Americans. As we will see in Chapters 5–7, such negative experiences also shape political capital formation by altering citizens' attitudes about democracy and how they participate in politics.

Support for regime principles

Our second legitimacy dimension is support for regime principles. What shapes the degree to which citizens support the basic underlying principles of democratic governance? Table 4.3 presents an analysis of the sources of such support.

TABLE 4.3. *Sources of support for regime principles – hierarchical
linear model*

Fixed Effect	t-ratio	P
System-Level Variable		
Intercept	43.410	0.000
History of democracy	2.222	0.067
Individual-Level Variables		
Women	−0.991	0.322
Age 21–30	−2.582	0.010
Age 31–40	−1.008	0.314
Age 41–50	−1.130	0.259
Age 51–60	−1.181	0.238
Age 61 and older	−0.925	0.356
Catholic	−0.238	0.812
Christian non-Catholic	−0.148	0.883
No religion	1.292	0.197
Primary education	1.065	0.288
Secondary education	2.955	0.004
College education	5.122	0.000
Postgraduate education	4.646	0.000
Wealth	−0.142	0.887
Media contact	3.995	0.000
Political information	5.230	0.000
Voted for presidential winner	−0.047	0.963
Interpersonal trust	7.255	0.000
Life satisfaction	−2.339	0.019
"Have you been the victim of some criminal act during the last year?" No = 0, yes = 1	1.563	0.118
"How safe from crime do you feel in your neighborhood?" 1 = not at all . . . 4 = much.	−1.324	0.186
"Has a public official solicited a bribe from you in the last year?" No = 0, Yes = 1	−0.200	0.842
Capital city resident	−2.865	0.005
Large city resident	−1.863	0.062
Medium city resident	−2.150	0.031
Small city/town resident	1.745	0.081

Note: Method of estimation: restricted maximum likelihood; $\sigma^2 = 303.72$; λ for intercept = 0.988; $\tau = 17.16$; P-value <.001; maximum number of level-1 units = 12,401 (unweighted); maximum number of level-1 units = 8; $r^{2(\text{level 1 and level 2})} = .051$; degrees of freedom system level = 6; d.f. individual level = 11,940.

Of all of the system-level values we modeled, once again only a nation's prior history of democracy contributed to greater support for democratic regime principles. This makes considerable sense on its face because there is strong evidence that institutions contribute a great deal to the development of political culture (Muller and Seligson 1994; Jackman and Miller 2004). To illustrate, Costa Rica and Panama have the highest levels of history of democracy (Vanhanen's mean democracy score 1900–89, Table 4.1), and we find that Costa Ricans and Panamanians have the highest average levels of support for regime democratic principles (Table 3.5). Meanwhile, Guatemala and El Salvador experienced the second and third lowest histories of democracy as measured by Vanhanen, and their citizens have the two lowest national mean scores for support for democratic regime principles. In short, the greater the nation's experience with democracy, the greater the commitment its citizens will manifest to fundamental democratic liberties in the contemporary era.

Few demographic factors have an impact on support for regime principles. Among the factors with little influence are sex, most age cohorts, religious denomination, and wealth. This means that support for basic democratic values is widely and deeply founded in these eight Latin American countries. We find no evidence that older citizens tend to support democratic principles less out of lingering loyalty to prior antidemocratic regimes. A more detailed analysis by country also failed to elicit any meaningful patterned effect of age on democratic regime principles.[11] Education, in contrast, especially at the more advanced secondary, college, and postgraduate levels, notably contributes to support for basic democratic regime norms. We expected this because of the extensive literature linking education to support for democratic principles (Jackman 1972). Being a resident of larger population centers, especially the capital city or a medium-sized city, significantly associates with lower support for regime principles, of course controlling for all other factors including education. This finding that rural and small-town residents are the strongest supporters of regime democratic principles will be echoed repeatedly in findings in this and later chapters. Together, they will suggest that

---

[11] A multiple regression analysis by age cohorts and with controls for sex and education (not shown here to conserve space) isolated only three national age-related effects: Guatemalans older than 60 are slightly but significantly less supportive of democratic regime principles than are the very youngest citizens, as are Hondurans aged 21 to 30. Panamanians aged 41 and older are slightly but significantly more supportive of democracy than the reference group of the very youngest citizens.

a tendency of scholars and observers to regard rural folk as antidemocratic or disengaged from politics is erroneous.

Persons with higher levels of media contact and political knowledge support democratic regime principles in these eight democracies. This suggests two possibilities: First, greater media contact and political information levels may indicate that those better informed about democracy in operation are more likely to embrace it. Second, a socialization effect may be operating as favorable media commentary about democracy inculcates greater citizen support for it.

Two effects shown in Table 4.3 are particularly noteworthy. As expected, more trusting individuals report higher support for regime democratic principles. One may assume that trusting one's neighbors would predispose a citizen to embrace democratic norms. It would be sensible to support broad political participation rights if one tends to trust the intentions of others (Uslaner and Brown 2005). The contrasting finding here is particularly telling. Those more satisfied with their lives, even holding constant all other factors including wealth, education, and personal experiences, are *less supportive* of the principles of a democratic regime. A similar finding has been reported previously among urban Central Americans using data from the early 1990s (Booth and Richard 1996). Thus, complacency with one's life situation may slightly undermine the legitimacy norm of support for a democratic regime. This too makes sense for citizens of highly socially and economically unequal societies such as these – those content with the sociopolitical order and their place within it might well look askance at the (potentially disruptive) participation of others.

Fear of crime, and crime and corruption victimization, while negatively signed, each fails to exert significant influence upon support for democratic regime principles. This shows that support for democratic participation rights is not as contingent upon crime and corruption-related experiences as we had expected. In Chapter 7 we also report that preference for elected government over unelected strongman rule is also unaffected by experiencing crime and corruption. When one notes that the absolute levels of support for regime principles and elected government are very high (ratios exceeding three to one) and little moved by experiencing crime or corruption, these findings suggest that fundamental commitment to democratic norms have become strongly ingrained in these countries. Citizens separate crime and corruption experiences, which do affect other legitimacy dimensions, from key democratic principles.

Support for regime institutions

Whether studied individually or collectively as part of a composite index, support for political institutions, our third dimension, is one of the most extensively researched forms of legitimacy. Table 4.4 presents the regression model for the sources of institutional legitimacy.

We expected system-level traits reflecting good performance in governance to contribute to higher levels of system support. Among our system-level measures, the World Bank Government Effectiveness Index (GEI) attempts to tap the following properties of governments: the quality of public services, the quality of the civil service and the degree of its independence from political pressures, the quality of policy formulation and implementation, and the credibility of the government's commitment to such policies (Kaufmann et al. 1999; Kaufmann et al. 2006).[12] Similarly, the delivery of social well-being (a high HDI or improving HDI) or democratic performance (a high Freedom House combined measures score) should affect support for institutions.

We modeled each of the selected variables separately for support for institutions and found that, as expected, the World Bank GEI contributed significantly and positively to institutional legitimacy. However, the other system-level variables did not. Three countries illustrate this relationship most clearly. Costa Rica, ranked at the top of the GEI among our eight countries (Table 3.1), enjoys the highest average citizen evaluation of its institutions (Table 3.5) in our sample. In sharp contrast, Nicaragua and Guatemala have the two lowest GEI rankings in our sample and receive the two lowest average citizen evaluations of their institutions. *This finding conforms strongly to our expectations that effective national institutions will enjoy popular support* and thus helps confirm the Easton-Lipset notion that legitimacy depends in part on the performance of institutions.

At the individual level of analysis, various demographic traits contribute to higher institutional support. As expected, women support national institutions somewhat more than men. We also found that both Catholic and protestant religious affiliations boost institutional support above that of those who profess no religion or non-Christian religions. This finding,

---

[12] Critics of the GEI produced by the World Bank question the independence of the sources as well as the possible business-oriented bias of the item (Kurtz and Schrank 2007). However, for our purposes, those concerns are not central because even if the underlying measures are not independent and have a probusiness bias, they indicate governance quality adequately for our purposes here (Kaufmann, Kraay, and Mastruzzi 2007).

TABLE 4.4. *Sources of support for regime institutions – hierarchical linear model*

Fixed Effect	t-ratio	P
System-Level Variable		
Intercept	42.378	0.000
World Bank Government Effectiveness Index	2.627	0.039
Individual-Level Variables		
Women	3.386	0.001
Age 21–30	−4.070	0.000
Age 31–40	−4.303	0.000
Age 41–50	−4.557	0.000
Age 51–60	−2.916	0.004
Age 61 and older	−3.641	0.000
Catholic	2.536	0.012
Christian non-Catholic	2.110	0.035
No religion	0.565	0.572
Primary education	−1.439	0.150
Secondary education	−2.904	0.004
College education	−2.674	0.008
Postgraduate education	−4.500	0.000
Wealth	−1.428	0.153
Media contact	2.401	0.017
Political information	−3.335	0.001
Voted for presidential winner	4.132	0.000
Interpersonal trust	7.810	0.000
Life satisfaction	5.231	0.000
"Have you been the victim of some criminal act during the last year?" No = 0, yes = 1	−4.016	0.000
"How safe from crime do you feel in your neighborhood?" 1 = not at all . . . 4 = much.	−7.767	0.000
"Has a public official solicited a bribe from you in the last year?" No = 0, Yes = 1	−5.413	0.000
Capital city resident	−7.233	0.000
Large city resident	−3.066	0.003
Medium city resident	−4.191	0.000
Small city/town resident	−1.636	0.102

Note: Method of estimation: restricted maximum likelihood; $\sigma^2 = 259.90$; λ for intercept = 0.983; $\tau = 10.596$; P-value <.001; Maximum number of level-1 units = 12,401 (unweighted); maximum number of level-1 units = 8; $r^{2(\text{level 1 and level 2})} = .072$; degrees of freedom system level = 6; d.f. individual level = 11,640.

fails to support, at least as far as the institutional legitimacy is concerned, the notion that members of evangelical religious groups have sharply different political views.

We found that several characteristics lowered institutional support: Compared to the very young, members of every older age cohort are less supportive of institutions, with the 31–40 and 41–50 age cohorts the least supportive of all. These patterns suggest that the youngest citizens – those most recently socialized by schools in patriotism and, on average, less responsible for others' well-being than their older cohorts – view national institutions uncritically. Advancing age appears to dampen the positive socialization effects of schooling and present citizens with life and economic challenges that lower their institutional evaluations.

The effect of education on institutional legitimacy is generally *negative*, as we had expected. Compared to the least educated, those with secondary, college, and especially postgraduate education are the least supportive of political institutions. Education, then, seems to give citizens analytical tools and information that leads them to evaluate institutional performance negatively. This reminds us of a legend about Nicaraguan dictator Anastasio Somoza García. When asked whether the government should spend more on education, Somoza reportedly replied, "No, I want them to be as ignorant as burros." The tyrant apparently understood well how education can breed criticism of underperforming institutions, of which the Somoza dynasty was a prime example.

Residents of larger cities and towns, and especially of the national capital, express lower support for national institutions than residents of small towns and rural areas. One wonders whether the increased proximity to government in Latin America afforded by living in capital cities – and thus possibly having greater information about its foibles – breeds contempt for institutions. Information is certainly more available the more urbanized an area is, and, as we suspected, greater political information decreases support for institutions, suggesting that familiarity indeed generates disapproval. Personal wealth has no impact on support for institutions.

When we turn to the experiences and attitudes of citizens, we find further support for our emerging impression that among our Latin American citizens' knowledge of government, personal information-handling skills, and proximity to government generate institutional *dis*approval. In contrast, while having more political information reduces support for national institutions, greater media contact increases support for institutions, other factors held constant. This runs contrary to a widely held belief that exposure (especially to television, a component of our measure) breeds cynicism among the public. Other factors held constant, it is the information rather than exposure that erodes support.

Research by Bratton and his colleagues using Afrobarometer data demonstrated that crime and the perception of corruption were linked to lower institutional support (Bratton et al. 2005: 101, 228–335). As we fully expected, Table 4.4 demonstrates that having been a crime victim, feeling unsafe in one's own neighborhood, and having been solicited for a bribe all strongly reduce support for political institutions. What more appropriate location to place the mistrust for the failures of government to keep citizens safe and act with integrity than on the very institutions of government charged with performing these functions? To the extent that these nations suffer from high crime and corruption their institutions will suffer from such critical attitudes of their citizens. Research on Latin America has found that the region has among the world's worst records on crime (Gaviria and Pagés 1999). Examining the data, we find that crime is indeed a serious problem for our respondents. As shown in Figure 4.1, in the year prior to the survey, between 12 and 17 percent of our respondents reported of having been crime victims.

Corruption is also a very serious problem, as disclosed in our survey results. As shown in Figure 4.2, based on a seven-item series of questions asking respondents whether in the year prior to the survey they had been asked to pay bribes to the police, in schools, in the health system, at work, and so forth, between 13 and 32 percent had suffered that experience. This compares with victimization rates in Western Europe of less than 1 percent of adults, as reported in U.N.-based surveys (United Nations 1999), or in Canada and the United States of less than 1 percent (Seligson 2008b).[13]

We consider in Chapter 5 what the implications of such lack of support might be for political participation – in particular whether crime victimization may contribute to protest, turmoil, or other possible precursors or facilitators of political instability.

We observe that both the trusting and the "life-satisfied" citizen tend strongly to be more supportive of government, a finding that conforms to much of the social capital literature (Inglehart 1990). And finally, having voted for the winner in the last presidential election encourages additional

---

[13] Further comparative data on corruption are found in Seligson (2001a), Seligson (2002b), Seligson and Recanatini (2003), Seligson (2006a).

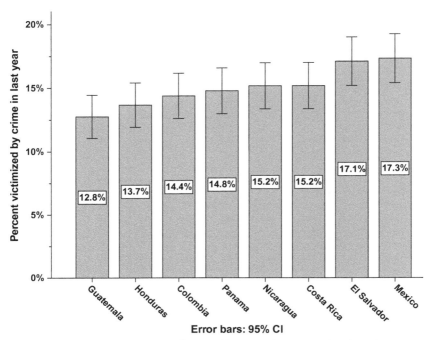

FIGURE 4.1. Survey respondents' self-reported victimization by crime

support for national institutions, further supporting the findings of Anderson and his coauthors (Anderson et al. 2005).

Evaluation of regime performance

We have measured citizen evaluation of regime performance in terms of perceptions of how the national economy is performing. This is appropriate because all governments, including those of the eight countries in this study, promote economic growth, enterprise, and employment creation in various ways. Table 4.5 presents our HLM analysis of the sources of citizen evaluation of regime performance.

Only one system-level variable proves to be related to citizen support for government performance – the dynamic measure of national GDP growth from 1990 to 2003. The better the economy performed in this regard, the more positive the citizens' evaluation of regime performance. For example, Panama and El Salvador had the highest mean citizen evaluations of regime economic performance legitimacy (Table 3.5), and both ranked among the top three in GDP change from 1990 through

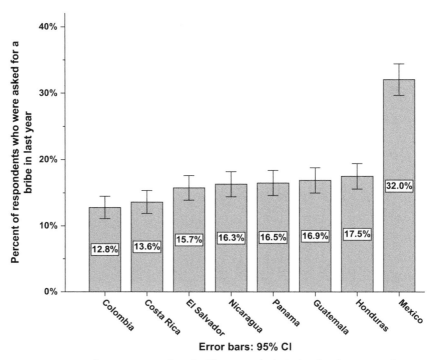

FIGURE 4.2. Survey respondents' self-reported victimization by corruption

2003 (Table 4.1). On the other end of the spectrum, the two worst-performing economies in GDP per capita increase were Nicaragua and Honduras, whose citizens gave them the two lowest mean regime performance evaluations. As we suspected and noted in Chapter 1, citizens are probably not very well attuned to absolute levels of GDP, but they do notice how their own national economy is performing compared to how it performed in the recent past. Citizens do, then, take note of the broad phenomenon of economic performance – most likely through personalized indicators such as employment opportunities, wages, the growth of their businesses and markets for their products and services – and transfer that view to their evaluation of their government's performance. Latin Americans may not be able to distinguish national economic performance well on a day-to-day basis, and we would not expect them to, but the evidence here shows that they certainly can do so over the span of a few years.

On the individual level, we see in Table 4.5 that women evaluate the performance of regimes much less positively than men. Thus, while

TABLE 4.5. *Sources of support for regime performance – hierarchical linear model*

Fixed Effect	t-ratio	P
System-Level Variable		
Intercept	35.184	0.000
GDP Growth 1990–2003	2.216	0.068
Individual-Level Variables		
Women	–5.522	0.000
Age 21–30	–5.317	0.000
Age 31–40	–7.400	0.000
Age 41–50	–9.219	0.000
Age 51–60	–7.838	0.000
Age 61 and older	–6.475	0.000
Catholic	1.490	0.136
Christian non-Catholic	1.302	0.193
No religion	–0.150	0.881
Primary education	–0.741	0.459
Secondary education	0.717	0.473
College education	3.016	0.003
Postgraduate education	1.338	0.181
Wealth	2.296	0.022
Media contact	0.061	0.952
Political information	–3.830	0.000
Voted for presidential winner	13.892	0.000
Interpersonal trust	2.323	0.020
Life satisfaction	11.641	0.000
"Have you been the victim of some criminal act during the last year?" No = 0, yes = 1	–2.185	0.029
"How safe from crime do you feel in your neighborhood?" 1 = not at all . . . 4 = much.	–7.562	0.000
"Has a public official solicited a bribe from you in the last year?" No = 0, Yes = 1	–1.680	0.092
Capital city resident	–2.119	0.034
Large city resident	–3.601	0.001
Medium city resident	–3.648	0.000
Small city/town resident	–1.579	0.114

Note: Method of estimation: restricted maximum likelihood; $\sigma^2 = 206.66$; λ for intercept = 0.989; $\tau = 12.263$; P-value <.001; Maximum number of level-1 units = 12,401 (unweighted); maximum number of level-1 units = 8; $r^{2(\text{level 1 and level 2})} = .076$; degrees of freedom system level = 6; d.f. individual level = 11,640.

women are more trusting of institutions, they evaluate effectiveness more negatively. This is no doubt an effect of women's generally worse standing in terms of earnings despite elevated economic responsibilities for families. Compared to the very youngest citizens, older cohorts view economic performance negatively. Cohorts with the major responsibility for larger families and the elderly (ages 31 and older) express much worse evaluations than the young. Education appears to matter little to regime performance evaluation except that those with college educations are more supportive. Wealth has a small positive effect on evaluation of regime performance.

Several personal experiences and attitudes contribute to negative views of a regime's performance: The more politically informed citizens are, the less positive their evaluations of regime performance. Crime victims, and especially those who feel unsafe in their own neighborhoods, also evaluate regime performance negatively. Residents of capital cities and intermediate-sized cities also negatively evaluate regime performance. We are not surprised by this finding because we surmise that insecurity bred by crime victimization and the fear of violence in one's neighborhood interferes with one's potential to earn a living. Crimes often result in property loss, and crime victimization may deprive workers of health and income. A perceived atmosphere of insecurity in one's neighborhood interferes with consumers' and merchants' willingness to circulate to places of commerce, to take economic risks, and to operate small businesses safely. Contrary to expectation, however, corruption victimization did not affect the evaluation of regime performance. This finding suggests to us once again the importance of disaggregating legitimacy. We have found previously that corruption victimization significantly reduces institutional support, a more general or diffuse measure of legitimacy. It does not, however, weaken the perception of regime performance. This highlights a clear separation in the impact of corruption on different legitimacy dimensions. Had we selected a single measure of legitimacy rather than our six-fold classification, this important distinction would have been lost.

The most striking finding shown in Table 4.5 is the t-ratio of almost 13.9 for having voted for the last winning president and a positive evaluation of regime economic performance. This high level of association suggests strongly that our respondents do not regard their governments as neutral arbiters of the economy and distributors of economic benefits. Other factors held constant, if an administration's electoral supporters view its performance to be so markedly better than those who did not vote for the incumbent president, one must surmise that there exist widespread economic payoffs (or at least the expectation thereof) for supporting the winning party and presidential candidate. Again, these results provide strong confirmation of findings by Anderson et al. (2005).

A sense of satisfaction with one's life also makes a very strong contribution to a positive evaluation of regime performance (t-ratio above 11.6). Even controlling for the myriad other factors in the model including income, those satisfied with their lives are much more prone than the dissatisfied to evaluate government performance positively.

Support for political actors

We measure this legitimacy dimension as evaluation of the performance of the incumbent president at the time of our surveys in 2004. Our theory leads us to expect that national contextual factors would influence the evaluation of incumbents less than short-term political factors because national context tends to vary over a relatively longer term. The results of the HLM modeling of all the system-level variables (see Table 4.1) confirm this expectation. None of the national-level performance variables had any effect on support for political actors independent of the individual-level variables also included in the model. As a result, we present in Table 4.6 an ordinary least squares regression model for the possible individual-level sources of citizen support for actors.[14]

The most notable finding in Table 4.6 is the very high association (t-ratio over 15.9) between having voted for the incumbent president and one's evaluation of the president's performance, even with all the other variables controlled for. This finding is in no way surprising, but its very face validity and strength vindicates our inclusion of this variable in the analysis. It demonstrates powerfully, as Anderson et al. (2005) argue, that in evaluating the legitimacy of political actors, one must take into account that those who voted for the incumbent president in the last election are significantly more likely to be more positive about the government than those who did not support the incumbent (whether they voted against the incumbent or merely did not vote). Our regression analysis allows us to

---

[14] In order to maintain the parallelism with the other regressions in this chapter, we do not include here country dummies, as we do in other chapters. We ran the regressions for the support for political actors, as well as support for local government (discussed below), with these dummies but found no important substantive variation in our findings that would have merited reporting a different form of the regression equations in this chapter.

TABLE 4.6. *Sources of support for political actors – ordinary least squares model*

Variable[a]	t-ratio	P
Women	.335	.738
Age 21–30	−4.373	.000
Age 31–40	−4.638	.000
Age 41–50	−5.146	.000
Age 51–60	−3.949	.000
Age 61 and older	−4.930	.000
Catholic	−.035	.972
Christian non-Catholic	−1.114	.265
No religion	−1.050	.294
Primary education	1.825	.068
Secondary education	.822	.411
College education	−3.936	.000
Postgraduate education	−4.844	.000
Wealth	8.604	.000
Media contact	.679	.497
Political information	−4.001	.000
Voted for presidential winner	15.936	.000
Interpersonal trust	8.081	.000
Life satisfaction	6.331	.000
"Have you been the victim of some criminal act during the last year?" No = 0, yes = 1	−1.731	.084
"How safe from crime do you feel in your neighborhood?" 1 = not at all... 4 = much	−4.181	.000
"Has a public official solicited a bribe from you in the last year?" No = 0, Yes = 1	−3.660	.000
Capital city resident	−3.794	.000
Large city resident	.863	.388
Medium city resident	1.645	.100
Small city/town resident	7.117	.000

Note: For this model R-square = .068; Standard Error of the Estimate = 22.389; d.f, 11,267; F = 31.494; N = 11,293.
[a] No contextual effects were detected for support for political actors, so this regression analysis is an OLS model containing only individual-level variables.

hold this powerful effect constant as we evaluate the other sources of support for actors.

Among the demographic factors, only greater personal wealth contributes to more support for the incumbent president. Perhaps the wealthy attribute some of their good fortune to those in power. Compared to the youngest age cohort (not included in the model but used as the base group), older citizens of all ages were less supportive. Compared to their less educated fellow citizens, those with college and postgraduate educations expressed much lower support for the incumbent president's performance.

Regarding personal experiences and attitudes, having higher levels of political information also correlates sharply negatively with support for actors. Those who are trusting and satisfied with their lives, as expected, evaluate the incumbent president more positively. Other factors held constant, citizens who feel unsafe in their own neighborhoods and those who recently have been asked for a bribe by a public official are markedly less supportive of the incumbents. This is quite consistent with what we expected. Governments that cannot establish or maintain a sense of safety among their citizens – a real problem for the regimes in Honduras and Colombia, for example – get poor performance marks from their citizens. The petty corruption of public officials also generates low evaluations for incumbent actors.

Support for local government

Support for local government adds a novel dimension to the study of political legitimacy. Municipal governments in Latin America largely resemble county governments in the United States. There are generally no other formal local governments equivalent to self-governing municipal corporations (U.S. towns, villages, and cities), except for some capital cities.[15] In the countries in our study, local governments are responsible for many basic public services including water, street lighting, sewers and sanitation, and streets and rural roads and traffic regulation. The *municipio* or *cantón* depends heavily upon central governments for revenue and is usually very strapped for locally generated funds. With their broad responsibilities and limited resources, these governments seem designed to perform poorly. Indeed, support for local government on our 100-point scale is the second lowest of all six dimensions with a score of 45.62 (see Figure 2.3).

---

[15] In some countries there are submunicipal district committees and even district *síndicos*, but they have little or no legislative or budgetary authority. Mexico, of course, is a federal system (the only one among our eight nations) and hence has state governments as well as local governments. Our study omitted consideration of state governments because they only exist in one case.

TABLE 4.7. *Sources of support for local government – ordinary least squares model*

Variable[a]	t-ratio	P
Women	3.386	.001
Age 21–30	−4.493	.000
Age 31–40	−3.600	.000
Age 41–50	−3.487	.000
Age 51–60	−4.362	.000
Age 61 and older	−5.457	.000
Catholic	1.428	.153
Christian non-Catholic	.485	.628
No religion	−.424	.671
Primary education	1.964	.050
Secondary education	3.222	.001
College education	2.241	.025
Postgraduate education	2.789	.005
Wealth	1.780	.075
Media contact	3.794	.000
Political information	−.615	.539
Voted for presidential winner	2.200	.028
Interpersonal trust	11.549	.000
Life satisfaction	5.683	.000
"Have you been the victim of some criminal act during the last year?" No = 0, yes =1	−2.434	.015
"How safe from crime do you feel in your neighborhood?" 1 = not at all . . . 4 = much.	−9.285	.000
"Has a public official solicited a bribe from you in the last year?" No = 0, Yes = 1	−3.276	.001
Capital city resident	−2.436	.015
Large city resident	−1.434	.152
Medium city resident	.600	.549
Small city/town resident	8.882	.000

R-square = .060; standard error of the estimate = 16.872; degrees of freedom = 11,267; F = 27.477; N = 11,293.
[a] No contextual effects were detected for Support for Local Government, so this regression analysis is an OLS model containing only individual-level variables.

Table 4.7 provides evidence on the sources of support for local government. We found no system-level variables affecting the legitimacy of local government, but we had not expected to. National-level performance factors are too remote to be seen by citizens as affecting the way municipal governments perform. Thus Table 4.7 presents here only the OLS model rather than the HLM results.

Turning to the individual-level factors, and beginning with demographic sources, we note that women evaluate local government more positively than do men. Wealth and religious affiliation have no impact on support for local government. Better-educated citizens (those with secondary, college, or postgraduate education) support local government *more* than do the less educated. This pattern is the reverse of that observed for several other national-level legitimacy dimensions, in which those most informed were less supportive. This finding again reinforces our contention that legitimacy should be studied using its multidimensional richness and complexity. Absent that approach, had we merged our six dimensions into only one or two, we would have missed completely this important variation in the role of education as a source of legitimacy norms.

Turning to experiences and attitudes, Table 4.7 shows that media contact positively affects local government support, but general political knowledge has no effect. Having voted for the incumbent president has a very slight positive effect on evaluating local governments, but it is minuscule compared to its effect on evaluating national actors. (Municipal elections in our eight countries are partisan, so partisanship may infuse this effect slightly. However, not all municipal elections coincide with national elections, so that a halo effect for local government of presidential choice is likely to be quite modest – and proves so here.)

Interpersonal trust strongly predicts support for local government (t-ratio = 11.549), as expected. This finding again is consistent with social capital research, especially that which regards interpersonal trust as logically affecting organizations "within arm's reach" of an individual, as are local governments in Latin America (Uslaner and Brown 2005). Also as expected, persons satisfied with their lives are strongly likely to evaluate local government positively, once again irrespective of all other factors in the model including their wealth, age, and education. Both being solicited for bribes and crime victimization reduce support for local government. Feeling unsafe in one's own neighborhood very strongly depresses citizens' evaluation of local government performance. Many municipalities have local security services of one kind or another, often auxiliary police forces. When citizens feel unsafe in their neighborhoods, they correctly lay some of the blame on municipal government.

The size of the community of residence provides the final set of variables to examine for effects on support for local government. One reasonably may assume that this factor could shape citizens' evaluations of local (municipal) government performance to a considerable degree. We anticipated possibly contending effects. For example, on the one hand in bigger cities municipal governments should have more resources and a larger investment in infrastructure, both of which argue for higher evaluations. On the other hand, smaller cities and towns should be more intimate and local officials much more accessible, perhaps also encouraging positive evaluations. The empirical pattern revealed fulfills the second expectation. Compared to the excluded reference category of rural areas and villages, smaller city and town governments had strongly more positive evaluations. Capital city governments had modestly negative evaluations compared to rural areas and villages. Therefore, these results reinforce the ones reported above regarding interpersonal trust. Even though larger local governments have more resources and can do more, people do not evaluate them nearly so well as governments in towns and smaller cities (Verba 1961).

DISCUSSION AND CONCLUSIONS

We conclude, as theory predicts, that different types of legitimacy arise from different sources. Conceptualizing legitimacy norms as multidimensional, as we have done and confirmed here, means that each type of legitimacy has its own particular referent, whether a perceived national political community, national government institutions, incumbent actors, or one's local government. These referents range from the relatively abstract and diffuse (democratic principles) to the very concrete (presidents, local government). We have also seen (Chapters 2 and 3) that citizens' appraisals of each distinct referent vary greatly among legitimacy dimensions and among countries. Thus, it is not surprising that we have found variant patterns of sources of legitimacy grounded in the specific nature of each dimension and concrete referent being evaluated. Voting for the winner in the last presidential election, for example, strongly affects evaluations of actors and regime performance for obvious reasons. Partisans tend to value or expect value from what their own candidate may accomplish. But voting for the last presidential winner has only a modest impact on evaluating the performance of local government, and none at all on whether a citizen agrees with fundamental democratic principles.

Table 4.8 summarizes the findings of the regression analyses of the six legitimacy dimensions and facilitates an overview of the extensive and complex material we have covered. The darker grey cells indicate positive relationships of the independent (source) variables, and the lighter grey

TABLE 4.8. *Summary of sources of legitimacy*

Variables	Political Community	Regime Principles	Regime Institutions	Regime Performance	Political Actors	Local Government
System-Level	History of Democracy	History of Democracy	Government Effectiveness	GDP Growth		
Micro level						
Women	4.825		3.386	−5.522		3.386
Age 21–30		−2.582	−4.070	−5.317	−4.373	−4.493
Age 31–40			−4.303	−7.400	−4.638	−3.600
Age 41–50			−4.557	−9.219	−5.146	−3.487
Age 51–60			−2.916	−7.838	−3.949	−4.362
Age 61 and older			−3.641	−6.475	−4.930	−5.457
Catholic			2.536			
Protestant			2.110			
No religion						
Primary education	3.314					
Secondary education	5.313	2.955	−2.904	3.016	−3.936	3.222
College education	2.416	5.122	−2.674		−4.844	2.241
Postgraduate education		4.646	−4.500		8.604	2.789
Wealth				2.296		3.794
Media contact	2.308	3.995	2.401			

(continued)

TABLE 4.8 (continued)

Variables	Political Community	Regime Principles	Regime Institutions	Regime Performance	Political Actors	Local Government
System-Level / Micro level	History of Democracy	History of Democracy	Government Effectiveness	GDP Growth		
Political information	3.643	5.230	-3.335	-3.830	-4.001	
Vote for winner	7.290		4.132	13.892	15.936	2.200
Interpersonal trust	7.996	7.255	7.810	2.323	8.081	11.549
Life satisfaction	7.415	-2.339	5.231	11.641	6.331	5.683
Crime victim	-2.310		-4.016	-2.185	-2.434	-2.434
Feels unsafe	-2.993		-7.767	-7.562	-4.181	-9.285
Corruption victim	-2.791		-5.413		-9.285	-3.276
Capital city resident		-2.865	-7.233	-2.119	-3.660	-2.436
Large city resident			-3.066	-3.601	-3.794	
Medium city resident		-2.150	-4.191	-3.648		
Small city/town resident					7.117	8.882

Key: blank cells = not significant; darker grey cells = positively significant; lighter grey cells = negatively significant; cell values = significant t-ratios.

cells signify negative relationships. The cell values are the t-ratios reported in Tables 4.2 through 4.7; blank cells represent statistically insignificant relationships.

Most categories of variables present mixed pictures. Turning first to the system-level independent variables, we found only a few with any effect. Prior experience with democracy elevates the sense of political community and support for democratic regime principles, both plausible outcomes. Government effectiveness elevates citizens' evaluations of regime institutions. GDP growth over a decade and a half prior to the surveys correlates positively with citizens' evaluations of regime economic performance. While these findings appeal to our common sense, the larger picture here is that, when properly modeled using HLM, few of the many contextual variables affect legitimacy. Neither the current levels of democracy, income inequality, GDP per capita, or HDI, nor the recent change in HDI affected any legitimacy dimension. This strongly suggests that for the eight countries we have studied most of legitimacy's sources arise from micro-level factors – the citizen's position in society, personal attributes, community type, personality, and experiences. Yet because our sample of countries is small, we cannot reject the possibility that with a larger sample of countries such contextual variables would turn out to be significant. One drawback of expanding the sample, however, would be that many other country-level factors such as shared history, language, culture, and institutions – now largely controlled – would begin to vary. This sample expansion thus would necessitate the incorporation of more system-level variables, and doing so would once again raise the case/variable ratio problem. For the moment, at least, we will need to accept the findings here as reasonable and consistent with our expectations and data.

The demographic factors shown in Table 4.8 reveal no wholly consistent patterns across all dimensions. Two sets of patterns are worthy of note, however. One is that older citizens almost always more negatively evaluate the more concrete legitimacy dimensions (regime institutions, performance, actors, local government) than the very youngest citizens aged 16 to 20. A second set of patterns in Table 4.8 involves education, which at the higher levels of attainment (secondary, college, and postgraduate) affect most dimensions of legitimacy. The significant effects, however, are not uniform among the different dimensions. More education correlates with a higher sense of national community and more support for democratic regime principles and local government. This pattern is also true for those with more political information. Even more important, having more education and more political knowledge each associates with lower evaluations of regime institutions and political actors. By contrast, the more knowledge and education one has in our eight Latin American nations, the worse the appraisal of the regime's leaders and institutions. What can it portend for these countries that having more education and information contribute to a national community and support for democracy, but also to disapproval of the concrete performance of their institutions and political leaders? We find in this pattern some cause for hope for the principles of national comity and democracy – values enhanced by education and knowledge. At the same time we also find cause for concern about the potential stability of these nations because their best educated and most informed citizens think badly of their performance.

The bigger the community in which citizens live, Table 4.8 reveals, the less likely they are to view most aspects of their regime positively. Large-scale urbanization and proximity to national government uniformly undermines political support in Latin America. In contrast, compared to rural and village dwellers, the residents of small cities and towns evaluate local governments and the president strongly more favorably, and strikingly more so than do residents of bigger communities and national capitals. We will return to this issue in subsequent chapters.

Another uniform pattern that stands out is the strong positive association between trusting one's neighbors and all six dimensions of legitimacy. Clearly more trusting citizens in these eight nations, other factors equal, are willing to give diverse aspects of their systems their approval. With our data we cannot readily determine whether interpersonal trust contributes to legitimacy or legitimacy to trust, or whether, as we suspect, there is a reciprocal relationship.[16] But direction of causality aside, these findings support the social capital literature's linking of interpersonal trust and political support.

When citizens have been victimized by crime or corruption, or when they believe their neighborhoods are unsafe, they rather consistently evaluate their governments negatively. The exception to this pattern is for support for democratic principles, an encouraging finding we will confirm using other measures in Chapter 7. Although insecurity, crime, and corruption do variously erode support for institutions, incumbents, and local government, they do not undermine support for democratic governance.

---

[16] To determine the direction of causality would require a two-stage least squares analysis, but we lack the appropriate instrumental variables to enable the application of that technique.

This exploration of the sources of legitimacy's six dimensions has uncovered several fascinating patterns, mostly consistent with expectations. The findings clearly show sufficient variation in sources across the six legitimacy dimensions to amply merit our multidimensional approach. But merely having determined that legitimacy has different dimensions, and different sources does nothing to demonstrate that legitimacy matters for political behavior, other attitudes, or political system stability. We now turn our attention to those subjects.

5

Legitimacy and Political Participation

The essence of democracy, according to the etymology of the word[1] and to classics of democratic theory, is *citizen participation in the rule of a political community* (Dahl 1956; Mill 1958; Aristotle 1962; Pateman 1970; Cohen 1973; Dahl 1998; Held 2001). Albeit central to the definition of democracy, political participation and its possible effects long have presented political scientists with what we might label the Goldilocks conundrum – the question of how much and what kinds of participation are too much, too little, or just right. On the one hand, many observers in the "too much" camp have expressed fears that excessive participation might overtax the capacity of states to manage it or respond effectively and thereby undermine political stability or produce bad policy (Schumpeter 1943; Almond and Verba 1963; Huntington 1968; Crozier, Huntington, and Watanuki 1975).[2] Those in the "too little" camp worry that low legitimacy might generate either too little system-reinforcing participation, too much protest, or too little supportive social and political capital for the health of democracies (Nye et al. 1997; Van Deth 1997; Pharr and Putnam 2000a; Putnam 2000; Putnam 2002).

These contending worries about participation and democracy – fears of both too much and too little participation for the good of democracy – focus attention directly on legitimacy. They force us to ask: Does legitimacy matter for political participation and for democracy, and if so, how

---

[1] "Democracy" derives from the Greek roots *demos*, which refers to the people, and *kratos*, meaning rule. That is, democracy literally means rule by the people (Held 2001).

[2] For an excellent discussion and bibliography of the classical literature, see Pateman (1970).

does it matter? As we noted in Chapter 1, the literature holds that legitimacy is central to the political stability of democracies. Legitimacy certainly *should* matter a great deal in new or unconsolidated democracies, such as some of the cases we study in this volume. Higher levels of public support for the political system (community, regime, institutions, and performance) should generate microlevel behaviors and attitudes that strengthen democratic regimes, while low legitimacy should weaken them. Support for government should increase citizens' willingness to comply with the law, their support for democracy, voluntary compliance with government, and various forms of political participation, and contribute to the consolidation of democratic regimes (Norris 1999a). Expressed from the negative side, many of the theorists we have already cited and others (Barnes and Kaase 1979; Kornberg and Clarke 1983) hold that low legitimacy could generate protest, unrest, and rebellion. According to Dalton (2004: 11), "public opinion has a practical impact on politics. . . . [I]f democracy relies on the participation of citizens as a basis of legitimacy and to produce representative decisions, then decreasing involvement as a consequence of distrust can harm the democratic process."

Norris challenges this received wisdom about the destabilizing potential of legitimacy for participation and rejects fears of sharp civic decline: "Not all indicators, by any means, point toward consistent and steady secular deterioration across all dimensions of political activism" (Norris 2002). She presents extensive evidence from many contemporary democracies of increased political participation in diverse arenas. Another perspective renders citizen participation virtually no threat to democracies at all. Przeworski et al. (2000), for example, argue that "no democracy has ever been subverted [i.e., broken down], not during the period we studied nor even before nor after, regardless of everything else, in a country with a per capita income higher than that of Argentina in 1975: $6,055. There is no doubt that democracy is stable in affluent countries." Thus according to this view, the stability of wealthy countries would be entirely independent of political legitimacy, participation, and attitudes because all that matters, to quote the lines from the musical *Cabaret*, is "money, money, money."

In order to confront the *effects puzzle*, then, we must ask: What kind of low or declining legitimacy erodes or undermines democracy, if any of it does at all? What are and where can we find the microsocial effects of the various legitimacy dimensions? Do low legitimacy levels increase antisystem behaviors while decreasing within-system participation vital for democracy? Does low legitimacy reduce support for democracy and increase norms justifying revolutionary challenges to the regime, coups d'etat, or confrontational political tactics? Do low levels of certain types of support shape political participation or institutions in specific ways that might, ultimately, undermine political stability?

The remainder of this book will seek answers to these questions about legitimacy's possible effects. In this chapter we focus on the behavioral aspect of the effects puzzle in the form of *political participation*. Then in Chapter 6 we will examine how legitimacy shapes confrontational and antisystem political *attitudes*. Finally, in Chapter 7 we examine how legitimacy affects citizens' demand for democracy and their perceptions of the supply of democracy in their particular countries.

THEORIES ABOUT LEGITIMACY AND POLITICAL PARTICIPATION

Two related yet somewhat contradictory arguments hold that both conventional and unconventional participation might operate either to strengthen or to weaken regimes. Having reviewed this literature in Chapter 1, we will summarize its key elements here. The first argument contends that citizens strongly supportive of regimes more likely would participate conventionally within institutional channels and vice versa. "Much commentary assumes that if people have little confidence in the core institutions of representative democracy . . . they will be reluctant to participate in the democratic process, producing apathy" (Norris 2002: 30). Within-system participation would tend to reinforce and stabilize extant institutions. Politically unsupportive citizens would pose no threat to regime institutions because they would make few demands upon the government. In essence, these arguments posit a linear and positive relationship between support and within-channels political activism: *Institutionally supportive citizens engage within the system and strengthen it, while disaffected citizens withdraw without weakening it.*

The second contention is that citizens with low legitimacy values more likely would engage in unconventional or protest participation. In short, a linear and positive relationship should exist between low political support and engaging in outside-of-channels participation and protest. For example, "It is widely believed that political cynicism fuels protest activity" (Norris 1999a: 261).[3] Thus, *citizens disaffected from democratic principles*

---

[3] See, however, the new argument by Norris, Walgrave, and Van Aelst (2005) that the theory that disaffection with the political system leads to protest "receives little, if any, support from the available systematic empirical studies of the survey evidence."

or institutions may protest or rebel, but supportive or neutral citizens generally do neither. In sum, large amounts of protest or confrontational participation motivated by low support for democracy or an elected regime's institutions could overtax them and provoke their decay. Low support and protest could encourage or contribute to elite efforts to overthrow democratic rulers or institutions. This excessive participation was central in the Huntingtonian (1968) theory of the causes of political decay. It provided a theoretical justification for those in the U.S. foreign policy establishment- who favored support for dictatorships in developing countries.

In examining these alternative theories, we have come to believe that most prior research has suffered from three main limitations. First, as we have argued elsewhere (Booth and Seligson 2005), hypotheses about legitimacy's behavioral effects have tended to dichotomize participation by focusing mainly on participation either within channels (voting or party activism) or outside of channels (protest or, more commonly studied, support for protest). While recognizing that political participation has many dimensions, prior research on legitimacy's effects has not systematically accommodated the full range and complexity of citizens' involvement and the multiple arenas in which it may occur. Nor has it yet fully explored multiple legitimacy dimensions' effects upon them.

Second, even though major prior studies of legitimacy's effects on participation, such as those by Norris (1999a) and Dalton (2004), have recognized legitimacy's multiple dimensionality, they have nevertheless largely examined the effect of support for institutions on participation, while not extensively examining effects of other legitimacy dimensions.[4] In this chapter, our treatment of the impact of legitimacy on political participation builds consistently from a multidimensional treatment of legitimacy, and we systematically examine their effects on six distinct modes of political participation. We do this because we theorize that not all dimensions of legitimacy should affect each mode of participation in the same way. Indeed, some legitimacy dimensions and participation modes might have no effect on participation at all, while others could have an important impact (Booth and Seligson 2005).

Third, a further advance over prior research emerges, again, from the Costa Rican pilot study we undertook for this book. We found there that

---

[4] In contrast, studies more attuned to the dimensionality of legitimacy (e.g., Rose, Shin, and Munro 1999; Canache 2002; Bratton, Mattes, and Gyimah-Boadi 2005) have focused their impact studies on other *political attitudes* – sometimes support for participation or protest – rather than on participation itself.

simple linear-positive assumptions cited above from the literature understate the possible range of legitimacy-participation effects by ignoring sharp differences of participation in diverse contexts. We discovered that Costa Ricans with low support were far from passive. They often participated in political arenas *other than* those afforded by formal, within-channel national institutions such as elections and partisan-campaign activism. Rather, they engaged in protests, civil society, and activities such as communal improvement efforts.

Fourth, as noted in Chapter 1, we distrust the assumptions of simple linearity made by most previous researchers. Why, we ask, would highly disaffected citizens of a democracy become inert or drop out of the political arena? We hypothesize that at least some disgruntled citizens, rather than doing nothing at all, might work for change within the system or strive to change the system. The evidence from Costa Rica revealed that citizens holding extremely polarized legitimacy positions (both high and low) might be moved to similarly high levels of participation. In contrast to those who feel indifferent about institutions, citizens who either *intensely approve or intensely disapprove* of government may each be moved to high levels of civic engagement.

In more technical terms, our pilot research and the logic we articulated above suggest to us that in a democracy, some legitimacy-participation functions might well be U-shaped. This relationship would likely exist, we believe, in formally democratic polities such as those in this study. It would be especially prevalent in a country with a good human rights climate, such as Costa Rica.[5] To our knowledge, other than our own pilot study neither theory nor empirical research has considered this possibility of a curvilinear participation-legitimacy relationship. Nor has theory explored what factors cause disaffected citizens to choose from a menu of five possible options – increasing their involvement in national-system politics (the behavior we characterize with the U-curve label), dropping out of national-system politics, changing their participation from national-system politics to organizational or communal arenas, adopting protest, or choosing to rebel.

We theorize that a citizen's expectation of experiencing repression by the regime might well shape such choices. Citizens who perceive themselves as

---

[5] In countries that are highly repressive, deterrents to all forms of participation can be so great as to stunt virtually any citizen activity. The low levels of protest behavior and other participation not mobilized by the state in the Stalinist Soviet Union or Nazi Germany illustrate the impact of extreme repression.

living in a democracy and thus do not expect repression would be likely to participate within-system channels and/or to protest whether they were satisfied *or* disgruntled citizens. In other words, the nonrepressive context allows all forms of participation to take place, unencumbered by significant fear of the consequences of that participation. Democracy formally invites citizen demand making so that, absent fear of repression, a disgruntled person might simultaneously use both within-system channels and protest to express demands and concerns to government. We believe that individuals, whether disgruntled or satisfied, may participate in diverse activities, often simultaneously. In contrast, fear of repression might affect one's decision about whether to engage in or drop out of politics. Repression's purpose, after all, is to discourage participation and demand making among those who disapprove of a regime (Arendt 1966). One logical and safe response to such a situation (and one consistent with the intentions of a repressive government) would be for a disgruntled citizen simply to withdraw from political participation and thus lower his/her risk of exposure to potentially horrific consequences.

Full abstinence from participation, however, would not satisfy the needs of many citizens. Most people, whether supportive of their regime or not, have interests that might benefit from collective action and cooperation with others. Thus, whether in repressive regimes or not (but more likely in repressive ones), citizens may shift participation arenas away from national-system politics to engage in local, communal, and civil society activism. In a prescient comment on a series of studies on political participation in Latin America in the 1970s, when much of the region was gripped by dictatorships, anthropologist Richard Adams argued that citizens did not stop participating but merely shifted the arena of that participation away from the national level, where the costs of repression were high, to the local level, where they could "get away with it" (Adams 1979). Citizens at the local level can work with their neighbors and local officials, network, and engage in collective problem solving below the radar of a repressive regime.[6] Our inclusion of a local dimension of legitimacy allows us to provide a direct test of this theory. Citizens disgruntled about regime performance or actors may, of course, protest more than those who feel satisfied on those dimensions. But for citizens to go further and rebel against a regime seems likely to require that they view

---

[6] Civil society activism can, of course, provide a vehicle for challenging repressive regimes, but that is only one of its potential functions (Foley 1996; Booth and Richard 1998a; Booth and Richard 1998b; Edwards, Foley, and Diani 2001).

their regime not only as deeply unsatisfactory but also as so repressive as to obviate other less risky means of seeking redress of grievances (Humphreys and Weinstein 2008).

A final theoretical issue involves the distribution of legitimacy norms among the population. When most people share high institutional or regime legitimacy norms, we expect that most citizens would take advantage of within-institution channels (voting, contacting officials, party activism). Their behavior might thus reinforce the system's institutions. In contrast, as we noted in Chapter 1, a larger share of citizens discontented with the democratic regime or institutions could affect national participation levels, for example, by depressing overall voter turnout rates or shifting participation to alternate arenas. Not all such participation need threaten extant political institutions, however. Both civil society engagement and community improvement activism can be very salutary for political institutions. Of course, large proportions of regime principles-, performance-, or institutions-disaffected citizens could also protest, support antisystem parties, or even engage in confrontational participation. With a high ratio of activist and antidemocratic malcontents to system supporters, the likelihood of protest or rebellion might increase. The protests could also encourage antidemocratic elites to conspire against system stability on the assumption that they might enjoy mass backing in a moment of turmoil. In contrast, a polarized, bimodal distribution of legitimacy norms would increase the potential for conflict between large numbers of both activist system supporters and activist malcontents. Mobilization and increased political activism might occur among those on the extremes, increasing the likelihood of violent conflict between pro- and antisystem citizens. One suspects that the situations in Haiti prior to the ouster of President Aristide in 2004 and in Bolivia in mid-2005 may well have involved such a polarized distribution of legitimacy norms driving pro- and anti-incumbent conflict.

We now turn to empirical analysis to consider the implications of legitimacy's dimensions for democracies. Already having identified six dimensions of political support and learned that there are varying levels of each type within and between countries, in this chapter we build on this foundation to examine legitimacy's specific effects on political participation. Then in Chapters 6 and 7 we explore legitimacy's impact on both antisystem and confrontational political attitudes and on support for democracy as a system of governance. These analyses will allow us eventually to determine whether citizen activists in Latin America, in Huntingtonian terms, may be overloading young democracies with excessive demands through their participation and whether their attitudes may serve to reinforce or undermine democratic regimes.

THE MEASURES OF PARTICIPATION

We have developed several measures of political participation, which scholars long ago discovered to be multidimensional (Verba et al. 1971; Verba and Nie 1972; Booth and Seligson 1976; Booth and Seligson 1978a; Booth and Seligson 1978b). Norris's recent *Democratic Phoenix* (2002), a major exploration of citizen political activism, also treats participation as multidimensional. In order to identify and measure the empirical dimensions (usually referred to as modes) of participation in our eight countries, we employed exploratory factor analysis of 13 civic engagement items and identified four modes of political participation: registration to vote and voting, partisan-campaign activism, contacting public officials, and communal activism.[7] Multiple measures of participation in four different organizations also provided an index of civil society activism.[8] Finally, the survey included a single item on protest participation, a direct measure of unconventional political activity. We then developed indexes for each of these six items and converted them into a scale ranging from zero to 100.[9] These six measures are our dependent variables for the analysis: voting-registration, contacting public officials, partisanship-campaigning, contacting public officials, civil society activism, and protest (see Appendix Table B.1 for details on the participation indices.)

---

[7] Following Verba and Nie (Verba et al. 1971; Verba and Nie 1972), and our own earlier research in Latin America (Booth and Seligson 1978b; Seligson and Booth 1979c; Seligson and Booth 1979b), we used exploratory factor analysis to examine the fourteen participation items. We ran this analysis on the pooled sample and on the eight individual countries and found the same structure. Voting was composed of reporting having voted in the most recent presidential election and being registered to vote. Contacting consists of reporting having contacted a legislator, or a local official, or having petitioned the municipal government. Partisanship-campaigning consists of frequency of attendance at political party meetings, trying to persuade another person how to vote, and working on an election campaign. Communal activism consists of affirmative responses to five items concerning contributing to community problem solving activities. See exploratory factor analysis confirming these dimensions in Appendix Table B.2. To save space, we did not include the essentially identical runs for each of the eight countries.

[8] Civil society activism consists of frequency of attendance in four types of organizations: school related, church related, community improvement, or commercial, professional, or producers groups.

[9] The zero to 100 metric is used to give all six participation variables a common scale to eliminate mathematical unit effects that can distort analytical results and because it is helpful for comparison purposes between modes.

We model political participation using the following independent variables, all of which have been either theorized or demonstrated empirically to affect political participation (see Appendix Table B.3 for details on these items). First, of course, given the focus of this book, we include the six indices of legitimacy norms we have developed.

To this basic set of predictors we added a critical control variable as to whether the respondent voted for the winner in the most recent presidential election. As noted in Chapter 4, recent research by Anderson et al. (2005) show that votes for the winner (or loser) can affect legitimacy norms and potentially strengthen the willingness of winners to participate while lowering the likelihood that losers will become engaged in politics. In our preliminary research we found this vote-for-the-winner variable to be related to at least some legitimacy norms. Therefore, we will assume that this partisan orientation might confound the propensity of legitimacy to shape participation in politics and will therefore control for it.

Anticipating that some relationships between legitimacy and participation might be curvilinear, we also include the squared term of each legitimacy dimension used in our regression analysis. Adding these variables allows us to determine whether each dimension of legitimacy has a quadratic (or U-shaped) relationship with each mode of political participation.

Given the strong evidence from prior research that socioeconomic status shapes participation in many countries, we included a number of sociodemographic and local context variables that indicate a citizen's position in society and access to resources critical to political participation: sex, age (operationalized as age cohorts), religious affiliation (operationalized as dummies for Catholic, protestant, none, other), formal education (entered as dummies for none, primary, secondary, college, postgraduate), personal wealth (an index of ownership of household appliances and access to basic services), and the population size of the community within which one resides (again, operationalized as dummies for rural/small town and small, medium, large, and capital city).

Beyond this basic list of predictors, we expanded our search to include several attitudes and experiences that, according to theory and prior research, influence participation in politics. These include the respondent's level of contact with the news media, level of political information (basic knowledge), interpersonal trust, level of satisfaction with one's life, having been a victim of a crime or bribe solicitation by a public official in the past year, and whether one fears crime in one's own neighborhood.

We also developed for analysis a number of contextual variables indicative of important static and dynamic aspects of national political and economic life. To capture the absolute and shifting natures of regime performance, we employ both static and dynamic measures of performance at the system level in our analyses. A classic theory holds that at higher levels of macrolevel economic development citizens should participate more in politics (Lipset 1961), although recent evidence suggests that this theory may be incorrect (Booth and Seligson 2008; Bratton 2008; Krishna 2008). At the level of economic performance alone, we employ both gross domestic product (GDP) per capita in absolute terms and changes in GDP per capita over time. We also consider economic distribution in terms of income inequality. Economic success in terms of positive GDP performance, if not translated into the distribution of wealth, could affect citizens' resource levels and improve their capacity to take part in politics. In addition, we wanted to measure how broad social conditions such as macrolevel education and health conditions might enable participation. Finally, because higher levels of systemic democracy should also encourage and facilitate participation, we include measures of political rights and liberties, government effectiveness, the rule of law, political stability, and the long-term history of democracy.

As discussed in Chapter 4, there are three main difficulties inherent using contextual variables in regression analysis – collinearity among the measures, applying the proper statistical techniques, and dealing with static versus dynamic contextual effects. Again, we have decided to employ a set of both static and dynamic context measures that are not collinear (listed in Appendix Table C.1), to use hierarchical linear modeling (HLM) as the appropriate statistical technique, and to examine each of the context variables one at a time to determine which, if any, may produce a statistically significant impact on our six participation modes. Finally, in order to identify and control for the impact of national context on participation as needed in the analysis, we developed national dummy variables (coded 0 and 1) for each of the nations in our pooled sample.

ANALYSIS AND RESULTS: LEGITIMACY'S EFFECTS ON PARTICIPATION

As summarized above, we hypothesized, following the standard literature, that more approving citizens might be more involved in within-system participation modes while more disaffected citizens might be more likely to protest. We also anticipated that disgruntled citizens might actually engage more in some within-system modes but do so in arenas outside the central government's purview (local government, communal problem solving, and civil society). Finally, based on our own findings from our pilot test in Costa Rica, we expected that some relationships between legitimacy and participation might be U-shaped, with both the most supportive and the most disaffected citizens participating more intensely than the indifferent.

Our analysis began with a variable-by-variable effort to determine, using hierarchical linear modeling, the impact of each context variable on each mode of political participation in our sample controlled for all the other individual-level variables. This effort yielded not a single significant contextual effect. We cannot conclude from this exercise, however, that context does not matter at all. Rather, given the standard that we have set for finding significant context-level predictors, as well as our relatively small number of cases, we simply did not find any.[10] We therefore conduct the remainder of the analysis employing ordinary least squares (OLS) regression analysis on the individual (microlevel variables only).

Because one may not reasonably ignore national context in pooled-sample studies, however, in our OLS regression models we include dummies for seven countries, using Costa Rica, the longest-standing democracy, as the reference case. Our purpose in including these dummies is not to focus on context per se. Rather, we use these variables to allow us to test for the possibility that the individual-level effects that we find in the pooled eight-nation dataset might be misleading. For example, if we find a significant relationship between legitimacy and participation, the result could be a true finding or it could be spurious, an artifact of a highly unusual variation in the pooled dataset in one or more countries. In other words, we might find, for example, that countries with higher levels of legitimacy have higher participation scores, while the *within-country* relationship *at the individual level* could in fact be insignificant. By including the country dummy variables we can control for this possibility in each of our regressions and filter out possibly confounding national-level effects. This will ensure that the legitimacy-participation relationships we seek to understand are robust.

Multiple OLS regression analysis, including several demographic, attitudinal, and experiential variables as controls, produced the following main findings, summarized in Table 5.1. First, and most important, legitimacy affects each mode of political participation; hence, *legitimacy clearly does matter in shaping political behavior.* Second, not all forms

---

[10] Indeed, if we alternatively use OLS and do not consider the misspecification effects of using both individual-level variables and context variables in a single OLS equation, we do find several significant context effects. We do not discuss these, however, as the HLM modeling shows that these results may well be misleading.

TABLE 5.1. *Summary of significant legitimacy effects on political participation – OLS models*

Independent Variable	Vote/ Register	Party Campaigning	Contact Public Officials	Communal Activism	Civil Society	Protest Participation
Political community	2.155					
Political community squared						
Regime principles		−3.184				3.680
Regime principles squared		4.226				
Regime institutions		2.795	3.070			
Regimes institutions squared			−2.785			
Regime performance		−4.813		−3.443	−2.666	−2.649
Regime performance squared		5.375		3.639	2.779	2.674
Political actors		−4.214				
Political actors squared		3.342				
Local government		−6.426	−6.740	−2.251		
Local government squared		7.999	9.178	4.297		
Mexico dummy		−4.983			−2.893	
Guatemala dummy	−8.893	.023			8.269	
El Salvador dummy		−4.599			−5.024	−5.903
Honduras dummy			−5.347	3.264	9.966	−3.133
Nicaragua dummy	3.945				3.695	3.280
Panama dummy	−4.517	2.372	−4.274		−8.039	
Colombia dummy			−3.411		2.282	
Voted for presidential winner[a]		7.301	3.235	2.241	3.774	7.051
Women		−6.081	−2.978	−7.723	7.823	−3.968
Age 21–30	35.889	2.501	3.528	3.006	5.020	−2.212
Age 31–40	39.037	3.456	6.903	9.108	13.087	
Age 41–50	37.941	4.784	7.376	10.356	12.737	

(continued)

TABLE 5.1. (continued)

Independent Variable	Vote/Register	Party Campaigning	Contact Public Officials	Communal Activism	Civil Society	Protest Participation
Age 51–60	35.468	3.625	7.276	7.977	7.485	
Age 61–95	32.986		4.580	6.796	4.691	6.586
Catholic	3.119				-3.401	8.330
Protestant						
No religion					-10.269	
Primary education	2.563	2.168				
Secondary education	3.159	3.218	2.162	4.308		
College education	5.856	3.900	3.729	3.906		
Postgraduate education	3.775	3.226	3.724	5.244	2.159	
Wealth	2.421		-4.646		-4.471	
Media contact	6.281	10.479	7.506	11.265	12.860	6.507
Political information	7.928	4.472		2.896	2.551	4.304
Interpersonal trust	2.017	-3.271	-2.187	3.885	3.472	
Life satisfaction		-2.150		2.870	3.181	-2.216
Victim of crime in last year		4.904	7.686	6.311	4.944	5.055
Fear crime in neighborhood			3.558	4.104	2.863	2.756
Solicited for bribe in last year		5.469	7.406	4.686	4.654	3.526
Capital city resident	-4.975	-6.185	-8.101	-10.191	-7.445	1.489
Large city resident	-4.672	-4.635	-7.242	-8.659	-6.868	
Medium city resident	-2.297	-2.380	-3.720	-11.411	-9.440	
Small city resident			2.120	-4.443	-6.329	

Note: Coefficients are t-ratios from Appendix A Tables A.7–A.12; t-ratios of ≥2.0 are statistically significant. Cells shaded in gray indicate a significant curvilinear relationship.

[a] Excluded from this model because this is a component of the dependent variable.

of legitimacy have a significant impact on participation. Among the six legitimacy dimensions that we have identified in this research project, the perception of a political community affects participation the least, influencing only voting.[11] In contrast, citizens' evaluation of regime performance has the most significant impacts, affecting four of six modes of participation, followed by support for local government, a dimension not included in prior research, which affects three modes of participation.

Twenty-three of the legitimacy-participation relationships examined reveal significant effects (Table 5.1). As anticipated, not all legitimacy norms affect all types of participation. Most importantly, in a striking finding with only a few exceptions, the main pattern of relationship between legitimacy and participation (in 31 percent of the possible 36 relationships) is U-shaped – that is, *both the most supportive and the most disaffected citizens are more active* than citizens holding middling legitimacy norms. Conversely, only one of 36 possible links between legitimacy and participation – that for political community and voting-registration – is linear and positive. We emphasize that *this is the only legitimacy-participation relationship conforming to the conventional hypothesis received from the literature.*[12]

Our final main finding is that these legitimacy-participation relationships are robust to specific country effects and to numerous other possibly intervening or confounding variables. A few country dummies stand out to isolate particular deviations in behavior (e.g., very low voting and registration in Guatemala, very high civil society engagement in Honduras, and very high protest levels in Colombia). Yet despite the inclusion of country dummies so that we can control for spurious local effects, the legitimacy influences on participation remain clearly defined and statistically significant.[13] As we will argue below, these findings have important implications for legitimacy theory.

---

[11] Political community is the legitimacy dimension that we previously determined varied least (had the smallest standard deviation) among the respondents in all eight countries in our sample (Appendix A.6).

[12] For all the models summarized in Table 5.1 for which squared legitimacy terms proved significant, their inclusion improved the models' explained variance (R-square). We have left all the squared terms in all the models presented for the sake of comparability.

[13] We first ran these regression models without country dummies (not shown to conserve space). Very few meaningful changes in legitimacy-participation effects appeared when the country dummies were added, as shown here. This suggests that the findings of the regressions without the country dummies are accurate representations of the true relationship between individual characteristics and participation.

Voting and registration

Voting has been the form of political participation most analyzed in political science. As revealed in Table 5.1 and in the more detailed data presented in Appendix A (Tables A.7–A.11), all other factors held constant, legitimacy norms have little effect on voting-related behavior. The exception is that citizens who perceive a national political community register and vote more than those who do not.

Guatemalans and Panamanians register and vote significantly less than do Costa Ricans, our reference case, while Nicaraguans vote more. Slightly more Catholics vote than do those in our reference category (a religious preference other than Catholic, protestant, or none). Sex does not affect registration and voting. Dramatically more citizens in all the age cohorts older than the youngest register and vote. All the education cohorts above the least educated group vote more than that group, especially the college educated. Wealth very slightly increases registration and voting, as do higher levels of interpersonal trust. Greater contact with the news media and higher levels of political information increase registration and voting. Crime victimization, fear of crime in one's own neighborhood, and being solicited for a bribe do not affect citizens' propensity to register and vote (although they affect almost all the other forms of participation). Finally, compared to residents of rural areas and small towns, the larger the city citizens live in, the less likely they are to appear on the electoral register and to vote.

Partisan and campaign activism

This mode of participation is defined by taking part in the meetings of political parties, trying to persuade others how to vote, and working on an election campaign. These activities engage a citizen with the institutionalized challenges of a democratic polity and electoral competition. Thus, it does not surprise us to discover that legitimacy norms exercise a greater influence on partisan and campaign activism than any other participation mode. Table 5.1 (see also Appendix Table A.8) reveals that greater support for regime institutions makes a simple linear-positive contribution to more partisan-campaign activism. The more interesting finding here, however, is that support for regime principles, positive evaluation of regime economic performance, support for political actors, and support for local government each manifests a strongly curvilinear relationship with partisan-campaign activity. The relationships are U-shaped, as indicated by a strong positive association between the statistically significant squared function of each and as further indicated by the statistically significant negative t-ratio for the linear legitimacy term.

To illustrate, Figures 5.1–5.4 graph the U-shaped legitimacy-participation relationships (absent controls for the other variables in the model). In all four dimensions of legitimacy, more citizens among the most and least approving of the system or its performance take part in party-campaign activities than citizens in the midrange of approval. Table 5.1 reveals these patterns to be robust to controls for all the other variables in the model, including national context dummies. Thus, both *strong approval of government performance and strong disapproval* motivate citizens to participate in electoral competition. The stronger the legitimacy position, negative and positive alike, the greater is the participation. In our eight Latin American democracies, therefore, both supportive and disaffected citizens engage more in electoral competition and partisanship than do indifferent citizens.

This finding makes sense on its face, even though prior researchers almost always predicted only the linear form of the relationship. In 2004 each of our respondents – especially the opponents of the party in power – could by dint of the adoption and practice of formal electoral

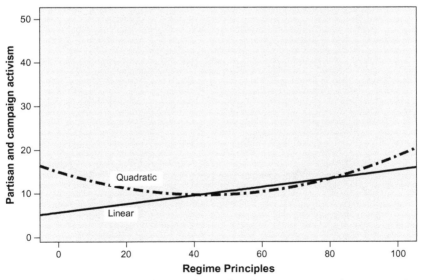

FIGURE 5.1. Linear and curvilinear relationships between support for regime principles and partisan and campaign activism

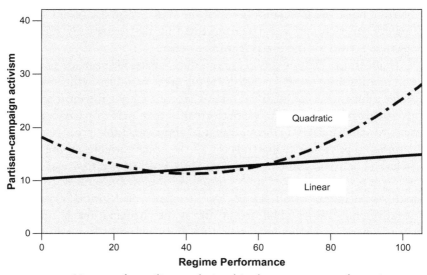

FIGURE 5.2. Linear and curvilinear relationships between support for regime performance and partisan and campaign activism

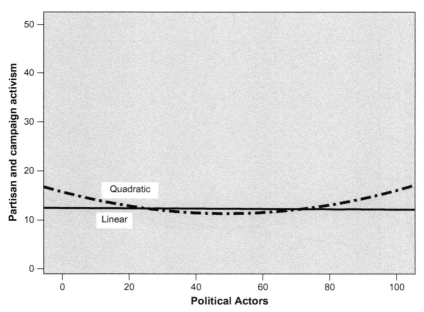

FIGURE 5.3. Linear and curvilinear relationships between support for political actors and partisan and campaign activism

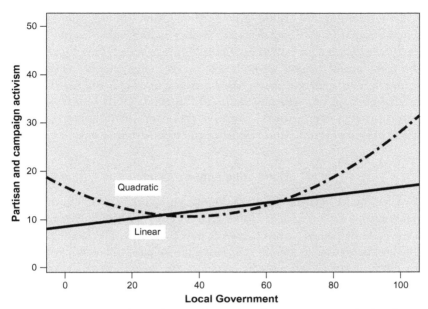

FIGURE 5.4. Linear and curvilinear relationships between support for local government and partisan and campaign activism

democracy freely engage in electoral efforts to unseat the government without falling victim to repression. While several of our countries were indeed flawed in their rights and liberties performance, all had embraced and encouraged electoral competition for power. The civil wars and repressive regimes that had wracked six of them in previous decades had ended. Even Colombia, with its long-lived civil war still under way, nevertheless allowed and indeed encouraged vigorous partisan and election campaign activism in hopes that insurgents might forego force and enter the legal political arena. In such political climates, citizens most frustrated by their government's performance in diverse areas and even those least committed to democratic regime principles should contend for political power through the electoral system rather than abandon it. Thus, in formal democracies with modest or little repression of participation (the condition of all of the nations in our sample), we find that disaffected citizens do not drop out of electoral contention (as the linear-positive hypothesis about participation suggests), but rather embrace it. This finding is consistent with that of Norris (2002) based on her empirical investigation of survey data from a wide variety of countries around the world.

Other findings in Table 5.1 merit mention. In our survey data, when compared to Costa Ricans, Mexicans and Salvadorans are less party-campaign active and Panamanians more active. Having voted for the presidential winner strongly encourages engagement, as do being a man, having media contact, being a victim of crime, and experiencing official corruption. Age and political information also increase party and campaign engagement. Negative influences include interpersonal trust, life satisfaction, and residence in larger urban areas.

Contacting public officials

Two legitimacy factors affect the contacting of public officials, and both relationships are curvilinear (Table 5.1). Support for local government has a strong U-shaped effect on contacting public officials. The fact that two of the three items used to measure the contacting of pubic officials involve local government actors undoubtedly enhances the strength of this relationship (see Figure 5.5). Those disgruntled about local government performance, even if not fighting city hall, at least contact and petition their local officials. Those who approve of local government also contact officials more.

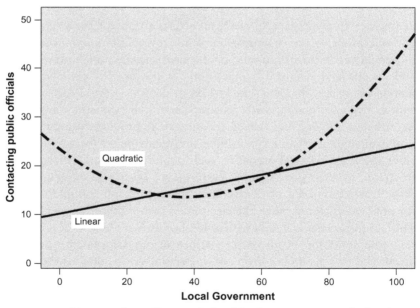

FIGURE 5.5. Linear and curvilinear relationships between support for local government and contacting public officials

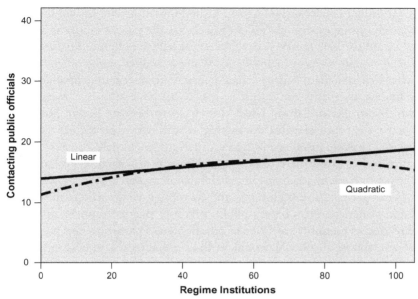

FIGURE 5.6. Linear and curvilinear relationships between support for regime institutions and contacting public officials

The unusual finding for contacting is that its curvilinear relationship with support for regime institutions (Figure 5.6) constitutes an *inverted* U. While this relationship is weak, it is significant, all other factors in the model accounted for. Those who are both most critical and most supportive of the institutions of national government tend to contact public officials the least while those in the indifferent middle contact government more. This inverted-U pattern is unique for our legitimacy-participation relationships. This may indicate clientelistic behavior – direct petitioning – that has fundamental differences from other participation modes. The pattern suggests to us that contacting local officeholders and legislators likely includes a fair amount of rent-seeking behavior in which citizens indifferent to national government performance seek to advance their personal interests by lobbying.

We examine first the influence of national and local contexts. Compared to the reference group of Costa Ricans, Hondurans, Panamanians, and Colombians contact officials significantly less. Compared to rural and small-town dwellers, our reference category, small-city residents contact officials more (probably due to the likely presence of municipal offices in such locales), while larger-city residents contact public officials sharply less.

Turning to microsocial factors, we find that older citizens contact more than the youngest cohort (no doubt because the younger citizens have yet to establish their families, develop a stake in the community, and build social capital, as have their elders). Women contact public officials somewhat less than men. More educated citizens contact public officials more, a finding that does not surprise us because education is a resource on which citizens can draw when they wish to become active politically. Media exposure elevates contacting, which we expected. In contrast, political information has no effect, other influences held constant, which surprised us given the importance political information levels have been shown to have in advanced industrial democracies.

Fear of crime and both crime and corruption victimization all mobilize Latin Americans to contact public officials. But we wonder about the direction of causality for bribe solicitation and contacting because the act of contacting an official would in itself enhance the opportunity to be solicited for a bribe. So we cannot be certain whether greater contacting takes place *because* individuals have been victimized by corruption, or whether contact with public officials makes them vulnerable to corruption.

Another finding of note is that wealth significantly *depresses* contacting public officials. Those who are poorer petition government more than those who are better off in our eight Latin American countries. Recall that we already have controlled for education, so this finding shows that citizens of the same level of education who are poorer are *more* likely to contact officials than richer citizens of that same level of education. We surmise this phenomenon arises from several sources. First, patron-client relationships abound in Latin American societies (Peeler 1998; Schneider 2007: 564), and they encourage the poor to seek resources from government. Cross-class patron-client relationships infuse parties and electoral organizations, so that officials often come into office linked to informal networks of poorer citizens by reciprocal expectations of payoffs for political support.[14] Second, some contacting involves seeking government expenditures for community improvement projects from which the

[14] This literature is vast, but see, for instance, Camp's (2007) bibliographic essay on clientelism, patronage, corporatism, and political recruitment in Mexico, and on other countries the multiple contributors to Mainwaring and Scully (1995), Mainwaring and Shugart (1997), and Wiarda and Kline (1996). Most observers concur that political patronship-clientelism have waned in recent decades in many countries and party systems, but also note that the rise of neopopulism in Latin America may be giving such cross-class relationships new life and new forms.

poor – disproportionately concentrated in infrastructure-poor smaller towns, rural areas, or poor urban districts – likely would need such support more than the wealthy. Indeed, as our research conducted in the 1970s showed, such demand making by the poor emerges out of needs that the richer elements of society simply do not have (Seligson and Booth 1979b). Moreover, wealthier citizens likely have intermediaries such as lobbyists and lawyers to contact officials for them, thus somewhat masking their involvement in this activity. Finally, countries that in our dataset demonstrate low levels of contacting (Honduras, Panama, and Colombia) likely have legislatures and municipalities that distribute fewer resources to petitioners than does the Asamblea Legislativa of the reference country Costa Rica, which has a strong pork-barrel tradition (Carey 1996; Booth 1998).

Communal activism

Citizens across Latin America – especially in poorer neighborhoods and rural hamlets – regularly engage in community improvement activities. They raise funds for and take part in building and keeping up town plazas and playing fields. These projects repair churches and schools, install public lighting, improve drainage, bridge creeks, and repair roads. They directly enhance their communities and the economic chances of their residents. Table 5.1 (and Appendix Table A.10) reveals that evaluation of regime performance and support for local government affect communal activism in the now-familiar U-shaped curvilinear pattern. So, once again, rather than dropping out of politics, those disgruntled with national economic performance and with local government instead direct their activism to the arena of their own communities and work to improve them. As expected, those satisfied with economic performance and local government also engage in community improvement (see Figure 5.7).

Hondurans, who live in one of the two poorest and most rural countries in our sample, engage in communal activism significantly more than do the citizens of the other countries. Rural and small-town residents are the most active communal improvers. Women are sharply less active than men in community improvement. Not surprisingly, people age 31 or older – those with the greatest economic and personal stake in their communities – are much more involved than the youngest voting-age residents. The more educated engage in more communal activism. Media contact elevates communal involvement sharply, as do crime victimization, corruption victimization, and fear of crime in one's own neighborhood. Interpersonal

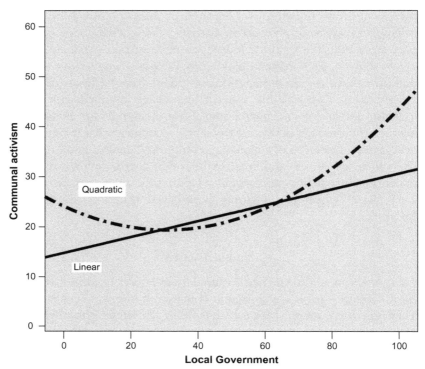

FIGURE 5.7. Linear and curvilinear relationships between support for local government and communal activism

trust and life satisfaction contribute to greater communal engagement (Uslaner and Brown 2005).

Civil society activism

Participation in organized groups constitutes our measure of civil society activism. We include in our index four kinds of associations: school, church-related, business-professional, and civic. Much of the interest in civil society and its connection to effective democracy has been sparked by Robert Putnam (Putnam 1993; Putnam 2002). Putnam's work has placed great emphasis on how civil society shapes social capital and cultural values, especially interpersonal trust. Putnam's work is, however, largely silent on the impact of legitimacy norms in explaining civil society. With a single exception, our research does not indicate that Putnam's exclusion of legitimacy as a predictor much weakened his arguments. Legitimacy norms have little effect on Latin Americans' engagement in civil society (Table 5.1 and

Appendix Table A.11) except for regime economic performance. For that type of legitimacy, we do find the familiar U-shaped curvilinear relationship that has emerged for other modes of participation. Here it is statistically significant but not strong. Those who are least satisfied with the government's economic performance and those who are most satisfied tend to participate in these organizations somewhat more intensely than do citizens indifferent about economic performance. The other dimensions of legitimacy (perception of a national community and support for regime principles, institutions, actors, and local government) do not affect civil society participation.

Other factors that stimulate engagement in civil society are the national and subnational contexts: Guatemalans, Hondurans, and Nicaraguans are more group involved than our Costa Rican reference group, while Salvadorans and Panamanians are sharply less so. Residents of small towns and rural areas take part in civil society far more than do residents of larger communities. Turning to demographic factors, being a Catholic or professing no religion reduces civil society activity despite the inclusion of church-related associations in the measure. Though less active in the communal improvement arena, women engage sharply more than do men in the groups we measure here. This makes sense because our index includes church- and school-related organizations that fall within the Latin American traditional sphere of women's responsibilities for child rearing and religious instruction. Other factors controlled, the poor engage more in the groups included in our measure than do their more prosperous neighbors.

Media contact and political knowledge associate with greater group activity. Persons who are more trusting and more life satisfied engage more in organizations. Finally, being a crime or corruption victim and fearing crime mobilize citizens to take part in organizations, probably in part seeking ways to manage or overcome these problems.

Protest participation

Many scholars regard taking part in protests as unconventional or outside-the-system political behavior. They conceive of protests as a challenge to governments and thus as the resort mainly of those alienated from the political system.[15] Following such logic, citizens with low legitimacy values would engage more in unconventional or protest – a simple linear-positive relationship between low political support and protest (e.g., Foley

---

[15] Indeed, in our early research on political participation, we referred to such actions as "unconventional" (Booth and Seligson 1979; Seligson 1979).

1996; Norris 1999a; Canache 2002; Booth 1991; Booth et al., 2006). Yet we find in our survey that, rather than correlating negatively with other forms of within-system participation such as voting, registration, contacting, and campaign activism, protest participation associates positively and significantly with these activities (Pearson's r = .21 with partisan-campaign activity, .18 with contacting, and .10 with registration-voting). This strongly suggests that, within these formally democratic Latin American countries, protesting constitutes not a regime-challenging activity but simply another tool that citizens employ to communicate with government.[16] This finding tempers the advice of Huntington (1968), whose perspective was taken as a warning for policy makers who might think of allowing such protests.

How, then, do legitimacy norms affect protest involvement?[17] Only two have significant effects (see Table 5.1, Figures 5.8 and 5.9, and Appendix Table A.12). First, both those who are more and those who are less committed to democratic regime principles protest more. This initially surprised us because it sharply deviates from a major prediction of the legitimacy literature. Virtually all prior studies have tested only a linear relationship and focused on the low-legitimacy respondents.[18] The second legitimacy dimension affecting protest behavior is the evaluation of regime economic performance, and again the relationship is U-shaped (Figure 5.9). Citizens who are both most dissatisfied and most satisfied with regime economic performance are more likely than the indifferent to protest.[19]

---

[16] Note that we are not claiming that all protest behavior is of this nature. Protest activities in Bolivia in the period 2000–05, for example, may well have been directed toward regime change.

[17] We also modeled this relationship using multinomial logistic regression (not shown to conserve space) because the dependent variable is ordered and has three response values: no protest, protest rarely, or protest a few times. Using no protest as the reference category we find that all but one of the significant predictors from OLS are also significant for the most frequent protestors. The exception is the relationship for regime principles. This essentially confirms the findings of the OLS regression, which we have included here for the sake of parallel presentation style and ease of interpretation.

[18] In his research on aggressive political participation in Germany, Muller (1979) found what he termed a "corner correlation" as depicted by the Gamma correlation coefficient. He focused on the respondents with extremely low system support and actual participation in violent political acts.

[19] Note that in Figure 5.9 the linear relationship plotted appears flat, indicating no influence of economic performance legitimacy with protest. Recall, however, that the illustration in Figure 5.9 represents the simple relationship between the two variables uncorrected for the other variables in the regression model. The t-ratio for the economic performance–protest relationship is −2.649 (Appendix Table A.12), indicating that with other variables accounted for the relationship is significant and negatively sloped.

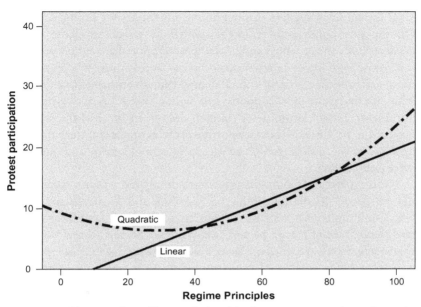

FIGURE 5.8. Linear and curvilinear relationships between support for regime principles and protest participation

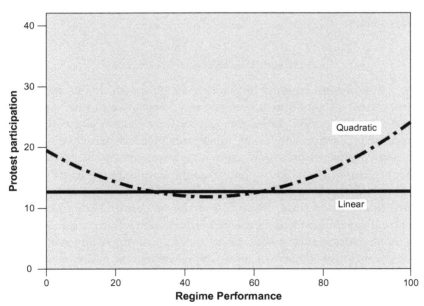

FIGURE 5.9. Linear and curvilinear relationships between support for regime performance and protest participation

These findings suggest countervailing potentials for political protest. On the one hand, protest might contribute to destabilizing conflict because both those who express the least support for regime principles (i.e., those with lower democratic norms) as well as those who express the most are prone to protest and challenge the government. On the other hand, we find those most supportive of regimes also more actively engaged in protesting. Such protests, of course, could be in favor of the regime or opposed to it. While regime-supportive protests might counterbalance the protests of the disaffected citizens, it also would set up a situation for increased conflict.

Nicaraguans and Colombians protest notably more than Costa Ricans, our reference population, while Salvadorans and Guatemalans protest less. Community size, religious affiliation, age, wealth, and interpersonal trust have little effect on protest involvement. Protest, therefore, rather than being merely a tool of the weak and the resource of the poor, pervades a broad array of social and demographic strata in our eight Latin American nations. Women and those expressing higher levels of life satisfaction protest less than men and the dissatisfied. Having college or postgraduate education elevates protest involvement, as do greater media contact and political knowledge. Logically, having voted for the government in power reduces protesting – after all, why demonstrate against a government one helped elect?

DISCUSSION AND CONCLUSIONS

The relationships explored in this chapter have provided us with some noteworthy insights into how legitimacy shapes six distinct modes of political participation. To summarize, we have found that, while all six types of legitimacy have some impact on political participation, their respective influence on citizen action is far from uniform. We have learned that perception of a national political community and support for political actors had the least influence on participation among the legitimacy dimensions. In contrast, evaluation of regime performance and support for local government had the greatest effects, each influencing at least half of the six participation modes. Legitimacy in its multiple dimensions does not always affect all forms of citizen engagement in the polity, nevertheless we have shown clearly that *legitimacy does matter for political participation*. This finding provides a first step toward addressing the puzzle of legitimacy's effects by linking system support to several forms of citizen engagement in the political arena.

The above findings make manifest that, consistent with the entire thrust of this book, *legitimacy must be studied as a multidimensional phenomenon* if we are to understand its importance properly. So much of the prior research has relied on a single support measure, and often only a single questionnaire item, to capture what we have shown in prior chapters to be complex and multidimensional. Thus, when some prior works have concluded that "legitimacy doesn't matter," we strongly suspect that part of the problem was that these studies did not understand or respect the multidimensional nature of the phenomenon.

Our findings go beyond proof that legitimacy does matter or, to be more precise, that some dimensions of legitimacy matter. We have also overturned key elements of the conventional wisdom as to the nature of the relationship between legitimacy norms and political participation. Our most striking finding is that, other factors in the models including national context held constant, 10 of the 13 significant legitimacy-participation effects proved to be not linear (negative or positive), as is widely hypothesized by the literature, but instead U-shaped. In twelve of them, *the most supportive and the most disaffected citizens engage in politics much more than those who are indifferent*. This discovery, we argue, has important implications for the theory on legitimacy's effects because it calls into question the three main hypotheses from the literature. First, it refutes the thesis that legitimacy is irrelevant for political behavior. Second, our data and analysis contradict the received wisdom that critical (low-legitimacy) citizens will not engage in politics, while the supportive (with high legitimacy values) will be more active. Here we have shown that the high-legitimacy part of the prediction is true, but that the political passivity prediction for disgruntled citizens is not true. Indeed, for citizens expressing low legitimacy norms, the opposite of the predicted happens – disaffected citizens become more rather than less involved in politics. This not only holds for participation within the channels of the national institutions – contacting officials, parties, and campaigns – but also prevails in other political arenas outside national channels – communal activism, civil society, and protest. Norris (2002: 223), writing of industrial democracies, uses a phrase apropos for our findings as well: "traditional electoral agencies linking citizens and the state are far from dead. And, like the phoenix, the reinvention of civic activism allows political energies to flow through diverse alternative avenues as well as conventional channels."

We find this conclusion important for our eight countries because these are cases in which citizen participation, especially protest participation, has been critically important in past insurrections and civil wars when these nations were not democracies (Booth et al. 2006). Yet, our findings, based on data from 2004 when each of our eight nations was formally democratic, demonstrate that even very high levels of alienation (expressed as extremely low scores on various legitimacy norms) produce *more* rather than less conventional participation. This contrast over time and political context suggests something important about our general notions of political participation. Modern social science still labors in the shadow of the early giants, and in the case of political participation, Durkheim's notions of political alienation still hold powerful sway (Durkheim and Bradbury 1947; Durkheim 1951). Durkheim argued that alienated individuals can become "anomic" and withdraw from politics. Such ideas undoubtedly shaped the widely held expectation we have cited so many times that low legitimacy could undermine industrial democracies. Yet here in several Latin American democracies, which arguably perform much worse than do richer and better established democracies, we find disaffected citizens actively engaged in multiple arenas, not merely protesting but participating in both formal political channels and civil society. The first inclination of the frustrated citizen of a democracy, we conclude, *is not anomie and passivity*, but *engagement*. Even in deeply flawed sociopolitical systems, democracy does what it is supposed to do – it allows the critical citizen to reach out to the government and others through multifaceted participation.

Recall that citizens in our nations were not rejecting democratic regime principles (support for these norms was strong in 2004), but they were critical of their political actors, institutions, local government, and national economic performance. Except for Costa Rica, these are fairly young democracies. While most citizens appeared to be patient in 2004, their patience may not be open ended. Persistent poor performance and resulting low legitimacy in a democratic setting may, of course, eventually nurture levels of disgruntlement that could provoke withdrawal from politics and perhaps even hostility toward democracy. Our data, however, do not at this juncture reveal a popular withdrawal from engagement in the diverse participation arenas available in Latin America. In the next chapters we will turn to the questions of how low legitimacy norms affect political attitudes and whether they might nurture antidemocratic sentiments or confrontational political attitudes.

The second major hypothesis undermined by our findings is that citizens expressing low legitimacy norms will be more prone to protest while those of high support will protest less. Here again we have shown that legitimacy's effect on protest is similar to its effect on other participation modes (with which, it should be recalled, protest is positively correlated). Protest, contrary to widely held expectations, occurs at high levels not only among critics of regime economic performance but also among its supporters. Finally, while we do identify two linear positive effects of legitimacy (political community on voting and regime institutions on partisan-campaign activity), by far the predominant pattern is that of high participation by politically engaged regime supporters and critics, rather than engaged supporters and disengaged critics.

The general lack of confirmation of the linear hypotheses, negative and positive, combined with the predominance of U-shaped influences of legitimacy on participation, provides another possible clue to the puzzle of legitimacy's effects. To the extent that our findings may be generalized to other countries, such as the industrialized democracies where much of the previous legitimacy research has been done, we speculate that the heretofore mystifying absence of detectable effects from declining support for institutions in such countries may be explained by the possibility that legitimacy has simply not fallen very low in such countries. As we will show in a later chapter, our Latin American countries manifest relatively lower legitimacy levels, at least where comparable measures are available. Thus legitimacy levels in high-performing industrial democracies simply may not in fact have fallen low enough to have revealed the U-shaped upturn in participation among the more extreme regime critics.

In democracies, those who are unhappy with their governments' performance are free to take part in politics with little fear of repression.[20] What we see among the critical Latin American citizens of our surveys reveals that, rather than withdrawing from participation or turning to protest, disaffected citizens participate and do so within national institutions and other salient arenas such as their communities and civil society. Thus, we surmise that, were legitimacy levels to fall low enough, the disgruntled citizens of industrial democracies might – like our Latin Americans – become more engaged in politics and/or shift the arenas of their activism to areas not studied by previous researchers. While they may also protest more, they may take part more in within-channel and nonconfrontational electoral competition, demand making, collective problem solving, and organizational activities.

---

[20] We of course recall campus shootings at Kent State and Jackson State universities and other instances of repression in the United States, and that is why we say little fear rather than no fear.

Such political activities by disaffected citizens do not necessarily threaten democratic stability. For these Latin American countries, at least at the time we surveyed them, we have found no evidence that the politically disgruntled undermine democratic institutions by their participation. Rather than disrupt the democratic political game or withdraw to the sidelines, the politically discontent remain in the game and in fact play harder to advance their goals. Some may engage in rent-seeking contacting activities, true, but others embrace electoral competition and party activity. Some find alternative arenas for participation and there contribute to community improvement and civil society. While disaffected citizens protest more than the indifferent, highly supportive citizens also protest and may thus provide a counterbalance of institutional support. Under such circumstances, protest behavior becomes another means for citizens to converse with the state and, because it comes from both critics and supporters, seems unlikely to undermine institutions. In sum, the heightened political engagement of the critical citizenry could affirm and strengthen political institutions rather than undermine them.

It is certainly true that within decades before our study political participation by some citizens of Nicaragua, Guatemala, El Salvador, Colombia, and even Honduras took on a violent and antiregime nature. But neither at the birth of their insurgencies nor during much of their worst political turmoil were any of these countries democracies. Indeed, in all cases but Colombia (and even there to some extent), the transition to a democratic regime and reduced political repression created an environment that eventually allowed or even encouraged broader participation. Most formerly rebellious citizens appear to have become more supportive of their evolved (newly democratic) regimes, abandoned rebellion, and embraced other modes of participation. It may, therefore, require extremely poor performance by a democratic government to create enough discontent to spawn rebellion.

Our tentative answer to the legitimacy effects puzzle (the question of why declining legitimacy has not destabilized democracies everywhere), based on what we have found so far, is that the disaffected citizens of democratic regimes usually do not withdraw from within-system politics or turn mainly to confrontational methods. Even though institutional support has declined in many democracies, fears that the sky would fall in democratic regimes or that protest and confrontation might overwhelm governments seem overblown. Indeed, we have found considerable evidence in our Latin American democracies (some of them very young and still rather turbulent) that those who have low regard for aspects of their political systems tend not to withdraw from politics within institutions. They are just about as likely as supportive citizens to become more politically active both within national institutional channels and in alternative arenas. Protesters are as likely to be system supporters as critics.

How can we account for the failure of most prior research to detect such a distinctive phenomenon? One answer may be that these legitimacy-participation effects occur only in Latin America, and therefore our research would suffer from what is called an "external validity" problem.[21] We doubt this, at least in part because to argue that a highly disgruntled citizen in any democracy might seek to improve his or her polity by becoming politically involved just makes good sense on its face. Why, one must ask, would reasonable citizens of a democracy who are frustrated with the actions of their government's president *not* work within the electoral arena to replace that incumbent? And further, why would individuals unhappy about economic performance not campaign against the incumbent, not strive to improve their own community infrastructure, or not join organizations to promote their own interests? These are reasonable choices for political action in democratic regimes. For these reasons, we believe that the failure of prior research to uncover the curvilinear patterns found here is a result of the simple failure to have anticipated them and tested for them.

We further believe that the failure to detect these patterns has occurred because much prior research focused fairly narrowly on support for institutions rather than on the broader multidimensional conception of legitimacy we have been able to employ. In well-established democracies, citizens' institutional support norms tend strongly toward the positive end of the support scale. In such skewed distributions, there would be relatively few disaffected citizens and thus scant evidence of how disgruntled citizens might actually conduct themselves. In our Latin American nations, in contrast, and over multiple dimensions of legitimacy, political support manifests more diverse distributions. Some of these legitimacy means even fall on the disapproving end of the legitimacy scales (Appendix Table A.6). This gave us an opportunity, not often available to previous researchers, to examine larger numbers of disaffected citizens and to consider them in more detail.

Finally, our findings also suggest that widely held assumptions about how disgruntled citizens might take part in politics have suffered from two

---

[21] An external validity problem occurs when a finding of a specific analysis derives from characteristics unique to the setting of the research or the particular dataset rather than being generalizable to all settings.

debilitating flaws. Treatments of participation and legitimacy that were too narrowly focused probably obscured the rich array of possible legitimacy-participation relationships. Skewed distributions of legitimacy in industrialized democracies may have obscured how disaffected citizens might participate in politics. Our study has overcome each of these problems and revealed a more nuanced picture of how political support shapes citizen action in democracies. Citizens may be critical of their systems, but that does not make them much more likely than their supportive fellow citizens to exit the political arena or attack the system. In fact, in democracies, the political engagement of disgruntled citizens may just as likely strengthen democratic institutions as threaten them. In the next chapter, we turn to the darker side of the equation, looking at what we call negative political capital.

6

Legitimacy and Negative Political Capital

We began this book by citing scholarship demonstrating that the United States and other established democracies have experienced a marked decline of the legitimacy of democratic institutions in recent decades. Many have asserted that low levels of key components of legitimacy (especially trust in institutions) would necessarily undermine or weaken democratic regimes. Yet, we also noted that very few democracies have failed despite low (and declining) legitimacy. We have identified this disjuncture between expected system-level consequences and low levels of legitimacy as part of the *legitimacy effects puzzle*. Why do predictions from such an important theory fall so wide of their mark?

In Chapter 5 we sought answers to the effects puzzle at the microlevel by exploring how legitimacy affects political participation. Treating participation as a form of political capital linking citizens to regimes by conveying demands and preferences, we encountered a pattern quite contrary to expectations from the literature. Disaffected citizens of our eight Latin American democracies do not drop out of conventional, within-system forms of participation but instead participate more than those of middling legitimacy levels and rather similarly to the most-supportive citizens. This gave us a partial answer to the effects puzzle: Democracies may not break down when legitimacy declines because most disaffected citizens do not disengage from within-system participation or attack the system. Rather, most disgruntled citizens engage the political system in diverse ways. Most such participation poses no threat to the institutional order and may actually reinforce or take pressure off

national institutions. Indeed, even for protest, both critical and supportive citizens in our sample engage in higher levels than those who hold
middling legitimacy norms.

But aspects of political capital other than participation also contribute
to regime stability. Citizens' attitudes also constitute a central aspect of
political capital related to democracy (Booth and Richard 1996; Booth
and Richard 1998b; Hetherington 2005). Diamond (1999) contends that
citizens' attitudes of support for democracy are central to the consolidation of democratic regimes and develop directly from their evaluations of
government performance. Norris (1999a) and Dalton (2004: 165–77) link
the perceived legitimacy of government to citizens' willingness to comply
with the law and their democratic norms. Indeed, much of the prior
research putatively linking legitimacy to protest participation did not
actually measure respondent participation at all, but measured *attitudes*
supportive of rebellion, protest, and political confrontation (Barnes and
Kaase 1979; Muller 1979; Thomassen 1989; Montero and Torcal 1990;
Morlino and Montero 1995; Dalton 1996; Linz and Stepan 1996; Rose,
Mishler, and Haerpfer 1998; Canache 2002).[1] The central hypothesis of
this literature is that citizens with low legitimacy norms will be more likely
to manifest negative political capital. They will be more likely to support
or endorse protest behavior, confrontational political tactics, and rebellion, and will be more likely to take the law into their own hands.[2] It
follows from this thesis that the greater the proportion of citizens holding
such attitudes, the more risk there will be for the survival of democracy. In
this chapter we put that speculation to a more rigorous test than has been
attempted to date.

MEASURING NEGATIVE POLITICAL CAPITAL

For the purposes of this chapter, we have developed four measures of
negative political capital. We structured them around a series of attitudes organized progressively from the most extreme forms of negative
political capital to attitudes that are milder yet still involve endorsing

---

[1] See the excellent discussions of the extensive literature and empirical findings on the
expected negative relationship between legitimacy norms and antidemocratic attitudes
and support for rebellion and confrontational political methods in Chapter 5 of Diamond
(1999) and Chapter 6 of Canache (2002).
[2] In the U.S. case Hetherington (1998, 2005) sees a decline in support for the incumbents
rather than mass protest as the outcome.

behaviors beyond within-system legal and political channels. In each case we focus on approval or disapproval of the behavior but do not measure the behavior itself (Chapter 5 examined protest). We focus only on attitudes here because we expected that in many of our countries, these extreme behaviors would be quite rare. Furthermore, such behaviors often are subject to social opprobrium, so we expected evasive and thus distorted answers had we asked the respondents to admit engaging in such behaviors themselves.

The first question, the most extreme, asks: "To what degree would you approve or disapprove [on a 10-point scale] that people participate in a group that wants to overthrow an elected government using violent means." Because this behavior involves violence and the abrogation of the principle of majority rule (the prompt calls for the overthrow of an *elected* government), it is the one item in the series that clearly taps into unequivocal hostility toward a democratically elected regime. Empirically, what our survey found is that approval of this form of behavior was not common. On the 1–10 scale, the mean for the eight-country sample was 2.5, with 58 percent of the respondents interviewed giving a reply of 1, that is, strongly disapprove. Moreover, 81.1 percent scored themselves below 5 (on the disapproving end of the continuum). Only 3.7 percent of the respondents scored themselves at 10 (strongly approve) on this item. Nonresponse was only 3 percent of the sample, leaving us 11,637 of 12,000 cases for the analysis. For purposes of comparability in subsequent analysis, we have converted this into a 0–100 scale (for details on this and other variables in the analysis, see Appendix Table B.3).

Our second item relates to the first in terms of content but provides for a much more mitigated justification for regime overthrow. It comes from a series of six questions:

Some people say that under certain circumstances the military would be justified in taking power via a coup d'etat [*golpe de estado* in the questionnaire]. In your opinion, would you justify a coup by the military:

1. in the face of very high unemployment?
2. in the face of a lot of social protest?
3. in the face of high crime?
4. in the face of high inflation, with excessive price increases?
5. in the face of a lot of corruption?
6. Do you think that at any time there could be sufficient reason for a coup, or do you think that there could never be sufficient reason for that?

This series of six questions produced many respondents willing to justify a coup. This might seem surprising in democracies, but given Latin America's long tradition of military coups, these results did not seem particularly remarkable. However, in the past most coups were justified on the basis of the need to provide social order in light of student or labor protests and unrest. Today, however, such factors seem far less important to citizens of the region than crime and corruption, two variables we have included as predictors throughout this book. For the pooled sample, the least common justification for a coup was social protests. In this case, 24.6 percent of the respondents justified it (with 8.8 percent missing). Nearly identical results were found for coups justified by high unemployment (25.0 percent, with 8.3 percent missing). Inflation and crime elicited more coup approval, 32.1 percent and 39.0 percent justifying it, respectively (7.9 percent missing). The highest level of justification of a coup was under conditions of high levels of corruption (41.9 percent, with 12.5 percent missing). The last question, the one framed in general terms and prompting respondents to think hypothetically about whether there might sometime be a reason for a coup, found 43.8 percent agreeing, with 10.9 percent missing. In order to tap the wide variation in these questions, we created an overall index in which each time a respondent said that a coup could be justified she received a score of 1, and each time that she rejected the idea, she was scored 0. We recalibrated the entire scale on a 0–100 basis to correspond to the 0–100 format used throughout this book. The mean score was 30.8.[3]

The third measure of negative political capital we call confrontational politics. The measure focuses on typical forms of civil disobedience found in the countries in our sample. It is comprised of three items in which respondents are once again asked to express their approval or disapproval, on a 1–10 scale, of a series of actions. The questions are

To what degree do you approve or disapprove

1. of people taking over factories, offices, and other buildings?
2. of people invading private property or land?
3. of people participating in a blockage of streets and highways?

---

[3] The computing formula recoded each response as 0 or 100, and then the six items were summed and a mean was taken and divided by six to produce a 0–100 scale. Respondents who did not give an answer to any of the six items were coded as missing. See Appendix Table B.3 for details on index construction and distribution.

Support for these three forms of civil disobedience was uniformly low on the 10-point scale. The lowest approval was for the item measuring support/opposition for invading private property. Slightly greater support was shown for takeovers of factories, offices, and other buildings. Respondents gave their greatest support, still well in the low end of the continuum, to blocking roads and highways. In the pooled sample, 86.3 percent of the valid respondents placed themselves in the negative range (i.e., scale score of 4 or lower) opposing the invasion of property item, with 59.5 percent of respondents registering the least possible approval. Only 1.8 percent gave the most positive response, and just 2 percent did not respond. Concerning attitudes toward taking over factories or other properties, 82.9 percent of the valid responses registered opposition. Some 55.0 percent scored at the extreme low end, and 2.8 percent at the extreme high end, with 2.6 percent registering no opinion. Finally, on the item measuring support for blocking streets and highways, 67.5 percent opposed, with 40.9 percent on the extreme negative end, 7.6 percent on the extreme positive end, and 2.0 percent offerning no opinion. For further analysis, we created an overall index of these three items using the same 0–100 transformation employed for the support for coup items.

The final measure of negative political capital evokes an increasingly popular form of activism in Latin America, namely, vigilantism. Citizens have been taking justice into their own hands in a number of countries. In Guatemala, lynching (*linchamiento*) is used to punish reputed criminals and has reached epidemic proportions (Seligson and Azpuru 2001; Sanford 2003; Seligson 2005a). Some participants in this form of direct action argue that since the state system of justice leaves the guilty unpunished, citizens should take action. Others view these lynchings as ways of settling personal grudges, often linked to romantic affairs, and having little to do with justice. To measure support for this form of citizen action, we used a single item, using the same 10-point approve/disapprove scale utilized in the other items in this section: "To what degree do you approve or disapprove (1–10) that people take justice into their own hands when the state does not punish criminals?"

On this item, in our pooled sample, 63.8 percent of the nonmissing respondents disapproved of vigilante actions, with 42.4 percent scoring at the lowest end (score of 1). However, 10.9 percent of respondents gave the strongest approval score (score of 10). Only 2.7 percent was missing (see Appendix Table B.3).

ANALYSIS AND RESULTS

Willingness to accept the violent overthrow of an elected government

What is the level of agreement with the proposition that it is acceptable to take part in a group using armed force to overthrow an elected regime? This is probably the most dramatic act a citizen would contemplate against his/her political system, one fraught with risks for rebelling participants and, of course, their targets. On a 0–100 scale, our pooled sample respondents averaged 17.1, so the overall support is quite low. Figure 6.1 reveals a range among countries from a low for Costa Rica of 8.4 to a high for Honduras of 24.0. Yet the value is greater than zero – about one-sixth of our respondents were willing to approve such action.

The literature leads us to expect a linear, negative relationship between higher legitimacy and citizens' support for the idea of an armed overthrow of an elected government. Table 6.1 presents a regression model for this variable incorporating indicators of citizens' legitimacy norms as well as familiar measures for their demographic/socioeconomic

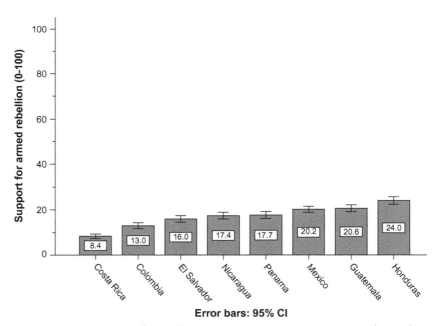

FIGURE 6.1. Approve of participation in a group using arms to overthrow the government

TABLE 6.1. *Predictors of willingness to accept the armed overthrow of an elected government (trimmed model) – OLS regression results*

Independent Variables[a]	t	Sig.
Constant	18.628	.000
Political community	−12.264	.000
Regime performance	−2.268	.023
Political actors	−3.380	.001
Local government	2.750	.006
Voted for presidential winner	−1.562	.118
Women	−3.095	.002
Age 21–30	−2.719	.007
Age 31–40	−6.243	.000
Age 41–50	−6.615	.000
Age 51–60	−6.626	.000
Age 61–95	−8.096	.000
Catholic	1.805	.071
Protestant	.745	.456
No religion	1.522	.128
Primary education	−1.740	.082
Secondary education	−2.808	.005
College	−2.658	.008
Postgraduate	−4.422	.000
Wealth	−2.341	.019
Media contact	1.171	.242
Political information	−6.354	.000
Interpersonal trust	−3.080	.002
Life satisfaction, low to high	−2.478	.013
Victim of crime in last year?	.971	.332
Fear crime in one's neighborhood?	.945	.345
Solicited for bribe in last year?	3.910	.000
Capital city resident	2.693	.007
Large city resident	2.321	.020
Medium city resident	1.303	.193
Small city resident	.498	.619
Mexico	5.336	.000
Guatemala	5.720	.000
El Salvador	4.151	.000
Honduras	9.350	.000
Nicaragua	1.412	.158
Panama	6.301	.000
Colombia	.734	.463

[a] R-square = .072; Model S.E. = 2.373; F = 23.149; model sig. = .0001
t-ratio significant at .05 or less are indicated in **boldface** type.

traits, and contextual and experiential variables.[4] Prior hierarchical linear modeling revealed that none of the system-level variables significantly affected citizens' support for armed overthrow of government, so we report ordinary least squares regression analysis and include national fixed effects to control for fixed national effects. Table 6.1 indicates that the greater one's sense of political community, evaluation of regime performance, and evaluation of political actors, the lower will be his tolerance for violent overthrow of an elected government. The effect is especially strong for perceiving a national political community (t-ratio of −12.3). The finding that runs counter to expectation involves support for local government, which has a weakly positive relationship for support for armed rebellion against an elected government. This finding surprised us, but given the low t-ratio we do not attribute great importance to it. Since the understanding of local government legitimacy remains uncharted terrain, giving meaning to these results will need to be the focus of future research.

Women, older citizens, those better off, and the more politically informed, trusting, and life-satisfied disapprove more of violent rebellion against an elected regime than do men, the poor, the politically less well informed, and those who are less trusting and satisfied with life. Once again we see that education has a marked effect, in this case likely contributing to political stability in the form of disapproval of violent rebellion. Compared to the reference country of Costa Rica, residents of five of the seven other countries are markedly more tolerant of the idea of armed rebellion (t-ratio between 4.0 and 7.0).

Those more inclined to embrace the idea of armed rebellion against an elected government include corruption victims and residents of larger cities and national capitals. As noted elsewhere, there is a widely held notion that rural residents seethe with revolutionary potential in Latin America. This image emerged at the time of the Cuban Revolution because Castro's rebel forces began their activities in remote mountain areas of the Sierra Maestra. The efforts by Ernesto "Ché" Guevara to stir revolution using his *foco* theory of insurgency also helped fuel the notion that

---

[4] The analysis summarized in Table 6.1 is an ordinary least squares regression model, trimmed to exclude two legitimacy norms (regime principles and regime institutions) found not to have a significant zero-order bivariate correlation with the dependent variable. These items were deleted to simplify analysis and interpretation. The reader should also note that the items in this and all subsequent regression models in this chapter were screened to assure that there were no collinear variables included.

the countryside was potentially a hotbed of radicalism, and the strategy spread to other nations (Wickham-Crowley 1992). Our empirical finding in this chapter, however, combines with what we have already learned in prior chapters to debunk that idea. Chapter 4 showed that rural and small-town residents tend to have higher legitimacy norms than do urban dwellers. Chapter 5 demonstrated that rural dwellers participate more in politics (except in protest) than urbanites. These findings empirically validate arguments by Mason (2004) and others (Scott 1976; Popkin 1979; Scott 1985; Stoll 1993) that peasants are difficult to mobilize into revolutionary movements. The findings further suggest that, in these eight countries, at least, and controlling for other factors, rural folk are not exceptionally aggrieved and indeed are more supportive and more positively engaged than their urban counterparts.

Although respondents report low levels of support for armed rebellion across all eight countries, Figure 6.1 indicates that Honduras, Mexico, and Guatemala have the highest levels of support for armed rebellion. Table 6.1 reveals that, other factors held constant, the country whose citizens have the greatest disposition to support an armed rebellion (highest t-ratio), compared to the reference case of Costa Rica, is Honduras. Colombians and Nicaraguans are not significantly higher than Costa Ricans in their aversion to armed rebellion.

Support for a coup d'etat

How much are respondents willing to justify a coup? Figure 6.2 compares levels of support for coups under certain circumstances (e.g., excessive crime, corruption) for the pooled sample. There we see that between 31 percent (for excessive social protests) and 52 percent (for high levels of corruption) say they might approve of a coup d'etat. While this may seem quite high to some readers, Latin America has a long tradition of military coups that has abated only in recent years. Moreover, we suspect that many of our respondents are likely to recall circumstances of great turmoil (unrest, hyperinflation) in recent decades. Times like those, which have afflicted all of our countries in recent decades, could place a prospective coup in a positive light for some respondents on the expectation that it would restore economic or political order or curtail inflation or crime. Social and political conditions in extremis, not at all unfamiliar in Latin America, could lead some citizens to imagine a military overthrow of the incumbent government as an acceptable way to restore order. Figure 6.3 indicates that, while coup support under conditions of high crime ranges widely, most national groups report between 40 and 56

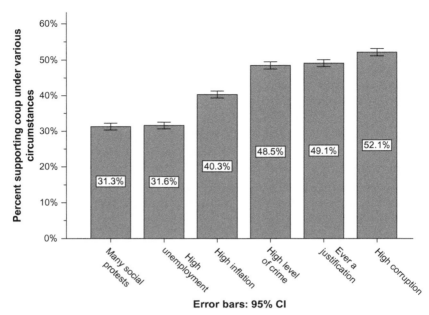

Error bars: 95% CI

FIGURE 6.2. Circumstances in which a coup d'etat might be justified

percent approval for a hypothetical coup. Hondurans and Salvadorans have the highest mean coup justification, Panama the lowest.

Following the logic of the legitimacy literature's main hypotheses, we expect hypothetical approval of a coup to be greater among citizens who express low levels of support for the regime. We reason that such disaffected citizens might have lower commitment to the retention of democracy and that they might express it as a willingness to justify or rationalize, under certain circumstances, a hypothetical military coup to topple the government.[5]

Our first finding based on HLM analysis was that no system-level variables affect willingness to justify a coup d'etat. We turn, therefore, to OLS regression with country dummies to account for national fixed effects. Table 6.2 presents a trimmed[6] regression analysis and reveals at

---

[5] Note that we did not ask whether the respondents would support a coup against their specific government. Rather we asked whether, under certain extreme hypothetical circumstances, a coup might be justified.

[6] The analysis summarized in Table 6.2 is an ordinary least squares regression model trimmed to exclude two legitimacy norms (regime principles and regime institutions) found not to have a significant zero-order bivariate correlation with support for coups.

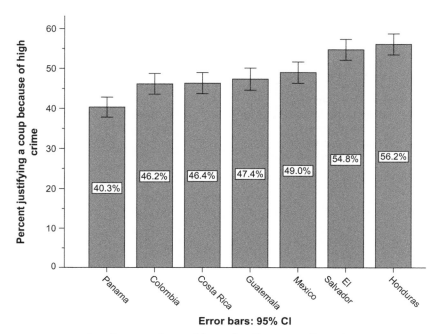

FIGURE 6.3. Percent who could ever justify a coup d'etat, by country

least some evidence supporting the proposition that citizens with the lowest legitimacy levels (that is, the lowest evaluations of the performance of parts of the system) would be the most likely to consider a coup to be acceptable. The hypothesized direction of influence (a negative relationship between coup justification and political support) prevails for all four legitimacy norms included in the model. Controlling for all the other variables in the model, the relationship is statistically significant only for evaluation of regime performance (t = −7.4) and political actors (t = −3.8). The citizens most critical about regime economic and political actor performance express a willingness to entertain a *hypothetical* overthrow of the regime.

Older citizens and those with college and postgraduate educations, high levels of interpersonal trust, life satisfaction, and political information approve significantly less than others of the idea of a coup d'etat. In contrast, crime victims, those fearful of crime in their neighborhoods, and corruption victims all are significantly more accepting of coups, revealing the corrosive effects of such negative experiences on the political capital of citizens. Residents of larger cities support coups more than any other sector. Interestingly, compared to the reference group of Costa Ricans,

TABLE 6.2. *Predictors of approval of coups d'etat (trimmed model) – OLS regression results*

Independent Variables[a]	t	Sig.
Constant	16.314	.000
Political community	-.926	.355
Regime performance	-7.440	.000
Political actors	-3.769	.000
Local government	-1.746	.081
Voted for presidential winner	-.288	.774
Women	-1.695	.090
Age 21–30	-1.817	.069
Age 31–40	-5.169	.000
Age 41–50	-6.422	.000
Age 51–60	-7.275	.000
Age 61–95	-9.620	.000
Catholic	2.206	.027
Protestant	1.850	.064
No religion	2.412	.016
Primary education	1.807	.071
Secondary education	.847	.397
College	-2.365	.018
Postgraduate	-5.700	.000
Wealth	-.387	.699
Media contact	3.390	.001
Political information	-5.816	.000
Interpersonal trust	-3.556	.000
Life satisfaction, low to high	-2.735	.006
Victim of crime in last year?	2.467	.014
Fear crime in one's neighborhood?	3.891	.000
Solicited for bribe in last year?	1.571	.116
Capital city resident	2.830	.005
Large city resident	3.722	.000
Medium city resident	.620	.535
Small city resident	1.346	.178
Mexico	-7.515	.000
Guatemala	-6.580	.000
El Salvador	1.524	.128
Honduras	-.846	.398
Nicaragua	-12.563	.000
Panama	-8.708	.000
Colombia	-4.926	.000

[a] R-square = .074; Model S.E. = 38.150; F = 22.812; model sig. = .0001
t-ratio significant at .05 or less are indicated in **boldface** type.

most other countries' residents are highly coup averse, with Nicaraguans, Panamanians, Mexicans, and Guatemalans expressing particularly intense disapproval. Salvadorans and Honduras are not significantly different from Costa Ricans in justifying a coup. While Latin Americans embrace democracy today, there remains a reservoir of acceptance of a coup by the armed forces as a potential source of rescue from crises of various sorts.

Approval of confrontational political tactics

Confrontational political tactics such as demonstrations, blocking streets and plazas, and even the occupation of public buildings constitute major tools of protest over politics and policy in Latin America. How much do citizens support such tactics? Figure 6.4 reveals a low general level of support; country mean scores, on the 0–100 scale, range from 13.8 for Costa Ricans to 25.5 for Hondurans. By and large, then, our Latin Americans tend to disapprove of confrontational political tactics, but a minority of the population does embrace them.

The literature predicts that disaffected citizens should be more prone than others to support the use of confrontational political tactics. That is, low legitimacy norms should correlate with a high confrontational orientation (a negatively signed relationship). Our first finding based on HLM analysis was that no system-level variables affect support for confrontational politics. We turn, therefore, to OLS regression using country dummies to account for national fixed effects (Table 6.3).[7] Surprisingly, only one variable conforms to expectation – those who perceive a national political community strongly oppose confrontational politics ($t = -16.8$). In sharp contrast, three of six legitimacy dimensions run counter to hypothetical expectations. Those who approve of regime democratic principles and of regime institutions significantly endorse confrontational political tactics (t-ratios of 13.1 and 9.8, respectively). Those who disapprove of local government's performance also significantly endorse confrontational tactics. Thus democrats, regime institution supporters, and local government supporters are much more willing to countenance confrontational or disruptive methodology than are other citizens. This

---

[7] The OLS models used in this chapter do not include the squared terms for the legitimacy dimensions employed for analyzing political participation in Chapter 5. This is because we had no theoretical expectation of or prior empirical evidence suggesting a reason to model attitudes this way.

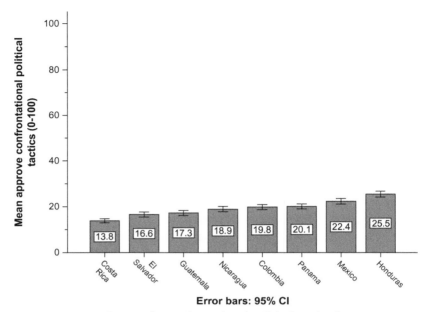

FIGURE 6.4. Support for confrontational political tactics, by country

pattern becomes less surprising on its face when we recall the evidence from Chapter 5 that protest correlates positively with all other forms of participation. This correlation reveals that those who vote, campaign, contact officials, or engage in civil society also protest from time to time. Thus protest is not simply the anomic behavior of the disgruntled citizen, but rather part of a Latin Americans' ordinary political repertoire. This confirms, we believe, that many who believe in democratic core values and institutions view protest and political confrontation (as distinct from rebellion) as normal and acceptable political actions.

Turning to other influences on support for confrontational political tactics in Table 6.3, we see that those who are older, have a postgraduate education, and are wealthier, more informed, and more trusting dislike this approach. In contrast, crime victims, residents of larger cities, and Hondurans, Mexicans, Panamanians, and Colombians approve of confrontational tactics.

Vigilantism

Citizens sometimes take the law into their own hands by lynching a person suspected of a crime. While this may happen in almost any society, it has

TABLE 6.3. *Predictors of approval of confrontational political tactics – OLS regression results*

Independent Variables[a]	t	Sig.
Constant	11.353	.000
Political community	−16.828	.000
Regime principles	13.134	.000
Regime institutions	9.810	.000
Regime performance	−1.287	.198
Political actors	−1.294	.196
Local government	4.211	.000
Voted for presidential winner	−3.878	.000
Women	−.582	.561
Age 21–30	−4.464	.000
Age 31–40	−7.584	.000
Age 41–50	−8.112	.000
Age 51–60	−8.678	.000
Age 61–95	−8.489	.000
Catholic	1.945	.052
Protestant	.738	.461
No religion	1.979	.048
Primary education	−.380	.704
Secondary education	−1.350	.177
College	−.867	.386
Postgraduate	−1.966	.049
Wealth	−4.912	.000
Media contact	1.068	.285
Political information	−7.980	.000
Interpersonal trust	−3.994	.000
Life Satisfaction, low to high	−.663	.507
Victim of crime in last year?	2.939	.003
Fear crime in one's neighborhood?	1.600	.110
Solicited for bribe in last year?	1.345	.179
Capital city resident	2.527	.012
Large city resident	2.440	.015
Medium city resident	1.781	.075
Small city resident	.628	.530
Mexico	5.858	.000
Guatemala	1.552	.121
El Salvador	1.822	.069
Honduras	10.246	.000
Nicaragua	−.233	.816
Panama	5.201	.000
Colombia	3.590	.000

[a] R-square = .104; Model S.E. = 21.016; F = 33.016; model sig. = .0001
t-ratio significant at .05 or less are indicated in **boldface** type.

reached epidemic proportions in some of the countries in our study in recent years when an effective security presence breaks down, especially after a civil conflict (Kincaid 2000). The use of vigilante "justice" or lynching is not, in itself, a political tool as practiced in Latin America but rather an expression of popular frustration at the absence of security in high crime areas. Citizens' willingness to endorse or embrace vigilantism appears to us to be a form of negative political capital that indicates a lack of willingness to obey the law and a lack of confidence that formal political institutions can provide for public order. We suspected that it might be related to legitimacy attitudes, anticipating that those most critical of the political system would be more prone to embrace vigilantism.

How strong is the approval of vigilantism among our respondents? Figure 6.5 shows approval levels on our approval "thermometer" ranging from 0 (lowest approval) to 100 (highest). The range for all the countries is between Colombia's lowest at 22.5 and El Salvador's highest at 36.2. While approval falls well below the scale midpoint for the pooled sample, the figure nevertheless reveals a substantial reservoir of tolerance for citizens taking the law into their own hands. Indeed, Costa Rica falls in the middle of the range, but as the error bars on Figure 6.5 demonstrate,

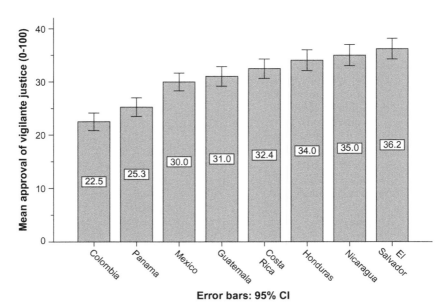

FIGURE 6.5. Approval of vigilantism, by country

Costa Ricans are not significantly less supportive of vigilantism than are Hondurans, Nicaraguans, or Salvadorans.

What effect does legitimacy have on citizen support for vigilantism? Our first finding based on HLM analysis was that no system-level variables affect approval of vigilantism. We turn, therefore, to OLS regression with country dummies to account for national fixed effects. Table 6.4 presents the results of an OLS multiple regression analysis of this variable.[8] The only significant legitimacy effect is that those who perceive a national community are less likely than others to approve of vigilante activity. We conclude that, other than a general identification with the national community, political support has no impact on this attitude. It seems to be an attitudinal dimension largely ungrounded in legitimacy attitudes.

Those significantly opposed to vigilantism include women, all older population cohorts, those with a secondary or higher education, the wealthier, the more informed, and the more trusting. Compared to the reference category of Costa Ricans who were excluded, Mexicans, Guatemalans, Panamanians, and Colombians are all significantly less approving of taking the law into one's own hands.

The sources of support for vigilantism shown in Table 6.4 are of particular interest. First, compared to anyone who self-identifies as having a religious affiliation or faith, persons professing no religion are slightly more apt to approve of vigilantism, all other factors in the model held constant. One may surmise that this effect stems from the impact of Latin America's predominant Christian sects' general teachings against using violence and favoring orderly social conduct. The other sources of support for vigilantism come from perceptions and experiences related to crime and corruption – believing one's own neighborhood is not safe and being either a crime victim or an official corruption victim. These findings straightforwardly reveal the value to a political system of successfully maintaining public safety and curtailing official corruption. Corruption, crime, and the fear of crime encourage citizens to consider taking the law into their own hands. If acted upon, of course, the vigilante impulse generates another crime, which could tend to cascade into ever-increasing social violence and a breakdown of the social contract. Finally, holding other factors in the model constant, Table 6.4 reveals that, compared to

---

[8] The analysis summarized in Table 6.4 is an OLS regression model trimmed to exclude two legitimacy norms (regime principles and regime institutions) found not to have a significant zero-order bivariate correlation with approval of vigilantism.

TABLE 6.4. *Predictors of vigilantism (trimmed model) – OLS regression results*

Independent Variables[a]	t	Sig.
Constant	15.596	.000
Political community	**−4.586**	.000
Regime performance	−1.912	.056
Political actors	−1.238	.216
Local government	−1.136	.256
Voted for presidential winner	1.383	.167
Women	**−4.304**	.000
Age 21–30	**−3.382**	.001
Age 31–40	**−6.187**	.000
Age 41–50	**−7.593**	.000
Age 51–60	**−8.089**	.000
Age 61–95	**−8.457**	.000
Catholic	1.237	.216
Protestant	−.878	.380
No religion	**2.638**	.008
Primary education	−1.470	.142
Secondary education	**−2.089**	.037
College	**−3.195**	.001
Postgraduate	**−3.885**	.000
Wealth	**−2.009**	.045
Media contact	1.367	.172
Political information	**−4.143**	.000
Interpersonal trust	**−3.362**	.001
Life Satisfaction, low to high	−1.882	.060
Victim of crime in last year	**2.959**	.003
Fear crime in one's neighborhood	**3.878**	.000
Solicited for bribe in last year	**4.762**	.000
Capital city resident	.769	.442
Large city resident	−.014	.989
Medium city resident	1.250	.211
Small city resident	.138	.890
Mexico	**−5.007**	.000
Guatemala	**−4.002**	.000
El Salvador	.872	.383
Honduras	−1.124	.261
Nicaragua	**−3.146**	.002
Panama	**−6.166**	.000
Colombia	**−7.991**	.000

[a] R-square = .051; Model S.E. = 35.162; F = 15.971; model sig. = .0001
t-ratio significant at .05 or less are indicated in **boldface** type.

the reference Costa Ricans, Panamanians and Mexicans are the least tolerant of vigilantism, while El Salvadorans and Hondurans are the most supportive of the idea of the use of vigilante justice.

DISCUSSION AND CONCLUSIONS

Attitudes that might undermine law and order, lead to violent challenges to the democratic regime, or encourage lynching are present in all eight nations at varying levels. There is considerably more tolerance for coups under certain hypothetical circumstances than for other negative political capital attitudes. Indeed, 49 percent of the pooled sample could imagine hypothetical circumstances in which a coup d'etat might be justified. (The reader understandably might be relieved that our respondents are ordinary citizens reacting to a hypothetical situation and not military officers in charge of troops, because in the latter circumstance coups might be much more common.) Perhaps better news for the potential stability of these young democratic regimes is that popular approval for armed rebellion, confrontational political tactics, and vigilantism are all much lower – indeed, well in the bottom end of each of these 100-point approval thermometer scales. And yet there remains a reservoir of approval of all three in each country. On the high end, over a third of Salvadorans approve of lynching, and roughly a quarter of Hondurans approve of both confrontational political methods and armed rebellion against an elected government.

We have found that legitimacy varies in both the strength and direction of its effects on negative political capital. Support for regime principles and regime institutions proved to be the least influential of the legitimacy norms. Each of them affects only one potentially disruptive political attitude, approval of confrontational tactics. Remarkably, their direction of causality is the opposite of what the literature hypothesized (see Table 6.5 for a summary of effects): Citizens with high support for democracy and national institutions tend rather strongly to approve of confrontational tactics. Apparently these citizens of eight Latin American countries do not view the techniques of confrontational protest to be inconsistent with democracy or national institutions. While this underscores the prospect that political turmoil in the form of protest will likely play a prominent role in Latin American democracies, it also suggests that protest does not necessarily menace either democracy as such or national institutions. Even Costa Rica, with its national image of calm and orderly politics, has a robust tradition of demonstrations and protests and usually of affirmative governmental response to such demands (Booth 1998).

196   *The Legitimacy Puzzle in Latin America*

TABLE 6.5. *Summary of effects on negative political capital*

Independent Variables	Approval of Overthrow	Approval of Coups	Confront. Tactics	Approve Vigilantism
Political community	-12.264		-16.828	-4.586
Regime principles			13.134	
Regime institutions			9.810	
Regime performance	-2.268	-7.440		
Political actors	-3.380	-3.769		
Local government	2.750		4.211	
Voted for presidential winner			-3.878	
Women	-3.095			-4.304
Age 21–30	-2.719		-4.464	-3.382
Age 31–40	-6.243	-5.169	-7.584	-6.187
Age 41–50	-6.615	-6.422	-8.112	-7.593
Age 51–60	-6.626	-7.275	-8.678	-8.089
Age 61–95	-8.096	-9.620	-8.489	-8.457
Catholic		2.206		
Protestant				
No religion		2.412	1.979	2.638
Primary Education				
Secondary Education	-2.808			-2.089
College	-2.658	-2.365		-3.195
Postgraduate	-4.422	-5.700	-1.966	-3.885
Wealth	-2.341		-4.912	-2.009
Media contact		3.390		
Political information	-6.354	-5.816	-7.980	-4.143
Interpersonal trust	-3.080	-3.556	-3.994	-3.362
Life satisfaction, low to high	-2.478	-2.735		
Victim of crime in last year		2.467	2.939	2.959
Fear crime in one's neighborhood		3.891		3.878
Solicited for bribe in last year	3.910			4.762
Capital city resident	2.693	2.830	2.527	
Large city resident	2.321	3.722	2.440	
Medium city resident				
Small city resident				
Mexico	5.336	-7.515	5.858	-5.007
Guatemala	5.720	-6.580		-4.002
El Salvador	4.151			
Honduras	9.350		10.246	
Nicaragua		-12.563		-3.146

Independent Variables	Approval of Overthrow	Approval of Coups	Confront. Tactics	Approve Vigilantism
Panama	6.301	−8.708	5.201	−6.166
Colombia		−4.926	3.590	−7.991

Key: blank cells = not significant; darker grey cells = negatively significant confirming hypothesis; lighter grey cells = positively significant disconfirming hypothesis; cell values = significant t-ratios.

While Figure 6.4 shows that Costa Ricans are the least supportive of protest among their neighbors in this study, their rate of protest participation remains quite similar to the overall sample mean.

Approval of local government affects negative political capital in the opposite direction from what was expected. Although the effects are modest, supporters of local government are slightly tolerant of rebellion and even more approving of confrontational political tactics. International aid programs in recent decades have dedicated considerable effort in all of the countries in our study to the strengthening of local government and the decentralization of democracy. Both the United States Agency for International Development and the German development agency (Gesellschaft für Technische Zusammenarbeit – GTZ) have made decentralization and the strengthening of local government a hallmark of their efforts in these countries. A rationale for such programs was that decentralization and building local government capacity might increase citizens' good experience with government and boost their positive political capital. Based on our findings alone, one might question the efficacy or even perhaps the advisability of such programs for building attitudes that favor democratic stability. Yet, Chapter 7 will reveal that approval of local actors correlates strongly with a positive perception of the level of democracy in one's country – the supply of democracy.

Among the legitimacy norms, perceiving a national political community exercises the most influence on negative political capital (Table 6.5). We expected what we found: Support for political community lowers approval for rebellion, confrontational tactics, and vigilantism. Greater support for political actors and national economic performance, also as expected, reduce support for armed rebellion and coups. This stands to reason on its face – citizens who are happy with the incumbent president or the nation's economic performance hardly would wish to see the regime attacked or overthrown.

We have noted with interest certain other patterns in the data. As citizens grow older they increasingly eschew all four forms of negative political capital. Education, higher standard of living, interpersonal trust, life satisfaction, greater political information, and small-town/rural residence also tend to curtail negative political capital. Professing no religion (slightly), being a crime victim, fearing crime in one's own neighborhood, being solicited for a bribe, and residing in a large city or national capital all enhance the chance of holding negative political capital norms.

Returning to the legitimacy puzzle, we ask how legitimacy affects negative social capital in our eight countries. On balance, legitimacy affects negative social capital more modestly and in somewhat more complex ways than the literature suggested. Only 11 of the 24 possible legitimacy–political capital relationships in Table 6.5 – less than half – were statistically significant. Moreover, for four of those the relationships were inverted from the expected. There are indeed effects and legitimacy dimensions that conform to the general prediction of the literature that disaffected citizens would have higher levels of negative social capital. A sense of national political community and positive evaluation of economic performance and political actors all tend to lower negative political capital. After all, why should people embrace or endorse a coup, violent rebellion, or taking the law into their own hands if they feel positively toward the national community or about its leaders or economy? Apparently these types of legitimacy are sufficiently high among our respondents that they give little support to rebellion and vigilantism.

In contrast, three other types of legitimacy fail to support the hypothesis that greater legitimacy should reduce negative social capital. Approval of regime democratic norms, of institutions, and of local government actually strengthen rather than reduce approval for confrontational political tactics. At first blush this deepens the legitimacy puzzle. Why, after all, would a citizen with greater approval of democracy and its national and local institutions protest more? This solid empirical fact, we believe, reveals an intriguing quirk of robust democratic expectations in these (mostly) young regimes. Citizens who value their democratic regime principles (i.e., hold basic democratic beliefs) and support both national and local institutions also endorse pressing demands on the state even with confrontational tactics. This bespeaks a latent confidence among the populace that their democratic governments will listen and respond with a modicum of respect or tolerance rather than with the violent repression that contributed so many dark pages to Latin America's national histories.

Implications for the individual countries warrant further comment. In examining negative political capital, we employed the oldest democracy, Costa Rica, as our reference case. Costa Ricans were more favorable toward coups and vigilantism than we had expected given the country's relative institutional health and the longevity of its democracy. They were also the most negative toward rebellion and confrontational political methods. The emergent picture of Costa Ricans reveals that they dislike confrontational political methods but could nevertheless justify a coup or citizens taking the law into their own hands under the right circumstances. On the latter point, because Costa Rica has no army, it has a constitutional provision for calling on citizen militias in crises. It has also historically had a largely unprofessional rural police filled through party patronage. Both factors may contribute to Costa Ricans' tolerance of vigilantism.

We have shown that political community suppresses support for rebellion and confrontational tactics. Even controlling for political community legitimacy, Hondurans rank very high on these two negative political capital norms. We have also learned that support for regime institutions and performance enhance support for confrontational tactics. Yet, even controlling for both, Hondurans report high support for confrontational political methods. Hondurans rank at or near the top in support for rebellion, political confrontation, and coup justification. These patterns suggest a potential reservoir of mass tolerance for potential coup plotters in Honduras. They also lead us to expect a particularly high propensity for mass protest and political turmoil in Honduran politics. To the extent that these political capital norms shape participation and encourage support for potential antidemocratic elites, we suspect that Hondurans' willingness to countenance rebellion and confrontation could tempt that country's antidemocratic elites to act against democracy to a degree greater than in most other countries in our study. Colombians and Panamanians, in contrast, ranked at or near the bottom on negative political capital norms. Our findings suggest that Panama and Colombia will tend toward less rather than greater political stability because antidemocratic elites there would find less potential mass tolerance than in several other countries.

We close this chapter by returning to Huntington's (1968) concern about whether too much demand might overload states and cause democratic decay. Here we encounter divided evidence about negative political capital. National community and positive evaluation of actors and economic performance strengthen attitudes that undergird democratic regimes by enhancing respect for the law and reducing support for rebellion and military adventurism. But supporters of democratic principles and national and local institutions favor confrontational political tactics. It is a cruel paradox that citizens who trust democracy and its institutions enough to protest might well overstretch state capacity or – more likely – that frequent protest might tempt civilian leaders or security forces to violate fundamental democratic practices with repression in order to curtail unruly popular demand making. Memories of Kent State, Jackson State, and similar episodes during the Viet Nam war period and of violent repression of civil rights activists in the United States remind us that, even in countries in which democracy is deeply entrenched, regimes can react with repression. We probe further the global implications of these findings in Chapter 7 by looking at the link between legitimacy and certain key attitudes about democracy.

7

Legitimacy and Democratic Values

We now ask whether legitimacy's effects include other values that might reinforce democracy, a counterpoint to the effects on negative political capital just discussed in Chapter 6. We ask this question because so far we have focused heavily on the impact of legitimacy on political participation as a result of our belief that citizen activism is the quintessential basis of all democratic rule. But, in this final substantive chapter, we wonder how deep is the commitment of citizens to democracy per se, and whether their legitimacy norms might undermine or strengthen a broad commitment to democracy. We saw in Chapter 5 that, for several forms of legitimacy, low levels contribute to higher participation rates. Do disgruntled activists pose a threat to democracy? Is their support for democracy as a system of government contingent upon how well they believe their rulers and institutions are performing? That is to say, we wonder, as did Huntington (1968), whether discontent with various aspects of the system could lead activist critics of a regime to participate in ways that could adversely affect democratic consolidation.

This book has explored the axiomatic assumption that legitimacy is a necessary (but clearly not sufficient) condition for the sustainability of democratic rule. We have accepted the literature's arguments that legitimacy is built, bit-by-bit, through effective regime performance, and that such support can erode over time. We worry, therefore, that if Huntington is correct, participation in developing democracies could place such a high level of stress on the regime that it would undermine support for democracy itself. In other words, is there an inevitable (or even frequent) conflict in developing democracies between the growth of legitimacy and the participation effects that we have shown that it induces, and thus the support for democracy per se? Indeed, we have found, somewhat to our surprise, that in these Latin American developing democracies both the most supportive and the least supportive citizens have the highest levels of political activism. While on one level it is encouraging that the most disaffected citizens take part within normal political channels in democracies, that fact also reinforces the Huntingtonian concern about their participation and its effects.

We also found in our exploration of the effects of legitimacy on negative political capital in Chapter 6 that legitimacy's effects partly deviate from expectations. As expected, higher political community beliefs lower most kinds of negative political capital; approval of both regime performance and political actors lowers approval for rebellion and coups. But contrary to expectations, higher support for regime principles and institutions and local government increases support for confrontational protest tactics. As for participation, legitimacy's effects on negative political capital are complex. We need, therefore, to go beyond the questions of citizens' methods of engagement and their views on appropriate political tactics. We must assess their commitment to democracy as political praxis: Are Latin Americans in our eight countries loyal or committed to democracy? If so, does legitimacy have anything to do with this? Do disaffected citizens express greater or less support for democratic governance?

To answer these questions, we explore the relationship between legitimacy and citizen belief in democracy. We approach belief in democracy from two perspectives. First, our study was conducted in Latin America, a region in which dictatorships have been all too common throughout its history. Indeed, six of our eight countries have experienced authoritarian rule within recent decades (Costa Rica and Colombia are the exceptions). Given this fact, we want to know whether higher levels of political legitimacy in these young democracies might help strengthen support for such regimes. To address this question, we borrow the approach taken by Michael Bratton and his colleagues (2005; Mattes and Bratton 2007), which focuses on the "demand" for and the "supply" of democracy in a given country. In essence, we ask: Does legitimacy among the citizens of developing democracies contribute to their preference or demand for elective government? We measure this demand for democracy as agreement that having an elected leader is always better than an unelected one. Second, we want to know whether those citizens who hold higher levels of legitimacy, measured with our survey items, also tend to believe that their political system provides them with a greater supply of democracy, to use terminology from Bratton et al. We assess how satisfied citizens say they are about how democracy is working in their countries, and then compare this to their demand.

We carry out this analysis taking advantage of the multifaceted notion of legitimacy that we have developed in this book and are fully aware of our findings about the complexity of legitimacy's effects. Given that complexity, we do not assume a priori that all forms of legitimacy necessarily will associate either with a preference for elected rulers or with the supply (perceived amount) of democracy. Nor do we assume that all dimensions of legitimacy will have the same level of impact on these variables.

LEGITIMACY AND OPPOSITION TO AUTHORITARIAN RULE

The eight-nation survey included an item measuring support/opposition to authoritarian rule that has clear face validity. We asked: "There are people who say that we need a strong leader who does not have to be elected by the vote. Other people say that even when things don't function well, electoral democracy, that is the popular vote, is always the best thing. What do you think?"[1] In our survey, most respondents selected the "elected democracy as always the best" alternative over the unelected strongman option, but there was statistically significant variation among the countries (see Figure 7.1). Hondurans (78.5 percent) and Guatemalans (82 percent) preferred elected government the least (although very large majorities in both supported it). Costa Ricans and Salvadorans exceeded 90 percent support. The relatively low support in Guatemala and Honduras signals a broader problem that we will find with these two countries later in this chapter. Yet, we need to stress here that even this "low" support is only relatively low because even in Honduras, where demand for democracy was weakest, more than three-quarters of respondents support electoral democracy over strongman rule. Guatemala and Mexico also have relatively low levels of demand for democracy, but in both countries more than four of five citizens prefer it to unelected leadership.

These univariate results, however, do not address our central question about the impact of legitimacy on the demand for electoral democracy. To do that, we must turn to a regression analysis. As predictors, we use all six dimensions of legitimacy described in Chapter 6. In addition, we deploy the same demographic and experiential variables used in previous chapters in which we sought to explain legitimacy's sources and links to various forms of participation and social capital. Table 7.1 presents the results of

---

[1] For the purposes of multivariate analysis below, preferring the popular vote was coded as a 1, and preferring a strong but unelected leader was coded 0. See Appendix Table B.3 for details on this item.

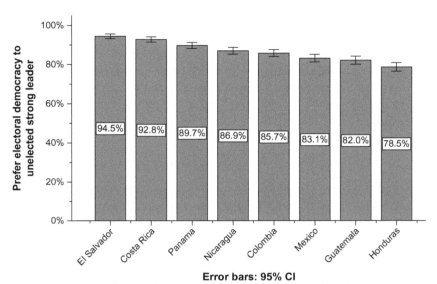

Error bars: 95% CI

FIGURE 7.1. Preference for electoral democracy over unelected strongman

the analysis. Several findings emerge. First, of the six dimensions of legitimacy, four significantly affect support for elected democratic rule and rejection of strongman rule. The legitimacy of national institutions and local government are insignificantly linked to the preference for an elected ruler. However, we note that, holding other factors constant, the relationship between the other four legitimacy norms and demand for democracy is not substantively very strong. We believe this demonstrates that the demand for democracy, manifestly high in all our countries, has become or is becoming a nearly universalized value, at least in these Latin American cases. As such it should be correlated only weakly, if at all, with performance evaluation. And that, in effect, is what Figure 7.1 and Table 7.1 reveal. This finding suggests that democratic systems contribute directly to their own legitimation by being less violent and repressive than authoritarian systems. Citizens, especially those with a memory of authoritarianism, thus will want democracy whether their government performs well or not (specific legitimacy). Except for Costa Ricans and Colombians, many of the middle-aged and older citizens we interviewed had lived in undemocratic and repressive states and thus could rationally compare authoritarian and democratic arrangements. Their preference for elected leaders remained strong even though those who evaluated system performance most highly favored democracy marginally more than those with low legitimacy norms.

TABLE 7.1. *Predictors of preference for elected leaders: logistic regression results*

Independent Variables	B	Sig.	Exp(B)^a
Political community	.023	.000	1.024
Regime principles	.007	.000	1.007
Regime institutions	.002	.401	1.002
Regime performance	.010	.000	1.010
Political actors	.006	.000	1.006
Local government	−.002	.305	.998
Voted for presidential winner	−.075	.245	.928
Women	.045	.465	1.046
Age 21–30	.281	.005	1.324
Age 31–40	.417	.000	1.517
Age 41–50	.472	.000	1.603
Age 51–60	.698	.000	2.010
Age 61–95	.437	.001	1.549
Catholic	−.114	.551	.892
Protestant	−.105	.596	.900
No religion	.025	.910	1.025
Primary Education	.037	.674	1.038
Secondary Education	.257	.009	1.294
College	.441	.003	1.554
Postgraduate	1.045	.000	2.844
Wealth	.009	.448	1.009
Media Contact	−.003	.025	.997
Political information	.007	.000	1.007
Interpersonal trust	.138	.000	1.148
Life satisfaction, low to high	.011	.781	1.011
Victim of crime in last year	.000	.988	1.000
Fear crime in one's neighborhood	−.008	.800	.992
Solicited for bribe in last year	−.315	.013	.730
Capital city resident	−.527	.000	.590
Large city resident	−.357	.001	.700
Medium city resident	−.339	.001	.712
Small city resident	−.543	.000	.581
Constant	−1.609	.000	.200

Note: Nagelkerke R-square = .082; estimation terminated at iteration number 6 because parameter estimates changed by less than .001; significant values for expectation of B – Exp(B) are indicated in **boldface**. Degrees of freedom for all variables = 1.

^{a} Exp(b) is the odds ratio for the variable; that is, knowing this variable's value, what improvement is there in predicting the value of the dependent variable.

Our second finding is that all age groups older than the youngest respondents were significantly more supportive of electoral democracy than were the very young. This is certainly somewhat reassuring, suggesting that as citizens age in Latin America they become more supportive of democracy. Older citizens have been found to be more supportive of democracy in other studies of Latin Americans (Booth and Richard 1996; Seligson and Macías 1996; Seligson et al. 2002). We also surmise that the older cohorts in most countries retain more memory of the brutality of authoritarian rule and thus prefer elected rulers. In contrast, a large proportion of the population in the region is young, and these youthful citizens express the lowest support for democracy. This fairly large segment is also the most likely to take part in protests but the least likely to take part in politics within channels (Chapter 5). The young, then, constitute a potentially politically volatile population – less committed to democracy, more committed to confrontational political methods, and more likely to protest. What we cannot know from this cross-sectional analysis is whether the young will emulate their elders and become more supportive as they grow older, or whether the youth of Latin America actually constitute a disenchanted group that as it ages will remain so. Were that true, the future for democracy in the region would be bleak.

Several personal characteristics matter in predicting support for democracy. While religious preferences make no difference, education matters considerably in the demand for democracy. As education increases beyond the primary school years, and as knowledge of political information increases, support for elected democracy over authoritarian regimes increases significantly. In contrast, material wealth has no effect on preference for democratic versus authoritarian government. As opposed to residing in any other area, living in a rural area increases support for democracy.

Of the attitudinal predictors, only interpersonal trust correlates with a stronger preference for electoral democracy, whereas life satisfaction does not. This finding for trust resembles that reported by other researchers reporting on numerous countries (Rose et al. 1999; Dalton 2004; Bratton et al. 2005: 247; Uslaner and Brown 2005). The presumption in the literature (see especially Putnam 2000) is that interpersonal trust is one of the essential by-products of civil society engagement and that it strengthens support for democracy and, ultimately, democratic systems (Uslaner and Brown 2005). Inglehart (1990), too, makes a similar argument that trust enhances support for democracy and the strength of democratic regimes. Other scholars argue, however, that the political context comes first, and that political rules and institutions shape culture (Jackman and Miller 2004). In this vein, Muller and Seligson (1994) contend that the existence of democracy contributes to higher average levels of interpersonal trust, rather than the reverse. In sum, we cannot determine from this evidence which way the causality runs between citizens' trust and their opposition to unelected strongman rule, but we note the association. Finally, Table 7.1 shows that corruption victimization decreases support for democratic rule. This finding makes sense on its face. Among the fundamental premises of democratic governance are the rule of law and the notion that citizens are legally equal and entitled to equal legal protection. Government and its representatives should play fairly and not discriminate among citizens. To encounter government corruption (i.e., be solicited for a bribe) is to undergo a corrosive and disappointing experience that undermines these principles of equitable treatment. The more often one is suborned for a bribe, the more likely it is that he/she would lose faith in basic egalitarian norms. Moreover, a desire to end corruption could lend itself easily to the notion that, in circumstances of rife corruption, one might embrace an avenging and powerful strongman leader to smite the corrupt and restore honesty to the public sector. This finding strongly suggests that political corruption may well constitute a real threat to democratic culture. The wider corruption victimization spreads, the greater the tendency among Latin Americans to prefer strongman rule.

THE PERCEIVED SUPPLY OF DEMOCRACY AND LEGITIMACY

A number of studies have focused on satisfaction with democracy as it operates in citizens' own particular countries – in essence, citizens' perception of the supply of democracy in their polity. A study of the impact of institutional configurations on citizen satisfaction with democracy (Anderson and Guillory 1997) reported a strong set of associations in advanced industrial democracies. Contributors to the volume on political legitimacy edited by Norris (1999b) also use this variable in their analyses. We drew the questionnaire item that we employ here directly from those studies: "In general, would you say that you are very satisfied, satisfied, dissatisfied, or very dissatisfied with the way that democracy works in [country]?" The difficulty with this item is that its interpretation may be ambiguous to respondents. Canache, Mondak, and Seligson (2001) found that its referent is somewhat ambiguous – respondents may be referring either to "democracy" or to their satisfaction with the government in power. For this reason, we decided to add two more items, also found in Norris (1999b), that

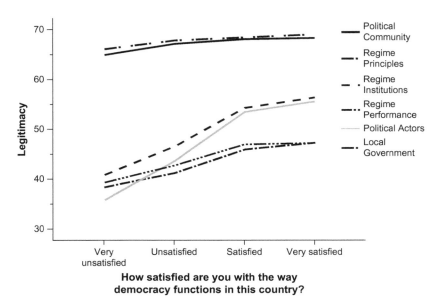

FIGURE 7.2. Impact of legitimacy on satisfaction with democracy

ensure the construct validity of our measure. Together the three can provide an overall index of the extent to which respondents find that the supply of democracy in their own country is adequate or wanting. We added: "In your opinion, [respondent's country] is very democratic, somewhat democratic, [only a] little democratic, or not at all democratic?" "Based on your experience from the last few years, [this country] has become more democratic, equally democratic, or less democratic?" These last two items seem unambiguously to measure the respondent's perception of the supply of democracy, so it is appropriate to examine the impact of legitimacy on each of them individually, and then, if the patterns seem clear, create an overall index of "supply of democracy."[2]

The patterns for all three variables are strikingly similar (see Figures 7.2–7.4). For each of them, increases in each one of the six dimensions of legitimacy are positively linked to greater supply of democracy. What differ are the intercepts and slopes of the lines. We demonstrated in Chapter 3 that the *levels* of legitimacy vary by dimension, with political community and regime principles consistently scoring at the top end of the scale, far above the other four dimensions. As a result, for these two variables there is not

[2] See Appendix Table B.3 for details on index construction and distribution characteristics.

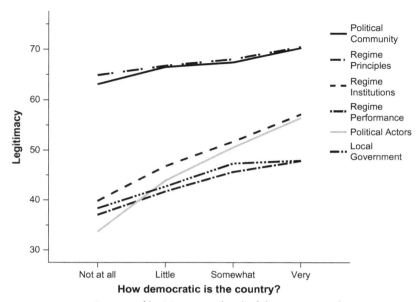

FIGURE 7.3. Impact of legitimacy on level of democracy in the country

much more "room to grow," as they are near the high end of the scaling metric. Even so, the slopes of the lines do vary, with a steeper slope indicating a stronger impact of legitimacy. Of the three supply items, only for the second, "How democratic is the country?" is there a relatively steep slope for the political community and regime principles dimensions of legitimacy, indicating a stronger impact of legitimacy on citizens' belief that the country is democratic than on the other two supply variables.

On the four remaining dimensions of legitimacy, each intercept for supply of democracy is lower and the "room to grow" is greater, and for some of these dimensions the growth is quite pronounced as legitimacy increases. Consider again the "How democratic is the country?" variable (Figure 7.3), and examine the regime institutions dimension. The slope is steep, rising from about 40 for those who say that the country is not at all democratic to about 55 for those who say it is very democratic. We find a similar pattern for support for political actors. These two legitimacy dimensions also have a marked effect on the first variable in the series, satisfaction with democracy, while the actors dimension has a sharper impact on the last measure of supply (country becoming more or less democratic, as shown in Figure 2.4).

Given the similarities in the patterns for all three democracy supply items, we tested all three items and determined that they formed a scale

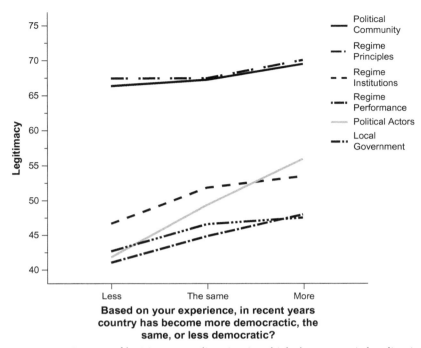

FIGURE 7.4. Impact of legitimacy on direction in which democracy is heading in the country

(see Appendix Table B.3 for details on index construction). Figure 7.5 presents the distribution of the democracy supply index by country. The scale ranges from a zero (no democracy perceived whatsoever) to 100 (the highest possible evaluation). Respondents report a lower supply of democracy in all countries than they do for their demand for democracy, which is also usually the case in the work reported by Bratton and Mattes in Africa. The range among countries is narrower than that for the demand for democracy. The eight countries supply means range between 50 and 60, compared to means between the upper 70s and low 90s on the demand for democracy. Colombians and Costa Ricans perceive the most democracy; Guatemalans, Mexicans, and Nicaraguans the least. So we see that in all countries there is a significant discrepancy between the preference for an elected leader and the perception that the country is supplying as much democracy as it might.

What determines citizens' perception of the supply of democracy, and do the various forms of legitimacy have anything to do with the levels? The results of a regression analysis of democracy supply are shown in Table

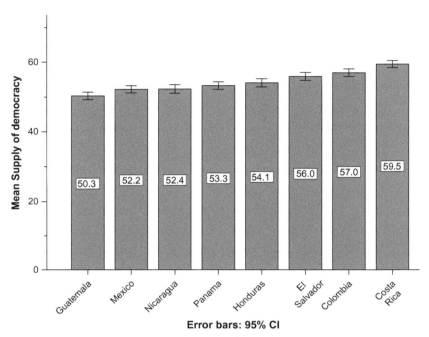

FIGURE 7.5. Perceived supply of democracy, by country

7.2. They show that legitimacy clearly predicts citizens' sense of the supply of democracy in their countries. Indeed, legitimacy shapes the perceived supply of democracy much more than it does the demand for democracy (Table 7.1). This reinforces our previous point that citizens' strong preference for democracy throughout our eight nations has become ingrained and much more independent of regime performance assessment than the perceived supply of democracy. In a sharp contrast, all six dimensions of legitimacy significantly predict the democracy supply index. By comparing the t-ratio, we see that evaluation of political actors exercises the strongest influence, followed closely by support for regime performance and regime institutions. Support for local government and political community both have significant but lesser influence on the perceived supply of democracy. In sum, these data provide clear evidence that, in these eight democracies, across all dimensions those perceiving their regimes to be more legitimate also believe their regimes to be more democratic.

Other variables play a role in predicting the perception of the supply of democracy. Importantly, while voting for the winning party in the presidential election prior to the survey increases citizens' sense of democracy supplied in our eight countries, its impact does not overwhelm the effects

TABLE 7.2. *Predictors of supply of democracy – OLS regression*

Independent Variables	t	Sig.
(Constant)	13.363	.000
Political community	4.784	.000
Regime principles	2.629	.009
Regime institutions	13.782	.000
Regime performance	14.626	.000
Political actors	18.423	.000
Local government	6.704	.000
Voted for presidential winner	4.247	.000
Women	-.363	.716
Age 21–30	.918	.359
Age 31–40	2.183	.029
Age 41–50	2.231	.026
Age 51–60	1.979	.048
Age 61–95	2.528	.011
Catholic	-.736	.462
Protestant	-.065	.948
No religion	-.966	.334
Primary education	-1.498	.134
Secondary education	-2.690	.007
College	-1.215	.224
Postgraduate	-2.497	.013
Wealth	-.296	.767
Media Contact	-1.207	.227
Political information	5.068	.000
Interpersonal trust	2.422	.015
Life Satisfaction, low to high	7.756	.000
Victim of crime in last year?	-.352	.725
Fear crime in one's own neighborhood?	-8.111	.000
Solicited for bribe in last year?	-1.741	.082
Capital city resident	-1.505	.132
Large city resident	-3.937	.000
Medium-sized city resident	-.132	.895
Small city resident	-3.893	.000

Note: $R^2 = .185$. $F = 76.342$; Significance $<.001$

of political legitimacy. Age, as shown in Table 7.2, also plays a role: Older citizens see a somewhat greater supply of democracy. Religious identification plays no role in the perceived supply of democracy, nor do crime, corruption victimization, or wealth. Thus, Latin Americans clearly are separating their view of the quality of democracy in their nations from the unhappy experiences of crime and corruption. We noted above that experiencing corruption actually increased the preference for strongman rule among survey respondents, probably because they believe a forceful leader could fight corruption. Here, however, victimization by corruption or crime does not affect how much democracy citizens perceive in their systems. This is, therefore, a somewhat contingent effect of corruption upon the desire for democracy.

Education plays a minor role, slightly elevating the tendency to perceive less democracy among some better-educated groups. Among the remaining predictors, the strongest is fear of crime in one's neighborhood, which considerably lowers the perceived supply of democracy. In contrast, interpersonal trust and, even more strongly, life satisfaction increase the amount of democracy perceived. Higher levels of political information associate with perceiving a greater supply of democracy. Finally, rural and small town residents perceive more democracy than do residents of some larger communities.

THE DEMOCRACY DEMAND-SUPPLY GAP

In all eight countries, citizens express a greater demand for democracy than they believe their political systems are supplying. Figure 7.6 plots the differences in demand and supply by country, which we interpret as democracy-favoring citizens' discontentment with getting enough democracy in their societies. We see that the gap or discrepancy is greatest in El Salvador, Panama, Nicaragua, and Costa Rica. The gap is the smallest in Honduras. One way to read the existence of a large demand-supply discrepancy is positively. Citizens want more democracy, not less. Thus, rather than serving to stimulate irresponsible or antidemocratic elites to undermine democracy, this dissatisfaction with the amount of democracy supplied may constitute a barrier to such actions. Despite perceived underperformance by the systems (supply), citizens nevertheless still strongly prefer democracy by a notable margin, which seems to us to provide clear evidence of a reservoir of support for the principle of elective leadership and discouragement to antidemocrats. If our argument is correct, then Honduras has a smaller reservoir of demand for democracy than the other countries. The four high-gap countries have a larger one that may redound in favor of their political stability.

We believe legitimacy norms should have something to do with this gap between the desire for democracy and its perceived level. In order to test the association between legitimacy and the demand-supply gap, we calculated the value of the gap by subtracting perceived supply from

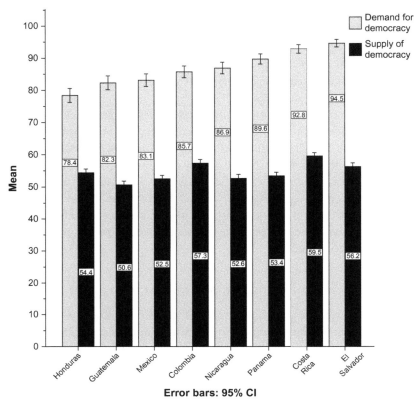

FIGURE 7.6. Perceived gap between the demand for and supply of democracy, by country

demand. We expected that if a government is performing poorly in the eyes of its citizens it should be reflected in larger values of this measure of unfulfilled democracy demand. We first correlated this new demand-supply gap variable with all six measures of legitimacy. We found something more complicated. The demand-supply gap associated positively with the more diffuse dimensions of legitimacy – perceived political community and support for democratic regime principles. In essence, a stronger commitment to the national community and to democracy adds to one's desire for more democracy. In contrast and as expected, we found negative associations between the gap and evaluations of specific support for institutions, actors, local government, and regime performance. Thus, the more negatively citizens evaluate the performance of specific parts of government, the more democracy they desire. Once again, the importance of disaggregating legitimacy into its various components provides important empirical payoffs.

To examine the relationship more closely, we then regressed the resulting value of the demand-supply gap on the six legitimacy norms. Bratton and his colleagues have shown that perceived participation rights strongly affect the perceived supply of democracy in African countries (Bratton et al. 2005: 247), so we added to this model controls for actual levels of political participation and dummies to isolate country effects. Indeed, the regression results, not shown to conserve space, confirmed the pattern reported above based on bivariate legitimacy-gap relationships. The controls for participation, in contrast, were not as influential when national fixed effects were included in the model. Country fixed effects, with Costa Ricans as the excluded reference group, demonstrated that Salvadorans most strongly preferred more democracy than they got in 2004. Hondurans, in contrast, had the smallest gap, and as we have shown in Figure 7.6 that gap was based on their expression of the lowest demand for democracy among the citizens of the eight nations. This pair of findings again suggests that El Salvador has relatively greater resources favoring stability despite its recent history of extreme violence. In contrast, Honduras, a relatively more stable country historically, had a smaller reservoir of demand for democracy over perceived supply that might protect democratic institutions.

HUNTINGTON'S QUESTION: LEGITIMACY, PARTICIPATION, AND DEMOCRACY

We return here to Huntington's question about whether political participation in developing democracies might place such stresses on a regime that it could undermine support for democracy itself. In other words, might there be a conflict within developing democracies between legitimacy and participation that could undermine citizens' support for democracy per se? We address this question by examining how multiple political participation modes affect the demand and perceived supply of democracy, controlling for the effect of our six legitimacy dimensions. The results of the analysis are presented in Table 7.3.

Looking first at the demand for democracy (preference for elected civilian government), we see that the logistic regression results show that political participation has little effect at all. Controlling for each mode of participation, the legitimacy dimensions, and country effects, only voting significantly affects citizens' demand for democracy and the effect is very small. Legitimacy, in contrast, does increase the preference for

TABLE 7.3. *Participation, legitimacy, and the perceived demand for and supply of democracy*

Participation Variables	Logistic Regression – Demand for Democracy		OLS Regression – Supply of Democracy	
	Expectation of (B)	Significance	t	Significance
Voting	1.004	.000	3.446	.001
Contacting public officials	1.002	.206	−2.187	.029
Communal activism	1.001	.393	−1.406	.160
Party and campaign activism	.997	.093	2.000	.046
Civil society activism	.999	.598	2.850	.004
Protest	1.000	.642	−3.653	.000
Legitimacy Dimensions				
Political community legitimacy	1.022	.000	4.973	.000
Regime principles legitimacy	1.007	.000	1.490	.136
Regime institutions legitimacy	1.001	.659	14.100	.000
Regime performance legitimacy	1.007	.001	17.156	.000
Political actors legitimacy	1.005	.002	19.801	.000
Local government legitimacy	1.000	.913	8.658	.000
Country Dummies				
Mexico	.500	.000	−8.112	.000
Guatemala	.526	.000	−7.575	.000
El Salvador	1.507	.009	−6.459	.000
Honduras	.407	.000	1.363	.173
Nicaragua	.645	.001	−3.157	.002
Panama	.782	.081	−3.463	.001
Colombia	.521	.000	−6.100	.000
Constant	.643	.068	19.221	.000

Note: Nagelkerke R-square = .079; R-square = .422

democracy, as one would expect given the central arguments of legitimacy theory. So, Latin Americans prefer elected governments whether they are politically active or not, but four of six forms of legitimacy strengthen the demand for democracy.

We analyze citizen perceptions of the supply of democracy using an ordinary least squares regression. The results in Table 7.3 present an interesting contrast to those for the demand for democracy in that, for five of six modes, participation does significantly affect the perceived supply, whereas for demand it had little effect. After controlling for legitimacy and country effects, more voting and campaign and party activism and less protesting associate with increased perceived democracy in their countries. Meanwhile contactors of public officials perceive lower levels of democracy supply.

What we see here, then, is that participation in certain arenas – voting, civil society, and campaign activity – goes with a stronger sense of the democracy supplied by the regime. Not protesting also goes with a stronger sense of democracy supply. The direction of causality is unclear: On the one hand, citizens' positive perception of regime democracy may encourage them to vote and engage in campaigning more and to protest less. On the other, participants may gain an increased sense of the democracy supplied by the political system based on the experience of freely taking part. Meanwhile, contactors of public officials perceive less democracy irrespective of legitimacy norms and country effects. Here we surmise that the direction of causality for this association is clearer – from attitude to behavior. One reasonably may assume that those who perceive less democracy will opt to make direct or personal pleas to officials to pursue their interests. Why bother voting or campaigning if one does not believe in the responsiveness of one's democratic regime? It may seem more efficacious to ask for benefits directly from officeholders.

What we find here gives us some comfort with respect to the issue Huntington raised. For most political arenas other than voting, most Latin Americans prefer elected civilian rule whether or not they take part in politics. The demand for democracy is not very participation dependent. The perceived supply of democracy is more participation dependent. Voters, civil society activists, and party-campaign activists – and those who protest less – perceive more democracy. We believe this demonstrates in these democracies, on balance, a positive political capital effect from engaging within the system, even controlling for legitimacy. In our eight countries, Huntington's fear that participation might undermine a preference for democracy does not materialize. Indeed, greater within-channel participation may well reinforce satisfaction with the level of democracy.

CONCLUSIONS

This chapter has asked two main questions about Latin Americans' legit-imacy norms and citizens' orientations toward democracy. First, do higher legitimacy levels contribute to the preference or demand for elective gov-ernment over unelected strongman rule? In short, does legitimacy affect how much citizens want democracy? And second, are citizens with higher legitimacy norms more inclined to believe that their political system pro-vides them with a greater supply of democracy? That is, does legitimacy affect how much democracy citizens think that they have?

In answering the first question we have found that Latin Americans prefer elected democracy to an unelected strongman by a ratio of about five to one, with some modest variation by country. For instance, Hondur-ans, Guatemalans, and Mexicans have a slightly lower preference for elec-ted democracy, while that of Salvadorans, Costa Ricans, and Panamanians are higher (Figure 7.1). Even when controlling statistically for the effects of legitimacy and political participation on demand for democracy, the coun-try dummies indicate that Hondurans, Mexicans, and Guatemalans prefer democracy less (Table 7.3). El Salvador stands out as the only country with demand for democracy scores well higher than those of Costa Ricans, even with controls for participation levels and legitimacy. We believe this is a remarkable and encouraging finding considering the country's recent history and its paucity of long-term experience with democracy.

As to whether legitimacy affects *how much* citizens prefer democracy, we have discovered that higher levels in four of six dimensions (commu-nity, regime principles, regime performance, and support for actors) con-tribute modestly to a greater demand for democracy. Even beginning with a large proportion favoring governance by elected leaders, we have found that the more positively citizens evaluate their democratic government's performance, the more likely they are to prefer democracy. This finding supports much of the theory of legitimacy and makes a great deal of logical sense as well. But it is important to understand that the effect of legitimacy norms is modest, contributing no more than 1–2 percent to the probability of predicting demand for democracy on a base of strong sup-port. Since demand is already so high, legitimacy norms had little room to increase this dependent variable.

As supporters of democracy in principle as a desirable form of govern-ment, we note with encouragement that even with only mediocre per-formance levels on certain legitimacy dimensions, citizens of our eight Latin American nations still manifest a strong positive bias for elected government and that low legitimacy levels do not undermine demand for democracy. Salvadorans' level of support for democracy strikes us as especially encouraging, considering the bitterness and violence of the civil conflict that raged there until 1992. Guatemalans and Mexicans, living in newer democracies that also have experienced or continue to suffer from high levels of violent political conflict, lag behind Costa Rica and El Salvador in preference for democracy over unelected rulers. But even where demand for democracy is weakest, support for elected rulers approaches or exceeds 80 percent. Democracy, we find, has a strong reservoir of support in the region and appears fairly resistant to low legitimacy norms. This finding suggests that the widely expressed concern among scholars about low or eroding legitimacy levels in democracies may be overblown.

Our second primary question in this chapter has been whether citizens who report higher levels of legitimacy are more inclined to believe that their political system supplies them with democracy. Here we have found that the answer is an unequivocal yes. The higher are citizens' legitimacy norms on all six dimensions, the more the democracy they perceive in their countries. Positive evaluation of actors, regime performance, and institutions contribute the most to the sense of supplied democracy. In contrast to the demand for democracy, we have found here that corruption victimization *does not* affect the perceived supply of democracy.

Therefore, we conclude that Latin Americans strongly prefer democracy to strongman rule. They also differentiate between a preference for democracy and how much democracy they believe that they have.[3] While corruption victimization does not affect how much democracy citizens believe that they have, it does undermine the preference for elected rulers. We conclude that official corruption is a serious problem in Latin America, not just in its own right but because it erodes support for democracy. Our findings indicate that the widespread political corruption, for which the region is known and which affects many of its citizens, is more than just an irritant. Corruption has a corrosive effect on citizen support for democracy. The bribe or *mordida* (literally "bite") comes not only out of citizens' pockets but also out of their willingness to support democratic governance. The strong majority support for elected rulers we observe here suggests that current corruption levels are unlikely to undermine any of these regimes any time soon. However, Figure 7.1 indicates

---

[3] Indeed, the simple bivariate correlation between the demand and supply of democracy indicators is only .089, so these are clearly independent concepts among our respondents.

that the reservoir of support is shallowest in Honduras, Guatemala, and Mexico.

All countries interested in conserving their democratic regimes would do well to take effective steps to curtail corruption on both large and small scales. While petty corruption may be tough to ferret out without increasing bureaucratic pay and institutional reform, it affects many citizens in diverse arenas of their lives. When citizens have to bribe a mail clerk to get a package, give a "tip" to a venal teacher to assure decent attention to their children in school, or pay a "fine" to a traffic cop for some illusory infraction, they lose respect for democracy.

Finally, participation within the political system's formal electoral channels and in civil society does not much affect the preference for civilian rule, which is broadly distributed within society. That the demand for democracy is largely invariant for participation levels suggests that it constitutes a strong cultural value in these eight countries and thus is not contingent upon the participation effort citizens put into the system. Whether politically active or not, Latin Americans prefer elected rulers to unelected strongmen by a wide margin. We view this as a sign of democratic consolidation. Participating within the system and in civil society does strengthen a citizen's sense of the supply (availability) of democracy in her own nation. Even despite modest or poor levels of performance for political actors, local government, and regime performance in most of our countries, within-channel activists do not reject elected rule (Huntington's fear) but embrace it. The gap between the demand for democracy and the perceived supply bespeaks a certain margin of comfort for democratic regimes – even underperforming regimes – in which their more active citizens view them positively. That margin of comfort is widest in El Salvador and Costa Rica and narrowest in Honduras.

One may speculate, along with Huntington and the legitimacy theorists, that regime performance might become so abysmal that it could undermine both citizens' preference for democracy and their sense that democracy even exists. Or the democracy gap could become so large or persist so long that it might eventually erode the preference for democracy. Honduras stands out as a poor performer in many areas of social and economic welfare and is thus a country where such effects might be expected. But as of 2004, even with the very poor objective conditions there, Hondurans still preferred democracy by a ratio of more than three to one, and they did so despite rating themselves at the low end of democracy supplied. Yet, as we will show in the next chapter, we do find reasons to be concerned over the future of democracy in Honduras.

8

The Sky Is Not Falling: The Puzzle Solved

We began this book with a puzzle, and we conclude by proffering a solution to it that works for eight Latin American nations. In Chapter 1 we wondered why so few advanced industrial democracies have broken down even though a raft of studies has both argued that legitimacy is critical for the survival of democracy and shown empirically that levels of legitimacy are declining in many countries. This anomaly between legitimacy theory and its failure to predict outcomes led us to speculate either that the theory has been faulty or partly so, or that the measurement of legitimacy has been at least partly faulty, or both. We set out to solve this puzzle by designing a research project that would, we hoped, allow us to understand the issues and point toward some clear solutions. In successive chapters we drew upon the work of others and added some ideas and findings of our own that allowed us to lay out partial answers to the puzzles. We conclude by reviewing what we have found (and how we have found it) so that we can, finally, offer our best solution to the legitimacy puzzle.

Our research design built upon but also differed from prior work in this area. Until recently most studies of legitimacy had been conducted in advanced industrial democracies.[1] This does not reflect some sort of failure of the discipline. Rather, it is best understood in terms of the old story about the tipsy partygoer returning home late at night and losing his door keys. When asked by a passerby why he was searching for the keys out in the street rather than near the door where he probably dropped the keys, his response was, "Well, the light is much better over here under the street lamp." So has it been with research on legitimacy and its impact. Until

---

[1] Welcome exceptions are Cleary and Stokes (2006) and Gilley (2009).

very recently, the bulk of research on the subject has attempted to understand legitimacy and its impacts precisely where the "street lamp" casts its glow but *not* where the keys to solving problem really lie. Advanced industrial democracies are rich with survey data, some spanning several decades, allowing for extensive exploration of the subject. Yet, these are countries in which democracy has become the "only game in town," to use Przeworski's (1986) well-known phrase. In some of them democracy emerged centuries ago, at least embryonically, while in others it has been the "only game" for the past half-century (Markoff 1995). These are among the wealthier countries in the world and are, research has shown (Seligson 1987b; Seligson 1997; Vanhanen 1997; Przeworski et al. 2000), so far above the threshold conditions under which democracy tends to develop and at which democratic breakdown could occur that it is simply unreasonable to assume that even sharply declining legitimacy levels would produce a cataclysm. In the rest of the world, in places where democratic experience is far newer and more limited and where recent instability has been commonplace, there have been many fewer "street lamps," by which we mean reliable data on legitimacy. Scientifically conducted surveys are only recently coming of age in these areas, and many problems of quality, validity, and reliability plague them (Seligson 2005b; Seligson 2005c; Seligson 2005d). Hence, our first decision was to conduct our research where we were likely to find the lost keys and to build our own "street lamp," or source of illumination. We decided to explore legitimacy theory and its measurement and effects in a region where the democratic tradition is more recent, economic conditions far less favorable, and civil wars, insurrections, guerrilla warfare, and military coups have all played a role in recent history. We emphasize that we are not the first researchers to move legitimacy research outside the established industrial democracies. Others paved the way by recognizing the value of examining political support in lower-performing and problematic political systems. Scholars recently have undertaken very significant studies involving legitimacy in new European democracies (Rose et al. 1998), Africa (Bratton, Mattes, and Gyimah-Boadi 2005), Asia (Shin 1999; Chu et al. 2008), and even Latin America (Canache 2002; Cleary and Stokes 2006). Still more research from developing and established democracies is in process (Seligson 2008b; Gilley 2009). We believe, however, that to date we have examined legitimacy more systematically and comprehensively than any previous study, whether in an industrial or a developing democracy, and thus our findings go farther toward answering the puzzles of legitimacy than have previously published efforts.

We also wish to emphasize that we did not select these eight countries randomly. Rather, we sought to build on our own comparative advantage because both authors are Latin Americanists who have concentrated the great bulk of our collective seven decades of research and fieldwork experience on these cases. In the classic tradition of comparative politics, we would like to believe that the years we have spent living in and researching these countries makes it possible for us to understand them and the data about them better than if we had just thrown darts at a world map to select the cases for our research.

For our country selection, we also saw great advantage in a design that could hold constant many factors whose variation all too often creates indeterminacy in cross-national comparative work. That is, when the cases vary substantially on a long list of key variables, the researcher often ends up with "more variables than cases," resulting in indeterminacy. Our study covered eight contiguous Latin American countries, each of which was predominantly or almost entirely Spanish speaking.[2] All had been former colonies of Spain and all have legal and institutional systems heavily influenced by that colonial heritage. Yet, the countries differ in certain ways that are relevant, or should be relevant, to legitimacy. First of all, they vary in terms of their experience with democracy. Costa Rica, of course, stands out among the eight countries studied here, with democratic antecedents dating back to the nineteenth century and with a democracy that became consolidated in the early 1950s. At the other extreme we have Mexico, a country that was ruled by a one-party regime up until 2000 when the PRI finally lost its hegemony.

South of Mexico lies Guatemala, a country ruled for decades by repressive military regimes enmeshed in a protracted guerrilla war. After a transitional period marked by continuing civil war and elected civilian governments in the 1980s and early 1990s, Guatemala's elites settled the civil war and adopted formal electoral democracy in 1996. El Salvador, Guatemala's neighbor to the south, also suffered brutal military rule for decades. A coup in 1979 set off an insurgency and violent civil war in the 1980s. El Salvador in 1992 achieved peace through an agreement that allowed competitive party politics and the reintegration of former insurgents into the electoral system. Honduras has oscillated between civilian and military rule, but with regimes far less repressive than those of

---

[2] Even in Guatemala, where Mayan and other indigenous languages are spoken, bilingualism is commonplace, such that only a small percentage of the population is monolingual indigenous language speaking (Guatemala Instituto Nacional de Estadística 1996).

Guatemala and El Salvador. Honduras likely avoided major unrest by establishing competitive democratic rule in the 1980s, and civilians consolidated their hold on the system in the mid-1990s.

Our sample of countries also includes Nicaragua, which, after rule for decades by a "sultanistic" dictatorship, has gone through dramatic shifts in regime type since the 1970s. Socialist revolutionaries seized power in 1979 and then faced a brutal counterrevolutionary civil war in the 1980s. Nicaragua's revolutionary government built a constitutional and electoral framework that allowed the revolutionaries' electoral defeat in 1990. Since then a succession of competitively elected regimes has followed. Panama long suffered from a cycle of serial military overthrow of its civilian regimes, a pattern broken by the U.S. invasion in 1989 and the establishment of competitive democracy. Colombia has been plagued by violence at least since the 1930s and has suffered from the region's longest guerrilla (and today narco-guerrilla) insurgency. Yet, following a 1958 agreement that provided for two decades of alternating power between the liberal and conservative parties, Colombia developed competitive party politics and civilian rule despite an ongoing and at times brutal insurgency.

The eight countries in our study vary in other ways as well, perhaps the most important differences being their regimes' abilities to "deliver the goods" to their populations. Once again, Costa Rica is the standout, with levels of social welfare, health, and education that are the envy of the region. Panama, too, has achieved impressive levels of welfare (Seligson and Franzoni forthcoming). At the other extreme are Guatemala and Honduras, whose governments have invested little in their own human capital and, not surprisingly, have populations with woeful basic indicators of infant mortality and literacy. Mexico is the industrial giant of the region, with ever-increasing trade ties with the United States. Capital flight, civil wars, and policy instability have kept Nicaragua's performance on providing for its citizens dismal, despite the revolution's efforts to advance education, basic services, and welfare. In short, our research design incorporates countries with many basic similarities of history and culture, yet with great divergence in experience with and levels of democracy. We expected, then, to find varying levels of legitimacy among these countries and that the consequences of low levels of legitimacy should matter. This concluding chapter briefly reviews the evidence we have gathered in our analytical chapters, examines the implications of the findings for individual countries, and then brings the weight of that evidence to bear on the central puzzle of the book.

SUMMARY OF FINDINGS

The structure of legitimacy

We began by exploring the dimensionality of legitimacy. We noted the scholarly evolution of the concept over time, from its initial conception as one-dimensional, to its broadening by Easton into "specific" versus "diffuse" support, and to its more recent expansion by Norris and by Dalton into five dimensions: political community, regime principles, regime performance, regime institutions, and political actors.

Our analysis benefited from key steps we took in the questionnaire design phase. We increased the robustness of measurement of the dimensions of the legitimacy in three ways. First, we collected and developed a large pool of items that would cover the legitimacy waterfront as broadly as possible. Many prior studies had limited themselves to asking only a few questions, which placed their focus on a limited notion of legitimacy and left validity highly dependent on only a few items. To our knowledge, no prior study has utilized a questionnaire as rich as the one we developed to measure legitimacy. In total, we deployed 23 survey items to measure legitimacy.

Second, unlike many (but certainly not all) prior studies, we insisted that each item be measured using multipoint scales. In many studies, questions have been asked in a simple agree/disagree format, one that not only severely truncates variation in response but also artificially disallows for any in-between attitudes. That strategy also increases the problem of acquiescence response set, whereby respondents tend to state agreement with many items irrespective of their feelings on the content of the item merely because they do not want to seem uncooperative. Our prior research in the Latin American environment revealed that acquiescence to interviewers by respondents of lower socioeconomic status can overstate seriously the proportion of positive responses. In our legitimacy variables, we never used items with fewer than five category responses (and then on only three of the items that eventually formed our indices). More often we utilized 7-point and 10-point response categories.[3]

---

[3] In an ideal world we would have used the same metric for all items, but since many of the items utilized in the 2004 survey had been used before by LAPOP in questions formulated as early as the late 1970s, we decided to retain the original coding schemes to allow comparability for longitudinal work. In each case in this volume, however, we converted *every one* of the legitimacy items into a 0–100 scale format so that it would be appropriate to compare their unstandardized coefficients in our regression analyses.

Finally, we have measured legitimacy (and many other key variables) using multiple items (survey questions) to increase their validity and reliability. We also have subjected them to construct reliability testing to assure that they are conceptually coherent. Many prior studies have used a single item to measure a construct as nuanced as legitimacy, so we have avoided that trap.

We began in 2002 with a pilot study in Costa Rica, described in Chapter 1. Using the survey data collected there, we used structural equation modeling (SEM) and found strong support for the five-dimensional legitimacy scheme plus a sixth dimension of support for local government. We have replicated this analysis here with our eight-nation study using 2004 survey data and have reconfirmed the validity of legitimacy as a multidimensional phenomenon. We concluded that approaches to legitimacy that do not follow the expanded Norris/Dalton approach are almost certainly missing important differences in the structure of the concept. The result of our analysis was a six-dimensional structure:

- Support for the Existence of a Political Community
- Support for Core Regime Principles
- Evaluation of Regime Performance
- Evaluation of Regime Institutions
- Evaluation of Local Government
- Evaluation of Political Actors

Thus, our first conclusion is that much of the measurement of legitimacy in prior work has been flawed, to a greater or lesser extent. Legitimacy typically has been conceived too narrowly. Much analysis has relied on too few or even single items to measure legitimacy norms. Most of it has captured only one or a very small number of dimensions. Our advantage and our methodological advance here has been to identify and develop measures of six distinct dimensions of legitimacy, each made up of multiple items and each in turn based on multichoice response patterns. Thus our indexes are stronger than in most prior research, and we know of no prior research that has used measures as finely graded and multidimensional as ours.

One problem that vexes all surveys is nonresponse. In truth, it is a problem for virtually all datasets in the social sciences; even such macrolevel data as GNP and voting records contain blanks. But survey respondents are always given the option of not responding to any given item, and thus analysts must develop a way of dealing with it.

Since legitimacy is the central variable of interest in our study, we decided to estimate the responses for those who did not answer questions in the legitimacy series using a multiple imputation technique, described in detail in Appendix E. This technique provides the best possible estimate as to what the missing response would have been based on all of the data in the study. By using this estimation technique, our final sample size for the legitimacy variables used for analysis throughout the book is the same as the entire initial sample actually drawn in the field. The only variation in sample size that then occurred was on the remaining variables in the study, used either as independent or dependent variables, for which we did not impute missing results.

Comparative levels of legitimacy

Our second conclusion has to do with the implications of the variation we found across these dimensions of legitimacy. By this we mean variation in three different senses: first, variation in *levels* of legitimacy among the six dimensions; second, variation in the *sources* of the six types of legitimacy; and finally and most importantly, variation in the *consequences* of legitimacy's several dimensions.

We find significant and sharp differences in the *levels* of legitimacy across dimensions as shown in Figure 8.1. The figure illustrates mean legitimacy levels (on a 0–100 basis) indicated by the large bars. (The smaller error bars shown on the top of the larger bars indicate the confidence intervals for each dimension of legitimacy.) In substantive terms, it is important to note the sharp distinction between the far higher level of support for political community and regime principles versus the other four dimensions. Indeed, the levels of these two dimensions are barely distinguishable from each other; only a half point separates them on a 0–100 scale. These two dimensions are the most general (diffuse) of the six and the ones on which our survey respondents disagreed little. All countries exhibited relatively high levels of belief in the existence of a political community as well as support for the core principle of democracy that people should be allowed to participate politically. This last finding is particularly important because it reveals very strong principled support among citizens for their nations as such and for the idea that they should be democratically governed. These data and others uncovered later in our study gainsay recently expressed apprehension that popular

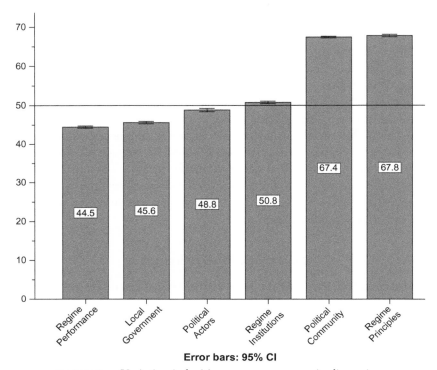

Error bars: 95% CI

FIGURE 8.1. Variation in legitimacy scores across six dimensions

support for democracy in Latin America has declined to dangerously low levels (Smith 2005; Diamond 2008).

Figure 8.1 also shows that on the other four dimensions, for the pooled sample of eight nations as a whole, only one other legitimacy dimension, regime institutions, produced a score that, on average, was in the high end of the 0–100 continuum.[4] The means for the other three dimensions fell in the low end of the continuum, with regime performance bringing up the rear. Thus, as legitimacy measures move away from the general dimensions (national community and support for democracy) and to more specific evaluations of actual performance by governments, our Latin American citizens become much more critical.

---

[4] Recall that the samples were all weighed equally (to an N of 1,500) so the means are true indications of the national sample results, giving equal weight to each country in the sample.

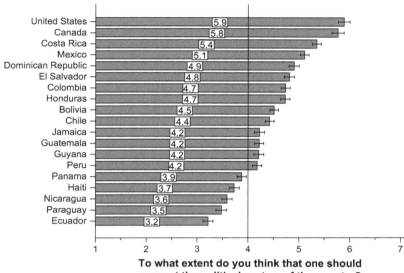

To what extent do you think that one should
support the political system of the country?

Sample size for all countries ca. 1,500 except U.S. and Canada ca. 600. Ecuador
and Bolivia ca. 3,000.
Error bars: 95% CI; Source: AmericasBarometer, 2006

FIGURE 8.2. Support for the political system, 2006 LAPOP sample

Legitimacy varies not only across types, but also among countries. Earlier chapters have covered this point in detail, but introducing a broader comparative framework here helps underscore the point. Consider the results of the index we developed here to measure support for regime institutions, our closest parallel to what Easton meant by "diffuse support." This index, based on five items that initially were developed for use in Germany by Muller (1979) and also employed in a sample in the New York City area in 1978, has been used repeatedly in Latin America by the LAPOP project. It provides a strong comparative base to support the contention that the countries in our present sample should vary among themselves while being meaningfully comparable to advanced industrial nations.

We can illustrate that there indeed exist important differences in legitimacy levels among the countries in our eight-nation study, other similar democratizing countries, and advanced industrial democracies by using data for 2006 from the AmericasBarometer that have recently become available. In Figure 8.2, a single item (identical to one we have used in our research) drawn from the support for regime institutions series is displayed using their original 7-point scale.[5] The comparison clearly reveals that, as our theory suggested, system support in the advanced industrial nations of Canada and the United States is far higher than in most of the emerging democracies in Latin America. Thus, the grave concerns so often expressed in academic papers and books about the legitimacy "crisis" faced by the advanced industrial democracies may be true only relative to their own presumably higher levels expressed at earlier time periods.

Compared to Latin America, the United States and Canada, at least, seem to be doing quite well in terms of institutional legitimacy. The results for the United States are especially illuminating because the survey was conducted in late 2006, just after that year's midterm elections. Recriminations against government ineptitude in the handling of Hurricane Katrina were widespread. With public opinion also running strongly against the war in Iraq, the Bush administration suffered a major defeat when the Republican Party lost control of both houses of Congress. It is therefore possible that the 2006 survey data on legitimacy were capturing an especially low point in popular opinion in the United States, one no doubt dragged down by highly unfavorable views of the government in Washington. Even so, the U.S. scores are significantly higher than those of any Latin American country (Costa Rica comes closest to the United States) and dramatically higher than several countries at the lower end of the scale.

Figure 8.2 also highlights the relative positions of the countries included in our eight-nation series. Costa Rica and Mexico are very clearly at the top, with El Salvador, Colombia, and Honduras in the middle range, and Guatemala near the bottom of the higher end (above the midpoint) of the scale. Panama and Nicaragua round out our eight cases, falling near the low end of the range of observed countries and below the scale mean. Still, the national sample means for Nicaragua and Panama remain some distance above that for Ecuador, a country seriously troubled over the last decade by repeated

[5] The 2006 sample included more countries, but the database lacks certain key legitimacy variables that would enable us to define and examine all six dimensions used in the 2004 study described in this book. The surveys for all of the Latin American countries followed the same sample design and identical working as was used in 2004, with face-to-face interviews of approximately 1,500 respondents per country, except Bolivia and Ecuador, where the sample was ca. 3,000 in each country. The United States and Canada, however, were covered by phone surveys using random-digit dialing to land-line phones, with translations into Spanish for the United States and French for Canada for the appropriate respondents, and samples of about 600 in each country.

irregular transfers of executive power and extreme violations of judicial independence.[6]

We emphasize that Figure 8.2 compares only a single variable from our list of 23 legitimacy items integrated into the dimensions examined throughout this book. Direct comparison with the ordering based on this single variable therefore could be misleading. Nonetheless, this single-variable comparison highlights two important points. First, legitimacy varies substantially among countries. Second, the countries we have selected to include in our eight-nation survey provide a wide range in legitimacy levels not available when samples are confined to long-established democracies in advanced industrial nations.

Sources of legitimacy

We next examined the sources of legitimacy and concluded that not all types of legitimacy arise from the same sources. Conceptualizing legitimacy norms as multidimensional, Chapter 4 demonstrates that each type of legitimacy has its own particular referent. Referents range from a national political community to particular local governments and from the relatively abstract idea of favoring democratic principles to the very concrete performance of particular presidents or economies. We found that voting for the winner in the last presidential election, for example, has a very strong effect on evaluating actors and regime performance for obvious reasons. A partisan tends to value or expect value from the accomplishments of his/her own party's candidates. But voting for the presidential winner has only modest impact on evaluating the performance of local government, and none at all on whether a citizen agrees with fundamental democratic principles. This last point is particularly important because it reveals that support for democracy as such is much more than a "winner's legitimacy" that is contingent on partisanship or ideological bias. Rather, citizens in our eight nations support democratic regime principles for their own sake.

We found that only a few system-level, or context, variables affect legitimacy. Prior experience with democracy elevates the sense of political community and support for democratic regime principles, both plausible outcomes. Government effectiveness elevates citizens' evaluations of

---

[6] We lack the space here to describe the Ecuadorian case in detail, but the interested reader should consult Seligson et al. (2006d) for an extensive study of survey data from that country.

regime institutions. Gross domestic product growth over a span of 14 years prior to the survey correlates positively with citizens' evaluations of regime economic performance. But we caution that, given our small sample of countries (as opposed to our reasonably large survey sample of respondents within each country), we risk committing what scientists call a "type II error" in which we fail to find something that actually exists. If we had had many more countries in the study and thus perhaps more contextual variation, we might have found that context mattered more. All we can say with our current sample is that most of legitimacy's sources arise from individual-level factors – the citizen's position in society, personal attributes, community type, personality, and experiences. The agenda for further research in this area is to expand the sample of countries considerably to enable a more thorough testing of country-level contextual variables.[7]

We also examined subnational-level contextual effects. We determined that the larger the population of the community in which one lives, the less likely it is that most aspects of the regime will be viewed positively. Proximity to national government clearly does not breed political support in Latin America. We do not argue that this will be a universal finding; in countries where central governments are more effective at "delivering the beef" and doing so equitably, we predict that community size might lose significance. Nevertheless, given the many unfilled needs of urban residents in the countries we are studying, including everything from poor trash collection and inadequate or nonexistent sewage disposal to potholed streets, rampant crime, inadequate schools, and substandard public health facilities, our findings suggest that urban dwellers in these eight Latin American countries, and probably in many more developing nations, are disgruntled.

We leave most other context variables, which would require developing indicators independent of the survey data, for another time (and perhaps another book). The range of context variables that could be explored is daunting, including macrolevel social, economic, and demographic variables, party preferences, historical voting patterns, and crime and corruption levels.[8] Of equal interest but likely even more difficult to tap are unique historical circumstances relating to regional conflicts, the popularity of political figures, and so forth. Context at the national, regional,

---

[7] We also should note that in most multilevel research combining survey and country-level data, most of the variation in the results is found in the individual-level data. In that sense, our results are consistent with the norm.

[8] For example, we found no impact of inequality, even though research in Europe has shown that it matters (Anderson and Singer 2008).

and local level may matter – indeed it may matter a great deal in explaining the sources of legitimacy. But the research program to untangle those effects more than we have done here is beyond the scope of this volume. It would require a very large sample of countries, but ones for which our six dimensions of legitimacy data are also available at the individual level.

We have far more confidence about the individual-level effects revealed by our analysis. All cohorts of older citizens almost always evaluate the more concrete legitimacy dimensions (regime institutions, performance, actors, local government) more negatively than do the very youngest citizens aged 16 to 20. Education affects most dimensions of legitimacy, but the patterns are not uniform across the six dimensions. Having more education correlates with a higher sense of national community and with more support for democratic regime principles and local government. This pattern also holds true for those with more political information. Even more important and in an interesting contrast, having more education and more political knowledge associate with lower evaluations of regime institutions and political actors. Thus, the more knowledge-management skills and information citizens in our eight Latin American nations have, the more harshly they appraise the regime's leaders and institutions.

These findings alone should send up a red flag to those who have evaluated legitimacy using a single dimension, or worse still, a single variable. If education associates positively with some dimensions of legitimacy and negatively with others, studies that agglutinate legitimacy into a single dimension seriously risk misinterpreting its sources and, by extension, misinterpreting the key ways in which individual traits raise or lower legitimacy.

Nonetheless, we did find that one frequently cited variable in the social-psychological literature, interpersonal trust for one's neighbors, strongly and positively associated with all six dimensions of legitimacy. Putnam's (1993) thesis, amplified by the impressionistic work of Fukuyama (1995) and studied intensively by others, seems borne out by our findings on legitimacy. The larger question of *how to build trust* is not addressed by our study. Moreover, we cannot be completely certain that, given the nature of our data, the causal arrow runs from trust to legitimacy. Indeed, we suspect that it may go the other way – countries that give their citizens reason to trust their political systems likely also encourage their citizens to trust one another. From a methodological point of view, untangling causality is a difficult process.

Another systematic finding affecting all but one dimension of legitimacy is the impact of crime and corruption. Those who have been asked

to pay bribes to public officials and those who believe that their neighborhoods are unsafe consistently evaluate the legitimacy of their political
system negatively. The only exception is support for core regime democratic principles. Those critical democratic values, we were relieved to
find, remained unaffected by corruption and crime, at least in this 2004
dataset. It follows, then, that regimes that seek to increase their legitimacy
must curtail crime and corruption.

Consequences of legitimacy: Its impact on political participation

Chapter 5 explored conflicting theories regarding the impact of legitimacy
on participation. Some theories hold that those who support the system
would participate while those who do not would withdraw from participation. Other theories place greater emphasis on those who hold low
legitimacy norms, arguing that such individuals do not withdraw, but
are more likely to engage in political protest. To test these propositions,
we looked at six distinct modes of political participation: registration to
vote and voting; partisan-campaign activism, contacting public officials,
communal activism, civil society activism, and protest behavior. We found
that legitimacy matters for political participation but, consistent with our
overall theme, different dimensions of legitimacy have different impacts
on participation. Table 8.1 summarizes these findings, along with other
effects of legitimacy.

Political community and support for political actors had the least effect
of the six legitimacy dimensions for political participation. In marked contrast, evaluation of regime performance and support for local government
had the greatest effects; each influenced at least half of the six participation
modes. While legitimacy in its multiple dimensions does not always impinge
upon all forms of citizen engagement in the polity, we nevertheless have
shown clearly that *legitimacy does matter for political participation.*

Our findings overturn key elements of the conventional wisdom about the
relationship between legitimacy norms and political participation. Most
strikingly, other factors in the models including national context held constant, 10 of the 13 significant legitimacy effects proved not to have a simple
linear form (negative or positive), as widely hypothesized by the literature.
Rather, 10 had a U-shaped relationship (and one an inverted U-shape). In
these twelve relationships, *the most supportive and the most disaffected
citizens engage in politics much more than do those who are indifferent.*

Our research has shown that disaffected citizens – those who express
low levels of legitimacy – do not withdraw from politics, as some theories

TABLE 8.1. *Summary of legitimacy's effects in eight Latin American nations*

Legitimacy Variables	Political Participation						Attitudes						Ratio of Significant Relationships
	Vote	Party-Camp. Activ.	Con-tact Publ. Off.	Com-munal Activ.	Civil Soc. Activ.	Pro-test Part.	Sup-port Rebel-lion	Sup-port Coup d'état	Sup-port Con-front.	Supp. Vigi-lan-tism	Dem-and for Demo-cracy	Perc. Supply of Democ.	
Political community	+						−			−	+	+	6/12
Regime principles		u				U			+		+	+	5/12
Regime institutions		+	n						+			+	4/12
Regime performance		u		U	u	U	−	−			+	+	8/12
Political actors		u					−	−			+	+	5/12
Local government		u	u	U			+		+		+	+	6/12

Key: "−" = significant negative relationship; "+" = significant positive relationship; "u" = significant U-shaped relationship; "n" = significant inverted U-shaped relationship. Grey shaded box indicates relationship with t-ratio of 9.00 or above (very strong).

have suggested. Rather, citizens expressing low legitimacy norms participate actively – the very opposite of such theories predictions. This holds
true not only for participation within the channels of national institutions – contacting officials, parties, and campaigns – but also prevails in
other political arenas such as communal activism, civil society, and protest. Indeed, we find that even very high levels of alienation from the
political system in our sample of countries consistently produce higher
rather than lower levels of participation. We thus dispel, at least for this
sample of countries, the notion that alienated individuals become "anomic" and withdraw from politics. We do note, however, that under nondemocratic situations of extreme repression (conditions not found in our
eight-nation sample) withdrawal from participation is, no doubt, the de-
fault option for all but the most risk-embracing individuals who would be
willing to sacrifice life and limb to challenge their regimes.

We did find, as the literature hypothesized, that disaffected citizens do
protest more while strong supporters of the system protest less. But more
generally, while we do identify two linear positive effects of legitimacy (political community on voting and regime institutions on partisan-campaign
activity – Table 8.1), by far the predominant pattern is that of *high participation by politically engaged regime supporters and by regime critics* rather
than the previously theorized high participation by supporters and low involvement by critics. The final section of this concluding chapter lays out the
implications of these findings for solving our overall legitimacy puzzle.

Consequences of legitimacy: Its impact on negative political capital

In Chapter 6 we examined legitimacy's effects on what we call negative
political capital, an array of attitudes about confrontational political
behaviors ranging from the extreme to the more commonplace. We first
examined support for an extreme measure, approval of attempting to
overthrow an elected government using violent means. We also asked
a series of questions about justification for a coup d'etat by the military
when the country is faced with stressors such as extensive social protests
and high levels of unemployment, crime, inflation, and corruption. We
also asked about approval of various forms of civil disobedience, including taking over factories and offices, invading private property, and blocking streets and highways. Finally, we asked about approval of vigilantism
(taking the law into one's own hands).

Once again we found that legitimacy matters and that its impact varies
across types; our findings are summarized in Table 8.1. Regime principles

and regime institutions legitimacy have the least effect on negative political capital. These findings appear counterintuitive because one would anticipate that people more supportive of democratic regime principles and national institutions would be less likely to manifest negative political capital values. In contrast, these legitimacy dimensions simply prove largely irrelevant to negative social capital.

One intriguing aspect of this missing connection between support for regime institutions and negative political capital arises because so much prior research relies heavily on some variant of support for regime institutions as its sole legitimacy measure. Our finding suggests that this previous work would have benefited from a broader view of legitimacy. Moreover, because support for institutions is the legitimacy dimension most often evaluated to trace legitimacy's evolution over time (Nye 1997; Seligson 2002a), researchers may well have been using the wrong measure. Other dimensions have much stronger links to social capital and participation. This problem may help account for the puzzling absence of a legitimacy effect upon regimes. If institutional legitimacy has little effect on attitudes and behavior in democracies, that alone might account for the absence of an observed legitimacy effect on system stability. What other legitimacy norms, if any, might matter more for political behavior and social capital norms thus remains to be determined.

Contrary to common expectations, high regime principles and regime institutions legitimacy values associate strongly with greater approval of some forms of negative political capital, especially support for confrontational tactics (including various forms of civil disobedience). Further, support for local government has a modestly positive association with support for rebellion and approval of confrontational political tactics. In contrast, the most influential dimension of legitimacy in predicting negative political capital is perception of the existence of a national political community. The stronger that norm is, the lower is the support for several forms of negative political capital. A similar pattern also was found for support for political actors and evaluation of regime economic performance.

Taken together, these findings paint a complex picture of legitimacy's effects on negative political capital. Those who perceive a national community and approve of incumbent actors and economic performance tend to have less negative political capital, a finding that corroborates the received wisdom on legitimacy's effects. Diverging from our expectations, however, some legitimacy dimensions produce effectively the opposite outcome. Institutional support, regime principles legitimacy, and support for local government associate with approval of confrontational political methods. Clearly, Latin American supporters of democratic regime principles and of their (however imperfect) democratic national political systems and local governments nevertheless feel comfortable with protest. Thus, no one should assume that Latin America's democrats and institutional loyalists will be politically passive or will embrace and employ only within-channels political means. Confrontation – protesting, occupying buildings, and blocking streets – makes up part of the culturally acceptable political toolkit of citizens of Latin American democracies. The implications of this finding are great: Policy makers, scholars, and the media would err seriously by imputing the protest or protesters in Latin America for any necessary repudiation of democracy or democratic institutions. Further, it would be just as incorrect to assume that rising support for democracy necessarily would reduce protest.

Other factors affecting negative political capital include an array of demographic and socioeconomic variables. Disturbingly, we found that younger citizens are more prone to negative political capital. We do not know whether this is cohort effect that young people might "grow out of" as they age and develop a greater stake in their communities. Alternatively, it might constitute a longer-term effect that eventually could increase negative political capital more generally in these countries as this cohort ages. We also uncovered the expected, but nonetheless troubling, finding that persons who are crime victims, fear crime, or have been victims of a bribe solicitation are more likely to support the negative tactics detailed in Chapter 6. Given the high levels of crime and corruption in Latin America (Fajinzylber, Lederman, and Loayza 1998; Gaviria and Pagés 1999; Seligson 2006a), it may well be that over time support for negative political capital will increase. On the other hand, greater levels of education, wealth, interpersonal trust, life satisfaction, and information all attenuate negative political capital, and because over time education and wealth are increasing, even if very slowly in some of our eight countries, these forces might countervail the increases in negative political capital being shaped by high crime and corruption levels.

Community size matters, with small-town and rural residents less likely to have high negative political capital levels. This finding gives credence to the notion that cities and city dwellers are more confrontational than are residents of small towns and the countryside. In Latin America, rural dwellers are systematically poorer and less well educated than urbanites, but rural life does nonetheless seem to stem negative political capital. Since Latin America has been urbanizing rapidly over the past few decades, this rural counterbalance to urban negative social capital may well be declining.

Consequences of legitimacy: Its impact on support for democracy

Chapter 7 examined legitimacy's effects on democratic values (Table 8.1 summarizes them). We raised the concern that political participation, which we found to be linked to legitimacy in many ways, might actually undermine democratic rule by overloading governments with excessive demand and disruptive protest. We drew this concern from Huntington's (1968) classic warning that in developing countries participation could overwhelm the capacity of the system to cope with it.

We structured our argument around the concepts of supply of/demand for democracy developed by Bratton et al. (2005). From that perspective, it is important to know both whether citizens are demanding democracy and how well they believe that their system supplies it. Our results demonstrated clearly that the levels of legitimacy we observed in these eight nations pose little threat to the demand for democracy. Strong majorities ranging from 78 to 90 percent, by country, preferred elected democracy to rule by an unelected strongman. Legitimacy nevertheless affected this preference: higher levels of political community, support for regime principles, support for regime performance, and support for political actors all contributed somewhat to greater preference for elected leaders. In these eight countries, then, Latin Americans' preference for elected rulers was only modestly contingent on legitimacy. Put another way, there was a high floor of preference for democracy; legitimacy raised or lowered it a bit, but did not appear to have the potential (that is, it had too weak an effect) to undermine a large majority's demand for democracy. We view this as very good news for those worried about democracy and its stability in Latin America. We note, however, that we have not examined here countries such as Bolivia and Ecuador where legitimacy is much lower and where the preference for democracy is uncertain.

We also examined the perceived supply of democracy using an index of respondents' evaluations of how democratic they believed their regimes to be. This analysis (summarized in Table 8.1) revealed that legitimacy mattered considerably for the perceived supply of democracy. All six legitimacy dimensions associated positively with perceived democracy. Regime principles, regime institutions, and regime performance had very strong relationships. Indeed, in one of the strongest patterns of influence found in our whole study of effects, citizens' legitimacy norms strongly influenced their sense of how democratic their nations are.

In sum, a democratic regime that is legitimate in all the meanings we have measured is likely to be viewed by its citizens as providing more democracy than is one with low legitimacy evaluations. Thus legitimacy – at least moderately good performance evaluations for different aspects of a regime – emerges as a factor likely to reinforce democracy. We know that Latin Americans strongly demand democracy, and here we see that the better they think their government is performing, the more democracy they believe they have. This pattern could well point to a beneficial circle that would contribute to the consolidation and entrenchment of democracy: *The people want democracy, and the better they believe their government is performing, the more democracy they will believe they have.*

On the cautionary side, however, this formulation hinges on the critical component of performance evaluation and reveals that the potential beneficial circle observed here is neither inevitable nor guaranteed. Returning to the cases of Ecuador or Bolivia, where both legitimacy and performance are much lower, legitimacy evaluation's effect on the demand for and supply of democracy may be profound and possibly negative. There, low legitimacy may have the potential to convert the beneficial cycle into a vicious one. In that case, very poor citizen evaluations of regime performance might undermine not only the perception of democracy supplied but also the demand for democracy itself, as some observers have feared.

We emphasize, however, that based on the data we analyze here such a scenario remains speculative. What we have in the eight nations in our study is evidence that legitimacy reinforces the perception of democracy supplied among people who strongly prefer elected leaders. We do not claim that this is necessarily a universal phenomenon. Indeed, we suspect that under certain scenarios and in some cases the vicious cycle may come into play.

IMPLICATIONS FOR THE EIGHT COUNTRIES

Theorists contend that legitimacy matters for regimes. Regimes whose citizens perceive a shared national community and agree on fundamental democratic rules of the game, and governments whose citizens approve of their performance, institutions, and leaders, should enjoy greater cooperation and compliance, and fewer system-threatening challenges from their people and elites. We have shown repeatedly, for the pooled sample of the eight nations, that the six legitimacy dimensions we have confirmed markedly affect citizens' political participation and key attitudes related to democracy, even when controlling for myriad other factors.

So far we have not focused very much on how, in practical terms, these patterns might affect the future of democratic political stability for the individual countries in our study. We understand the risks of prediction in the social sciences and know that expert opinion is notoriously unreliable (Tetlock 2005). Nonetheless, to demonstrate the practical utility of legitimacy theory and to advance our exploration, we will try our hand at prediction. This effort should provide further insight into the risk of instability for the eight countries we are studying. We recognize that the effort is speculative[9] but believe that even if we miss the mark our predictions may help us better understand the challenges ahead for appropriate use of the data we have gathered and analyzed.

How legitimacy might affect regime stability appears less than obvious owing to the puzzling absence of visible effects of the industrial democracies' declining institutional legitimacy and to the complex effects of legitimacy we have uncovered. Unfortunately, our cross-national data, all from 2004, do not allow us to investigate the dynamics of national legitimacy over time. We also know that mass publics' legitimacy norms constitute only part of the equation of democratic stability. Compared to developed democracies, young and developing democracies typically have modest political institutionalization and weak elite commitment to democratic norms. Far more than in developed democracies, young democracies' political elites, security forces, and external actors can all play critical roles. They more easily can promote a military or executive coup d'etat or undermine support for a democratic regime than can elites in more established democracies.

We will now try to explain how legitimacy norms are likely to affect political stability in our eight nations. We showed earlier that legitimacy affects various democratic behaviors and norms, including citizen participation and support for democracy. We believe these effects point the way toward legitimacy's prospective import for system stability in our Latin American countries. We overlay low legitimacy levels across multiple support dimensions and examine whether citizens who are *disgruntled in several distinct ways simultaneously* may exhibit combinations of

---

[9] There is, of course, an entire and highly lucrative industry built around evaluating the political risks facing businesses, development projects, and whole nations. We suspect that much risk analysis is intuitive and based on less solid foundation research and theorizing than we have brought to bear here. On the other hand, the effort and cost we have expended to undergird this study would likely be prohibitive for that industry.

behaviors and attitudes that could affect system stability. The pooled data analysis has detected some of the probable effects arising from certain legitimacy dimensions, especially antidemocratic values, confrontational political norms, and political participation.

We hypothesize that citizens with combined low legitimacy levels on multiple dimensions might also harbor beliefs and behave in ways that could contribute to political turmoil or, even more likely, facilitate the actions of antidemocratic elites. In a situation of widespread low legitimacy on multiple dimensions, strategically positioned elites might feel emboldened to use multiple dimensions of discontent as a pretext to curtail democratic liberties or to attempt to overthrow a democratic regime (Cameron 1998). The executive coup by Alberto Fujimori in Peru (Seligson and Carrión 2002; Carrión 2006) provides the prototype: Fujimori capitalized on public discontent driven by the serious threats to the system posed by the Sendero Luminoso guerrillas (in today's parlance, "terrorist group") to justify extinguishing democracy. Years earlier, the threat of insurgents in Uruguay and Guatemala had provided similar justifications for executive coups. Alternatively, in a country with few politically discontented citizens, elite justification for neutering or extinguishing democracy would ring hollow and likely would garner less support from the public, the military, or other strategically placed elites.

Venezuela, a country outside our set of cases, starkly illustrates the implications of low levels of legitimacy across several dimensions. Venezuelan elites in 1958 broke sharply with the country's long tradition of dictatorship when they signed the Punto Fijo agreement. This established power sharing between the two leading prodemocracy factions of the day (Peeler 1985; Peeler 1992; Karl 1997; Schneider 2007), and the resulting "pacted democracy" proved stable and apparently well institutionalized for decades (Higley and Gunther 1992). Venezuela eventually became Latin America's second oldest democracy, following only Costa Rica (Gastil 1989; Karatnycky 2000; Kelly 2001). Yet, as with many pacts, this one obsolesced. The original parties to the deal shared power, but they also largely excluded all newcomers from the system. This comfortable arrangement enabled both leading factions to grow increasingly corrupt, which gradually eroded the entire system's legitimacy (Martz and Baloyra 1976; Baylora 1979; Baloyra and Martz 1979; Baloyra 1987; Romero 1997; Canache and Kulisheck 1998; Canache 2002; Hawkins and Hansen 2006). In that context, the emergence in the 1990s of Hugo Chávez, a charismatic military figure and critic of the system, struck a resonant chord among a Venezuelan public alienated from the leading parties

(Hawkins 2003; Hawkins and Hansen 2006). Even though Chávez burst onto the scene with a failed 1992 coup attempt for which he was prosecuted and sent to jail, Venezuelans later overwhelmingly ignored that antidemocratic behavior and elected him president in 1999. Once in power, Chávez began what Diamond (Diamond et al. 1997; Diamond 1999b) has termed the "hollowing out" of democracy by whittling away at representative liberal institutions, restraints on the executive, and the rule of law. Many Latin Americanists believe that Evo Morales in Bolivia and Rafael Correa in Ecuador, to varying degrees, have emulated Chávez's model. Each has promoted constitutional changes that weaken traditional checks and balances and strengthen the presidency. We believe these cases exemplify contemporary efforts in Latin America to emasculate democracy by way of what Schedler (2006) has termed "electoral authoritarianism" in which democracy is limited to elections but little else.

Our intent in this section, therefore, is to look for evidence of perceptions of illegitimacy across three key dimensions of our six-fold schema. We believe that, where substantial proportions of a nation's population hold such notions, the opportunity for either electoral authoritarianism or a regime breakdown caused by the protest/executive coup cycle may increase. Of course, for antidemocratic elements to harvest such opportunities, many other factors would need to be in place, not the least of which is finding a popular candidate to lead the effort. Yet, charismatic leaders have a way of emerging in times of stress, as recent research has shown (Merolla, Ramos, and Zechmeister 2007).

To examine whether multiple dissatisfactions (holding multiple low legitimacy norms) might hold danger for our eight democracies, we now broaden our view. We consider whether a combination of low legitimacy norms on three key dimensions, if sufficiently widespread, may erode democracy or promote authoritarian or quasi-authoritarian regimes, perhaps of the "electoral dictatorship" variety noted above. After considering all six dimensions of legitimacy, we believe three have the most salience for the kinds of attitudes and behaviors we wish to explore: regime principles, support for regime institutions, and evaluation of regime performance. We exclude the other three from consideration for the following reasons: Local government legitimacy does not focus on *national* institutions. Perception of political community was so high in all eight countries that it identified very few respondents with low legitimacy values. Finally, the evaluation of actors seemed too narrowly focused on an individual officeholder, the president. Presidents can be relatively easily replaced by an election in all our countries (indeed, most have term limits). We thus believe this aspect of performance fails to capture the requisite scope of displeasure with government institutions in general, which citizens cannot easily replace.

Our theory is straightforward: First, for the survival of a democratic polity, a majority of citizens should support the core principles of democracy as such. If the people do not value democracy for its own sake, elites seeking to undermine democracy will almost certainly meet less resistance. Second, we know that regime performance evaluations affect more types of political participation and attitudes than do any other legitimacy mode. Satisfaction/dissatisfaction with the regime's ability to "deliver the bacon," therefore, potentially motivates more citizen political action and drives more negative attitudes than do other types of legitimacy. Third, institutional legitimacy is critical because, presidential popularity notwithstanding, support for national democratic institutions would stand as an obstacle to antidemocratic elites' or military attacks on a constitutional order. A lack of popular support for democratic institutions could make democracies vulnerable.

We hypothesize that when a large percentage of the population of a country is *triply satisfied* with the regime in terms of support for democratic regime principles, evaluation of national political institutions, and approval of the regime's performance, the weight of their shared attitudes will serve as a bulwark against threats to democratic rule. We further hypothesize that when an important percentage of the population of a country is *triply dissatisfied* – unsupportive of democratic principles, critical of national political institutions, and displeased with the regime's performance – the weight of their shared attitudes could encourage authoritarian challenges to liberal democracy. But what about citizens who hold mixed or conflicted positions on these three legitimacy dimensions? We believe that they are less likely to play an important role in democratic stability because their crosscutting legitimacy norms would give them dissonant motivations that might restrain them from action and confound their political attitudes.

Of course, we do not yet know how large the triply dissatisfied population must be for these low levels of legitimacy norms to matter. We are in uncharted terrain here, and cannot specify magnitudes a priori. We begin, therefore, by simply identifying the absolute proportions of triply disgruntled citizens and of those who are triply satisfied, as well as the ratio between them, and then considering their potential to influence the political system. We believe that these proportions and their ratio to each other will provide telltales for stability, especially through their impact on citizen participation. As we already have shown, those with low regime performance and regime principles legitimacy norms do not drop out of the system but actually engage in high levels of partisan, protest, and civil society activism. Within democracies, then, participation by such triply disgruntled citizens may become particularly important to the extent that they equal or outnumber the triply satisfied and not only fail to support prodemocracy actors but actually embrace those who promise to restrict (or even eliminate) democracy. Indeed, under extreme circumstances, a high proportion of triply dissatisfied citizens who outnumber the triply satisfied might signal, as they may have in the executive coups in Peru and Uruguay, the existence of a core group willing to endorse extreme measures. Of course, should the triply dissatisfied *oppose rather than support* rebellion or military intervention and should they prefer elected governments, their potential utility to would-be antidemocratic elites would be small.

What proportion of citizens is triply dissatisfied?

We explore the potential impact of the proportion of triply dissatisfieds first by dividing our eight-nation sample between citizens who support versus those who do not support democratic regime principles (those above or below the regime principles scale midpoint of 50), those who are satisfied versus unsatisfied with regime performance (above or below the scale midpoint of 50), and those who positively versus negatively evaluate national political institutions (above/below 50 on the scale.) Having a combination of a score either above the mean on all three dimensions or below the mean on all three thus defines the populations of triply satisfied versus triply unsatisfied. Depending on their content, the political behaviors and attitudes of these two types of citizens likely will hold particular import for democratic stability. If the triply dissatisfied lack behaviors and attitudes threatening to democracy, the legitimacy norms would define only a *latent* potential to contribute to instability. But if the triply dissatisfieds actually hold antidemocratic values and actively participate in politics, they could, we believe, link low legitimacy to system-disruptive conditions and invite elite subversion of democracy.

We begin with the relative proportions of the triply dissatisfied versus triply satisfied and of their respective shares of the overall citizen population. Each has implications for the impact of legitimacy on democracy, but in certain combinations we think that they could be of great import. For the sake of illustration, if – ceteris paribus – there were twice as many triply dissatisfied citizens in a country as triply satisfied citizens, the political activism and views of the triply dissatisfied might favor or encourage antidemocratic actions by civilian elites, a restive military, or even a portion of the military (Kling 1956; Putnam 1967; Lowenthal and Fitch 1986; Seligson 2008a). But this ratio obviously would matter more (or less) depending upon the overall share of the population that was triply dissatisfied. Two scenarios help clarify this point. In the first instance, assuming the same hypothetical 2:1 ratio of triply disgruntled citizens to triply satisfied ones, if only 10 percent of all citizens were triply dissatisfied and 5 percent triply satisfied, the relative impact of both groups combined on the polity as a whole likely would be small. If, in contrast, 40 percent of all citizens were triply dissatisfied while only 20 percent were triply satisfied, the potential impact of the disgruntled on stability likely would be large. A situation in which four out of 10 citizens are performance unhappy, uncommitted to democracy, and institutionally dissatisfied could portend great risks for extant democratic institutions. Note, of course, that we offer these proportions and their impact only speculatively at this point because we know of no benchmark research on which we can norm these estimates. In most of the developing world, datasets of the type we have gathered for this study simply have not existed, so estimates until now have not been possible.

Table 8.2 presents the distribution of triply dissatisfied and triply satisfied citizens in our sample by country. Very noteworthy is that in the pooled sample only 7 percent of the respondents are triply disgruntled, while 19 percent are triply satisfied. In Costa Rica and Panama the share of triply dissatisfieds is 3 percent or less. It falls between 5 and 7 percent in Mexico, El Salvador, Nicaragua, and Colombia. Two countries, however, have much higher proportions of triply dissatisfieds – Guatemala (15 percent) and Honduras (12 percent). Most of our eight countries, therefore, have minute percentages of triply disgruntled citizens, a fact that supports the overall theme of this chapter that indeed "the sky is not falling." In two countries, however, the ratio of those with multiple dissatisfactions, while not high in absolute terms, is much higher than in the other six countries. How can one explain this finding?

We showed in Chapter 3 that Honduras and Guatemala suffer from very poor performance in various economic, social, political, and security areas, and here we see that each has comparatively high proportions of triply dissatisfied citizens. The Honduran and Guatemalan cases thus bear particular scrutiny as we move forward. We are somewhat puzzled, based on their objective comparative performance problems,

TABLE 8.2. *Triply dissatisfied and triply satisfied respondents (percent), and ratio of triply dissatisfied to triply satisfied[a] on regime principles, regime performance, and institutional support, by country*

Country	Triply Dissatisfied as Percent of All Citizens	Triply Satisfied as Percent of All Citizens	Ratio Triply Dissatisfied to Satisfied
Mexico	6	16	.38
Guatemala	15	11	1.37
El Salvador	5	26	.21
Honduras	12	8	1.57
Nicaragua	7	13	.53
Costa Rica	2	29	.08
Panama	3	27	.11
Colombia	6	22	.26
Pooled sample	7	19	.37

[a] Triply dissatisfied respondents fall below the midpoint (50 points) on the 0–100 point legitimacy scale on all three of regime principles, regime performance, and institutional support. Triply satisfied respondents fall above the 50-point legitimacy scale midpoint on all three of regime principles, regime performance, and institutional support.

that Colombia and Nicaragua do not manifest greater numbers than they do of citizens expressing multiple dissatisfaction. We will return to these cases below.

The last column of Table 8.2 presents the ratio of triply dissatisfied to triply satisfied citizens, by country. Given that both groups are likely to contain political activists, we believe it is important for system political stability to consider whether there are more performance-dissatisfied, antidemocratic, and institutionally unsupportive citizens in a country than performance-satisfied, democratic, and institutionally supportive ones. We theorize that a ratio of triply dissatisfieds to triply satisfieds approaching or greater than 1.0 could indicate an activist population potentially amenable to antidemocratic appeals by coup plotters (civilian or military) or candidates for office antagonistic to a democratic regime. With this dissatisfieds-to-satisfieds ratio above 1.0, the triply dissatisfieds would outnumber the activist citizenry that we expect to be more sup-portive of democracy.

The triply disgruntled outnumber the triply satisfied only in Guate-mala and Honduras, and the ratio of the triply dissatisfied to the triply satisfied is well above 1.0 in only those two cases (Guatemala ratio = 1.37; Honduras ratio = 1.57). Note also that the overall percentage of such triply dissatisfied citizens in Honduras (12 percent) and Guatemala (15 percent) is nearly double to over seven times greater than the percentage of the triply dissatisfieds in the six other countries. Once again, this application of our theory strongly suggests that Guatemala and Honduras demonstrate greater risk for unrest, political turmoil, and support for antidemocratic regimes than do the other countries based on this indicator.[10]

To those who might argue that a mere 12–15 percent of a population that is very dissatisfied is too small to matter for political stability, we counter that the activists in virtually all rebellions consist of a tiny minority of the population. Further, motivated antidemocratic elites who potentially could draw support or encouragement from one eighth of the population, we believe, would be significantly advantaged by the presence of these disgruntled citizens. Moreover, if the deeply disgruntled sharply outnumber the most institution supportive, democratic, and performance satisfied, their utility to antidemocratic elite actors would be magnified.

Thus our combination of three legitimacy indicators has helped us flag two of our eight countries as potentially problematic for political stability. But what about the opposite condition? In which countries are legitimacy-related threats to instability and appeals of authoritarian rule the lowest? If our argument is correct, Costa Rica is clearly (and not surprisingly) the least likely to suffer from such risks because its triply dissatisfied elements are indeed minuscule (2 percent) while the triply satisfied are quite numerous (29 percent). We believe this finding strongly explains why Costa Rica has not suffered political instability despite its documented erosion of institutional support over recent decades (Seligson 2001d; Seligson 2002a). Three other countries have high percentages of triply satisfied citizens: Panama (27 percent), El Salvador (26 percent) and Colombia (22 percent). Further, Mexico, El Salvador, Nicaragua, Colombia, Costa Rica, and Panama all have lower percentages of triply dissatisfieds than Honduras and Guatemala, and considerably lower ratios of triply disgruntled to triply satisfied citizens. Our theory suggests, therefore, that these other six countries all have stronger prospects for political stability than Honduras and Guatemala.

[10] We suspect that Bolivia, Ecuador, and Venezuela are three other cases in which we would find similar ratios. LAPOP studies of Bolivia and Ecuador have shown extremely low levels of legitimacy (Seligson 2001c; Seligson 2002a; Seligson 2003; Seligson, Catsam, et al. 2004; Pérez-Liñán, Ames, and Seligson 2006; Seligson, Cordova, et al. 2006; Seligson, Donoso, et al. 2006). However, analyses of those cases fall outside the scope of this book.

How do the triply dissatisfied behave and what are their attitudes?

So far we have been dealing with the latent *potential* for instability that the triply discontented might generate based simply upon their proportions in the population. Our argument in Chapters 5 through 7, however, has been that legitimacy shapes *concrete political behavior and values* in ways that may reinforce or undermine democracy. Thus, particular behaviors and attitudes give a directional content to the latent potential implicit in legitimacy norms. Low legitimacy may help antidemocratic elites more easily pursue democracy-damaging schemes. For example, the multiple disgruntled public may embrace and applaud antidemocratic elite behavior or may mobilize in the streets or polling places in support of antidemocratic projects and candidates. Were we to discover that the triply dissatisfied population indeed both was politically very active and harbored attitudes corrosive to democracy (e.g., high levels of support for rebellion, confrontational political tactics, willingness to justify coups, or low preference for elected leaders), then their potential threat to a democratic regime and their potential utility to antidemocratic elites would be high. Were we to discover, in contrast, that little difference in such activism or values existed between the triply dissatisfied and other citizens, or that the triply dissatisfied held values that were conducive to democracy and stability, we would conclude that their legitimacy positions mattered little for democratic stability. Thus we now examine the *content of the political activism and attitudes* among three types of citizens – the triply disgruntled, the triply satisfied, and citizens with mixed (some high and some low) legitimacy norms.

Figure 8.3 compares key political behaviors and attitudes among the triply disgruntled, mixed, and triply satisfied citizens for the pooled sample. It illustrates our argument before we turn again to individual countries. We hypothesize that a scenario favorable to political instability would reveal sharp differences between the triply disgruntled and other citizens (that is, the slopes of the lines in the graph would be steep). Moreover, we would expect that in an instability-prone democracy, triply disgruntled citizens might manifest high levels of support for rebellion and confrontational political tactics as well as elevated political activism.

Figure 8.3 reveals that the differences among the groups amount to only a few scale points on any of these political capital variables. Considering behaviors, the triply dissatisfied engage slightly less in party-campaign activism and protest than do the triply satisfied and citizens with mixed legitimacy norms. In contrast, the triply dissatisfied are slightly

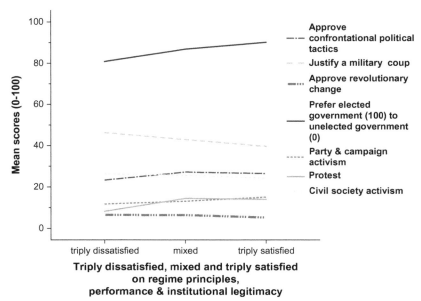

FIGURE 8.3. Political participation and attitudes by combined legitimacy norms, pooled sample

more active in civil society than are the triple satisfied. Thus, for the pooled sample, levels of legitimacy make very modest differences in participation levels, and some of them run counter to expectations. Turning to attitudes, the triply dissatisfieds indicate slightly more willingness to justify a coup d'etat and endorse armed rebellion than do the triply satisfied. With respect to the willingness to endorse revolutionary change, however, the level is extremely low for all groups. The mean score in these eight countries on endorsing revolutionary change is only 6.4 out of a possible 100. Further, the differences among the groups' means fail to achieve statistical significance; they only range from the triply satisfieds at 5.7 out of 100 mean approval of revolutionary change to the triply dissatisfieds' only slightly higher score of 7.1. Figure 8.3 further shows that the triply dissatisfied express less support for confrontational political tactics such as strikes, protests, or occupying buildings than do the triply satisfieds. This runs counter to our hypothesis that the triply dissatisfied might approve of confrontation considerably more than do other citizens.

Overall, then, for all countries combined the slopes of these lines are relatively flat, meaning that one's position on the multiple-legitimacy scale we use does not identify sharply different participation-related attitudinal and behavior patterns. In short, the *content* of the democracy-related political behavior and attitudes of the high-legitimacy versus low-legitimacy groups suggests little that would contribute to political instability.

Returning to the country level, another way to examine the possible roles of citizens with multiple low legitimacy positions is to consider how much total weight their political participation carries in the political system compared to that of citizens who report consistently high legitimacy positions. Our rationale is that the total number of political actions of a triply disgruntled population might matter considerably for overall political stability. We ask: Of all the participation in the polity, how much is the triply disgruntled segment contributing compared to the triply satisfieds? Do the triply disgruntled join groups more frequently, engage more people in party and campaign activity, and protest more than the triply satisfied? Further, do the patterns in the data confirm our suspicion that Guatemala and Honduras may have more potential problems for political stability than the other countries?

To measure overall participation we simply add up all the reported acts of participation among the triply disgruntled and the triply satisfied by country and compare them. This produces a total (rather than mean) participation value for each type of activism by legitimacy group for each nation. Figures 8.4–8.6 present these summed scores of party and campaign activism, civil society involvement, and protest participation, respectively, by country. These graphs clearly suggest that Honduras and Guatemala are more at risk for turmoil and offer populations more amenable to antiregime political appeals than other countries and that Costa Rica, El Salvador, Panama, and Colombia are less so.

Each of these figures shows that the total amount of political activism contributed by the triply disgruntled (the dark-shaded bars) in both Guatemala and Honduras nearly equals or exceeds that of the triply satisfied. In the other six countries, in contrast, the self-reported sum of all protest, all partisan activism, and all civil society activism undertaken by the triply satisfied is much greater than that of the triply dissatisfied. Thus the least satisfied in Honduras and Guatemala were not withdrawn from the political arena in 2004. Quite the contrary, they took part more in elections and campaigns and joined organizations more than did their triply satisfied fellow citizens. In Guatemala, the sum of protest by the triply dissatisfied was only slightly less than was that of the triply satisfied. In Honduras the triply disgruntled engaged in more protest overall than did the triply satisfied. To the extent that it persists, this near parity of participation between the most- and least-satisfied citizens in Guatemala

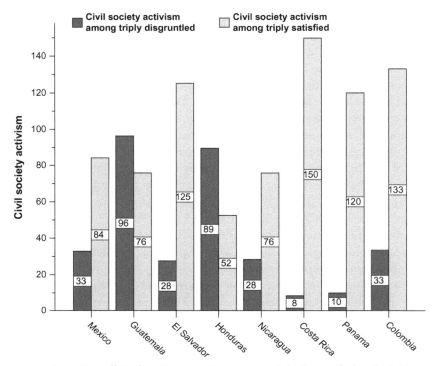

FIGURE 8.4. Overall civil society activism among triply dissatisfied and triply satisfied respondents, by country

and Honduras, we believe, is not by itself likely to derail democratic politics. But such a relatively large and disgruntled activist minority could place a very significant number of frustrated and mobilized citizens at the disposal of antidemocratic elites were a charismatic figure like Hugo Chávez or Evo Morales to materialize. A situation in which the overall participation contributed by the triply disgruntled *far exceeded* that of the triply satisfied (note that we have no case in which those conditions prevailed) might indeed be destabilizing in and of itself by overwhelming the political involvement of those much more content with the system.

Finally, a more detailed examination of the attitudes of Hondurans and Guatemalans adds further evidence that even in these *potentially* problematic cases, there was still little in the 2004 distribution of attitudes to suggest a problematic reservoir of antidemocratic feeling. When we compared the mean levels of support for coups and revolutionary change among Hondurans and Guatemalans by multiple satisfaction/dissatisfaction levels, we found that only support for confrontational tactics was

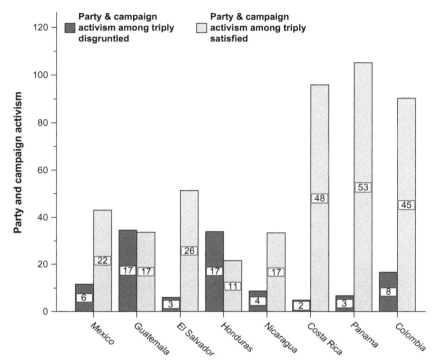

FIGURE 8.5. Overall partisan and campaign activism among triply dissatisfied and triply satisfied respondents, by country

significantly different among the three groups. Support for revolutionary change was very low across the board and not significantly different among the legitimacy groupings. To reiterate: Guatemala and Honduras had many more citizens in the triply dissatisfied category and their ratios of triply dissatisfied to triply satisfied citizens were both high in 2004. Nevertheless, the key political capital attitudes held by these least-satisfied citizens did not differ appreciably from other citizens with higher legitimacy values. Thus despite the large shares of triply disgruntled citizens in Guatemala and Honduras, the attitudes they held as of 2004 would have offered little encouragement to potential antidemocratic elites.

In sum, recent configurations of negative political capital attitudes among the triply dissatisfied in Guatemala and Honduras indicated only a latent potential to contribute to instability. However, as we have noted, antidemocratic populist political entrepreneurs recently have arisen elsewhere in Latin America. Indeed, in Guatemala in 2003 just such a person, the former military dictator and right-wing populist Efraín Ríos Montt,

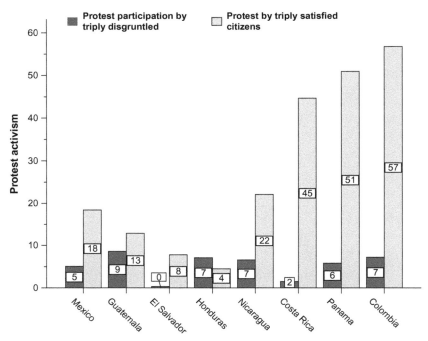

FIGURE 8.6. Overall protest activism among triply dissatisfied and triply satisfied respondents, by country

sought to return to the presidency via the ballot. Despite legal maneuvering and violent street protests organized on behalf of his candidacy, the Constitutional Court disqualified Rios Montt by upholding a constitutional provision against former members of de facto governments holding the presidency. Using propaganda and popular mobilization, other such figures could incite antidemocratic feelings and action among the disgruntled. Among our eight countries, however, we would assess their prospects for success as significantly higher in Honduras and Guatemala.

In contrast to Guatemala and Honduras, in three other cases overall participation by the triply satisfied far exceeded that by the triply dissatisfieds. In Costa Rica, Panama, and Colombia the triply satisfieds contributed several times more participation to the system than the triply disgruntled. Support for rebellions was low among all groups in these three countries. Support for rebellion was significantly higher among the triply dissatisfied only in Colombia. Bear in mind that the percentage of the triply disgruntled citizenry in each of these three countries was tiny, between 2 and 6 percent, and dwarfed by the percentage of those who were triply satisfied. We believe these patterns of a high ratio of triply satisfied to triply dissatisfied, combined with tiny differences among legitimacy groups, constitute a strong buttress to the stability of the political systems of Costa Rica, Panama, and Colombia.

The remaining cases (Mexico, El Salvador, and Nicaragua) fall somewhere between the other two sets of countries. In each, the overall participation of the triply satisfied citizenry exceeded that of the triply disgruntled, a positive sign for stability. The political participation of those who evaluated their systems more positively outstripped that of those who were most disgruntled on all three of our legitimacy dimensions, but in none of the three was there quite so large a reservoir of participation among the most satisfied citizens as in Costa Rica, Panama, and Colombia. Support for revolutionary change was low across all legitimacy categories at around 5 scale points out of 100 in El Salvador and 7 out of 100 in Nicaragua. The size of the triply disgruntled citizenries was smaller in both than that of the most satisfied. Even protest participation among the most disgruntled was very low. In Mexico support for revolutionary change among the most disgruntled was comparatively high at around 14 out of 100 on the scale, but still only one in 16 Mexicans fell into this small segment.

Our use of multiple legitimacy norms allows us tentatively to separate our eight countries into three expected risk categories based on the size and relative weight of their triply disgruntled citizenries and their levels of political participation as measured in 2004. The lowest risk group includes Colombia, Costa Rica, and Panama. The intermediate risk group includes Nicaragua, Mexico, and El Salvador. At the greatest risk of political instability are Guatemala and Honduras. In 2004, however, not even the large segments of triply disgruntled citizens in the two higher latent-risk countries held high levels of negative political capital. Nevertheless, Rios Montt and the possibility of a yet-to-appear antidemocratic demagogue like Chávez or Fujimori in either country exemplify the kinds of actors we believe could mobilize a potent threat to Honduran and Guatemalan democracy by mobilizing citizens with low legitimacy norms.

In conclusion we discuss two other countries where our analysis has revealed a legitimacy-based risk for democracy somewhat different from what we expected based on their political and economic histories. The first of these is Nicaragua, a country plagued by a record of economic performance so abysmal that we expected to find it at a high risk of instability. Nicaraguan economic performance actually lost substantial ground over the period of revolutionary and counterrevolutionary turmoil (1979–early

1990s), and very little recovery has occurred since then (Booth 1985). Why, then, are more Nicaraguans not triply disgruntled?

We believe that the answer lies in the fact that Nicaragua has recently experienced a major social revolution. In 1979 the Sandinistas overthrew the Somoza dynasty in a bloody insurrection. When they took power and implemented their revolution, some of their opponents (the *contras* or counterrevolutionaries) mounted a protracted civil war fueled in part by U.S. support. Thus between the mid-1970s and 1990, Nicaragua experienced an insurrection followed by a decade of revolution and counterrevolutionary violence. The resulting carnage and social disruption, pervasive throughout Nicaraguan society, affected the psychology of Nicaraguans to a degree that is difficult to overstate (Seligson and McElhinny 1996).

We believe that the searing experience of the revolution mitigated the very poor performance of the Nicaraguan economy, which otherwise might have produced high proportions of triply dissatisfied citizens. First, some Nicaraguans gained a sense of pride and accomplishment from taking part in the revolution or supporting it, and thus they likely have a greater sense of efficacy than they might have based solely on the country's dismal economic performance. Similarly, those who opposed the revolution and eventually voted the Sandinistas out may also feel a sense of accomplishment that transcends national economic performance. Second, Nicaraguans in general may suppress their discontent out of fear of rekindled political violence. Prior research on Mexico discovered that memories of the Mexican Revolution of 1910 passed across generations to the grandchildren of the revolution. Even that inherited fear of revolution dampened support for revolutionary change as late as the 1970s, despite high levels of political dissatisfaction among Mexicans (Seligson and Stevenson 1996). A combination of these factors rooted in the revolutionary experience could well be keeping legitimacy norms higher and levels of negative political capital lower in Nicaragua than in the other countries.

And finally, Colombia also seems anomalous in that it has experienced decades of civil war and contemporary narco-guerrilla conflict. We expected that this violent history would have generated a higher proportion of triply dissatisfied Colombians and that the country would have fallen into the middle risk group with Mexico and Nicaragua. Yet in Colombia only 6 percent of the population is triply dissatisfied. How might this low value be explained? We believe that the answer to this riddle is that, despite its political turmoil, Colombia's economic performance has been reasonably good in recent decades. Moreover, in spite of the protracted guerrilla insurgency and narco-violence, Colombia's electoral democratic political institutions have likely retained popular support by withstanding the protracted armed challenge and continuing to function.

SOLVING THE PUZZLE

We offer our solution to the legitimacy puzzle by returning to our initial question: Why do democratic regimes not collapse when legitimacy is low? Our first conclusion is that our multidimensional approach to defining legitimacy enabled us to determine that citizens do not see a monolithic political system in which they either have faith or do not. Rather, citizens can believe strongly in their political communities and have strong beliefs in regime principles, all the while being disgruntled about regime performance and/or national political leaders. Similarly, they can feel positively or negatively about their local governments. While these legitimacy dimensions correlate somewhat with each other, for most of the dimensions the relationship with each of the others is weak. It is thus difficult to predict an individual's position on one legitimacy dimension by his/her position on another.

We conclude that political regimes do not collapse when legitimacy is low partly because legitimacy is a far more nuanced and variegated concept than it was conceived of until recently. Legitimacy's various dimensions do not operate in lockstep with each other and their impact on participation and attitudes varies in complex ways. We found that among the dimensions of legitimacy that are significant predictors of participation and other attitudes, many influences are not in the direction originally expected. Equally surprising and arguably more important, most of the participation-legitimacy links are curvilinear. It is, therefore, quite likely that in medium- or high-performing democracies citizens are not upset enough about multiple issues to make low legitimacy norms on one or another dimension as threatening as much of the previous literature suggests that they are. Indeed, when it occurs, low legitimacy may lead some individuals to participate more *within* channels, thus having the real (but previously unanticipated) potential of reinforcing and strengthening democratic institutions.

Further, high support for democratic regime principles associates with high protest and high support for confrontational tactics. Thus the strategy of promoting adherence to democratic values embraced increasingly by many foreign aid donor nations in their foreign assistance programs will not necessarily contribute to political quiescence. Quite the contrary, citizens who believe deeply in democracy, our data show, are more likely to engage in protest and confrontational tactics than citizens with only middling levels of support for democratic norms. In sum, legitimacy is multidimensional and its impacts on participation and attitudes are simply too complex to summarize in the unidimensional and linear theories of much of the previous literature.

Moreover, we have found that the most commonly used metric for legitimacy, namely, support for national institutions, is the dimension that has the *fewest significant links to the behaviors and attitudes we have studied*. In only one-third of the 12 relationships we examined does institutional support matter. Institutional support elevates party and campaign activism, support for confrontational tactics, and perception of the supply of democracy.[11] One hardly can overstate the implications of this finding for previous research on legitimacy. If prior researchers have been using as their metric of citizen support the *least influential* of the legitimacy norms, what does it imply for their conclusions? At a minimum, we suspect that this finding may go a very long way toward explaining why there has been no apparent impact of low or declining institutional legitimacy on democratic regimes. To borrow Gertrude Stein's oft quoted phrase, it is possible that with respect to institutional support "there is no there there."

Our findings reveal that in the eight Latin American nations included in our sample rather than institutional support, citizen *evaluation of regime economic performance is the most important legitimacy dimension*. It affects four of six participation variables, all with the U-shaped relationship in which both the most supporting *and* the most disaffected citizens become more engaged in partisan, communal, civil society, and protest activities. Moreover, higher regime performance evaluation lowers support for rebellion and coups while it increases both the demand for democracy and the perception of its supply. This finding, we believe, has powerful implications for future efforts to evaluate the impact of legitimacy on political regimes. One critical variable that should be employed is evaluation of economic performance, not support for institutions. It may be that, because these eight nations have levels of wealth well below the advanced industrial democracies examined in nearly all prior studies of legitimacy, economic performance matters more in our cases than it does

[11] Institutional support also has the only inverted U-shaped relationship we discovered with contacting officials.

in the others. We are not certain that this is true, considering that so much of the literature until the recent advances made by Norris, Gilley and Dalton restricted legitimacy to its institutional dimension alone. We suspect, that our findings are replicable among developing nations generally.

Two other legitimacy dimensions affect about half of the key political attitudes and behaviors we have studied. First, *evaluation of local officials* has a sharp U-shaped effect on partisanship, contacting, and communalism. It also correlates with a greater perceived supply of democracy. Intriguingly, however, positive evaluations of local officials also correlate with higher support for rebellion and for confrontational tactics. We remain somewhat uncertain about just how and why, with so many possibly intervening individual (and some contextual) effects controlled for, the evaluation of local government links conceptually or empirically to high negative social capital. One possibility is that leftists (perhaps more prone to rebellion and confrontation) have had more success in winning local mayoralties than national government offices in Mexico, Colombia, Nicaragua, El Salvador, and Guatemala. The recent sharp shift to the left in many countries in Latin America also could be having an important effect on this dynamic (Seligson 2007).

Second, a sense of *political community* has an effect not unlike that often predicted in the literature for institutional support – it increases voting, demand for democracy, and the perception of the supply of democracy. Political community also associates with lower levels of negative social capital – support for rebellion, confrontational tactics, and vigilantism.

We also draw a second conclusion to help us solve the puzzle of why democratic regimes do not collapse when legitimacy is low. Even in countries like several of ours where regime performance is far from stellar, legitimacy does not fall to extremely low levels at which it would threaten stability of the regime. This does not mean that there is no lower limit below which low levels of legitimacy would undermine democratic stability. Extremely low levels of legitimacy recently have been found in both Bolivia and Ecuador (countries recently included in the AmericasBarometer surveys from which we drew the 2004 data analyzed in this book). While an examination of those cases is beyond the scope of this volume, Bolivia and Ecuador have been politically unstable for a number of years. In each case, successive presidents were elected and then forced to leave office by popular protests or by actions of legislatures operating under constitutional crises. The resulting "musical chairs" administrations have revealed one chief executive after another who found himself without a seat when the music stopped playing. Even so, although presidents in these countries have been forced from power, constitutional forms continue, and elections remain relatively free and fair.

The institutions of liberal democracy in Venezuela, once among the most admired democracies in the region, have eroded steadily under the leadership of President Hugo Chávez. Early public opinion studies showed that many years prior to Chávez' rise to power, Venezuelans were expressing deep-seated alienation from their political system (Baylora 1979). The public opinion studies that followed showed ongoing legitimacy problems (Canache and Kulisheck 1998; Canache 2002). Despite all of this turmoil, formal electoral democracy continues in Venezuela, although fair and important questions can be raised about the quality of democracy beyond the dimension of elections.

Our eight cases included a wide range of regimes, from long-established consolidated democracies (Costa Rica) to very new ones (Mexico) and even to one case of a country particularly battered by abysmal economic performance (Nicaragua). Yet, the range of variation we could cover here was not infinite, and only careful multidimensional analysis of the varieties of legitimacy in an even wider range of cases can contribute to a fuller picture.

A FINAL WORD

We draw several broader conclusions from our findings. First, to the extent that one may generalize our findings to other countries such as the industrialized democracies, where much of the previous legitimacy research has been done, legitimacy levels there may simply not be low enough for there to be any meaningful negative effects on citizens' behavior and attitudes. Indeed, in our eight countries, which arguably perform much worse on economic, social, and political metrics than most industrial democracies, we find no legitimacy-driven crises.

In democracies, citizens unhappy with their governments' performance are free to take part in politics without significant fear of repression. What we have found is that in Latin America, "critical citizens," to use Norris's (1999b) apt term, participate rather than withdraw from participation or turn to protest. They engage within national institutions as well as in other salient arenas such as civil society and their communities. Of course, were legitimacy levels to fall low enough in industrial democracies, their disaffected citizens – like our Latin Americans – might become *more* engaged in politics and/or shift the arenas of their activism to areas not previously studied. While they might protest more, they might also take part more in within-channel and nonconfrontational electoral competition, demand making, collective problem solving, and organizational activities. Thus, if generalizable to all democracies, the patterns we have observed may attenuate or mitigate the long feared system-level implications of low or eroded legitimacy in industrial democracies. Political activities by disaffected citizens in democracies thus may not necessarily threaten democratic stability.

For our eight Latin American countries we have found no evidence that the participation of politically disgruntled citizens undermines democratic institutions. Rather than disrupt the democratic political game or withdraw to the sidelines, the politically discontent stay in the game and play harder to advance their goals. They take part in elections, contact officials, and find alternative participatory arenas in local government and civil society. While disaffected citizens do protest more than the indifferent, highly supportive citizens also protest – and thus provide a counterbalance of institutional support and action. Under such circumstances, protest behavior becomes simply another means by which citizens communicate with the state. Because it comes from both critics *and* supporters of the system, protest as such seems less likely to undermine institutions than it would if only the deeply disaffected protested. Indeed, the heightened political engagement of the disgruntled citizenry could affirm and strengthen political institutions rather than undermine them.

Our answer to the legitimacy effects puzzle of why declining legitimacy has not destabilized democracies is this: *Absent the threat of major repression, disaffected citizens in democracies do not usually withdraw from within-system politics or turn mainly to confrontational methods.* Even though institutional support has declined in many democracies, fears that the sky would fall in democratic regimes or that protest and confrontation might overwhelm governments thus seem overblown, so long as the repressive apparatus of the state remains in check. We also note that in the not-too-distant past, many of the nations we studied unleashed furious attacks on civilians, in turn unleashing protracted unrest and even civil war (Booth 1991; Stoll 1993).

Why has most prior research failed to find such a distinctive phenomenon and solve the legitimacy puzzle? Perhaps these legitimacy-participation effects occur only in Latin America. We doubt this, however, simply because it just makes good sense to argue that a critical citizen in any democracy might seek to improve his or her polity by becoming politically involved. In a democracy, citizens frustrated with the actions of their president may easily and safely work within the electoral arena to oust that undesirable actor from power. Individuals unhappy about economic performance can campaign against the incumbent, strive to improve their own community infrastructure, and join organizations to promote their own interests or promote change. In democratic regimes these are reasonable options – options unavailable in repressive regimes that aggressively suppress participation and thus may drive citizens to drop out or make desperate choices. We believe that the failure of prior research to uncover the curvilinear patterns found here is a result of the simple failure to look for the right thing in the right places – multiple aspects of legitimacy within democracies with divergent performance and legitimacy ranges. The failure also comes because legitimacy theorists have overlooked the ways in which formal democracy allows disgruntled citizens safely to protest, vote, and campaign against incumbents in ways unavailable in nondemocracies.

We further conclude that prior failures to detect these patterns occurred because so much of the earlier research focused fairly narrowly on support for institutions rather than on the broader multidimensionality of legitimacy we have been able to employ. (Thanks to the more recent work of several scholars, notably Norris and Dalton, the field has improved in this regard.) In well-established democracies, citizens' institutional support norms tend strongly toward the positive end of the support scale. In such skewed distributions, there would be relatively few disaffected citizens and thus scant evidence of how disaffected citizens might actually conduct themselves. In our Latin American nations, in contrast, and over multiple dimensions of legitimacy, political support manifests much broader distributions. On some dimensions, the population means approach or fall below the center of the support scales. This has given us an opportunity, rarely available to previous researchers, to identify and study many disaffected citizens in detail.

This returns us one final time to Huntington's (1968) concern that too much demand might overload states and cause democratic decay and breakdown. We have seen that the evidence for negative political capital is divided. National community and positive evaluation of actors and regime economic performance strengthen attitudes that undergird democratic regimes by enhancing respect for the law and reducing support for rebellion and military intervention. In contrast, supporting democratic principles and national and local institutions increases support for confrontational political tactics. It is a fascinating paradox that, when citizens trust democracy and its institutions enough to engage in protest, this behavior might then overstretch state capacity. It is probably even more likely that frequent protest persuades nervous leaders or security forces to violate fundamental democratic principles by repressing what they view as unruly popular demand making. It is out of such action and reaction that democratic stability can, ultimately, begin to disintegrate. We bear in mind that Latin America stands out as a region of the world marked by repeated cycles of democracy and dictatorship. We only hope that this time around, with democracy established and functioning in nearly all of the region, the cycle has been broken for good.

Appendix A: Supporting Data and Analyses for Chapters 1–5

TABLE A.I. *Variables and dimensions of political legitimacy, Costa Rica, 2002*

Object of Support (listed from most general to most specific)	Operationalization of Variables	MM Mean	Standard Deviation
Existence of a political community	1. To what degree are you proud to be a Costa Rican? (7-point scale: recoded into a great deal = 100...not at all = 0).	84.90	18.48
	2. To what degree do you agree that in spite of our differences, we Costa Ricans have a lot of things and values that unite us as a country? (7-point scale: recoded into very much agree = 100...very much disagree = 0).	96.75	12.97
	Group mean	90.83	15.73
Support for core regime principles	I am going to read you a list of some actions or things that people can do to achieve their goals and political objectives. Please tell me to what degree do you approve or disapprove of people taking these actions: (10-point scale, 0 = strongly disapprove; 10 = strongly approve, transformed to a 0–100 range)		
	1. That people participate in a legally permitted demonstration.	73.29	30.22

(continued)

TABLE A.1 *(continued)*

Object of Support (listed from most general to most specific)	Operationalization of Variables	MM Mean	Standard Deviation
	2. That people participate in a group that tries to resolve community problems.	86.32	21.98
	3. That people work in an election campaign for a party or candidate	78.58	26.56
	Group mean	79.35	21.78
Regime performance	1. How would you rate, in general, the economic situation of the country? (5-point scale: recoded into very good = 100...very poor = 0)	41.00	19.06
	2. Do you think that the economic situation of the country is better, about the same or worse that it was a year ago? (5-point scale: recoded into much better = 100...much worse = 0)	37.90	32.90
	3. Do you think that over the next 12 months that the economic situation of the country will be better, the same or worse than it is now? (5-point scale: recoded into much better = 100...much worse = 0)	45.04	37.35
	Group mean	41.27	22.57
Regime institutions (diffuse support)	All of the following are on a 7-point scale: 0 = none...7 = much, transformed into 0–100):		
	1. How much do you think the courts of Costa Rica guarantee a fair trial?	57.26	24.22
	2. How much do you respect the political institutions of Costa Rica?	77.65	24.62
	3. How much do you think citizens' basic rights are well protected by the Costa Rican political system?	61.11	24.40
	4. How proud do you feel to live under the Costa Rican political system?	75.10	23.62
	5. How much do you think one should support the Costa Rican political system?	75.05	23.38
	Group mean	69.23	24.05

Object of Support (listed from most general to most specific)	Operationalization of Variables	MM Mean	Standard Deviation
Support for regime institutions	6. How much do you trust the Supreme Electoral Tribunal?	76.32	241.16
	7. How much do you trust the Legislative Assembly?	56.88	27.83
	8. How much do you feel well represented by your provincial legislative deputies?	45.28	27.87
	9. How much do you trust the political parties?	38.99	26.93
	10. How much do you trust the Supreme Court?	60.36	25.79
	Group mean	*55.59*	*19.74*
Support for local government	1. How much trust do you have in the municipality? (7-point scale: 0 = none...100 = much)	48.86	26.32
	2. Would you say that the services that the municipality is providing the people of your canton (county) are very good (100), good (75), neither good nor bad (50), bad (25), very bad (0)?	46.66	23.04
	3. How do you think they have treated you or your neighbors when you have gone to the municipality to do some business? Very well (100), well (75), neither well nor badly (50), badly (25), very badly (0).	55.73	22.69
	4. Do you think that the mayor and municipal council respond to the people's wishes always (100), most of the time (75), some of the time (50), almost never (25), never (0)?	34.54	21.53
	Group mean	*46.44*	*23.40*
Support for political actors or authorities	All on a 7-point scale (nothing = 0... much = 100): Referring to the government of Miguel Angel Rodríguez, how much did that government:		
	1. Fight poverty?	48.23	25.81
	2. Promote economic development?	52.14	25.46
	3. Combat government corruption?	42.51	27.40
	4. Fight crime?	46.13	27.90
	5. Promote democratic principles?	55.18	24.77
	Group mean	*46.69*	*23.15*

TABLE A.2. *Varimax rotated principle components solution for legitimacy variables, pooled eight-nation sample[a]*

Items	Component					
	1 Support for Regime Institutions	2 Support for Political Actors	3 Support for Local Government	4 Support for Regime Principles	5 Perceive a Political Community	6 Support for Regime Performance
B43 How proud are you to be a ____ (e.g. citizen of Guatemala)?	.048	.034	.034	.043	.726	−.012
pn2 How much do you agree that, in spite our differences, we ____s have much in common?	.060	.134	.024	.364	.544	−.036
e5 How much do you agree that people should participate in demonstrations allowed by law?	.025	−.056	.025	.791	−.074	−.020
e8 How much do you approve or disapprove that people should take part in a group seeking to resolve community problems?	.004	.007	−.007	.771	.234	−.019
e11 How much do you approve or disapprove that people should work on election campaigns for a political party or candidate?	.219	.048	.023	.684	.098	.083
soct1r How do you view the economic situation of the country?	.144	.110	.107	−.014	−.066	.743
soct3r How do you believe the country's economic situation will be a year from now, better or worse than it is now?	.049	.141	.087	.042	.070	.741

b1 How much do you believe that the courts of justice in ___ (respondent's country) guarantee a fair trial?	.599	.088	.036	.083	−.110	−.007
b2 How much respect do you feel for the political institutions of ___ (respondent's country)?	.509	.057	.029	.060	.362	.057
b3 How well do you believe the basic rights of the citizen are well protected by the political system of ___ (respondent's country)?	.658	.118	.063	−.004	.070	.113
b4 How proud do you feel to live under the political system of ___ (respondent's country)?	.636	.140	.040	−.047	.306	.176
b6 How much do you think one should support the political system of ___ (respondent's country)?	.547	.108	.021	.029	.398	.173
b11 How much confidence do you have in the ___ (respondent's national electoral authority)?	.608	.068	.022	.088	.160	.143
b13 How much confidence do you have in the ___ (respondent's national legislature)?	.685	.169	.114	.027	−.007	−.026
b21 How much confidence do you have in the political parties?	.633	.139	.130	.069	−.180	.040
b31 How much confidence do you have in the Supreme Court of Justice?	.692	.189	.157	.104	.022	−.062
b32 How much confidence do you have in your municipality?	.482	.128	.487	.041	.103	−.074
sgl1r How much satisfaction do you feel with the quality of local government service?	.089	.020	.687	−.040	.110	.109

(continued)

TABLE A.2 (*continued*)

Items	Component					
	1 Support for Regime Institutions	2 Support for Political Actors	3 Support for Local Government	4 Support for Regime Principles	5 Perceive a Political Community	6 Support for Regime Performance
np1br How much do you believe your municipal officials pay attention to what the people ask for in municipal council meetings?	.073	.079	.791	.020	-.050	.050
np1cr If you had a complaint about a local problem and took it to a member of the municipal council, how much attention would be paid to it?	.101	.084	.765	.056	-.027	.081
n1 How well do you believe President ____ (of respondent's country) fights poverty?	.245	.816	.087	-.020	.012	.193
n9 How well do you believe President ____ fights corruption in the government?	.218	.829	.104	-.007	.077	.048
n3 How well do you believe President ____ promotes and protects democratic principles?	.287	.820	.079	.048	.135	.122

Notes: Extraction Method: Principal Component Analysis. Rotation Method: Varimax with Kaiser Normalization. Cells shaded in grey indicate variables that define the given factor.
[a] Rotation converged in 7 iterations.

TABLE A.3A. *Oblimin rotated principle components solution for legitimacy variables, pooled eight-nation sample structure matrix, with factor correlation matrix*

Items	Component					
	1 Support for Regime Institutions	2 Support for Regime Principles	3 Support for Local Government	4 Support for Political Actors	5 Perceive a Political Community	6 Support for Regime Performance
B43 How proud are you to be a ____ (e.g. citizen of Guatemala)?	.113	.113	.050	.109	.729	.043
pn2 How much do you agree that, in spite our differences, we ____ s have much in common?	.137	.418	.053	.198	.570	.014
e5 How much do you agree that people should participate in demonstrations allowed by law?	.053	.780	.036	−.026	−.024	−.036
e8 How much do you approve or disapprove that people should take part in a group seeking to resolve community problems?	.061	.786	.010	.048	.282	−.014
e11 How much do you approve or disapprove that people should work on election campaigns for a political party or candidate?	.270	.706	.077	.147	.159	.107
soc1r How do you view the economic situation of the country?	.197	−.010	.173	.229	−.036	.761
soc3r How do you believe the country's economic situation will be a year from now, better or worse than it is now?	.120	.050	.144	.242	.096	.759
b1 How much do you believe that the courts of justice in ____ (respondent's country) guarantee a fair trial?	.598	.124	.131	.247	−.060	.057

(continued)

TABLE A.3A *(continued)*

Items	Component					
	1 Support for Regime Institutions	2 Support for Regime Principles	3 Support for Local Government	4 Support for Political Actors	5 Perceive a Political Community	6 Support for Regime Performance
b2 How much respect do you feel for the political institutions of ____ (respondent's country)?	.544	.135	.116	.237	.403	.137
b3 How well do you believe the basic rights of the citizen are well protected by the political system of ____ (respondent's country)?	.678	.059	.174	.321	.122	.198
b4 How proud do you feel to live under the political system of ____ (respondent's country)?	.677	.036	.156	.357	.354	.275
b6 How much do you think one should support the political system of ____ (respondent's country)?	.595	.111	.123	.310	.444	.263
b11 How much confidence do you have in the ____ (respondent's national electoral authority)?	.633	.153	.127	.268	.213	.220
b13 How much confidence do you have in the ____ (respondent's national legislature)?	.704	.088	.226	.362	.046	.067
b21 How much confidence do you have in the political parties?	.642	.110	.234	.315	-.127	.114
b31 How much confidence do you have in the Supreme Court of Justice?	.721	.170	.270	.388	.079	.038
b32 How much confidence do you have in your municipality?	.538	.102	.558	.312	.136	.022

sgl1r How much satisfaction do you feel with the quality of local government service?	.161	−.010	.696	.139	.109	.163
np1br How much do you believe your municipal officials pay attention to what the people ask for in municipal council meetings?	.149	.038	.798	.185	−.049	.104
np1cr If you had a complaint about a local problem and took it to a member of the municipal council, how much attention would be paid?	.180	.078	.779	.201	−.020	.138
n1 How well do you believe President _____ (of respondent's country) fights poverty?	.360	.014	.198	.869	.051	.306
n9 How well do you believe President _____ fights corruption in the government?	.335	.033	.205	.866	.111	.167
n3 How well do you believe President _____ promotes and protects democratic principles?	.411	.097	.195	.889	.180	.248

Notes: Extraction Method: Principal Component Analysis. Rotation Method: Oblimin with Kaiser Normalization. Cells shaded in lighter grey indicate variables that define the given factor. Darker grey shading indicates variables with loadings split between factors.

TABLE A.3B. *Factor correlation matrix, eight-nation pooled sample oblimin rotation (for solution in Table A.3A)*

Dimensions	1	2	3	4	5	6
1 Support for regime institutions	1.000	.143	.243	.417	.156	.174
2 Support for political actors	.143	1.000	.051	.077	.158	−.005
3 Support for local government	.243	.051	1.000	.234	.014	.129
4 Support for regime principles	.417	.077	.234	1.000	.128	.242
5 Perceive a political community	.156	.158	.014	.128	1.000	.093
6 Support for regime performance	.174	−.005	.129	.242	.093	1.000

TABLE A.4A. *Oblimin rotated principle components solution for legitimacy variables, Guatemala (structure matrix), with factor correlation matrix*[a]

Items	Components					
	1 Support for Institutions (specific)	2 Regime Principles	3 Political Actors/ Economic Evaluation	4 Local Government	5 Support for Institutions (diffuse)	6 Political Community/ Economic Evaluation
B43 How proud are you to be a citizen of Guatemala?	.144	.202	-.144	.086	-.167	-.548
pn2 How much do you agree that, in spite our differences, we Guatemalans have much in common?	.201	.485	-.253	.028	-.332	-.426
e5 How much do you agree that people should participate in demonstrations allowed by law?	.136	.786	-.062	-.012	-.076	-.078
e8 How much do you approve or disapprove that people should take part in a group seeking to resolve community problems?	.058	.806	-.104	-.015	-.137	-.247
e11 How much do you approve or disapprove that people should work on election campaigns for a political party or candidate?	.200	.738	-.160	.155	-.255	.014
soc11 How do you view the economic situation of the country?	.096	-.011	-.116	.093	-.042	.682
soc3r How do you believe the country's economic situation will be a year from now, better or worse than it is now?	-.133	.013	-.526	.316	-.293	.199
b1 How much do you believe that the courts of justice in Guatemala guarantee a fair trial?	.594	.114	-.251	.174	-.305	-.134

(continued)

TABLE A.4A (continued)

Items	Components					
	1 Support for Institutions (specific)	2 Regime Principles	3 Political Actors/ Economic Evaluation	4 Local Government	5 Support for Institutions (diffuse)	6 Political Community/ Economic Evaluation
b2 How much respect do you feel for the political institutions of Guatemala?	.249	.142	-.179	.107	-.748	-.218
b3 How well do you believe the basic rights of the citizen are well protected by the political system of Guatemala?	.509	.071	-.258	.101	-.598	.076
b4 How proud do you feel to live under the political system of Guatemala?	.431	.163	-.254	.155	-.717	.075
b6 How much do you think one should support the political system of Guatemala?	.212	.309	-.286	.093	-.750	-.084
b11 How much confidence do you have in the Supreme Electoral Tribunal?	.548	.153	-.292	.184	-.394	-.126
b13 How much confidence do you have in the National Congress?	.720	.096	-.230	.151	-.319	.005
b21 How much confidence do you have in the political parties?	.605	.218	-.220	.202	-.222	.278
b31 How much confidence do you have in the Supreme Court of Justice?	.765	.227	-.269	.223	-.299	-.005
b32 How much confidence do you have in your municipality?	.5121	.217	-.288	.543	-.373	-.042

sgl1r How much satisfaction do you feel with the quality of local government service?	.150	.012	-.096	.717	-.171	.165
np1br How much do you believe your municipal officials pay attention to what the people ask for in (municipal council) meetings?	.149	.002	-.188	.718	.000	-.003
np1cr If you had a complaint about a local problem and took it to a member of the municipal council, how much attention would be paid?	.077	.062	-.154	.758	-.076	-.052
n1 How well do you believe President Oscar Berger fights poverty?	.265	.067	-.855	.177	-.220	.076
n9 How well do you believe President Oscar Berger fights corruption in the government?	.268	.180	-.819	.141	-.237	-.101
n3 How well do you believe President Oscar Berger promotes and protects democratic principles?	.282	.198	-.870	.198	-.304	-.066

Notes: Extraction Method: Principal Component Analysis. Rotation Method: Oblimin with Kaiser Normalization.
[a] Lighter grey shading indicates main associated items with a particular factor; darker grey shading indicates split (divided loadings) across two factors.

TABLE A.4B. *Component correlation matrix, Guatemala oblimin rotation (for solution in Table A.4A)*

Component	1	2	3	4	5	6
1. Support for regime institutions	1.000	.178	−.239	.180	−.342	−.013
2. Support for political actors	.178	1.000	−.156	.055	−.207	−.145
3. Support for local government	−.239	−.156	1.000	−.237	.319	−.002
4. Support for regime principles	.180	.055	−.237	1.000	−.165	.062
5. Perceive a political community	−.342	−.207	.319	−.165	1.000	.057
6. Support for regime performance	−.013	−.145	−.002	.062	.057	1.000

Notes: Extraction Method: Principal Component Analysis. Rotation Method: Oblimin with Kaiser Normalization.

TABLE A.5A. *Oblimin rotated principle components solution for legitimacy variables, Colombia (structure matrix), with factor correlation matrix*[a]

Items	Component					
	1 Support Regime Institutions	2 Support Regime Principles	3 Support Political Actors	4 Support for Local Government	5 Political Community/ Diffuse Support	6 Support for Regime Performance
B43 How proud are you to be a citizen of Colombia?	.038	.144	.038	.084	.776	.075
pn2 How much do you agree that, in spite our differences, we Colombians have much in common?	.102	.406	.323	.015	.064	.009
e5 How much do you agree that people should participate in demonstrations allowed by law?	.117	.769	-.006	.017	.059	.006
e8 How much do you approve or disapprove that people should take part in a group seeking to resolve community problems?	.066	.821	.100	.036	.137	-.021
e11 How much do you approve or disapprove that people should work on election campaigns for a political party or candidate?	.268	.646	.157	.136	.174	.095
soct1r How do you view the economic situation of the country?	.159	-.004	.140	.146	.037	.844
soct3r How do you believe the country's economic situation will be a year from now, better or worse than it is now?	.161	.062	.334	.124	.153	.730
b1 How much do you believe that the courts of justice in Colombia guarantee a fair trial?	.645	.115	.180	.026	-.006	.118

(continued)

TABLE A.5A *(continued)*

Items	Component					
	1 Support Regime Institutions	2 Support Regime Principles	3 Support Political Actors	4 Support for Local Government	5 Political Community/ Diffuse Support	6 Support for Regime Performance
b2 How much respect do you feel for the political institutions of Colombia?	.523	.226	.228	.084	.345	.021
b3 How well do you believe the basic rights of the citizen are well protected by the political system of Colombia?	.611	.035	.323	.222	.260	.097
b4 How proud do you feel to live under the political system of Colombia?	.629	.072	.405	.157	.556	.183
b6 How much do you think one should support the political system of Colombia	.497	.118	.395	.140	.630	.154
b11 How much confidence do you have in the National Electoral Council?	.706	.144	.285	.191	.187	.206
b13 How much confidence do you have in the National Congress	.706	.102	.298	.213	.121	.144
b21 How much confidence do you have in the political parties?	.717	.096	.172	.227	.027	.173
b31 How much confidence do you have in the Supreme Court of Justice?	.712	.201	.249	.247	.331	.127
b32 How much confidence do you have in your municipality?	.614	.130	.196	.395	.274	.183

sgl1r How much satisfaction do you feel with the quality of local government service?	.202	.052	.102	.458	.166	.278
np1br How much do you believe your municipal officials pay attention to what the people ask for in municipal council meetings?	.184	.039	.028	.831	.017	.080
np1cr If you had a complaint about a local problem and took it to a member of the municipal council, how much attention would be paid?	.175	.049	.124	.835	.089	.097
n1 How well do you believe President Alvaro Uribe fights poverty?	.293	.030	.816	.108	.071	.310
n9 How well do you believe President Alvaro Uribe fights corruption in the government?	.285	.151	.810	.105	.212	.215
n3 How well do you believe President Alvaro Uribe promotes and protects principles?	.347	.127	.883	.125	.197	.219

Notes: Extraction Method: Principal Component Analysis. Rotation Method: Oblimin with Kaiser Normalization.
[a] Medium grey shading indicates main items associated with a particular factor; darker grey shading indicates split (divided loadings) across two factors; lightest grey shading indicates very weak association with a dimension for a variable expected to be linked to it.

TABLE A.5B. *Component correlation matrix, Colombia oblimin rotation (for solution in Table A.5A)*

Component	1 Support for Institutions (specific)	2 Regime Principles	3 Political Actors/ Economic Evaluation	4 Local Government	5 Support for Institutions (diffuse)	6 Political Community/ Economic Evaluation
1 Support for regime institutions	1.000	.155	.328	.240	.241	.179
2 Support for political actors	.155	1.000	.141	.049	.134	.005
3 Support for local government	.328	.141	1.000	.093	.194	.219
4 Support for regime principles	.240	.049	.093	1.000	.129	.179
5 Perceive a political community	.241	.134	.194	.129	1.000	.088
6 Support for regime performance	.179	.005	.219	.179	.088	1.000

Note: Extraction Method: Principal Component Analysis.

TABLE A.6. *Mean legitimacy scores by dimension and country, 2004*

Legitimacy Dimension	Mexico	Colombia	Costa Rica	El Salvador	Guatemala	Honduras	Nicaragua	Panama	Pooled Sample Mean	Std. Dev.	Range among Nations
Political community	63.4	67.4	72.3	69.9	64.0	65.3	67.7	69.2	67.4	12.3	8.3
Regime principles	64.2	68.1	73.4	64.0	59.3	65.8	71.0	76.5	67.8	18.4	14.1
Regime performance	42.9	47.7	46.5	48.0	43.2	36.2	41.4	49.7	44.5	15.3	13.5
Regime institutions	53.8	49.8	58.9	54.4	45.7	49.2	45.6	48.8	50.8	17.1	13.3
Local government	45.7	55.0	45.0	46.9	45.3	44.5	41.0	41.5	45.6	17.4	14.0
Political actors	53.7	61.0	55.0	53.1	50.2	38.1	42.3	37.4	48.8	23.2	18.6

TABLE A.7. *Legitimacy effects on voting and registration – ordinary least squares model*[a]

Variable	B Coeff.	Error	beta	t	P
Political community	.249	.116	.100	2.155	.031
Political community squared	−.137	.095	−.066	−1.433	.152
Regime principles	.010	.077	.006	.125	.901
Regime principles squared	.022	.062	.017	.359	.720
Regime institutions	.099	.072	.056	1.363	.173
Regimes institutions squared	−.090	.071	−.051	−1.259	.208
Regime performance	−.054	.084	−.027	−.635	.526
Regime performance squared	.071	.088	.034	.806	.420
Political actors	−.018	.050	−.014	−.360	.719
Political actors squared	.031	.050	.024	.624	.533
Local government	−.081	.063	−.046	−1.277	.202
Local government squared	.082	.065	.045	1.252	.211
Mexico dummy	−.009	1.121	.000	−.008	.993
Guatemala dummy	−10.472	1.178	−.112	−8.893	.000
El Salvador dummy	1.425	1.120	.016	1.273	.203
Honduras dummy	−.610	1.174	−.007	−.520	.603
Nicaragua dummy	4.852	1.230	.052	3.945	.000
Panama dummy	−5.056	1.119	−.056	−4.517	.000
Colombia dummy	−2.354	1.232	−.026	−1.912	.056
Voted for presidential winner[b]					
Women	−.457	.534	−.008	−.857	.392
Age 21–30	33.097	.922	.491	35.889	.000
Age 31–40	37.718	.966	.523	39.037	.000
Age 41–50	39.420	1.039	.482	37.941	.000
Age 51–60	40.571	1.144	.430	35.468	.000
Age 61–95	39.506	1.198	.400	32.986	.000
Catholic	5.006	1.605	.076	3.119	.002
Protestant	2.669	1.683	.036	1.585	.113
No religion	.253	1.838	.002	.138	.890
Primary education	2.054	.801	.030	2.563	.010
Secondary education	2.820	.893	.045	3.159	.002
College education	7.463	1.274	.072	5.856	.000
Postgraduate education	5.996	1.588	.041	3.775	.000
Wealth	.284	.117	.031	2.421	.016
Media contact	.072	.011	.061	6.281	.000
Political information	.093	.012	.084	7.928	.000
Interpersonal trust	.572	.284	.018	2.017	.044
Life satisfaction	−.054	.353	−.001	−.153	.878
Victim of crime in last year	.000	.007	.000	.008	.993
Fear crime in your neighborhood	−.022	.274	−.001	−.082	.935
Solicited for bribe in last year	−.104	1.234	−.001	−.084	.933
Capital city resident	−4.099	.824	−.058	−4.975	.000

Variable	B Coeff.	Error	beta	t	P
Large city resident	−4.611	.987	−.047	**−4.672**	.000
Medium city resident	−1.989	.866	−.024	**−2.297**	.022
Small city resident	.945	.906	.011	1.043	.297

Notes: For this model, R-squared = .208; Standard Error of the Estimate = 26.970; d.f. 11,100; F = 66.680; N = 11,244. Significant coefficients in bold.
[a] No contextual effects were detected; this regression analysis is an OLS model containing only individual-level variables.
[b] Voted for winner excluded from this model as component of dependent variable.

TABLE A.8. *Legitimacy effects on partisan and campaign activism – OLS model*[a]

Variable	B Coeff.	Error	beta	t	P
Political community	−.006	.085	−.003	−.066	.948
Political community squared	−.053	.070	−.038	−.753	.452
Regime principles	−.180	.057	−.160	**−3.184**	.001
Regime principles squared	.192	.045	.212	**4.226**	.000
Regime institutions	.148	.053	.123	**2.795**	.005
Regimes institutions squared	−.060	.052	−.051	−1.154	.249
Regime performance	−.298	.062	−.222	**−4.813**	.000
Regime performance squared	.347	.065	.246	**5.375**	.000
Political actors	−.154	.037	−.173	**−4.214**	.000
Political actors squared	.122	.037	.136	**3.342**	.001
Local government	−.297	.046	−.250	**−6.426**	.000
Local government squared	.382	.048	.308	**7.999**	.000
Mexico dummy	−4.090	.821	−.066	**−4.983**	.000
Guatemala dummy	.020	.864	.000	.023	.982
El Salvador dummy	−3.780	.822	−.061	**−4.599**	.000
Honduras dummy	−.289	.863	−.005	−.335	.738
Nicaragua dummy	1.159	.902	.018	1.285	.199
Panama dummy	1.949	.822	.031	**2.372**	.018
Colombia dummy	1.806	.904	.029	**1.997**	.046
Voted for presidential winner	2.961	.406	.069	**7.301**	.000
Women	−2.378	.391	−.058	**−6.081**	.000
Age 21–30	1.703	.681	.037	**2.501**	.012
Age 31–40	2.471	.715	.050	**3.456**	.001
Age 41–50	3.672	.768	.066	**4.784**	.000
Age 51–60	3.061	.844	.047	**3.625**	.000
Age 61–95	1.605	.884	.024	1.817	.069
Catholic	.255	1.166	.006	.219	.827
Protestant	−.465	1.225	−.009	−.379	.704

(continued)

TABLE A.8 *(continued)*

Variable	B Coeff.	Error	beta	t	P
No religion	.240	1.339	.003	.179	.858
Primary education	1.272	.587	.027	**2.168**	**.030**
Secondary education	2.105	.654	.050	**3.218**	**.001**
College education	3.644	.934	.051	**3.900**	**.000**
Postgraduate education	3.760	1.165	.037	**3.226**	**.001**
Wealth	−.149	.086	−.024	−1.735	.083
Media contact	.088	.008	.109	**10.479**	**.000**
Political information	.038	.009	.051	**4.472**	**.000**
Interpersonal trust	−.680	.208	−.032	**−3.271**	**.001**
Life satisfaction	−.557	.259	−.021	**−2.150**	**.032**
Victim of crime in last year?	.027	.005	.046	**4.904**	**.000**
Fear crime in your neighborhood?	−.272	.200	−.013	−1.356	.175
Solicited for bribe in last year?	4.929	.901	.051	**5.469**	**.000**
Capital city resident	−3.737	.604	−.078	**−6.185**	**.000**
Large city resident	−3.346	.722	−.051	**−4.635**	**.000**
Medium city resident	−1.509	.634	−.026	**−2.380**	**.017**
Small city resident	.720	.664	.012	1.084	.279

Notes: For this model, R-squared = .083; Standard Error of the Estimate = 19.805; d.f. 11,248; F = 22.736; N = 11,293. Significant coefficients in bold.

[a] No contextual effects were detected; this regression analysis is an OLS model containing only individual-level variables.

TABLE A.9. *Legitimacy effects on contacting public officials – OLS model*[a]

Variable	B Coeff.	Error	beta	t	P
Political community	−.112	.112	−.050	−.999	.318
Political community squared	.101	.092	.055	1.098	.272
Regime principles	.050	.075	.034	.665	.506
Regime principles squared	.026	.060	.022	.442	.659
Regime institutions	.215	.070	.136	**3.070**	**.002**
Regimes institutions squared	−.191	.069	−.123	**−2.785**	**.005**
Regime performance	−.139	.082	−.079	−1.698	.090
Regime performance squared	.164	.085	.089	1.930	.054
Political actors	.010	.048	.009	.208	.835
Political actors squared	−.031	.048	−.026	−.639	.523
Local government	−.411	.061	−.265	**−6.740**	**.000**
Local government squared	.578	.063	.356	**9.178**	**.000**
Mexico dummy	−.846	1.083	−.010	−.781	.435
Guatemala dummy	−.701	1.140	−.008	−.615	.539
El Salvador dummy	−1.623	1.084	−.020	−1.497	.134
Honduras dummy	−6.085	1.138	−.074	**−5.347**	**.000**

Variable	B Coeff.	Error	beta	t	P
Nicaragua dummy	−1.096	1.189	−.013	−.922	.357
Panama dummy	−4.632	1.084	−.057	**−4.274**	**.000**
Colombia dummy	−4.067	1.192	−.050	**−3.411**	**.001**
Voted for presidential winner	1.730	.535	.031	**3.235**	**.001**
Women	−1.536	.516	−.028	**−2.978**	**.003**
Age 21–30	3.166	.897	.053	**3.528**	**.000**
Age 31–40	6.506	.943	.101	**6.903**	**.000**
Age 41–50	7.467	1.012	.102	**7.376**	**.000**
Age 51–60	8.098	1.113	.096	**7.276**	**.000**
Age 61–95	5.338	1.165	.060	**4.580**	**.000**
Catholic	−1.103	1.540	−.019	−.717	.474
Protestant	−.866	1.616	−.013	−.536	.592
No religion	−3.254	1.767	−.032	−1.842	.066
Primary education	−.029	.774	.000	−.038	.970
Secondary education	1.866	.863	.034	**2.162**	**.031**
College education	4.596	1.233	.050	**3.729**	**.000**
Postgraduate education	5.725	1.537	.043	**3.724**	**.000**
Wealth	−.527	.113	−.065	**−4.646**	**.000**
Media contact	.083	.011	.078	**7.506**	**.000**
Political information	.015	.011	.016	1.355	.175
Interpersonal trust	−.252	.274	−.009	−.921	.357
Life satisfaction	−.747	.341	−.021	**−2.187**	**.029**
Victim of crime in last year?	.055	.007	.073	**7.686**	**.000**
Fear crime in your neighborhood?	.941	.264	.035	**3.558**	**.000**
Solicited for bribe in last year?	8.810	1.190	.070	**7.406**	**.000**
Capital city resident	−6.453	.797	−.103	**−8.101**	**.000**
Large city resident	−6.903	.953	−.080	**−7.242**	**.000**
Medium city resident	−3.111	.836	−.042	**−3.720**	**.000**
Small city resident	1.857	.876	.024	**2.120**	**.034**

Notes: For this model, R-squared = .070; Standard Error of the Estimate = 26.100; d.f. 11,228; F = 18.840; N = 11,273. Significant coefficients in bold.
[a] No contextual effects were detected; this regression analysis is an OLS model containing only individual-level variables.

TABLE A.10. *Legitimacy effects on communal activism – OLS model*[a]

Variable	B Coeff.	Error	beta	t	P
Political community	.102	.139	.037	.737	.461
Political community squared	−.055	.115	−.024	−.476	.634
Regime principles	.016	.092	.009	.172	.863
Regime principles squared	.007	.074	.005	.090	.928

(continued)

TABLE A.10 *(continued)*

Variable	B Coeff.	Error	beta	t	P
Regime institutions	−.003	.087	−.002	−.038	.970
Regimes institutions squared	.030	.085	.016	.357	.721
Regime performance	−.349	.101	−.158	**−3.443**	.001
Regime performance squared	.385	.106	.166	**3.639**	.000
Political actors	−.005	.060	−.004	−.092	.927
Political actors squared	.002	.060	.001	.025	.980
Local government	−.170	.076	−.087	**−2.251**	.024
Local government squared	.336	.078	.165	**4.297**	.000
Mexico dummy	−1.318	1.343	−.013	−.982	.326
Guatemala dummy	2.322	1.415	.022	1.642	.101
El Salvador dummy	−1.656	1.345	−.016	−1.231	.218
Honduras dummy	4.608	1.412	.045	**3.264**	.001
Nicaragua dummy	1.354	1.476	.013	.917	.359
Panama dummy	1.243	1.345	.012	.924	.355
Colombia dummy	.272	1.480	.003	.184	.854
Voted for presidential winner	1.488	.664	.021	**2.241**	.025
Women	−4.942	.640	−.073	**−7.723**	.000
Age 21–30	3.349	1.114	.044	**3.006**	.003
Age 31–40	10.656	1.170	.132	**9.108**	.000
Age 41–50	13.009	1.256	.142	**10.356**	.000
Age 51–60	11.022	1.382	.104	**7.977**	.000
Age 61–95	9.827	1.446	.089	**6.796**	.000
Catholic	.210	1.909	.003	.110	.912
Protestant	−.150	2.004	−.002	−.075	.940
No religion	−3.210	2.191	−.025	−1.465	.143
Primary education	1.504	.961	.019	1.566	.117
Secondary education	4.612	1.071	.066	**4.308**	.000
College education	5.972	1.529	.051	**3.906**	.000
Postgraduate education	10.001	1.907	.061	**5.244**	.000
Wealth	−.235	.141	−.023	−1.668	.095
Media contact	.155	.014	.117	**11.265**	.000
Political information	.041	.014	.033	**2.896**	.004
Interpersonal trust	1.321	.340	.038	**3.885**	.000
Life satisfaction	1.216	.424	.027	**2.870**	.004
Victim of crime in last year	.056	.009	.060	**6.311**	.000
Fear crime in your neighborhood	1.346	.328	.040	**4.104**	.000
Solicited for bribe in last year	6.911	1.475	.044	**4.686**	.000
Capital city resident	−10.076	.989	−.128	**−10.191**	.000
Large city resident	−10.230	1.181	−.094	**−8.659**	.000
Medium city resident	−11.838	1.037	−.126	**−11.411**	.000
Small city resident	−4.829	1.087	−.051	**−4.443**	.000

Notes: For this model, R-squared = .087; Standard Error of the Estimate = 32.410; d.f. 11,248; F = 23.909; N = 11,293. Significant coefficients in bold.

[a] No contextual effects were detected; this regression analysis is an OLS model containing only individual-level variables.

TABLE A.11. *Legitimacy effects on civil society activism – OLS model[a]*

Variable	B Coeff.	Error	beta	t	P
Political community	.072	.079	.043	.908	.364
Political community squared	−.040	.065	−.029	−.611	.541
Regime principles	−.013	.053	−.012	−.246	.806
Regime principles squared	.020	.042	.022	.467	.640
Regime institutions	.057	.049	.048	1.152	.250
Regimes institutions squared	−.048	.049	−.041	−.984	.325
Regime performance	−.154	.058	−.117	**−2.666**	**.008**
Regime performance squared	.167	.060	.121	**2.779**	**.005**
Political actors	−.008	.034	−.009	−.235	.814
Political actors squared	.010	.034	.012	.306	.760
Local government	.000	.043	.000	−.006	.995
Local government squared	.085	.044	.071	1.919	.055
Mexico dummy	−2.212	.764	−.036	**−2.893**	**.004**
Guatemala dummy	6.658	.805	.107	**8.269**	**.000**
El Salvador dummy	−3.846	.766	−.064	**−5.024**	**.000**
Honduras dummy	8.008	.804	.131	**9.966**	**.000**
Nicaragua dummy	3.105	.840	.050	**3.695**	**.000**
Panama dummy	−6.155	.766	−.102	**−8.039**	**.000**
Colombia dummy	1.923	.842	.032	**2.282**	**.022**
Voted for presidential winner	1.426	.378	.034	**3.774**	**.000**
Women	2.850	.364	.071	**7.823**	**.000**
Age 21–30	3.185	.634	.071	**5.020**	**.000**
Age 31–40	8.716	.666	.182	**13.087**	**.000**
Age 41–50	9.108	.715	.167	**12.737**	**.000**
Age 51–60	5.886	.786	.094	**7.485**	**.000**
Age 61–95	3.864	.824	.059	**4.691**	**.000**
Catholic	−3.693	1.086	−.085	**−3.401**	**.001**
Protestant	.507	1.140	.010	.445	.657
No religion	−12.800	1.246	−.169	**−10.269**	**.000**
Primary education	−1.049	.547	−.023	−1.918	.055
Secondary education	−.664	.609	−.016	−1.090	.276
College education	1.122	.870	.016	1.289	.197
Postgraduate education	2.344	1.086	.024	**2.159**	**.031**
Wealth	−.358	.080	−.059	**−4.471**	**.000**
Media contact	.101	.008	.127	**12.860**	**.000**
Political information	.020	.008	.028	**2.551**	**.011**
Interpersonal trust	.672	.194	.032	**3.472**	**.001**
Life satisfaction	.767	.241	.029	**3.181**	**.001**
Victim of crime in last year	.025	.005	.045	**4.944**	**.000**
Fear crime in your neighborhood	.535	.187	.026	**2.863**	**.004**
Solicited for bribe in last year	3.907	.840	.042	**4.654**	**.000**
Capital city resident	−4.191	.563	−.089	**−7.445**	**.000**
Large city resident	−4.619	.673	−.072	**−6.868**	**.000**
Medium city resident	−5.576	.591	−.100	**−9.440**	**.000**
Small city resident	−3.916	.619	−.069	**−6.329**	**.000**

Notes: For this model, R-squared = .163; Standard Error of the Estimate = 48.570; d.f.
11,229; F = 48.570; N = 11,274. Significant coefficients in bold.
[a] No contextual effects were detected; this regression analysis is an OLS model containing
only individual-level variables.

TABLE A.12. *Legitimacy effects on protest participation – OLS model[a]*

Variable	B Coeff.	Error	beta	t	P
Political community	.091	.132	.034	.687	.492
Political community squared	−.091	.109	−.042	−.839	.402
Regime principles	−.160	.088	−.092	−1.824	.068
Regime principles squared	.260	.071	.186	3.680	.000
Regime institutions	.027	.082	.014	.322	.748
Regimes institutions squared	−.053	.081	−.029	−.653	.514
Regime performance	−.255	.096	−.123	−2.649	.008
Regime performance squared	.269	.101	.123	2.674	.008
Political actors	−.032	.057	−.023	−.562	.574
Political actors squared	−.022	.057	−.016	−.393	.694
Local government	−.009	.072	−.005	−.119	.906
Local government squared	.091	.074	.048	1.229	.219
Mexico dummy	−1.651	1.273	−.017	−1.297	.195
Guatemala dummy	−.905	1.341	−.009	−.675	.500
El Salvador dummy	−7.491	1.269	−.079	−5.903	.000
Honduras dummy	−4.201	1.341	−.043	−3.133	.002
Nicaragua dummy	4.591	1.399	.047	3.280	.001
Panama dummy	.229	1.287	.002	.178	.859
Colombia dummy	9.844	1.396	.105	7.051	.000
Voted for presidential winner	−.529	.631	−.008	−.839	.402
Women	−2.415	.609	−.038	−3.968	.000
Age 21–30	−2.342	1.059	−.033	−2.212	.027
Age 31–40	−1.846	1.111	−.024	−1.661	.097
Age 41–50	.044	1.195	.001	.037	.970
Age 51–60	1.046	1.315	.010	.796	.426
Age 61–95	−.062	1.377	−.001	−.045	.964
Catholic	−.476	1.817	−.007	−.262	.794
Protestant	−1.284	1.907	−.016	−.673	.501
No religion	.215	2.081	.002	.103	.918
Primary education	−1.665	.916	−.023	−1.818	.069
Secondary education	.827	1.018	.013	.813	.416
College education	9.557	1.451	.088	6.586	.000
Postgraduate education	15.017	1.803	.098	8.330	.000
Wealth	−.198	.134	−.021	−1.480	.139
Media contact	.085	.013	.068	6.507	.000
Political information	.058	.013	.050	4.304	.000
Interpersonal trust	−.160	.324	−.005	−.493	.622
Life satisfaction	−.893	.403	−.021	−2.216	.027
Victim of crime in last year	.043	.008	.048	5.055	.000
Fear crime in your neighborhood	.860	.312	.027	2.756	.006
Solicited for bribe in last year	4.934	1.399	.033	3.526	.000
Capital city resident	1.404	.943	.019	1.489	.137
Large city resident	.184	1.122	.002	.164	.870
Medium city resident	−.560	.990	−.006	−.566	.572
Small city resident	.757	1.034	.008	.732	.464

Notes: For this model, R-squared = .092; Standard Error of the Estimate = 30.394; d.f. 10,932; F = 24.706; N = 10,977. Significant coefficients in bold.
[a] No contextual effects were detected; this regression analysis is an OLS model containing only individual-level variables.

Appendix B: Variables Used in the Analyses

TABLE B.I. *Political participation indexes*

Variables	Description of Variables and Index Construction	Mean	Std. Deviation
Voting and registration	Index combining having voted in most recent presidential election (no = o, yes = 50) and having registered to vote (no = o, yes = 50), range o–100.	82.28	30.23
Party and campaign activism	Index combining having worked for a campaign (no = o, yes = 33.33), having tried to persuade another how to vote (no = o, yes = 33.33), and attendance at political party meetings (no = o ... frequently = 33.33), range o–100.	12.30	20.52
Contact public officials	Index combining having contacted a legislator, contacted a municipal council member, or petitioned the municipal government (no = o, yes = 33.33 for each), range o–100.	16.31	26.88
Communal activism	Index combining having taken part in five different community improvement related activities (no = o, yes = 20 for each), range o–100.	22.03	33.71
Civil society activism	Index combining measures of frequency of attendance at meetings of church-related, school-related, civic, and professional groups; range o–100.	25.41	20.14

(continued)

TABLE B.1 *(continued)*

Variables	Description of Variables and Index Construction	Mean	Std. Deviation
Protest participation	Reported having participated in a protest in the last year (no = 0, at least once = 50, more than once = 100).	12.70	31.65

TABLE B.2. *Exploratory factor analysis of variables with multiple indicators, excluding protest and civil society (pooled eight-nation sample); rotated component matrix(a)*

Variables	Component			
	1	2	3	4
	Communal Activism	Contacting Public Officials	Voting	Campaign and Party Activism
cp5r Communal activism cp5 recoded	.916	.096	.074	.031
cp5ar Donate materials recoded	.763	.029	.025	.041
cp5br Donated materials recoded	.831	.096	.085	.014
cp5cr Attended community meetings recoded	.823	.150	.096	.032
cp5dr Organize comm. group recoded	.712	.176	.099	.021
cp2r Petitioned legislator recoded	.069	.631	.169	−.016
cp4r Contacted local official recoded	.138	.780	.032	.057
np2r Petitioned government recoded	.150	.723	.073	.047
vb1r Registered to vote recoded	.033	.009	−.002	.840
vb2r Voted last presidential election recoded	.049	.067	.105	.817
Party act partisan activism – (cp13 recoded)	.098	.088	.602	−.013
pp1r Persuade vote	.043	.063	.704	.040
pp2r Work for campaign	.081	.104	.740	.086

Notes: Extraction Method: Principal Component Analysis. Rotation Method: Varimax with Kaiser Normalization. Cells shaded in grey indicate variables that define the factor.

TABLE B.3. *Additional variables and indices used in the analysis*

Variables	Description of Variables and Index Construction	Mean	Std. Deviation
Perceive a political community	Index based on combining replies to two items: Range 0–100.	67.61	12.10
Political community squared	Perceive a political community index squared and renormed (divided by 100) to provide a range 0–100.	47.18	14.69
Support regime (democratic) principles	Range 0–100.	68.03	18.31
Regime principles squared	Support regime (democratic) principles index squared and renormed (divided by 100) to provide a range 0–100.	49.63	22.79
Support for regime institutions	Range 0–100.	50.87	17.08
Regime institutions squared	Support for regime institutions index squared and renormed (divided by 100) to provide a range 0–100.	28.80	17.34
Support for regime performance	Range 0–100.	44.53	15.36
Regime performance squared	Support for regime performance index squared and renormed (divided by 100) to provide a range 0–100.	22.19	14.61
Support for political actors	Range 0–100.	49.09	23.16
Political actors squared	Support for political actors index squared and renormed (divided by 100) to provide a range 0–100.	29.46	23.01
Support for local government	Range 0–100.	45.76	17.37
Local government squared	Support for local government index squared and renormed (divided by 100) to provide a range 0–100.	23.96	16.62

(continued)

TABLE B.3 (continued)

Variables	Description of Variables and Index Construction	Mean	Std. Deviation
Women	Respondent is a male = 0, female = 1.	.51	.49
Age 21–30	Respondent of age 21–30 years (no = 0, yes = 1).	.27	.44
Age 31–40	Respondent of age 21–30 years (no = 0, yes = 1).	.22	.41
Age 41–50	Respondent of age 21–30 years (no = 0, yes = 1).	.16	.36
Age 51–60	Respondent of age 21–30 years (no = 0, yes = 1).	.11	.32
Age 61–95	Respondent of age 21–30 years (no = 0, yes = 1).	.10	.30
Catholic	Respondent identifies self as "Catholic" (no = 0, yes = 1)	.69	.46
Protestant	Respondent identifies self as "Protestant" (no = 0, yes = 1)	.20	.40
No religion	Respondent identities self as having "no religion" (no = 0, yes = 1)	.07	.26
Primary education	Respondent has completed up to grade 6 (no = 0, yes = 1).	.25	.43
Secondary education	Respondent has completed high school (no = 0, yes = 1).	.38	.48
College education	Respondent has completed college (no = 0, yes = 1).	.09	.29
Postgraduate education	Respondent has completed postgraduate education (no = 0, yes = 1).	.04	.20
Wealth	Index of personal wealth in terms of artifacts possessed in respondent's home (telephone, microwave, computer, automobiles, etc.... 1 point for each). Range 0–14.	4.94	3.34
News media exposure	Index of exposure to news by listening to the radio, watching television, and reading the newspaper. Calculated by taking the mean score of answers concerning frequency: never = 0, rare occasions = 33, once or twice a week = 67, everyday = 100. Range = 0–100.	55.89	25.70
Score on political information quiz	Index of level of political information, calculated as the percent of correct answers given to four items: president of the United States, number of political subdivisions of respondent's own country, length of the presidential term of the respondent's country, and the name of the president of Brazil. Range 0–100.	53.98	27.82

Variable	Description		
Interpersonal trust	Index constructed by adding scores for the responses to three items: (a) "Speaking of the people from around here, would you say that the people of the community are very trustworthy (1), somewhat trustworthy (.67), little trustworthy (.33), or not trustworthy?" (0); (b) "Do you believe most people are concerned only with themselves, or do you believe that most people generally try to help their fellow man?" Self-concerned (0), help others (1); "Do you believe the majority of people, if given an opportunity, would try to take advantage of you (0), or would not take advantage of you (1)?" Range 0–3.	2.82	.96
Life satisfaction, low to high	Respondent's answer to the following item: In general, how satisfied are you with your life? "Would you say that you find yourself very satisfied (4), somewhat satisfied (3), a little unsatisfied (2), very unsatisfied (1)?" Range = 1–4.	3.27	.76
Victimized by crime in last year	"Have you been the victim of some sort of crime in the last twelve months?" Yes = 100, no = 0. Range 0–100.	15.24	35.94
Fear of crime in one's neighborhood	"Speaking of the neighborhood where you live, and thinking about the possibility of becoming a victim of an assault or robbery, do you feel very safe (4), somewhat safe (3), somewhat unsafe (2), very unsafe (1)?" Range = 1–4.	2.29	.99
Solicited for bribe by public employee	"Has a public employee solicited a bribe from you during the last year?" (1 = yes), (0 = no).	.05	.21
Capital city resident	(no = 0, yes = 1)	.24	.42
Large city resident	(no = 0, yes = 1)	.10	.31
Medium city resident	(no = 0, yes = 1)	.15	.36
Small city resident	(no = 0, yes = 1)	.14	.35
Voted for winner	Indicator of whether respondent voted for the winning candidate (current incumbent) in the last presidential election before the survey; calculated from reported presidential vote. Voted for the incumbent president = 1; did not vote or voted for another candidate = 0. Range = 0–1.	.35	.47

(continued)

Variables	Description of Variables and Index Construction	Mean	Std. Deviation
Approve armed overthrow	To what degree would you approve or disapprove [on a 10-point scale] that people participate in a group that wants to overthrow an elected government using violent means? Answer options range in 10 even increments from "not at all" = 0 to completely" = 100."	17.10	27.45
Justify coup	This is an index calculated as the mean of respondent answers to the following items: "Some people say that under certain circumstances the military would be justified in taking power via a coup d'etat [golpe de estado in the questionnaire]. In your opinion, would you justify a coup by the military: 1. In the face of very high unemployment? In the face of a lot of social protest? In the face of high crime? In the face of high inflation, with excessive price increases? In the face of a lot of corruption? Do you think that some time there could be sufficient reason for a coup, or do you think that there could never be sufficient reason for that?" Any answer approving of a coup is scored 100, any answer disapproving is scored zero. Range = 0–100.	41.64	39.65
Approve confrontational political tactics	This is an index calculated as the mean of respondent answers to the following items: "To what degree do you approve or disapprove: Of people taking over factories, offices, and other buildings? Of people invading private property or land? Of people participating in a blockage of streets and highways?" Answer options range in 10 even increments from "not at all" = 0 to "completely" = 100. Range = 0–100.	19.28	22.29

Support for vigilantism	This is the respondent's reply to an item asking "To what degree do you approve or disapprove that people take justice into their own hands when the state does not punish criminals?" Answer options range in 10 even increments from "not at all" = 0 to "completely" = 100. Range = 0–100.	30.77	36.07
Perceived supply of democracy	This is an index calculated as the mean of respondent answers to the following items: "In general, would you say that you are very satisfied, satisfied, dissatisfied, or very dissatisfied with the way that democracy works in [country]? In your opinion, [country] is very democratic, somewhat democratic, [only a] little democratic, or not at all democratic? [and] Based on your experience from the last few years, [country] has become more democratic, equally democratic, or less democratic?" Answers for each allow a range from not at all (scored 0) to very (scored 100). Range 0–100.	54.41	21.68
Demand for democracy	This is the respondent's reply to an item asking: "There are people who say that we need a strong leader who does not have to be elected by the vote. Other people say that even when things don't function well electoral democracy, that is the popular vote, is always the best thing. What do you think?" Those who opted for an elected leader scored 100; those preferring an unelected strongman scored 0.	86.77	33.88

Appendix C: System-level Performance Measures

TABLE C.1. *System-level performance measures, eight Latin American nations*

	Human Development Index (HDI) 2003	Percent Change in UNDP HDI 1975–2003	Gross Domestic Product Per Capita 2003	Percent GDP Per Capita Change 1990–2003	GDP Per Capita (PPP) 2003	Vanhanen Mean Democracy Score 1900–1989	World Bank Government Effectiveness Index	Gini Index of Income Inequality	Freedom House – Combined (scale polarity reversed)
Mexico	0.814	1.18	6121	16.8	9168	2.05	61.9	54.6	10.00
Guatemala	0.663	1.30	2009	13.2	4148	2.52	32	59.9	6.00
El Salvador	0.722	1.22	2277	25.2	4781	2.54	35.6	53.2	9.00
Honduras	0.667	1.29	1001	2.4	2665	2.53	27.3	55.0	8.00
Nicaragua	0.69	1.18	745	10.8	3262	3.19	17.5	43.1	8.00
Costa Rica	0.838	1.12	4352	31.2	9606	8.81	66.5	46.5	11.00
Panama	0.804	1.13	4319	28.8	6854	4.69	53.6	56.4	11.00
Colombia	0.785	1.19	1764	4.8	6702	4.2	45.4	57.6	6.00

Sources: Freedom House (2004), United Nations Development Program (2005), World Bank Institute (Kaufmann et al. 2006), Vanhanen (1997).

Appendix D: Nonsampling Errors, Sampling Errors, and Design Effects for the Eight-Nation Survey[1]

Every survey that uses a sample of respondents rather than the entire population of possible respondents (i.e., the "universe") is affected by two types of error: *nonsampling* and *sampling errors*. Both are important and affect the accuracy of the results, but only the sampling errors can be quantified. Nonsampling errors, namely, those that are made during the collection and processing of data, are ones that researchers can attempt to minimize. In this study, we made every attempt to control nonsampling errors. We did extensive pretesting of the survey instrument to help improve comprehension on the part of the respondents. In the end, we produced 23 major redrafts and many more minor drafts before we began the surveys. Good training of interviewers helps ensure uniform application of the questionnaire. Supervision of fieldwork reduces nonsampling error, as it helps to ensure that interviews are carried out according to the standards established by the researchers. Careful coding and checking of coding helps ensure that errors are minimized. A clean database was achieved by utilizing data entry software that had built-in range codes, so that "wild codes" were not possible; in addition, double entry by different data entry clerks was used to check for typing errors made during the data entry process.

---

[1] This discussion draws on technical appendices prepared by Juan Pablo Pira and Luis Rosero for the 2004 surveys. Discussions of individual country design effects are contained in the various country studies that were written by the national teams. Electronic copies are available in English and Spanish at www.lapopsurveys.org. The calculations of the design effects for the eight-nation survey were done by the authors of this volume.

Sampling errors stem from the fact that only a sample is interviewed, not the whole population. Sampling error is the measure of variability among all the possible samples that could be employed using the same technique. As it is impossible to know the results of all possible samples, we estimate these errors from the variance. Contrary to popular belief, the sampling error does not depend only on the number of cases but also on the technique that was employed to choose respondents.

Sampling error is complex to report, since the error differs for each ratio or proportion estimated within a study, and the error that is reported for a sample is the error estimated for a statistic known as the sampling variable. The sampling error for a particular statistic is calculated as the square root of the population variance of the statistic. In order to estimate this error, it is necessary to consider the way in which the sample was designed. As explained in Chapter 2 of this volume, the samples were country stratified and clustered rather than simple random. Simple random sampling (SRS) is infrequently used. As far as we know, it is never used in large national samples such as the ones we have developed for this study because it would be too costly and highly inefficient. To examine the impact of deviating from SRS, we can compare the results we obtained from the field to what we would have obtained via SRS and thereby determine the "design effect" of the survey. A simple random sample is the one that would be obtained if the interviewees were to be chosen from a roster with the names of all the available adults.

A stratified sample is usually more accurate than an SRS. This is to say that a stratified sample allows for more precision than does an unrestricted random sample. A clustered sample is considerably cheaper than an SRS, but it is also less accurate. In the survey we used for this study, a complex sample that combined the characteristics of a stratified sample and those of a clustered sample was employed. In this way, the loss of accuracy that occurs when costs are reduced by the use of clustering is in part compensated by stratification. The measure that expresses the way in which a complex sample compares with an SRS is known as the "design effect," usually abbreviated as DEF. DEF is the quotient of the variance obtained by a complex sampling divided into the variance obtained by an SRS. The design effect compares the accuracy of a complex sample with that of a simple random sample design. A value of 1 indicates that the variance obtained by using the complex sample is the same as that obtained by the SRS. In those cases in which the complex sample appears to be more efficient, a value below 1 is obtained for DEF. If the value of DEF is higher than 1, which is what happens in most cases, the complex sampling is less efficient than the SRS, as the effects of clustering reduce the accuracy. Usually it is considered adequate to have values for DEF between 1 and 2, although occasionally there are some indicators in which the value of DEF can exceed 4. High values for DEF emerge for variables that are very similar within each cluster but vary considerably across clusters.

The presence of very high design effects would suggest the need to employ techniques that take them into account for the significance tests. In the case of this study, as shown in Table D.1, the majority of the design effects for variables of interest were found between 1 and 2; this suggests that the use of an assumed SRS does not have a significant impact in the quality of the conclusions.

Table D.1 summarizes the standard errors and design effects for selected variables and indexes of the survey. In most cases, the cluster design for this survey was very efficient. On the key demographic variable of gender, the design proved extremely efficient. In no county was the DEF higher than .58 above what would have been achieved by SRS, and in three of the countries the sample design was far more efficient than SRS. Family size, measured by mean number of children, also demonstrated the efficiency of the sample with low design effects. Similarly, marital status had low design effects with two of the countries more efficient than SRS. On our key dependent variables – the six measures of political legitimacy – in most countries and for most indicators the DEF ranged between 1 and 2, indicating that our sample design produced only a small increase in the confidence intervals that would have been achieved had we used SRS. We do take note that on three of the dimensions for Mexico and on only one dimension (local government) for Guatemala, Nicaragua, and Colombia did the DEF rise above 2.0, which would be our benchmark for an ideally efficient design. Also, on one dimension (regime institutions), in Panama the DEF was slightly over 2.0. These results indicate that the combined effect of stratification and clustering was more efficient than a simple random design, which, in any event, would have been impossible because of the unacceptably high cost.

TABLE D.I. *Design effects for demographic and legitimacy indicators*

Country	Sex	Mean # of Children	Marital Status	Political Community	Regime Principles	Regime Performance	Regime Institutions	Local Government	Political Actors
Mexico	1.16	1.61	1.06	3.29	2.63	1.82	2.87	3.07	3.86
Guatemala	0.37	1.11	.95	1.52	1.24	1.37	1.25	2.06	1.49
El Salvador	.60	1.35	.95	1.08	1.20	1.58	1.47	1.28	1.42
Honduras	1.09	1.43	1.44	1.81	1.91	1.57	1.76	1.76	1.71
Nicaragua	0.47	.90	1.37	.99	1.49	1.96	1.55	2.14	1.55
Costa Rica	1.58	1.28	1.16	1.21	1.20	1.25	1.15	1.76	1.14
Panama	1.06	1.31	1.24	1.51	1.53	1.09	2.17	1.69	1.90
Colombia	0.39	1.31	1.18	1.63	1.61	1.57	1.67	2.40	1.79

Appendix E: Method of Constructing the Legitimacy Factor Scores

Once we determined (using the factor analysis and structural equation models) the complete six-dimensional structure of political legitimacy, it became necessary to engage in a data reduction exercise in order to continue with the rest of this research project. That is, given the large number of variables that defined the various aspects of political legitimacy in this dataset, it would have been unwieldy to attempt to employ them all in examining the sources and consequences of legitimacy. Moreover, from a theoretical perspective, we argue that the items being studied do in fact form dimensions. We therefore did not want to work with individual variables but only with summary indices of variables reflecting those dimensions.

This required us to confront the problem of missing data. Virtually all surveys include respondents who fail to answer at least some of the questions put to them, whether from unwillingness to respond, lack of sufficient information to respond, or inability to comprehend the question. One solution to this often vexing problem is to use the "listwise" deletion technique, in which a missing response to any one survey question results in that entire case (respondent) being deleted from the analysis. A second technique, "pairwise" deletion, removes the case only when one or both of the values are missing for any pair of correlations. Both approaches assume that missing data occur completely at random and that there are no patterns or biases in what is missing. But we actually know that assumption is rarely true in practice. For example, if a respondent does not tell us about her vote in one election, she is not likely to tell us about a vote in another election. When the randomness assumption is thus violated, as it normally is with both pairwise and listwise deletion methods, the regression estimates are biased.

Several considerations drove us to develop legitimacy indexes that would remain true to our theory and to the empirical underpinnings of the project while minimizing most effectively the challenges of nonresponse and the inherent interrelatedness of the six dimensions uncovered by our analysis here. Because our solutions to these two problems are themselves interrelated, we cover them together. First, because the structural equations approach (confirmatory factor analysis) that we used was based on maximum-likelihood estimation, a method that inherently operates by estimating the values for missing data (i.e., nonresponse of a respondent to the items in the series), we decided to create indices for our key legitimacy variables that estimated missing scores. Second, because we would employ the six indices of legitimacy throughout study, we decided to maintain a constant sample size on those variables in all of our analyses. Failing that, the multiple regression analyses we would later employ could vary sharply in the number of cases that they covered. They would thus tend toward idiosyncratic results rather than the robust solutions we hoped to present. Third, the current wisdom is that in estimating values for missing data, the most appropriate approach is to rely on data from *all* of the variables in a study rather than to use only the values of the nonmissing to impute the missing value (e.g., using means estimation based on the means of the nonmissing cases on a given variable). The reasoning behind this is that the missing data ought to reflect the full pattern of information for each respondent rather than the pattern of responses merely for the scales on which the missing data points are located. State-of-the-art scholarship in this area encouraged us to use that approach. Fourth, because we had found the factors and latent structures that emerged from our analysis to be both theoretically and empirically related to each other, we wished the index representing each factor to reflect that reality.

A final consideration was that we wanted to be able to return to our original dataset for all of the analyses in the study in their original (i.e., unimputed) form. Imputation of missing data by our method here, in which all missing values in the dataset are estimated, can produce anomalous results for certain kinds of variables, such as fractional point estimates for variables in which the only legal responses are whole integers. (For example, an estimated value for a question in which the only possible actual answers are "yes" = 1 or "no" = 0 might be estimated at .34, a nonsensical value). Imputation can also produce values above or below the scale of responses (with negative values for questions that have only positive scores). In contrast, this estimation method would not constitute a problem for the continuous interval-level indices we would need for legitimacy dimensions. So, we decided to retain to our dataset's original *un*imputed values for all other variables in the sample once we had imputed the values for the legitimacy dimensions, and to use imputation to estimate missing values in order to maximize the sample size on our central variables.

In order to accomplish these goals, we first used expectation-maximization estimation (EM) to impute missing data for all of our legitimacy variables when we encountered nonresponse. With this method, we assumed a normal distribution for the variables on which there were some missing data. The dataset is first run through the E step, which produces estimates of the missing data, and then the "M" step, in which maximum-likelihood estimates are produced. We did this for all of the variables in our dataset after first dividing the pooled sample into eight country files so that the estimates would be generated by the respondents in each country. We then produced indexes for each of our six dimensions using factor scores that allowed intercorrelation (nonorthogonality) among the resulting dimensions. By following this method, we are able to produce an index score for 100 percent of the respondents in the study on our key legitimacy variables, with scores that genuinely reflect the theoretical and empirical reality of the nonorthogonal nature of the six dimensions.

Our final step was to save the index scores for the six legitimacy index variables and then to add them back to the *unimputed* pooled original dataset. This means that when we perform regression analysis in this study, we do so with index scores for all of the cases for the variables of critical interest here, namely, the six dimensions of political legitimacy. Missing data in the regression analyses for the other variables included in the regressions are treated using listwise deletion, which in most cases results in only a small loss of cases. The loss is small because our macro-level data contain 0 percent missing, while the microlevel socioeconomic and demographic control variables for the 12,000 cases in the sample contain very little missing data. Only when we are using predictors or dependent attitudinal/behavioral variables do we encounter any significant percentage of missing data, but it is our practice to exclude any of those variables if they produce a large drop in the regression N.

References

Abramson, Paul R., and Ronald Inglehart. "The Development of Systemic Support in Four Western Democracies." *Comparative Political Studies* 2(1970): 419–42.

Adams, Richard Newbold. "The Structure of Participation: A Commentary." In *Politics and the Poor: Political Participation in Latin America*, edited by Mitchell A. Seligson and John A. Booth. New York: Holmes and Meier, 1979.

Almond, Gabriel A. "Review of Ronald Rogowski, 'Rational Legitimacy: A Theory of Political Support'." *American Political Science Review* 71, no. 1 (1977): 330–32.

Almond, Gabriel A. "The Intellectual History of the Civic Culture Concept." In *The Civic Culture Revisited*, edited by Gabriel A. Almond and Sidney Verba. Boston: Little, Brown, 1980.

Almond, Gabriel A., and Sidney Verba. *The Civic Culture: Political Attitudes and Democracy in Five Nations*. Princeton, N.J.: Princeton University Press, 1963.

Almond, Gabriel A., and Sidney Verba, eds. *The Civic Culture Revisited*. Boston: Little, Brown, 1980.

Anderson, Christopher J., Andre Blais, Shaun Bowler, Todd Donovan, and Ola Listhaug. *Loser's Consent: Elections and Democratic Legitimacy.* Oxford: Oxford University Press, 2005.

Anderson, Christopher J., and Christine A. Guillory. "Political Institutions and Satisfaction with Democracy: A Cross-National Analysis of Consensus and Majoritarian Systems." *American Political Science Review* 91(1997): 66–81.

Anderson, Christopher J., and Matthew M. Singer. "The Sensitive Left and the Impervious Right: Multilevel Models and the Politics of Inequality, Ideology, and Legitimacy in Europe." *Comparative Political Studies* 41, no. 4–5 (2008): 564–99.

Anderson, Thomas P. *Matanza: El Salvador's Communist Revolt of 1932.* Lincoln: University of Nebraska Press, 1971.

Andrews, George Reid. *Afro-Latin America, 1800–2000.* New York: Oxford University Press, 2005.

Arendt, Hannah. *The Origins of Totalitarianism.* New ed. New York: Harcourt, 1966.

Aristotle. *Politics (Aristotle's Politics)*. Translated by Richard Robinson. Oxford: Clarendon Press, 1962.

Atkins, G. Pope. *Latin America in the International Political System*. Boulder, Colo.: Westview Press, 1989.

Baloyra, Enrique. "Criticism, Cynicism, and Political Evaluation: A Venezuelan Example."*American Political Science Review*, no. 73 (1979): 987–1002.

Baloyra, Enrique. *El Salvador in Transition*. Chapel Hill: University of North Carolina Press, 1982.

Baloyra, Enrique. "Public Opinion and Military Coups and Democratic Consolidation in Venezuela." In *Democracy in Latin America: Colombia and Venezuela*, edited by Donald L. Herman. New York: Greenwood Press, 1987.

Baloyra, Enrique A., and John D. Martz. *Political Attitudes in Venezuela: Societal Cleavages and Political Opinion*. Austin: University of Texas Press, 1979.

Barnes, Samuel, and Max Kaase. *Political Action: Mass Participation in Five Western Democracies*. Beverly Hills: Sage, 1979.

Bermeo, Nancy Gina. *Ordinary People in Extraordinary Times: The Citizenry and the Breakdown of Democracy*. Princeton, N.J.: Princeton University Press, 2003.

Bollen, Kenneth. "Issues in the Comparative Measurement of Political Democracy." *American Sociological Review* 45, no. 14 (1980): 370–90.

Booth, John A. "Rural Violence in Colombia, 1948–1963." *Western Political Quarterly* 27, December (1974): 657–79.

Booth, John A. "Are Latin Americans Politically Rational? Citizen Participation and Democracy in Costa Rica." In *Citizen and State: Political Participation in Latin America*, edited by John A. Booth and Mitchell A. Seligson. New York: Holmes and Meier, 1978.

Booth, John A. *The End and the Beginning: The Nicaraguan Revolution*. Boulder, Colo.: Westview Press, 1985.

Booth, John A. "Socioeconomic and Political Roots of National Revolts in Central America." *Latin American Research Review* 26, no. 1 (1991): 33–73.

Booth, John A. *Costa Rica: Quest for Democracy*. Boulder, Colo.: Westview Press, 1998.

Booth, John A. "Sociopolitical Violence, Protest, and Antidemocratic and Confrontational Norms in Eight Latin American Nations." Paper presented at the Latin American Studies Association, San Juan, Puerto Rico, March 17, 2006.

Booth, John A. "Political Parties in Costa Rica: Democratic Stability and Party System Change in a Latin American Context." In *Party Politics in New Democracies*, edited by Paul Webb and Stephen White. Oxford: Oxford University Press, 2007.

Booth, John A., and Patricia Bayer Richard."Repression, Participation and Democratic Norms in Urban Central America." *American Journal of Political Science* 40, no. 4 (1996): 1205–32.

Booth, John A., and Patricia Bayer Richard. "Civil Society and Political Context in Central America." *American Behavioral Scientist* 42, September (1998a): 33–46.

Booth, John A., and Patricia Bayer Richard. "Civil Society, Political Capital, and Democratization in Central America." *Journal of Politics* 60, no. 3 (1998b): 780–800.

Booth, John A., and Patricia Bayer Richard. "Revolution's Legacy: Residual Effects on Nicaraguan Participation and Attitudes in Comparative Context." *Latin American Politics and Society* 48, no. 2 (2006a): 117–40.

Booth, John A., and Patricia Bayer Richard. "Violence, Participation, and Democratic Norms: Prospects for Democratic Consolidation in Post-Conflict Central America." In *Sustaining the Peace: War Prevention and Peacebuilding in Post Conflict Societies*, edited by James A. Meernik and T. David Mason. London: Routledge, 2006b.

Booth, John A., and Mitchell A. Seligson. "Political Participation in Latin America: An Agenda for Research." *Latin American Research Review* 11, Fall (1976): 95–115.

Booth, John A., and Mitchell A. Seligson. "Images of Participation in Latin America." In *Citizen and State: Political Participation in Latin America*, edited by John A. Booth and Mitchell A. Seligson. New York: Holmes and Meier, 1978a.

Booth, John A. and Mitchell A. Seligson, eds. *Citizen and State: Political Participation in Latin America*. Vol. I. New York: Holmes and Meier, 1978b.

Booth, John A., and Mitchell A. Seligson. "The Political Culture of Authoritarianism in Mexico: A Reevaluation." *Latin American Research Review* 19, no. 1 (1984): 106–24.

Booth, John A., and Mitchell Seligson. "Political Culture and Democratization: Evidence from Mexico, Nicaragua and Costa Rica." In *Political Culture and Democracy in Developing Countries*, edited by Larry Diamond. Boulder: Lynne Reinner, 1994.

Booth, John A., and Mitchell A. Seligson. "Political Legitimacy and Participation in Costa Rica: Evidence of Arena Shopping." *Political Research Quarterly* 59, no. 4 (2005): 537–50.

Booth, John A., and Mitchell A. Seligson. "Inequality and Democracy in Latin America: Individual and Contextual Effects of Wealth on Political Participation." In *Poverty, Participation and Democracy*, edited by Anirudh Krishna. Cambridge: Cambridge University Press, 2008.

Booth, John A., Mitchell A. Seligson and Miguel Gómez Barrantes. *The Structure of Democratic Legitimacy*. Paper presented at the Midwest Political Science Association, Chicago, Ill., April 2005.

Booth, John A., Christine J. Wade, and Thomas W. Walker. *Understanding Central America: Global Forces, Rebellion and Change*. Boulder, Colo.: Westview Press, 2006.

Bratton, Michael. "Poor People and Democratic Citizenship in Africa." In *Poverty, Participation and Democracy: A Global Perspective*, edited by Anirudh Krishna. Cambridge: Cambridge University Press, 2008.

Bratton, Michael, Robert Mattes, and E. Gyimah-Boadi. *Public Opinion, Democracy, and Market Reform in Africa, Cambridge Studies in Comparative Politics*. New York: Cambridge University Press, 2005.

Cameron, Maxwell A. "Self-Coups: Peru, Guatemala, and Russia." *Journal of Democracy* 9, no. 1 (1998): 125–39.

Camp, Roderic A. "The Cross in the Polling Booth: Religion, Politics and the Laity in Mexico." *Latin American Research Review* 29, no. 3 (1994): 69–100.

Camp, Roderic A. *Politics in Mexico*. New York: Oxford University Press, 2007.

Canache, Damarys. *Venezuela: Public Opinion and Protest in a Fragile Democracy*. Coral Gables, Fla.: North-South Center Press at the University of Miami, 2002.

Canache, Damarys, and Michael R. Kulisheck, eds. *Reinventing Legitimacy: Democracy and Political Change in Venezuela*. Westport, Conn.: Greenwood Press, 1998.

Canache, Damarys, Jeffrey Mondak, and Mitchell A. Seligson. "Measurement and Meaning in Cross-National Research on Satisfaction with Democracy." *Public Opinion Quarterly* 65(2001): 506–28.

Cardoso, Ciro F.S., and Héctor Pérez Brignoli. *Centro America y la economía occidental (1520–1930)*. San José: Editorial Universidad de Costa Rica, 1977.

Carey, John M. *Term Limits and Legislative Representation*. Cambridge: Cambridge University Press, 1996.

Carothers, Thomas. *In the Name of Democracy: U.S. Policy Toward Latin America in the Reagan Years*. Berkeley: University of California Press, 1991.

Carrión, Julio, ed. *The Fujimori Legacy: The Rise of Electoral Authoritarianism in Peru*. University Park, Pa.: Pennsylvania State University Press, 2006.

Caspi, Dan, and Mitchell A. Seligson. "Toward an Empirical Theory of Tolerance: Radical Groups in Israel and Costa Rica." *Comparative Political Studies* 15(1983): 385–404.

Central Intelligence Agency. *World Factbook*. Central Intelligence Agency, 2005. Available from www.cia.gov/cia/publications/factbook/index.html [accessed July 19, 2005].

Cho, Wonbin. "Institutions, Partisan Status, and Citizens' Political Support in Emerging Democracies." Ph.D. dissertation, Michigan State University, 2005.

Chu, Yun-han, Michael Bratton, Marta Lagos, Sandeep Shastri, and Mark Tessler. "Public Opinion and Democratic Legitimacy." *Journal of Democracy* 19, no. 2 (2008): 74–87.

Chu, Yun-han, and Min-hua Huang. "A Synthetic Analysis of Sources of Democratic Legitimacy."Asia Barometer Working Paper Series: No. 41, 47. Taipei: AsiaBarometer, National Taiwan University and Academia Sinica, 2007.

Citrin, Jack. "The Political Relevance of Trust in Government." *American Political Science Review* 68(1974): 973–88.

Citrin, Jack. "Democracy and trust." *Political Psychology* 23, no. 2 (2002): 402–04.

Citrin, Jack, and Christopher Muste. "Trust in Government." In *Measures of Political Attitudes*, edited by John P. Robinson, Phillip R. Shaver, and Lawrence S. Wrightsman. San Diego, Calif.: Academic Press, 1999.

Cleary, Matthew R., and Susan Carol Stokes. *Democracy and the Culture of Skepticism: Political Trust in Argentina and Mexico*. Russell Sage Foundation Series on Trust vol. 11. New York: Russell Sage Foundation, 2006.

Cohen, Carl. *Democracy*. New York: The Free Press, 1973.

Coleman, James S. *Foundations of Social Theory*. Cambridge, Mass.: Harvard University Press, 1990.

Coleman, Kenneth M. *Diffuse Support In Mexico: The Potential for Crisis.* Beverly Hills: Sage Publications, 1976.

Comisión de la Verdad. *De la locura a la esperanza: La guerra de doce años en El Salvador. Informe de la Comisión de la Verdad para El Salvador.* San Salvador: Editorial Universitaria, Universidad de El Salvador, 1993.

Córdova, Ricardo, and José M. Cruz. *Cultura-política de la democracia en El Salvador:* 2006, edited by Mitchell A. Seligson. San Salvador: Instituto Universitario de Opinión Pública (IUDOP- UCA), 2007.

Cornelius, Wayne A. "Urbanization and Political Demand-Making: Political Participation among the Migrant Poor in Latin American Cities." *American Political Science Review* 68, no. 3 September (1974): 1125–46.

Cornelius, Wayne A., Todd A. Eise3nstadt, and Hane Hindley, eds. *Subnational Politics and Democratization in Mexico.* La Jolla, Calif.: Center for U.S.-Mexican Studies, University of California, San Diego, 1999.

Craig, Stephen C. *The Malevolent Leaders: Popular Discontent in America.* Political Cultures Series. Boulder, Colo.: Westview Press, 1993.

Crook, Richard, and James C. Manor. *Democracy and Decentralization in South Asia and West Africa: Participation, Accountability, and Performance.* Cambridge: Cambridge University Press, 1998.

Crozier, Michael, Samuel P. Huntington, and Joji Watanuki. *The Crisis of Democracy: Report on the Governability of Democracies to the Trilateral Commission.* New York: New York University Press, 1975.

Cuesta, José. "Political Space, Pro-Poor Growth and Poverty Reduction Strategy in Honduras: A Story of Missed Opportunities." *Journal of Latin American Studies* 39, no. 2 (2007): 329–54.

Dahl, Robert A. *A Preface to Democratic Theory.* Charles R. Walgreen Foundation Lectures. Chicago: University of Chicago Press, 1956.

Dahl, Robert A. *Polyarchy: Participation and Opposition.* New Haven, Conn.: Yale University Press, 1971.

Dahl, Robert A. *On Democracy.* New Haven, Conn.: Yale University Press, 1998.

Dalton, Russell J. *Citizen Politics: Public Opinion and Political Parties in Advanced Industrial Democracies.* Chatham, N.J.: Chatham House, 1996.

Dalton, Russell J. "Political Support in Advanced Industrial Democracies." In *Critical Citizens: Global Support for Democratic Government*, edited by Pippa Norris. New York: Oxford University Press, 1999.

Dalton, Russell J. "Value Change and Democracy." In *Disaffected Democracies: What's Troubling the Trilateral Countries?*, edited by Susan J. Pharr and Robert D. Putnam. Princeton, N.J.: Princeton University Press, 2000.

Dalton, Russell J. *Democratic Challenges, Democratic Choices: The Erosion of Political Support in Advanced Industrial Democracies.* Oxford: Oxford University Press, 2004.

Davis, Charles L., and Kenneth M. Coleman. "Who Abstains?: The Situational Meaning of Nonvoting." *Social Science Quarterly* 64 (1983): 764–76.

Della Porta, Donatella. "Social Capital, Beliefs in Government, and Political Corruption." In *Disaffected Democracies: What's Troubling the Trilateral Countries?*, edited by Susan J. Pharr and Robert D. Putnam. Princeton, N.J.: Princeton University Press, 2000.

Dennis, Jack, Leon Lindberg, Donald McCrone, and Rodney Stiefbold. "Political Socialization to Democratic Orientations in Four Western Systems." *Comparative Political Studies* 1(1968): 71–101.

Dennis, Jack, and Donald J. McCrone. "Preadult Development of Political Party Identification in Western Democracies." *Comparative Political Studies* 3(1970): 243–63.

Diamond, Larry Jay. *Developing Democracy: Toward Consolidation*. Baltimore, Md.: Johns Hopkins University Press, 1999.

Diamond, Larry Jay. *The Spirit of Democracy: The Struggle to Build Free Societies Throughout the World*. New York: Henry Holt and Company, 2008.

Diamond, Larry Jay, Marc F. Plattner, Yun-han Chu, and Hung-mao Tien, eds. *Consolidating the Third Wave Democracies: Regional Challenges*. Baltimore, Md.: Johns Hopkins University Press, 1997.

Dunkerley, James. *Power in the Isthmus: A Political History of Modern Central America*. London: Verso, 1988.

Durham, William H. *Scarcity and Survival in Central America: Ecological Origins of the Soccer War*. Stanford, Calif.: Stanford University Press, 1979.

Durkheim, Émile. *Suicide: A Study in Sociology*. Glencoe, Ill.: Free Press, 1951.

Durkheim, Émile, and William C. Bradbury. "Selected Readings of Anomie." Unpublished, 1947.

Easton, David. *A Framework of Political Analysis*. Englewood Cliffs, N.J.: Prentice-Hall, 1965a.

Easton, David. *A Systems Analysis of Political Life*. New York: Wiley, 1965b.

Easton, David. "A Re-Assessment of the Concept of Political Support." *British Journal of Political Science* 5(1975): 435–57.

Easton, David, Jack Dennis, and Sylvia Easton. *Children in the Political System: Origins of Political Legitimacy*. Chicago: University of Chicago Press, 1980.

Eaton, Kent. "Decentralization, Democratization and Liberalization: The History of Revenue Sharing in Argentina, 1934–1999." *Journal of Latin American Studies* 33, no. 1 (2001): 1–28.

Eaton, Kent. *Politics Beyond the Capital: The Design of Subnational Institutions in South America*. Stanford, Calif.: Stanford University Press, 2004.

Edwards, Bob, Michael W. Foley, and Mario Diani, eds. *Beyond Tocqueville: Civil Society and the Social Capital Debate in Comparative Perspective*. Hanover, N.H.: University Press of New England, 2001.

Elkins, Zachary, and John Sides. "The Vodka is Potent, but the Meat is Rotten: Evaluating Equivalence in Cross-National Survey Data." Paper presented at the American Political Science Association, Chicago, Ill., August 30–September 1 2007.

Fajinzylber, Pablo, Daniel Lederman, and Norman Loayza. *Determinants of Crime Rates in Latin America and the World: An Empirical Assessment*. Washington, D.C.: The World Bank, 1998.

Falleti, Tulia. "A Sequential Theory of Decentralization: Latin American Cases in Comparative Perspective." *American Political Science Review* 99, no. 3 (2005): 327–46.

Finkel, Steven, Edward Muller, and Mitchell A. Seligson. "Economic Crisis, Incumbent Performance and Regime Support: A Comparison of Longitudinal

Data from West Germany and Costa Rica." *British Journal of Political Science* 19(1989): 329–51.

Fischel, Astrid. *Consenso y represión: una interpretación sociopolítica de la educación costarricense.* San José de Costa Rica: Editorial Costa Rica, 1990.

Foley, Michael W. "Laying the Groundwork: The Struggle for Civil Society in El Salvador." *Journal of Interamerican Politics and World Affairs* 38(1996): 67–104.

Freedom House. "Freedom in the World 2003: Country and Related Territory Reports 2004." Available from http://freedomhouse.org/research/freeworld/2003/countries.htm [accessed June 6, 2005].

Fuchs, Dieter. "The Democratic Culture of Unified Germany." In *Critical Citizens: Global Support for Democratic Government,* edited by Pippa Norris. Oxford: Oxford University Press, 1999.

Fuchs, Dieter, Giovanna Guidorossi, and Palle Svensson. "Support for the Democratic System." In *Citizens and the State,* edited by Hans-Dieter Klingemann and Dieter Fuchs, 323–53. Oxford: Oxford University Press, 1995.

Fukuyama, Francis. *Trust: The Social Virtues and the Creation of Prosperity.* New York: The Free Press, 1995.

Gamson, William A. *Power and Discontent.* Homewood, Ill.: Dorsey, 1968.

Gans, Curtis B. "President Bush, Mobilization Drives Propel Turnout to Post-1968 High, Kerry, Democratic Weaknesses Shown." Committee for the Study of American Elections, November 4, 2004. Available from http://www.fairvote.org/reports/CSAE2004electionreport.pdf [accessed June 4, 2005].

Gastil, Raymond D. *Freedom in the World: Political Rights and Civil Liberties, 1988–1989.* Lanham, Md.: Freedom House, 1989.

Gaviria, Alejandro, and Carmen Pagés. "Patterns of Crime Victimization in Latin America." Paper presented at the Inter-American Development Bank Conference on Economic and Social Progress in Latin America, Washington, D.C., 1999.

Gibney, Mark. "Notes on Levels of Political Terror Scale." 2005a. Available from www.unca.edu/politicalscience/faculty-staff/gibney_docs/Political Terror Scale.doc [accessed March 12, 2005].

Gibney, Mark. "Political Terror Scale." University of North Carolina Asheville, 2005b. Available from www.unca.edu/politicalscience/faculty-staff/gibney_docs/pts.xls [accessed March 12, 2005].

Gibson, James L. "Challenges to the Impartiality of the State Supreme Courts: Legitimacy Theory and 'New Style' Judicial Campaigns." *American Political Science Review* 102, no. 1 (2008): 59–75.

Gibson, James L., and Gregory A. Caldeira. "Changes in the Legitimacy of the European Court of Justice: A Post-Maastricht Analysis." *British Journal of Political Science* 28, no. 1 (1998): 63–91.

Gibson, James L., Gregory A. Caldeira, and Lester Kenyatta Spence. "Measuring Attitudes toward the United States Supreme Court." *American Journal of Political Science* 47, no. 2 (2003): 354–67.

Gibson, James L., Gregory A. Caldeira, and Lester Kenyatta Spence. "Why Do People Accept Public Policies They Oppose?: Testing Legitimacy Theory with a Survey-Based Experiment." *Political Research Quarterly* 58, no. 2 (2005): 187–201.

Gil, Federico G. *Latin American-United States Relations.* New York: Harcourt Brace Jovanovich, 1971.

Gilley, Bruce. "The Meaning and Measure of State Legitimacy: Results for 72 Countries." *European Journal of Political Research* 45, no. 3 (2006): 499–525.

Gilley, Bruce. *The Right to Rule: How States Win and Lose Legitimacy.* New York: Columbia University Press, 2009.

Gramsci, Antonio, and Quintin Hoare. *Selections From Political Writings, 1921–1926: With Additional Texts by other Italian Communist Leaders.* Minneapolis: University of Minnesota Press, 1990.

Grayson, George W. *The Mexico-U.S. Business Committee: Catalyst for the North American Free Trade Agreement.* Rockville, Md.: Montrose Press, 2007.

Guatemala Instituto Nacional de Estadística. *República de Guatemala: Características generales de población y habitación: Cifras definitivas.* Guatemala, C.A.: Instituto Nacional de Estadística, 1996.

Gudmondson, Lowell. *Costa Rica Before Coffee: Society and Economy on the Eve of the Export Boom.* Baton Rouge: Louisiana State University Press, 1986.

Hall, Carolyn, Héctor Pérez Brignoli, and John V. Cotter. *Historical Atlas of Central America.* Norman, Okla.: University of Oklahoma Press, 2003.

Hardin, Russell. "Trusting Persons, Trusting Institutions." In *The Strategy of Choice,* edited by Richard J. Zeckhauser. Cambridge, Mass.: MIT Press, 1991.

Hartlyn, Jonathan. *The Politics of Coalition Rule in Colombia.* Cambridge Latin American Studies 66. Cambridge: Cambridge University Press, 1988.

Hawkins, Kirk A. "Populism in Venezuela: The Rise of Chavismo." *Third World Quarterly* 24, no. 6 (2003): 1137–60.

Hawkins, Kirk A., and David R. Hansen. "Dependent Civil Society: The Círculos Bolivarianos in Venezuela." *Latin American Research Review* 41, no. 1 (2006): 102–32.

Hayen, Goran, and Michael Bratton, eds. *Governance and Politics in Africa.* Boulder, Colo.: Lynne Reinner Publishers, 1992.

Held, David. "Democracy." In *The Oxford Companion to Politics of the World,* edited by Joel Krieger. Oxford: Oxford University Press, 2001.

Herreros, Francisco, and Henar Criado. "The State and the Development of Social Trust." *International Political Science Review* 29, no. 1 (2008): 53–71.

Heston, Alan, Robert Summers, and Bettina Aten. "Penn World Table, Version 6.1.," 2002. Available from http://pwt.econ.upenn.edu/ [accessed July 27, 2005].

Hetherington, Marc J. "The Political Relevance of Political Trust." *American Political Science Review* 92, no. 4 (1998): 791–808.

Hetherington, Marc J. *Why Trust Matters: Declining Political Trust and the Demise of American Liberalism.* Princeton, N.J.: Princeton University Press, 2005.

Hibbing, John R., and Elizabeth Theiss-Morse. *Congress as Public Enemy: Public Attitudes toward American Political Institutions.* Cambridge Studies in Political Psychology and Public Opinion. Cambridge: Cambridge University Press, 1995.

Hibbing, John R., and Elizabeth Theiss-Morse, eds. *What Is It about Government that Americans Dislike?* Cambridge Studies in Political Psychology and Public Opinion. Cambridge: Cambridge University Press, 2001.

Hibbing, John R., and Elizabeth Theiss-Morse. *Stealth Democracy: Americans' Beliefs About how Government Should Work.* Cambridge Studies in Political Psychology and Public Opinion. Cambridge: Cambridge University Press, 2002.

Higley, John, and Richard Gunther, eds. *Elites and Democratic Consolidation in Latin America and Southern Europe*. New York: Cambridge University Press, 1992.

Hiltunen de Biesanz, Mavis, Richard Biesanz, and Karen Zubris de Biesanz. *Los costarricenses*. San José, Costa Rica: Editorial Universidad Estatal a Distancia, 1979.

Hiskey, Jon, and Mitchell A. Seligson. "Pitfalls of Power to the People: Decentralization, Local Government Performance, and System Support in Bolivia." *Studies in Comparative International Development* 37, no. 4 (2003): 64–88.

Historical Clarification Commission. "Guatemala: Memory of Silence." Guatemala City: Historical Clarification Commission, 1999.

Holmberg, Soren. "Down and Down We Go: Political Trust in Sweden." In *Critical Citizens: Global Support for Democratic Governance*, edited by Pippa Norris. Oxford: Oxford University Press, 1999.

Humphreys, Macartan, and Jeremy M. Weinstein. "Who Fights? The Determinants of Participation in Civil War." *American Journal of Political Science* 52, no. 2 (2008): 436–55.

Huntington, Samuel P. *Political Order in Changing Societies*. New Haven, Conn.: Yale University Press, 1968.

Inglehart, Ronald. "The Renaissance of Political Culture." *American Political Science Review* 82, no. 4 (1988): 1203–30.

Inglehart, Ronald. *Culture Shift in Advanced Industrial Society*. Princeton, N.J.: Princeton University Press, 1990.

Inglehart, Ronald. *Modernization and Postmodernization: Cultural, Economic and Political Change in 43 Societies*. Princeton, N.J.: Princeton University Press, 1997a.

Inglehart, Ronald. "Postmaterialist Values and the Erosion of Institutional Authority." In *Why People Don't Trust Government*, edited by Joseph Nye Jr., Philip D. Zelikow, and David C. King. Cambridge, Mass.: Harvard University Press, 1997b.

Inglehart, Ronald. "Postmodernization Erodes Respect for Authority, but Increases Support for Democracy." In *Critical Citizens: Global Support for Democratic Government*, edited by Pippa Norris. Oxford: Oxford University Press, 1999.

Inglehart, Ronald, and Christian Welzel. *Modernization, Cultural Change, and Democracy*. New York: Cambridge University Press, 2005.

Interamerican Development Bank. *Country Reports*. Interamerican Development Bank, 2004. Available from www.iadb.org/countries/index.cfm?language=English [accessed July 18, 2005].

Jackman, Robert W. "Political Elites, Mass Politics, and Support for Democratic Principles." *Journal of Politics* 34, no. 3 (1972): 752–64.

Jackman, Robert W., and Ross Alan Miller. *Before Norms: Institutions and Civic Culture*. Ann Arbor: University of Michigan Press, 2004.

Jonas, Susanne. "Democratization Through Peace: The Difficult Case of Guatemala." *Journal of Interamerican Studies and World Affairs* 42, no. 4 (2000): 9–38.

Karatnycky, Adrian. "The 1999 Freedom House Survey: A Century of Progress." *Journal of Democracy* 11, no. 1 (2000): 187–200.

Karl, Terry Lynn. *The Paradox of Plenty: Oil Booms and Petro-States*. Studies in International Political Economy 26. Berkeley: University of California Press, 1997.

Kaufmann, Daniel, Arat Kraay, and Massimo Mastruzzi. "Growth and Governance: A Reply." *Journal of Politics* 69, no. 2 (2007): 555–62.

Kaufmann, Daniel, Arat Kraay, and Pablo Zoido-Lobatón. "Governance Matters." Vol. 2196, Policy Research Working Paper. Washington, D.C.: World Bank, 1999.

Kaufmann, Daniel, Arat Kraay, and Pablo Zoido-Lobatón. *Governance Matters V: Governance Indicators for 1996–2005*, edited by World Bank. Washington, D.C., 2006.

Kelly, Phil. *The Fitzgibbon-Johnson Index: Specialists' View of Democracy in Latin America, 1945–2000*. Emporia, Kans.: Emporia State University, 2001.

Kincaid, A. Douglas. "Demilitarization and Security in El Salvador and Guatemala: Convergences of Success and Crisis." *Journal of Interamerican Studies and World Affairs* 42, no. 4 (2000): 39–58.

Kling, Merle. "Towards a Theory of Power and Political Instability in Latin America." *The Western Political Quarterly* 9(1956): 21–35.

Klingemann, Hans-Dieter. "Mapping Political Support in the 1990s: A Global Analysis." In *Critical Citizens: Global Support for Democratic Government*, edited by Pippa Norris. Oxford: Oxford University Press, 1999.

Kornberg, Allan, and Harold D. Clarke., eds. *Political Support in Canada: The Crisis Years*. Durham, N.C.: Duke University Press, 1983.

Kornberg, Allan, and Harold D. Clarke. *Citizens and Community: Political Support in a Representative Democracy*. Cambridge: Cambridge University Press, 1992.

Krishna, Anirudh. "Do Poor People Care Less for Democracy? Testing Individual-level Assumptions with Individual-level Data from India." In *Poverty, Participation and Democracy*, edited by Anirudh Krishna. Cambridge: Cambridge University Press, 2008.

Krosnick, Jon A. "Maximizing Questionnaire Quality." In *Measures of Political Attitudes*, edited by John P. Robinson, Phillip R. Shaver, and Lawrence S. Wrightsman. San Diego, Calif.: Academic Press, 1999.

Kurtz, Marcus J., and Andrew Schrank. "Growth and Governance: Models, Measures and Mechanisms." *Journal of Politics* 69, no. 2 (2007): 538–54.

LaFeber, Walter. *Inevitable Revolutions: The United States in Central America*. New York: W.W. Norton, 1983.

Lagos, Marta. "Latin America's Smiling Mask." *Journal of Democracy* 8, no. 3 (1997): 125–38.

Lagos, Marta. "Latin America's Diversity of Views." *Journal of Democracy* 19, no. 1 (2008): 111–25.

Lane, Robert Edwards. *Political Ideology: Why the American Common Man Believes What He Does*. New York: Free Press of Glencoe, 1962.

Levy, Daniel C., Kathleen Bruhn, and Emilio Zebadúa. *Mexico: The Struggle for Democratic Development*. 2nd ed. Berkeley: University of California Press, 2006.

Lijphart, Arend. "The Structure of Inference." In *The Civic Culture Revisited*, edited by Gabriel A. Almond and Sidney Verba. Beverley Hills: Sage, 1989.

Linz, Juan J., and Alfred Stepan. *Problems of Democratic Transition and Consolidation: Southern Europe, South America, and Post-Communist Systems.* Baltimore, Md.: Johns Hopkins University Press, 1996.

Lipset, Seymour Martin. *Political Man: The Social Bases of Politics.* Expanded ed. Baltimore, Md.: Johns Hopkins University Press, 1981 [1961].

Lora, Eduardo, and World Bank. *The State of State Reform in Latin America.* Stanford, Calif., and Washington, D.C.: Stanford University Press and World Bank, 2007.

Lowenberg, Gerhard. "The Influence of Parliamentary Behavior on Regime Stability: Some Conceptual Clarifications." *Comparative Politics* 3(1971): 177–200.

Lowenthal, Abraham F., and John Samuel Fitch. *Armies and Politics in Latin America.* Rev. ed. New York: Holmes & Meier, 1986.

MacLeod, Murdo J. *Spanish Central America: A Socioeconomic History, 1520–1720.* Berkeley: University of California Press, 1973.

Magaloni, Beatrix. *Voting for Autocracy: Hegemonic Party Survival and its Demise in Mexico.* Cambridge: Cambridge University Press, 2007.

Mahoney, James. *The Legacies of Liberalism: Path Dependence and Political Regimes in Central America.* Baltimore, Md.: Johns Hopkins University Press, 2001.

Mainwaring, Scott, and Timothy R. Scully, eds. *Building Democratic Institutions: Party Systems in Latin America.* Stanford: Stanford University Press, 1995.

Mainwaring, Scott, and Matthew Soberg Shugart, eds. *Presidentialism and Democracy in Latin America.* Cambridge: Cambridge University Press, 1997.

Markoff, John. *The Great Wave of Democracy in Historical Perspective.* Cornell Studies in International Affairs, Western Societies Papers 34. Ithaca, N.Y.: Cornell University, 1995.

Martz, John D. *Colombia: A Contemporary Political Survey.* Westport, Conn.: Greenwood Press, 1975.

Martz, John D., and Enrique A. Baloyra. *Electoral Mobilization and Public Opinion: The Venezuelan Campaign of 1973.* Chapel Hill, N.C.: University of North Carolina Press, 1976.

Mason, T. David. *Caught in the Crossfire: Revolution, Repression, and the Rational Peasant.* Lanham, Md.: Rowman and Littlefield, 2004.

Mattes, Robert, and Michael Bratton. "Learning about Democracy in Africa: Awareness, Performance, and Experience." *American Journal of Political Science* 51, no. 1 (2007): 192–217.

McAllister, Ian. "The Economic Performance of Governments." In *Critical Citizens: Global Support for Democratic Government*, edited by Pippa Norris. Oxford: Oxford University Press, 1999.

Merolla, Jennifer, Jennifer Ramos, and Elizabeth Zechmeister. "Crisis, Charisma and Consequences: Evidence from the 2004 U.S. Presidential Election." *Journal of Politics* 69, no. 1 (2007): 30–42.

Meyer, Michael C., William L. Sherman, and Susan M. Deeds. *The Course of Mexican History.* 8th ed. New York: Oxford University Press, 2007.

Mill, John Stuart. *Considerations on Representative Government.* Indianapolis: Bobbs-Merrill, 1958.

Miller, Arthur H. "Political Issues and Trust in Government." *American Political Science Review* 68(1974): 951–72.

Miller, Arthur, H., and Ola Listhaug. "Political Performance and Institutional Trust." In *Critical Citizens: Global Support for Democratic Government*, edited by Pippa Norris. Oxford: Oxford University Press, 1999.

Mishler, William, and Richard Rose. "Five Years After the Fall: Trajectories of Support for Democracy in Post-Communist Europe." In *Critical Citizens: Global Support for Democratic Government*, edited by Pippa Norris. Oxford: Oxford University Press, 1999.

Mishler, William, and Richard Rose. "What Are the Origins of Political Trust? Testing Institutional and Cultural Theories in Post-Communist Societies." *Comparative Political Studies* 34, no. 1 (2001): 30–62.

Molina Jiménez, Iván, and Fabrice Lehoucq. *Urnas de lo inesperado: Fraude electoral y lucha política en Costa Rica*. San José, Costa Rica: Editorial de la Universidad de Costa Rica, 1999.

Mondak, Jeffery J. "Developing Valid Knowledge Scales." *American Journal of Political Science* 32(2001): 224–38.

Montero, A.P., and David J. Samuels, eds. *Decentralization and Democracy in Latin America*. South Bend, Ind.: University of Notre Dame Press, 2004.

Montero, José R., and Mariano Torcal. "Voters and Citizens in a New Democracy: Some Trend Data on Political Attitudes in Spain." *International Journal of Public Opinion Research* 2, no. 2 (1990): 116–40.

Montgomery, Tommie Sue. *Revolution in El Salvador: Origins and Evolution*. Boulder, Colo.: Westview, 1982.

Montgomery, Tommie Sue. *Revolution in El Salvador: From Civil Strife to Civil Peace*. Boulder, Colo.: Westview Press, 1994.

Morlino, Leonardo, and José Ramón Montero. "Legitimacy and Democracy in Southern Europe." In *The Politics of Democratic Consolidation: Southern Europe in Comparative Perspective*, edited by Richard P. Gunther, P. Nikiforos Diamandouros, and Hans-Jürgen Puhle. Baltimore, Md.: Johns Hopkins University Press, 1995.

Muller, Edward N. "Correlates and Consequences of Beliefs in the Legitimacy of Regime Structures." *Midwest Journal of Political Science* 14(1970a): 392–412.

Muller, Edward N. "The Representation of Citizens by Political Authorities: Consequences for Regime Support." *American Journal of Political Science* 64(1970b): 1149–66.

Muller, Edward N. *Aggressive Political Participation*. Princeton, N.J.: Princeton University Press, 1979.

Muller, Edward N., and Thomas O. Jukam. "On the Meaning of Political Support." *American Political Science Review* 71(1977): 1561–95.

Muller, Edward N., Thomas O. Jukam, and Mitchell A. Seligson. "Diffuse Political Support and Antisystem Political Behavior: A Comparative Analysis." *American Journal of Political Science* 26(1982): 240–64.

Muller, Edward N., and Mitchell A. Seligson. "Civic Culture and Democracy: The Question of the Causal Relationships." *American Political Science Review* 88(1994): 635–54.

Muller, Edward N., and Carol Williams. "Dynamics of Political Support-Alienation." *Comparative Political Studies* 13(1980): 33–59.

Nathan, Andrew. "Political Culture and Diffuse Regime Support in Asia." Working Paper Series 43, edited by Asia Barometer Project Office, 38. Taipei, 2007.

Newton, Kenneth. "Social and Political Trust in Established Democracies." In *Critical Citizens: Global Support for Democratic Government*, edited by Pippa Norris. Oxford: Oxford University Press, 1999.

Newton, Kenneth, and Pippa Norris. "Confidence in Public Institutions: Faith, Culture, or Performance?" In *Disaffected Democracies: What's Troubling the Trilateral Countries?*, edited by Susan J. Pharr and Robert D. Putnam. Princeton, N.J.: Princeton University Press, 2000.

Nickson, R. Andrew. *Local Government in Latin America*. Boulder, Colo.: Lynne Reinner Publishers, 1995.

Nolan-Ferrell, Catherine. "The State, Civil Society, and Revolutions: Building Political Legitimacy in Twentieth-Century Latin America." *Latin American Research Review* 39, no. 3 (2004): 294–304.

Norris, Pippa. "Conclusions: The Growth of Critical Citizens and its Consequences." In *Critical Citizens: Global Support for Democratic Government*, edited by Pippa Norris. New York: Oxford University Press, 1999a.

Norris, Pippa, ed. *Critical Citizens: Global Support for Democratic Government*. Oxford: Oxford University Press, 1999b.

Norris, Pippa. "Introduction: The Growth of Critical Citizens?" In *Critical Citizens: Global Support for Democratic Government*, edited by Pippa Norris. Oxford: Oxford University Press, 1999c.

Norris, Pippa. "Institutional Explanations for Political Support." In *Critical Citizens: Global Support for Democratic Government*, edited by Pippa Norris. Oxford: Oxford University Press, 1999d.

Norris, Pippa. "The Impact of Television on Civic Malaise." In *Disaffected Democracies: What's Troubling the Trilateral Countries?*, edited by Susan J. Pharr and Robert D. Putnam. Princeton, N.J.: Princeton University Press, 2000.

Norris, Pippa. *Democratic Phoenix: Reinventing Political Activism*. Cambridge: Cambridge University Press, 2002.

Norris, Pippa, and Ronald Inglehart. *Sacred and Secular: Religion and Politics Worldwide*. Cambridge Studies in Social Theory, Religion, and Politics. Cambridge: Cambridge University Press, 2004.

Norris, Pippa, Stefaan Walgrave, and Peter Van Aelst. "Who Demonstrates? Antistate Rebels, Conventional Participants, or Everyone?" *Comparative Politics* 37(2005): 189–205.

Nye Jr., Joseph. "The Decline of Confidence in Government." In *Why People Don't Trust Government*, edited by Joseph Nye Jr. Cambridge, Mass.: Harvard University Press, 1997.

Nye Jr., Joseph, and Philip D. Zelikow. "Reflections, Conjectures and Puzzles." In *Why People Don't Trust Government*, edited by Joseph Nye Jr., Philip D. Zelikow, and David C. King. Cambridge, Mass.: Harvard University Press, 1997.

Nye Jr., Joseph, Philip D. Zelikow, and David C. King, eds. *Why People Don't Trust Government*. Cambridge, Mass.: Harvard University Press, 1997.

Otake, Hideo. "Political Mistrust and Party Dealignment in Japan." In *Disaffected Democracies: What's Troubling the Trilateral Countries?*, edited by Susan J. Pharr and Robert D. Putnam. Princeton, N.J.: Princeton University Press, 2000.

Paige, Jeffrey M. "Coffee and Power in El Salvador." *Latin American Research Review* 28, no. 3 (1993): 7–40.

Paige, Jeffery M. *Coffee and Power: Revolution and the Rise of Democracy in Central America.* Cambridge, Mass.: Harvard University Press, 1997.

Pateman, Carole. *Participation and Democratic Theory.* New York: Cambridge University Press, 1970.

Paxton, Pamela. "Social Capital and Democracy: An Interdependent Relationship." *American Sociological Review* 67(2002): 254–77.

Paxton, Pamela. "Association Memberships and Generalized Trust: A Multilevel Model Across 31 Countries." *Social Forces* 86, no. 1 (2007): 47–76.

Payne, J. Mark. *Democracies in Development: Politics and Reform in Latin America.* 2nd ed. Washington, D.C.: Inter-American Development Bank and International Institute for Democracy and Electoral Assistance, 2007.

Peeler, John. *Latin American Democracies: Colombia, Costa Rica, and Venezuela.* Chapel Hill, N.C.: University of North Carolina Press, 1985.

Peeler, John. "Elite Settlements and Democratic Consolidation in Latin America: Colombia, Costa Rica, and Venezuela." In *Elites and Democratic Consolidation in Latin America and Southern Europe*, edited by John Higley and Richard Gunther. New York: Cambridge University Press, 1992.

Peeler, John. *Building Democracy in Latin America.* Boulder, Colo.: Lynne Reinner Publishers, 1998.

Pérez, Orlando J. "Elections Under Crisis: Background to Panama in the 1980s." In *Elections and Democracy in Central America, Revisited*, edited by Mitchell A. Seligson and John A. Booth. Chapel Hill, N.C.: University of North Carolina Press, 1995.

Pérez, Orlando J. *Post-invasion Panama: The Challenges of Democratization in the New World Order.* Lanham, Md.: Lexington Books, 2000.

Pérez-Brignoli, Héctor. *A Brief History of Central America.* Berkeley: University of California Press, 1989.

Pérez-Liñán, Aníbal, Barry Ames, and Mitchell A. Seligson. "Strategy, Careers and Judicial Decisions: Lessons from the Bolivian Courts." *Journal of Politics* 68, no. 2 (2006): 284–95.

Pharr, Susan J. "Officials' Misconduct and Public Distrust: Japan and the Trilateral Democracies." In *Disaffected Democracies: What's Troubling the Trilateral Countries?*, edited by Susan J. Pharr and Robert D. Putnam. Princeton, N.J.: Princeton University Press, 2000b.

Pharr, Susan J., and Robert D. Putnam, eds. *Disaffected Democracies: What's Troubling the Trilateral Countries?* Princeton, N.J.: Princeton University Press, 2000a.

Pharr, Susan J., Robert D. Putnam, and Russell J. Dalton. "A Quarter-Century of Declining Confidence." *Journal of Democracy* 11, no. 2 (2000c): 5–25.

Pitkin, Hannah. *The Concept of Representation.* Berkeley: University of California Press, 1967.

Popkin, Samuel L. *The Rational Peasant: The Political Economy of Rural Society in Vietnam.* Berkeley: University of California Press, 1979.

Preston, Richard Arthur, E. Donald Briggs, Allan Kornberg, and Harold D. Clarke. *Political Support in Canada: The Crisis Years: Essays in Honor of*

Richard A. Preston. A Duke University Center for International Studies publication. Durham, N.C.: Duke University Press, 1983.

Pritchett, Lant, and Daniel Kaufmann. "Civil Liberties, Democracy, and the Performance of Government Projects." *Finance and Development* 35, no. 1 (1998): 26–29.

Przeworski, Adam. "Some Problems in the Study of the Transition to Democracy." In *Transitions from Authoritarian Rule*, edited by Guillermo O'Donnell, Philippe C. Schmitter, and Lawrence Whitehead. Baltimore, Md.: Johns Hopkins University Press, 1986.

Przeworski, Adam, Michael E. Alvarez, Jose Antonio Cheibub, and Fernando Limongi. *Democracy and Development: Political Institutions and Well-Being in the World, 1950–1990.* Cambridge: Cambridge University Press, 2000.

Putnam, Robert D. "Toward Explaining Military Intervention in Latin America." *World Politics* 20, no. 1 (1967): 83–110.

Putnam, Robert D. *Making Democracy Work: Civic Traditions in Modern Italy.* Princeton, N.J.: Princeton University Press, 1993.

Putnam, Robert D. "Tuning In, Tuning Out: The Strange Disappearance of Social Capital in America." *PS: Political Science and Politics* 28, no. 4 (1995): 664–83.

Putnam, Robert D. *Bowling Alone: The Collapse and Revival of American Community.* New York: Simon & Schuster, 2000.

Putnam, Robert D. *Democracies in Flux: the Evolution of Social Capital in Contemporary Society.* Oxford: Oxford University Press, 2002.

Putnam, Robert D., Susan J. Pharr, and Russell J. Dalton. "Introduction: What's Troubling the Trilateral Democracies?" In *Disaffected Democracies: What's Troubling the Trilateral Countries?*, edited by Susan J. Pharr and Robert D. Putnam. Princeton, N.J.: Princeton University Press, 2000.

Rahn, Wendy M., and Thomas J. Rudolph. "A Tale of Political Trust in American Cities." *Public Opinion Quarterly* 69(2005): 530–60.

Rodríguez-Raga, Juan Carlos, and Mitchell A. Seligson. *La cultura política de la democracia en Colombia, 2004.* Nashville, Tenn.: Vanderbilt University, 2004.

Rogowski, Ronald. *Rational Legitimacy: A Theory of Political Support.* Princeton, N.J.: Princeton University Press, 1974.

Romero, A. "Rearranging the Deck Chairs on the Titanic: The Agony of Democracy in Venezuela." *Latin American Research Review* 32, no. 1 (1997): 7–36.

Ropp, Steve C. *Panamanian politics: From Guarded Nation to National Guard, Politics in Latin America.* New York and Stanford, Calif.: Praeger and Hoover Institution Press, 1982.

Ropp, Steve C. "Leadership and Political Transformation in Panama: Two Levels of Regime Crisis." In *Central America: Crisis and Adaptation*, edited by Steve C. Ropp and James A. Morris. Albuquerque: University of New Mexico Press, 1984.

Ropp, Steve C. "Panama: New Politics for a New Millennium." In *Latin American Politics and Development*, edited by Howard Wiarda and Harvey F. Kline. Boulder, Colo.: Westview Press, 2007.

Rose, Richard, William Mishler, and Christian Haerpfer. *Democracy and Its Alternatives: Understanding Post-Communist Societies.* Oxford: Oxford University Press, 1998.

Rose, Richard, Doh C. Shin, and Neil Munro. "Tensions Between the Democratic Ideal and Reality: South Korea." In *Critical Citizens: Global Support for Democratic Government*, edited by Pippa Norris. Oxford: Oxford University Press, 1999.

Rosenberg, Mark B. "Democracy in Honduras: The Electoral and the Political Reality." In *Elections and Democracy in Central America, Revisited*, edited by Mitchell A. Seligson and John A. Booth. Chapel Hill, N.C.: University of North Carolina Press, 1995.

Rosenstone, Steven J., and Mark Hansen. *Mobilization, Participation and Democracy in America*. New York: Macmillan, 1993.

Sánchez, Fernando F. "Dealignment in Costa Rica: A Case Study of Electoral Change." University of Oxford, 2003.

Sanford, Victoria. *Buried Secrets: Truth and Human Rights in Guatemala*. New York: Palgrave Macmillan, 2003.

Sartori, Giovanni. "Concept Misformation in Comparative Politics." *American Political Science Review* 64, no. 4 (1970): 1033–53.

Schedler, Andreas. *Electoral Authoritarianism: The Dynamics of Unfree Competition*. Boulder, Colo.: Lynne Rienner Publishers, 2006.

Schlesinger, Stephen C., and Stephen Kinzer. *Bitter Fruit: The Story of the American Coup in Guatemala*. Rev. and expanded ed. David Rockefeller Center Series on Latin American Studies 4. Cambridge, Mass.: Harvard University, David Rockefeller Center for Latin American Studies, 2005.

Schneider, Ronald M. *Latin American Political History: Patterns and Personality*. Boulder, Colo.: Westview Press, 2007.

Schoultz, Lars. *Human Rights and United States Policy Toward Latin America*. Princeton, N.J.: Princeton University Press, 1981.

Schoultz, Lars. *National Security and United States Policy Toward Latin America*. Princeton, N.J.: Princeton University Press, 1987.

Schoultz, Lars. *Beneath the United States: A History of U.S. Policy Toward Latin America*. Cambridge, Mass.: Harvard University Press, 1998.

Schumpeter, Joseph A. *Capitalism, Socialism, and Democracy*. London: Allen and Unwin, 1943.

Scott, James C. *The Moral Economy of the Peasant: Rebellion and Subsistence in Southeast Asia*. New Haven: Yale University Press, 1976.

Scott, James C. *Weapons of the Weak: Everyday Forms of Peasant Resistance*. New Haven: Yale University Press, 1985.

Seligson, Amber L. "*When Democracies Elect Dictators: Motivations for and Impact of the Election of Former Authoritarians in Argentina and Bolivia.*" Ph.D. dissertation, Cornell University, 2002a.

Seligson, Mitchell A. "Unconventional Political Participation: Cynicism, Powerlessness, and the Latin American Peasant." In *Politics and the Poor: Political Participation in Latin America*, edited by Mitchell A. Seligson and John A. Booth. New York: Holmes and Meier, 1979.

Seligson, Mitchell A. *Peasants of Costa Rica and the Development of Agrarian Capitalism*. Madison and London: University of Wisconsin Press, 1980.

Seligson, Mitchell A. "On the Measurement of Diffuse Support: Some Evidence from Mexico." *Social Indicators Research* 12(1983): 1–24.

Seligson, Mitchell A. *El campesino y el capitalismo agrario de Costa Rica*. 2nd rev. ed. San José, Costa Rica: Editorial Costa Rica, 1984.

Seligson, Mitchell A. "Costa Rica and Jamaica." In *Competitive Elections in Developing Countries*, edited by Myron Weiner and Ergun Ozbudun. Durham, N.C.: Duke University Press, 1987a.

Seligson, Mitchell A. "Development, Democratization and Decay: Central America at the Crossroads." In *Authoritarians and Democrats: The Politics of Regime Transition in Latin America*, edited by James M. Malloy and Mitchell A. Seligson. Pittsburgh, Penn.: University of Pittsburgh Press, 1987b.

Seligson, Mitchell A. "Thirty Years of Transformation in the Agrarian Structure of El Salvador, 1961–1991." *Latin American Research Review* 30, no. 3 (1995): 43–74.

Seligson, Mitchell A. "The Vanhanen Thesis and the Prospects for Democracy in Latin America." In *Prospects for Democracy: A Study of 172 Countries*, edited by Tatu Vanhanen. London: Routledge, 1997.

Seligson, Mitchell A. "Corruption and Democratization: What Is To Be Done?" *Public Integrity* 3, no. 3 (2001a): 221–41.

Seligson, Mitchell A. "Costa Rican Exceptionalism: Why the 'Ticos' Are Different." In *Citizen Views of Democracy in Latin America*, edited by Rodric Ai Camp. Pittsburgh, Penn.: University of Pittsburgh Press, 2001b.

Seligson, Mitchell A. *La cultura política de la democracia en Bolivia: 2000*. La Paz, Bolivia: Universidad Católica Boliviana, 2001c.

Seligson, Mitchell A. "¿Problemas en el Paraíso? La erosión el apoyo al sistema político en Costa Rica, 1978–1999." In *La democracia de Costa Rica ante el siglo XXI*, edited by Jorge Rovira Más. San Pedro de Montes de Oca, Costa Rica: Editorial de la Universidad de Costa Rica, 2001d.

Seligson, Mitchell A. "Trouble in Paradise: The Impact of the Erosion of System Support in Costa Rica, 1978–1999." *Latin American Research Review* 37, no. 1 (2002a): 160–85.

Seligson, Mitchell A. "The Impact of Corruption on Regime Legitimacy: A Comparative Study of Four Latin American Countries." *Journal of Politics* 64 (2002b): 408–33.

Seligson, Mitchell A. "The Renaissance of Political Culture or the Renaissance of Ecological Fallacy." *Comparative Politics* 34(2002c): 273–92.

Seligson, Mitchell A. *Auditoria de la democracia: Bolivia, 2002*. La Paz, Bolivia: Universidad Católica Boliviana, 2003.

Seligson, Mitchell A. "Democracy on Ice: The Multiple Paradoxes of Guatemala's Peace Process." In *The Third Wave of Democratization in Latin America: Advances and Setbacks*, edited by Francis Hagopian and Scott Mainwaring. Cambridge: Cambridge University Press, 2005a.

Seligson, Mitchell A. "Encuestas y democratización." *Este País (Mexico)*, no. 168 (2005b): 4–13.

Seligson, Mitchell A. "Improving the Quality of Survey Research in Democratizing Countries." *PS: Political Science and Politics* 38, no. 1 (2005c): 51–56.

Seligson, Mitchell A. "Mejorando la calidad de la investigación por medio de encuestas en los países en democratización." *Revista de Ciencias Sociales (Costa Rica)* 108(2005d): 79–90.

Seligson, Mitchell A. "The Measurement and Impact of Corruption Victimization: Survey Evidence from Latin America." *World Development* 34, no. 2 (2006a): 381–404.

Seligson, Mitchell A. *The Political Culture of Democracy in Mexico, Central America, and Colombia, 2004.* Nashville, Tenn.: Latin American Public Opinion Project, Vanderbilt University, 2006b.

Seligson, Mitchell A. "The Rise of Populism and the Left in Latin America." *Journal of Democracy* 18, no. 3 (July 2007): 81–95.

Seligson, Mitchell A. "The 'Kling Thesis': An Early Effort at Systematic Comparative Politics." *Political Research Quarterly* 61, no. 1 (2008a): 17–19.

Seligson, Mitchell A., ed. *Challenges to Democracy in Latin America and the Caribbean: Evidence from the AmericasBarometer 2006–07.* Nashville, Tenn.: Latin American Public Opinion Project, 2008b.

Seligson, Mitchell A., and John A. Booth. "Development, Political Participation and the Poor in Latin America." In *Politics and the Poor: Political Participation in Latin America*, edited by Mitchell A. Seligson and John A. Booth. New York: Holmes and Meier, 1979a.

Seligson, Mitchell A., and John A. Booth. "Structure and Levels of Political Participation in Costa Rica: Comparing Peasants with City Dwellers." In *Politics and the Poor: Political Participation in Latin America*, edited by Mitchell A. Seligson and John A. Booth. New York: Holmes and Meier, 1979b.

Seligson, Mitchell A., and John A. Booth, eds. *Politics and the Poor: Political Participation in Latin America*, New York: Holmes and Meier Publishers, 1979c.

Seligson, Mitchell A. and John A. Booth. "Political Culture and Regime Type: Evidence from Nicaragua and Costa Rica." *Journal of Politics* 55, no. 3 (1993): 777–92.

Seligson, Mitchell A., John A. Booth, and Miguel Gómez Barrantes. "Os contornos da cidadanía crítica: Explorando a legitimidade democrática." *Opinião Pública* 12, no. 1 (2006): 1–37.

Seligson, Mitchell A., and Julio Carrión. "Political Support, Political Skepticism and Political Stability in New Democracies: An Empirical Examination of Mass Support for Coups D'Etat in Peru."*Comparative Political Studies* 35, no. 1 (2002): 58–82.

Seligson, Mitchell A., Marcus Catsam, Andrew Lotz, Daniel Moreno, and A. Polibio Córdova C. *Auditoría de la democracia: Ecuador, 2004.* Quito, Ecuador: Ediciones CEDATOS, Universidad San Francisco de Quito, FLACSO Quito, Universidad Espíritu Santo, Guayaquil, Universidad de Guayaquil, 2004.

Seligson, Mitchell A., Annabelle Conroy, Ricardo Córdova Macías, Orlando J. Pérez, and Andrew Stein. "Who Votes in Central America? A Comparative Analysis." In *Elections and Democracy in Central America, Revisited*, edited by Mitchell A. Seligson and John A. Booth. Chapel Hill, N.C.: University of North Carolina Press, 1995.

Seligson, Mitchell A., Abby B. Córdova, Juan C. Donoso, Daniel Moreno, Diana M. Orcés, and Vivian Schwarz-Blum. *Auditoría de la democracia: Bolivia, 2006*, edited by Mitchell A. Seligson. Cochabamba: Latin American Public Opinion Project (LAPOP), 2006.

Seligson, Mitchell A., and Ricardo Córdova Macías. "Integration and Disintegration in Central America: From 1950–1990." In *Changing Boundaries in the Americas: New Perspectives on the US-Mexican, Central American, and South American Borders*, edited by Lawrence A. Herzog. San Diego: Center for US-Mexican Studies, 1992.

Seligson, Mitchell A., and Ricardo Córdova Macías. *El Salvador: Entre guerra y la paz, una cultura política en transición*. San Salvador: IDELA and FundaUngo, 1995.

Seligson, Mitchell A., and Ricardo Córdova Macías. "Nicaragua 1991–1995: Una cultura política en transición." In *Cultura política y transición democrática en Nicaragua*, edited by Ricardo Córdova Macías. Managua: Fundación Ebert, Fundación Guillermo Ungo, Instituto de Estudios Nicaraguenses y Centro de Análisis Socio-Cultural, 1996.

Seligson, Mitchell A., Juan Carlos Donoso, Daniel Moreno, Diana Orcés, and Vivian Schwarz-Blum. *Auditoría de la democracia: Ecuador, 2006*, edited by Mitchell A. Seligson. Quito, Ecuador: Ediciones CEDATOS, 2006.

Seligson, Mitchell A., and Miguel B. Gómez. "Ordinary Elections in Extraordinary Times: The Political Economy of Voting in Costa Rica." In *Elections and Democracy in Central America*, edited by John A. Booth and Mitchell A. Seligson. Chapel Hill, N.C.: University of North Carolina Press, 1989.

Seligson, Mitchell A., Agustín Grijalva, and Polibio Córdova. *Auditoría de la democracia: Ecuador*. Quito, Ecuador: Ediciones CEDATOS, Universidad Andina Simón Bolívar and Universidad de Guayaquil, 2002.

Seligson, Mitchell A., Earl Jones, and Edgar Nesman. "Community and Cooperative Participation among Land Reform Beneficiaries in Honduras." *Journal of Rural Cooperation* 12, nos. 1–2 (1984): 65–87.

Seligson, Mitchell A., and Juliana Martínez Franzoni. "Limits to Costa Rican Heterodoxy: What Has Changed in 'Paradise?'" In *The Politics of Democratic Governance in Latin America: Clues and Lessons*, edited by Scott Mainwaring and Timothy Scully. Palo Alto, Calif.: Stanford University Press, forthcoming.

Seligson, Mitchell A., and Vincent McElhinny. "Low Intensity Warfare, High Intensity Death: The Demographic Impact of the Wars in El Salvador and Nicaragua." *Canadian Journal of Latin American and Caribbean Studies* 21, no. 42 (1996): 211–41.

Seligson, Mitchell A., and Edward N. Muller. "Democratic Stability and Economic Crisis: Costa Rica 1978–1983." *International Studies Quarterly* 31(1987): 301–26.

Seligson, Mitchell A., and Francesca Recanatini. "Governance and Corruption." In *Ecuador: An Economic and Social Agenda in the New Millennium*, edited by Vicente Fretes-Cibils, M. Giugale Marcelo, and José Roberto López-Cálix. Washington, D.C.: World Bank, 2003.

Seligson, Mitchell A., and Linda Stevenson. "Fading Memories of the Revolution: Is Stability Eroding in Mexico?" In *Polling for Democracy: Public Opinion and Political Liberalization in Mexico*, edited by Roderic Ai Camp. Wilmington, Del.: Scholarly Resources Press, 1996.

Shin, Doh C. *Mass Politics and Culture in Democratizing Korea*. Cambridge: Cambridge University Press, 1999.

Smith, Peter H. *Talons of the Eagle: Dynamics of U.S.–Latin American Relations.* New York: Oxford University Press, 1996.

Smith, Peter H. *Democracy in Latin America: Political Change in Comparative Perspective.* New York: Oxford University Press, 2005.

Stanfield, David, Edgar Nesmanr, Alexander Coles, and Mitchell A. Seligson. "The Honduras Land Titling and Registration Experience." *Land Tenure Center Research Paper*, Madison, Wisc.: Land Tenure Center, University of Wisconsin, Madison, 1990.

Stein, Andrew. "The Consequences of the Nicaraguan Revolution for Political Tolerance among the Mass Public, Catholic Priests and Secular Elites." *Comparative Politics* 30, no. 3 (1998): 335–53.

Stoll, David. *Is Latin America Turning Protestant?: The Politics of Evangelical Growth.* Berkeley: University of California Press, 1990.

Stoll, David. *Between Two Armies in the Ixil Towns of Guatemala.* New York: Columbia University Press, 1993.

Sudman, Seymour. "Probability Sampling with Quotas." *Journal of the American Statistical Association* 61(1966): 749–71.

Sunshine, Jason, and Tom Tyler. "The Role of Procedural Justice and Legitimacy in Shaping Public Support for Policing." *Law and Society Review* 37, no. 3 (2003): 513–48.

Tetlock, Philip. *Expert Political Judgment: How Good is It? How Can We Know?* Princeton, N.J.: Princeton University Press, 2005.

Thomassen, Jacques. "Economic Crisis, Dissatisfaction, and Protest." In *Continuities in Political Action*, edited by M. Kent Jennings and Jan van Deth. Berlin: de Gruyter, 1989.

United Nations. *Global Report on Crime and Justice*, edited by Graeme Newman. New York: Oxford University Press, 1999.

United Nations Development Program. *Human Development Report* 2005. United Nations, 2005. Available from http://hdr.undp.org/reports/global/2005/pdf/HDR05_HDI.pdf [accessed May 18, 2006].

United States Department of the Army. *Country Studies: Colombia* 1988. Available from http://countrystudies.us/ [accessed July 19, 2005].

Uslaner, Eric M., and Mitchell Brown. "Inequality, Trust and Civic Engagement." *American Politics Research* 33, no. 6 (2005): 868–94.

Van Deth, Jan Willem, ed. *Private Groups and Public Life: Social Participation, Voluntary Associations, and Political Involvement in Representative Democracies.* London: Routledge, 1997.

Vanhanen, Tatu. *Political and Social Structures: Part 1, American Countries 1850–1973.* Tampere, Finland: Institute of Political Science, 1975.

Vanhanen, Tatu. *Prospects of Democracy: A Study of 172 Countries.* London: Routledge, 1997.

Véliz, Caudio. *The Centralist Tradition in Latin America.* Princeton, N.J.: Princeton University Press, 1980.

Verba, Sidney. *Small Groups and Political Behavior: A Study of Leadership.* Princeton, N.J., Princeton University Press, 1961.

Verba, Sidney. "The Citizen as Respondent: Sample Surveys and American Democracy." *American Political Science Review* 90, no. 1 (1996): 1–7.

Verba, Sidney, and Norman H. Nie. *Participation in America: Political Democracy and Social Equality.* New York: Harper and Row, 1972.

Verba, Sidney, Norman H. Nie, and Jae-On Kim. *The Modes of Democratic Participation: A Cross-National Comparison. Vol. 1, Comparative Politics Series.* Beverly Hills, Calif.: Sage Publications, 1971.

Verba, Sidney, Norman H. Nie, and Jae-On Kim. *Participation and Political Equality: A Seven-Nation Study.* New York: Cambridge University Press, 1978.

Walker, Thomas W. *Nicaragua: The Land of Sandino.* Boulder, Colo.: Westview, 1981.

Warren, Mark E. *Democracy and Trust.* Cambridge: Cambridge University Press, 1999.

Weatherford, M. Stephen. "Measuring Political Legitimacy." *American Political Science Review* 86, no. 1 (1992): 149–66.

Weber, Max. *Politics as a Vocation*: Fortress Press, 1965.

Webre, Stephen. *José Napoleón Duarte and the Christian Democratic Party in Salvadoran Politics: 1960–1972.* Baton Rouge, La.: Louisiana State University Press, 1979.

Werner, Simcha B. "The Development of Political Corruption in Israel." In *Political Corruption: A Handbook*, edited by Arnold J. Heidenheimer, Michael Johnston, and Victor T. LeVine. New Brunswick, N.J.: 1989.

Weyland, Kurt. "Neoliberalism and Democracy in Latin America: A Mixed Record." *Latin American Politics and Society* 46, no. 1 (2005): 135–64.

Wiarda, Howard J., and Harvey F. Kline, eds. *Latin American Politics and Development.* Boulder, Colo.: Westview Press, 1996.

Wickham-Crowley, Timothy. *Guerrillas and Revolution in Latin America: A Comparative Study of Insurgents and Regimes since 1956.* Princeton: Princeton University Press, 1992.

Williams, Philip J., and Knut Walter. *Militarization and Demilitarization in El Salvador's Transition to Democracy.* Pittsburgh, Penn.: University of Pittsburgh Press, 1997.

Wilson, Bruce M. *Costa Rica: Politics, Economics, and Democracy.* Boulder, Colo.: Lynne Rienner Publishers, 1998.

Woodward, Ralph Lee Jr. *Central America: A Nation Divided.* New York: Oxford University Press, 1976.

World Bank. *Guatemala, Investing for Peace: A Public Investment Review.* Report No. 16392-GU. Washington, D.C.: World Bank, 1997.

Yashar, Deborah J. *Demanding Democracy: Reform and Reaction in Costa Rica and Guatemala, 1870s–1950s.* Stanford: Stanford University Press, 1997.

Zimbalist, Andrew S., and John Weeks. *Panama at the Crossroads: Economic Development and Political Change in the Twentieth Century.* Berkeley: University of California Press, 1991.

About the Authors

John A. Booth is Regents Professor of Political Science at the University of North Texas. His research examines democratization, political attitudes and behavior, and political violence and revolution, concentrating especially on Central America, Mexico, and Colombia. In addition to his four coedited volumes and fourteen articles and chapters with this study's coauthor Mitchell Seligson, he is the author of *Understanding Central America: Global Forces, Rebellion, and Change* (fourth edition 2006 coauthored with Christine J. Wade and Thomas W. Walker), *Costa Rica: Quest for Democracy* (1998), *The End and the Beginning: The Nicaraguan Revolution* (second edition 1985). He has published articles in a wide array of scholarly journals in the United States and Latin America, as well as numerous anthology chapters.

He was an Associate Editor of *International Studies Quarterly* from 2004 through 2008 and serves on the editorial board of *Latin American Politics and Society;* he previously served on the editorial boards of the *Latin American Research Review* and *Political Research Quarterly*. He received a Fulbright-Hays fellowship (Costa Rica 1979–80) and taught at the National Autonomous University there. He has consulted for the United Nations Electoral Assistance Division, U.S. Agency for International Development, U.S. Department of State, Foreign Service Institute, and other U.S. government agencies, and for the Inter-American Dialogue, Washington Office on Latin America and other organizations and firms. He served on several election observation and peace settlement follow-up delegations in Central America from 1984 to 2001 and was program chair for the XVII International Congress of the Latin American Studies Association (1992). He chaired the Political Science Department of the

University of North Texas from 1986 to 1990 and was interim chair of Foreign Languages and Literatures at UNT from January 2003 through May 2004.

Mitchell A. Seligson is the Centennial Professor of Political Science at Vanderbilt University and a Fellow of the Vanderbilt Center for Nashville Studies. He founded and directs the Latin American Public Opinion Project (LAPOP), which conducts the AmericasBarometer surveys that currently cover 20 countries in the Americas. LAPOP has conducted over 100 surveys of public opinion, mainly focused on democracy, in many countries in Latin America, but has also included projects in Africa and the Balkans (see www.LapopSurveys.org).

Prior to joining the faculty at Vanderbilt, Seligson held the Daniel H. Wallace Chair of Political Science at the University of Pittsburgh and also served there as director of the Center for Latin American Studies. He has been a Fulbright Fellow and has received grants and fellowships from the Social Science Research Council, the Rockefeller Foundation, the Ford Foundation, The Mellon Foundation, The Howard Heinz Foundation, The Danforth Foundation, the U.S. Department of Education, USAID and others, and has published over 140 articles, 14 books, and dozens of monographs. He has consulted for USAID, the World Bank, the UNDP, and the IADB. He recently served on the National Academy of Sciences panel studying the impact of foreign assistance and democracy, is an appointed member of the Organization of American States (OAS) Advisory Board of Inter-American Program on Education for Democratic Values and Practices, is a founding member of the International Advisory Board of the Afrobarometer, and a member of the editorial board of the *European Political Science Review*. Earlier, he served on the editorial board of the *Latin American Research Review*. His most recent book is *Development and Underdevelopment, the Political Economy of Global Inequality* (fourth edition), coedited with John Passé-Smith. He has chaired or cochaired over 25 Ph.D. dissertations.

Index

acquiescence response set, 225
activism. *See specific forms of activism.*
Adams, Richard, 149
Africa, 2, 4, 35–6, 41, 210, 222
Afrobarometer, 16, 18, 48, 111, 128
Afro-Latin populations, 69
age
  and civil society activism, 167
  and cohort effects, 107
  and communal activism, 165
  and confrontational political tactics, 191
  and contacting officials, 164
  and coup d'etat support, 187, *188*
  and democracy support, 204, *205*, 206, 212, *212*, 233
  and legitimacy levels, 114, *139*
  and local government support, *136*
  and negative political capital, *196*, 197, 238
  and partisan and campaign activism, 162
  and political actor support, *134*, 135
  and political community perception, *120*
  and political participation, 152, *155–6*
  and protest activism, 170
  and rebellion support, *183*

and regime institutions support, *126*, 127
and regime performance support, *131*, 132
and regime principles support, *122*, 123, 123n. 11
and vigilantism, 193, *194*
and voting, 158
aggregation of data, 23
agriculture, 70, 82, 84, 87–8, 90–91, 93–94, 99
Albania, xix
Alemán, Arnoldo, 92
Alliance for Progress, 71, 83, 84, 90–91
Almond, Gabriel, 15, 19, 38
AmericasBarometer, 229, 229–30
Arbenz, Jacobo, 71, 82
Arellano, Oswaldo López, 88
"arena shopping," 34
Arévalo, Juan José, 82
Argentina, 4, 5
Arias, Arnulfo, 97–8
Arias, Óscar, 27
Aristide, Jean-Bertrand, 23, 150
Armas, Carlos Castillo, 82
Armed Forces of the Colombian Revolution (FARC), 101
Asamblea Legislativa, 165
Asia, 4, 35–6, 222
AsiaBarometer, 16, 18

and political community perception, 121

political performance, 76, 77

population characteristics, 73, 74

and protest activism, 20, 170, 174, 254

and rebellion support, *182*

and regime performance support, 129–30

and regime stability, 251

and relative levels of support, 61

and sample size, 45

and social development, 75, *75*

and structure of legitimacy, 57

and U.S. interventionism, 71–2

and vigilantism, 192, *192*, *193*, 195

elections and voting

and case selection, 103

and Colombia, 100

and confrontational political tactics, 190, *191*

and Costa Rica, 25, 28, 34, 93 94–5

and coup d'etat support, *188*

and democracy support, *205*, 211, 215–16, 216, 217, 220, 243–4

and disaffected citizenry, 261

and El Salvador, 86

"electoral authoritarianism," 24, 243

and Guatemala, 157

and Honduras, 88

and legitimacy levels, 138, *140*, *155*– 6, *158*, 234

and local government support, *136*, 137

measures of, 33, 33n. 26

and Mexico, 79

and negative political capital, 196

operationalizing, 151n. 7

and partisan and campaign activism, 161, *162*

and personal attitudes, 116

and political actor support, 133–4, *134*

and political community perception, *120*, 121, *259*

and political participation, 150, 151n. 7, 152, *155*, 157, 174

and protest activism, 168, 170

and rebellion support, *183*

and regime institutions support, 126, 129

and regime performance support, *131*, 132–3

and regime principles support, *122*

in selected countries, 73

and vigilantism, *194*

voter turnout rates, 22, 23, 25n. 18, 26n. 19, 27–8

elites

and antidemocratic sentiment, 243–4

in Colombia, 100

common features of cases, 70

in Costa Rica, 94

and coup d'etat, 23–4, 242–3

and disaffected citizenry, 245–6, 249

in Honduras, 87

in Nicaragua, 90

and political participation, 150

and protest activism, 147

and regime stability, 241

Endara, Guillermo, 98

ethnic minorities, xxi, 69, 96–7, 121

Eurobarometer, 16, 48

Europe, 4, 7, 222

evangelicals, 114, 127

executive power, 56

external validity problem, 175, 175n. 21

factor analysis, 29–33, 30n. 24, *31*, 31n. 25, 33n. 26, 40–41, 49, 54–5, 54n. 12, *55*, 151n. 7

Farabundo Martí National Liberation Front (FMLN), 85–86

federalism, 56, 73, 135n. 15

Figueres, José María, 27

Figueres Ferrer, José "Pepe," 94

foco theory of insurgency, 184–5

Fox, Vicente, 72, 80

Freedom House, 11n. 9, 17, 24–5, 76n. 7, 76, 77, 89, 93, 98, *110*, 125

selected countries, 74, 74
and survey translations, xxi
industrial democracies, 173, 222, 230, 260
infant mortality, 75, 76, 89, 93, 99, 224
inflation, *186*
Inglehart, Ronald, 11, 11n. 10, 206–7
Institutional Revolutionary Party (Mexico), 72
institutions. *See* regime institution support
instrumental contacting, 33, 33n. 26, 34
Inter-American Development Bank (IADB), xix
Inter-American Reciprocal Defense Treaty, 71
interpersonal trust. *See* trust
intraclass correlation, 47, 118n. 10
Iraq War, 230
isthmian canal 95–6. *See also* Panama Canal

Jamaica, 229
Japan, 67
Juárez, Benito, 78

Kish, Leslie, xxi
Klingemann, Hans-Dieter, 13, 43
Korea, 7

la violencia, 100
labor, 87, 93–4
land ownership, 82, 87
Lane, Robert, 3
language issues, xviii–xix, xxi, 36, 36n. 27, 44, 46n. 9, 223, 223n. 2
latent factors, 30n. 24, 31–2, 54–6
Latin American Public Opinion Project (LAPOP), xviii–xix, xix–xx, 68, 225n. 3, 229, 229, 248n. 10
LatinoBarometer, 44n. 7
legislatures, 11–12, 73
legitimacy. *See* dimensional structure of legitimacy; specific dimensions of legitimacy
Liberal Party (Colombia), 100

Liberal Party of Honduras (PLH), 87–8
liberal regimes, 84
life expectancy, 75, 89, 93, 99, 103
life satisfaction
and civil society activism, 167
and communal activism, 166
and confrontational political tactics, *191*
and coup d'etat support, 187, *188*
and democracy support, 212
and legitimacy levels, 117, *140*
and local government support, *136*, 137
and negative political capital, *196*, 198, 238
and partisan and campaign activism, 162
and political actor support, 134, 135
and political community perception, 121
and political participation, 152, *156*
and protest activism, 170
and rebellion support, *183*, 184
and regime institutions support, *126*, 128
and regime performance support, *131*, 133
and regime principles support, 122, 124
and vigilantism, *194*
Lipset, Seymour Martin, 1, 66–7
Listhaug, Ola, 18
literacy, 75, 75, 93, 224
local government support
in Colombia, 101
and communal activism, 165, *166*
and community size, 117–18
and confirmatory factor analysis, *31*, 32, 55
and confrontational political tactics, 189, *191*
and contacting officials, 162, *162*
and country variation, 133n. 14
and coup d'etat support, *188*

Lightning Source UK Ltd.
Milton Keynes UK
UKHW041549280419
341740UK00001B/50/P